"I love myself when I am laughing.
And then again when I am looking mean and impressive."

—*Zora Neale Hurston, in a letter
to Carl Van Vechten, December 10, 1934, referring to a series
of photographs he had taken of her.*

ZORA NEALE HURSTON, outstanding novelist, journalist, folklorist, and critic, was, between 1920 and 1950, the most prolific black woman writer in America. The intellectual and spiritual foremother of a generation of black women writers, Hurston believed in the beauty of black expressions and traditions and in the psychological wholeness of black life.

But Zora Neale Hurston was a woman ahead of her time. Although her work was praised by some when it appeared, many critics attacked it, focusing more on Hurston's lifestyle and personality—her audaciousness, independence, arrogance—than on her writing.

This volume is an essential part of a recent reevaluation of Hurston, an attempt to grant her her rightful place among the major American writers of the 1930s and 1940s. The first anthology of Hurston's work ever published, *I Love Myself When I Am Laughing* . . . contains fourteen remarkable selections chosen for their literary quality and historical significance.

The collection includes original commentary by Alice Walker and Mary Helen Washington, two black writers in the forefront of the Hurston revival. Their writings and the selections in this anthology provide illuminating insights into Hurston—the writer, the person—as well as into American social and cultural history.

I Love Myself

When I Am Laughing...

And Then Again When I Am Looking Mean and Impressive

A ZORA NEALE HURSTON READER

Edited by Alice Walker

Introduction by Mary Helen Washington

THE FEMINIST PRESS

Library of Congress Cataloging in Publication Data:
Hurston, Zora Neale.
    I love myself when I am laughing.
    Includes bibliographical references.
    1. Hurston, Zora Neale, in fiction, drama, poetry, etc. I. Walker, Alice, 1944–
II. Title.
PZ3.H9457Iad   [PS3515.U789]   813'.5'2   79-17582
ISBN 0-912670-56-8   ISBN 0-912670-66-5 pbk.

This project is supported by a grant from the National Endowment for the Arts in Washington, D.C., a federal agency.

With special acknowledgment to the following people for their kind assistance: Bill Dorsch, Ellen Dorsch, Carolyn G. Heilbrun, Ann McGovern, Rose Rubin, Barbara Sussman

Grateful acknowledgment is made for permission to reprint the following copyrighted material: **From the book** *Dust Tracks on a Road* by Zora Neale Hurston. Copyright 1942 by Zora Neale Hurston. Copyright © renewed 1970 by John C. Hurston. Reprinted by permission of J.B. Lippincott Company. **From the book** *Jonah's Gourd Vine* by Zora Neale Hurston. Copyright 1934 by Zora Neale Hurston. Copyright © renewed 1962 by John C. Hurston and Joel Hurston. Reprinted by permission of J.B. Lippincott Company. **From the book** *Moses, Man of the Mountain* by Zora Neale Hurston. Copyright 1939 by Zora Neale Hurston. Copyright © renewed 1967 by John C. Hurston and Joel Hurston. Reprinted by permission of J.B. Lippincott Company. **From the book** *Mules and Men* by Zora Neale Hurston. Copyright 1935 by Zora Neale Hurston. Copyright © renewed 1963 by John C. Hurston and Joel Hurston. Reprinted by permission of J.B. Lippincott Company. **From the book** *Tell My Horse* by Zora Neale Hurston. Copyright 1938 by Zora Neale Hurston. Copyright © renewed 1966 by John C. Hurston and Joel Hurston. Reprinted by permission of J.B. Lippincott Company. **From the book** *Their Eyes Were Watching God* by Zora Neale Hurston. Copyright 1937 by J.B. Lippincott Company. Copyright © renewed by John C. Hurston and Joel Hurston. Reprinted by permission of J.B. Lippincott Company.

Grateful acknowledgment is made for permission to use the following photographs: **Front cover, back cover, and frontispiece,** photographs by Carl Van Vechten, from the James Welden Johnson Memorial Collection of Negro Arts and Letters, Collection of American Literature, Beinecke Rare Book and Manuscript Library, Yale University. **Pages vi and 6,** courtesy of Dr. Herbert Sheen. **Pages 26 and 174,** photographs by Prentiss Taylor, from the James Welden Johnson Memorial Collection of Negro Arts and Letters, Collection of American Literature, Beinecke Rare Book and Manuscript Library, Yale University. **Page 150,** courtesy of Everette Hurston. **Page 296,** courtesy of Jane Belo Estate.

This book was typeset in Garamond and Avant Garde Gothic by Talbot Typographics, Inc.; it was printed by Mark IV Press, Ltd.

Jacket and text design by Susan Trowbridge

TABLE OF CONTENTS

DEDICATION
By Alice Walker

On Refusing to Be
Humbled by Second Place
in a Contest You Did Not Design:
A Tradition by Now

A FRIEND OF MINE called one day to tell me that she and another woman had been discussing Zora Neale Hurston and had decided they wouldn't have liked her. They wouldn't have liked the way—when her play *Color Struck!* won second prize in a literary contest at the beginning of her career—Hurston walked into a room full of her competitors, flung her scarf dramatically over her shoulder, and yelled "COLOR..R.R STRUCK..K.K!" at the top of her voice.

Apparently it isn't easy to like a person who is not humbled by second place.

Zora Neale Hurston was outrageous—it appears by nature. She was quite capable of saying, writing, or doing things *different* from what one might have wished. Because she recognized the contradictions and complexity of her own personality, Robert Hemenway, her biographer, writes that Hurston came to "delight" in the chaos she sometimes left behind.

Yet for all her contrariness, her "chaos," her ability to stir up dislike that is as strong today as it was fifty years ago, many of us love Zora Neale Hurston.

We do not love her for her lack of modesty (that tends to amuse us: an assertive black person during Hurston's time was considered an anomaly); we do not love her for her unpredictable and occasionally weird politics (they tend to confuse us); we do not, certainly, applaud many of the *mad* things she is alleged to have said and sometimes actually did say; we do not even claim never to dislike her. In reading through the thirty-odd-year span of her writing, most of us, I imagine, find her alternately winning and appalling, but rarely dull, which is worth a lot. We love Zora Neale Hurston for her work, first, and then again (as she and all Eatonville would say), we love her for herself. For the humor and courage with which she encountered a life she infrequently designed, for her absolute disinterest in becoming either white or bourgeois, and for her *devoted* appreciation of her own culture, which is an inspiration to us all.

Reading *Their Eyes Were Watching God* for perhaps the eleventh time, I am still amazed that Hurston wrote it in seven weeks; that it speaks to me as no novel, past or present, has ever done; and that the language of the characters, that "comical nigger 'dialect'" that has been laughed at, denied, ignored, or "improved" so that white folks and educated black folks can understand it, is simply beautiful. There is enough self-love in that one book—love of community, culture, traditions—to restore a world. Or create a new one.

I do not presume to judge or defend Zora Neale Hurston. I have nothing of finality to say of Hurston the person. I believe any artist's true character is seen in the work she or he does, or it is not seen. In Hurston's work, what she was is revealed. The purpose of this anthology is to present enough of that work so that the reader can make up her or his own mind.

Is *Mules and Men* racist? Or does it reflect the flawed but nonetheless beautifully creative insights of an oppressed people's collective mythology? Is "The Gilded Six-Bits" so sexist it makes us cringe to think Zora Neale Hurston wrote it? Or does it make a true statement about deep love functioning in the only pattern that at the time of its action seemed correct? Did Zora Neale Hurston never question "America" or the status-quo, as some have accused, or was she questioning it profoundly when she wrote phrases like "the arse-and-all of Democracy"? Is Janie Crawford, the main character in *Their Eyes Were Watching God*, light-skinned and silken-haired because *Hurston* was a colorist, as a black male critic has claimed, or because Hurston was not blind and therefore saw that black men (and black women) have been, and are, colorist to an embarrassing degree?

Is Hurston the messenger who brings the bad news, or is she the bad news herself? Is Hurston a reflection of ourselves? And if so, is that not, perhaps, part of our "problem" with her?

I think we are better off if we think of Zora Neale Hurston as an artist, period—rather than as the artist/politician most black writers have been required to be. This frees us to appreciate the complexity and richness of her work in the same way we can appreciate Billie Holiday's glorious phrasing or Bessie Smith's perfect and raunchy lyrics, without the necessity of ridiculing the former's addiction to heroin or the latter's excessive love of gin.

Implicit in Hurston's determination to "make it" in a career was her need to express "the folk" and herself. Someone who knew her has said: "Zora would have been Zora even if she'd been an Eskimo." That is what it means to be yourself; it is surely what it means to be an artist.

It is instructive to consider the lives of Zora Hurston and Bessie Smith (whom no one, it seems, thought to ask what *she* thought of things like integration!) particularly in relation to the white "patrons of the Negro" they both knew. There is a wonderful story told of how Bessie Smith once attended a Carl Van Vechten party which that reigning patron of Negro Art threw in her honor. As she entered, never having seen Carl or Fania Van Vechten before (and dragging her full length, white ermine on the floor behind her, an ermine purchased with money from her bestselling records), Fania Van Vechten flung herself into Bessie's arms. Bessie knocked her flat, exclaiming over a glass of straight gin: "I never *heard* of such shit!"

Bessie Smith knew shit when she saw it, and from Zora Hurston's work, we can assume she did too. Yet she never knocked anyone flat for having the audacity to patronize her, nor does she ever complain in print about the hypocrisy she must have borne. The difference between Hurston and Smith? One's work—singing, to which one could dance or make love—supported her. The other's work—writing down the unwritten doings and sayings of a culture nobody else seemed to give a damn about, except to wish it would more speedily conform to white, middle-class standards—did not.

Financial dependency is the thread that sewed a cloud over Hurston's life, from the time she left home to work as a maid at fourteen to the day of her death. It is ironic that *this* woman, who many claimed sold her soul to record the sources of authentic, black American folk art (whereas it is apparently cool to sell your soul for a university job, say, or a new car) and who was made of some of the

universe's most naturally free stuff (one would be hard pressed to find
a more nonmaterialistic person), was denied even a steady pittance,
free from strings, that would have kept her secure enough to do her
best work.

It has been pointed out that one of the reasons Zora Neale Hurston's work has suffered neglect is that her critics never considered her
"sincere." Only after she died penniless, still laboring at her craft,
still immersed in her work, still following *her* vision and *her* road, did
it begin to seem to some that yes, perhaps this woman *was* a serious
artist after all, since artists are known to live poor and die broke. But
you're up against a hard game if you have to die to win it, and we
must insist that dying in poverty is an unacceptable extreme.

We live in a society, as blacks, women, and artists, whose contests
we do not design and with whose insistence on ranking us we are
permanently at war. To know that second place, in such a society, has
often required more work and innate genius than first, a longer, grim-
mer struggle over greater odds than first—and to be able to fling your
scarf about dramatically while you demonstrate that you know—is to
trust your own self-evaluation in the face of the Great White Western
Commercial of white and male supremacy, which is virtually everything we see, outside and often inside our own homes. That Hurston
held her own, literally, against the flood of whiteness and maleness
that diluted so much other black art of the period in which she
worked is a testimony to her genius and her faith.

As black women and as artists, we are prepared, I think, to keep
that faith. There are other choices, but they are despicable.

. Zora Neale Hurston, who went forth into the world with one dress
to her name, and who was permitted, at other times in her life, only a
single pair of shoes, rescued and recreated a world which she labored
to hand us whole, never underestimating the value of her gift, if at
times doubting the good sense of its recipients. She appreciated us, in
any case, *as we fashioned ourselves.* That is something. And of all the
people in the world to be, she chose to be herself, *and more and more
herself.* That, too, is something.

So this book is dedicated to Zora Neale Hurston. And it is sent
off to her wherever she is now in the universe with the good wishes
and love of all those who have glimpsed her heart through her work,
as well as those who gave joyfully of their thought and scholarship and

feelings to make this collection an offering from more relatives than one: the intrepid and sharp Mary Helen Washington, the brave and brilliant Barbara Smith, the thoughtful and insistent Gloria Hull, the women of The Feminist Press, Robert Allen and Robert Hemenway, and me.

ALICE WALKER   *October, 1978*
San Francisco

INTRODUCTION
By Mary Helen Washington

Zora Neale Hurston:
A Woman Half in Shadow

"She walked into my study one day by telephone appointment; carelessly, a big-boned, good-boned young woman, handsome and light yellow."
—Fannie Hurst, Zora Hurston's employer; novelist[1]

"Zora was rather short and squat and black as coal."
—Theodore Pratt, writer for the Florida Historical Society[2]

"She was reddish light brown."
—Mrs. Alzeda Hacker, a friend of Zora Hurston[3]

WHETHER ZORA NEALE HURSTON was black as coal, light yellow, or light brown seems to have depended a great deal on the imagination and mind set of the observer. These three divergent descriptions of her color serve as a paradigm for the way Zora Hurston, the personality, and Zora Hurston, the writer, has been looked upon by the world which judged her. Outstanding novelist, skilled folklorist, journalist, and critic, Zora Hurston was for thirty years the most prolific black woman writer in America. And yet, from what has been written about her, it would be difficult to judge the quality of her work or even to know what color she was.

In all of the various personality sketches, full-length literary studies, forewords, and afterwords inspired by Hurston, there is a broad range of contradictory reactions. There were those who saw her as a highly reserved and serious writer, so private that few people ever knew correct age or that she had been married several times; she was also described as loud and coarse, playing the happy darky role to entertain whites. Some critics put her writing in the same category as minstrel shows; others praised her as the most significant "unread" author in America. One critic wrote that her work reveals an uncon-

scious desire to be white. But a student who heard Hurston speak at
Bennett College in 1941 said that what the students were most impressed with was this woman's deep sense of racial pride.

Certainly nothing ever written about her or her work is lukewarm.
Partly, this is attributable to her own unique personality. From the
anecdotes and apocryphal tales told about Hurston, one must conclude
that she was nothing if not controversial, highly outspoken, arrogant,
independent, and eccentric. She was also a black woman determined,
in the period between 1920 and 1950, to have a career as a writer,
which in itself was eccentric. Though she lived in controversy, died
penniless, and was out of print for thirty years, Zora Neale Hurston
did indeed establish herself as a writer and folklorist. In her thirty-year
career, she published four novels, two books of folklore, an autobiography, numerous stories, articles, and plays.

To a large extent, the attention focused on Zora Hurston's controversial personality and lifestyle have inhibited any objective critical
analysis of her work. Few male critics have been able to resist sly innu-
endos and outright attacks on Hurston's personal life, even when the
work in question was not affected by her disposition or her private
affairs. But these controversies have loomed so large in the reviews of
her work that once again the task of confronting them must precede
any reappraisal or reevaluation of her highly neglected work. Jumping
up and down in the same foot-tracks, as Zora would call it.

Three recent literary events signaled the end of the inadequate,
sometimes venomous, often highly inaccurate, assessment of Hurston's
life and work: the appearance of Robert Hemenway's excellent and
thoroughly researched book, *Zora Neale Hurston: A Literary Biography*;[4] the reissue of Hurston's finest novel, *Their Eyes Were Watching God*;[5] and the publication of this volume, *I Love Myself When I
Am Laughing*, . . . These are three important steps in bringing Hurston
to the place her mother meant for her to occupy when she urged Zora
to "jump at de sun."

Questions and controversies have surrounded Hurston and her
career since she stepped into New York City in 1925 to join the Harlem Renaissance. Like the "lyin' tales" Hurston collected in her folklore research, some have become as familiar as legend and have the
same degree of veracity. But still the questions must be posed and
answered if one is to understand the richly complicated Zora Hurston.
How did this poor, unschooled girl from a peasant background in the

all-black town of Eatonville, Florida, manage, in the early 1900s, to get to Howard University, Barnard College, and Columbia University, and eventually become one of the shapers of the important black literary and cultural movement of the twenties, the Harlem Renaissance? Is there any truth to the often-made accusation that Hurston played the obsequious role of the swinging, happy darkie in order to sustain the financial support of wealthy white patrons? Did Hurston deliberately avoid any condemnation of racism in order not to offend white friends? What is the truth behind the 1948 morals charge that she sexually abused a ten-year-old boy? How did this celebrant of black folk culture become, in later years, a right-wing Republican, publicly supporting a staunch segregationist and opposing the 1954 Supreme Court desegregation decision? Why, in the last decade of her life, did she remove herself from all her acquaintances and contacts and die in poverty in a Florida county welfare home?

Any probing of the life and times of Zora Neale Hurston must begin in the town of Eatonville, Florida, where she was born, *probably* around 1901.[6] Incorporated in 1886 as an all-black town, Eatonville, Florida, five miles from Orlando, was, according to Hurston's autobiography, a "pure Negro town—charter, mayor, council, town marshal and all."[7] It was neither ghetto, nor slum, nor black bottom, but a rich source of black cultural traditions where Zora would be nourished on black folktales and tropical fruits and sheltered from the early contacts with racial prejudice that have so indelibly marked almost all other Afro-American writers. It was a sheltering for which Hurston paid dearly, as it caused her to develop attitudes that were out of the mainstream, particularly in the protest years of the forties.

The most critical fact of Zora Neale Hurston's childhood was that her mother, Lucy Hurston, who encouraged her daughter's indomitable and creative spirit, died when Zora was nine. In the years that followed, Zora went from one relative to another and was eventually rejected by her father and his new wife. She hired herself out as a domestic in several homes, and, around the age of fourteen, she joined a Gilbert and Sullivan traveling dramatic troupe as a wardrobe girl and maid, ending up, after eighteen months, in Baltimore. There she enrolled in Morgan Academy (now Morgan State University), with one dress, a change of underwear, a pair of oxfords, and the intelligence and drive that were her hallmarks.[8] After graduation in June 1918, she went on to Howard University in Washington, D.C. She received an associate degree in 1920, though she studied intermittently at Howard until 1924, getting A's in courses she liked, and F's in those she didn't.[9]

During her years in school, Zora Hurston was frequently in debt, though she worked at all sorts of jobs from a manicurist in a Washington barber shop to a maid for distinguished black families. Throughout her life, Hurston would not be a stranger to either debt or hard work. In 1950, when she was a noted American writer, she was discovered "masquerading" as a maid for a wealthy white woman in a fashionable section of Miami.[10] Though she claimed she was temporarily "written out" and wanted the experience for an article about domestics, the truth was she was living in a shabby studio, had received a number of rejection slips for stories, was hustling speaking dates and borrowing from friends, and was flat broke. These were some of the most critical facts of her adult life. On the other hand, during her earlier writing period, Zora Hurston was extremely adept at finding people to give her money to further her career, a talent which sparked the accusation that she pumped whites for money, compromising her own dignity in the process. Fellow artist Langston Hughes, who for years was supported by the same white woman as Hurston, said that "In her youth she was always getting scholarships and things from wealthy white people, some of whom simply paid her just to sit around and represent the Negro race for them, she did it in such a racy fashion. . . . To many of her white friends, no doubt, she was a perfect 'darkie'. . . ."[11]

Behind that spurious comment was an old feud between these one-time good friends over their collaboration in writing the play *Mule Bone*. Each accused the other of stealing a part of the play. Robert Hemenway concludes, in his biography of Hurston, that while most of the play was Hurston's work, she reneged on the partnership when Hughes tried to include a third party, a woman, in the deal. Hughes's self-serving, chauvinistic remark about the incident, "Girls are funny creatures," was designed to make Hurston look childish and fickle, rather than like a colleague who felt betrayed, however mistaken she might have been.[12]

Critic Nathan Huggins gives Hurston the same kind of going over in his book, *Harlem Renaissance*.[13] Huggins says Hurston thrived on her dependent relationship to an elderly white patron, Mrs. R. Osgood Mason, and deliberately played the role of the simple, childlike primitive. In his critical evaluation of Hurston, Huggins devotes an entire page to Wallace Thurman's satire of Hurston in his book, *Infants of the Spring*, in which Thurman caricatures Hurston as Sweetie Mae Carr, a Negro opportunist cutting the fool for white folks in order to get her tuition paid and her stories sold. Nearly every word of the four and one-half pages on Zora Hurston is taken up with whether or not Hurston's "darky act" was real or put-on, and there is little effort by Huggins to examine her literary contributions to the period.

There are other invasions of Hurston's personality under the guise of critical commentary. Theodore Pratt of the Florida Historical Society says she was pampered and spoiled, having been given too many scholarships, fellowships, and grants. And Darwin Turner's lengthy critique of Hurston in his book, *In a Minor Chord*, makes clear that, like previous critics, he intends to evaluate Hurston's work on the basis of her personality. Turner describes her as a "quick-tempered woman, arrogant toward her peers, obsequious toward her supposed superiors, desperate for recognition and reassurance to assuage her feelings of inferiority...." Then he concludes: "It is in reference to this image that one must examine her novels, her folklore, and her view of the Southern scene."[14] It is ironic and telling that in his critique of Renaissance writer Jean Toomer in the very same book, Turner does not evaluate Toomer's work on the basis of his marriage to a white woman or his refusal to be identified with blacks after the publication of *Cane*. On the contrary, Turner delicately tiptoes around that controversy and declares that Toomer's vehement insistence that he was neither "Negro" nor Caucasian—but a member of the "American" race—is "philosophically viable and utterly sincere."[15] Few critics ever considered Hurston's idiosyncratic views "philosophically viable," and even fewer excused her because she was sincere. Although Darwin Turner blames Zora Hurston's obscurity on the fact that she got sandwiched in between the exotic primitivism of the Harlem Renaissance and the protest mood of the forties, another possibility suggests itself: she was a black woman whose entire career output was subjected to the judgment of critics, both white and black, who were all men.

Much of the criticism of Zora Hurston that was commonplace from the twenties on seems to have stemmed from her early relationship with a white patron. Just what did go on between Zora Hurston and Mrs. R. Osgood Mason of Park Avenue, New York, and why did it inspire such severe and, in some cases, venomous attacks on Hurston?

According to the letters she wrote to the wealthy Mrs. Mason, Zora Hurston signed a contract on December 8, 1928, granting her a monthly allowance of two hundred dollars so that she could collect folklore in the South, gathering materials for her first book. The contract stipulated that Hurston's folklore collections would become Mrs. Mason's exclusive property, and that she would exercise full control over Hurston's work because she felt Hurston could not be trusted to know best what to do with it.[16] Over a period of five years, Mrs. Mason gave Hurston approximately fifteen thousand dollars for her work and self-support.[17] Although the entire collection, except for the contract, is a one-way correspondence—all of the letters between them are from Hurston to Mrs. Mason—there is a great deal about Mrs. Mason that can be read between the lines. She must have been an extremely controlling woman because Zora Hurston was kept walking a tightrope so as not to offend her. Hurston wrote an article in which she said that "white people could not be trusted to collect the lore of others," and "Godmother" Mason was so upset that Hurston had to hastily explain that "Godmother" was not included in that remark.[18] "Godmother" encouraged a childlike dependency from those under her patronage and demanded obedience and loyalty in return for the monthly checks. Hurston felt that she could not make a move in her career without this woman's permission, and, according to the terms of the contract, she was absolutely correct.

The letters reveal some unpleasant things about Hurston too. She was capable not only of surviving the terrible constrictures of this arrangement, but of dredging up some pretty self-serving flattery for the woman she addressed variously as "Dearest Godmother," "little mother of the primitive world," "the immaculate conception," and "a glimpse of the holy grail." Some letters sound almost mystical, as though Hurston is petitioning favors from a high priestess. This poetic tribute to Mrs. Mason, dated Sunday morning, 1931, would be humorous in its excessiveness if it were not also so hopelessly servile:

Out of the essence of my Godmother
Out of the True one
Out of the Wise one I am made to be
From her breath I am born
Yes, as the world is made new by the breath of Spring
And is strengthened by the winds of Summer

The Sea is stirred by its passion
Thus, I have taken from the breath of your mouth
From the vapor of your soul I am made to be
By the warmth of your love I am made to stand erect
You are the Spring and Summer of my existence.[19]

The next letter, dated August 14, 1932, begins:

Now about the money, Godmother.

Beneath all the subterfuge and posturing in these letters is one cold, inescapable fact: Zora was hard-pressed for the money for her career. She needed to travel to the South to spend time with people who knew the folk stories and would tell them only to trusted friends. Few black scholars had the kind of money to finance such an expedition. But even the contract with Mrs. Mason did not relieve Hurston of money worries. At one time she had to itemize her expenses for Mrs. Mason to show her how she was handling the money. She had to account for such obvious necessities as shoe repair, car fare, and medicine; even a box of Kotex is listed. Once or twice she mentions the intestinal problem that was beginning to trouble her, in order to justify buying medication for treatment. In a letter dated April 27, 1932, Hurston was reduced to begging "Godmother darling" for a pair of shoes;

I really need a pair of shoes. You remember that we discussed the matter in the fall and agreed that I should own only one pair at a time. I bought a pair in mid-December and they have held up until now. My big toe is about to burst out of my right shoe and so I must do something about it.[20]

There are many letters from this period documenting Hurston's efforts to become self-supporting. She staged concerts and plays in order to make money on her own, and at one point proposed utilizing her culinary skills by becoming a "chicken specialist," making chicken soup, salad, à la king, and supplying hot chicken at a moment's notice to fifty to one hundred customers—"an exclusive mouth to mouth service" to New York's finer hostesses.[21] In her efforts to economize, she washed her face with laundry soap and ignored a growing and painful stomach ailment.

If one thinks of the arrogant, individualistic woman who once went after her domineering stepmother with a hatchet, then these letters are strangely un-Hurston-like. But Zora Hurston was fiercely determined to have a career, no matter what or who had to be sacrificed. In consideration of that determined will, perhaps the most Hurston-like statement in the whole passel of letters is one which is unintentionally revealing of the use to which Mrs. Mason had been put: "I shall wrassle me up a future or die trying."[22]

Zora Hurston had been able to "wrassle up" a scholarship to Barnard College, where she studied under the noted anthropologist, Dr. Franz Boas. Later she continued to work under him at Columbia University. Her association with "Papa" Franz, as she called him, was partly responsible for sending Hurston back to her hometown of Eatonville in 1927 to do formal folklore research. There was a gold mine for a folklorist, a rich storehouse of authentic tales, songs, and folkways of black people—unresearched by any black scholar until Hurston. Thus began the unique effort of Zora Neale Hurston to tell the tales, sing the songs, do the dances, and repeat the raucous sayings and doings of the Negro farthest down.[29] It was out of this material that Hurston would fashion her career as folklorist and novelist.

The decade of the thirties was the meridian of Hurston's career. In 1935, she published her first book of folklore, *Mules and Men,* based on material she collected in Florida and Louisiana. A classic in form and style, *Mules and Men* goes far beyond the mere reproduction of the tales; it introduces the reader to the whole world of jook joints, lying contests, and tall-tale sessions that make up the drama of the folk life of black people in the rural South. The tales are set in the framework of a story in which Hurston herself is a character. The other characters, who in conventional folklore collections are merely informants, are real personalities in *Mules and Men,* exposing their prejudices, love affairs, jealousies, while they tell the old stories about how black people got black or how John outwitted Ole Massa during slavery. In her first novel, *Jonah's Gourd Vine,* also published in the thirties, Zora Hurston continued to use the folk life of Eatonville as the essential experience. Loosely based on the lives of her parents, *Jonah's Gourd Vine* presents one of Hurston's many powerful women characters—Lucy Pearson, wife of the town's philandering preacher, John Pearson. On her deathbed, Lucy Pearson is such a strong-willed woman that John is afraid to be in the same room with her, and with

the advice she gives Isis (probably Zora), she bequeaths the spirit to
her daughter: "You always strain tuh be de bell-cow, never be de tail
uh nothin'."[24] With these publications and the ones that were to follow in the thirties, Zora Hurston had begun to take her work in directions that would earn her both high praise and severe censure. In an
era when many educated and cultured blacks prided themselves on re-
moving all traces of their rural black origins, when a high-class
"Negro" virtue was not to "act one's color," Zora not only celebrated
the distinctiveness of black culture, but saw those traditional black
folkways as marked improvements over the "imaginative wasteland of
white society."[25]

Then, in 1937, came the novel in which Hurston triumphed in
the art of taking the imagery, imagination, and experiences of black
folk and making literature—*Their Eyes Were Watching God.* Hurston
says in her autobiography that she wrote the novel in seven straight
weeks in the Caribbean after a love affair ended, and, though the circumstances were difficult, she tried to "embalm" the novel with all of
her tenderness for this man.

Perhaps because the novel's main character, Janie Woods, has a
succession of husbands and finally finds joy and fulfillment in her
third marriage, the novel has generally been thought of as a love story
about love. On a much deeper and more important level, however, its
theme is Janie's search for identity, an identity which finally begins to
take shape as she throws off the false images which have been thrust
upon her because she is both black and woman in a society where
neither is allowed to exist naturally and freely. Hurston uses two images from nature to symbolize Janie's quest: the horizon and the blos-
soming pear tree. One, the horizon, suggests that the search is an
individual quest; the other, the pear tree in blossom, suggests a fulfillment in union with another. Janie describes her journey to find herself
in a language that takes us deep into black folk traditions:[26]

Ah been a delegate to de big 'ssociation of life. Yessuh! De Grand Lodge,
de big convention of livin' is just where Ah been dis year and a half y'all ain't
seen me.[27]

Folk language, folkways, and folk stories work symbolically in the
novel as a measure of a character's integrity and freedom. Those characters whose self-esteem and identity are based on illusion and false

values are alienated from the black folk community, and, conversely, those, like Janie herself, who struggle against those self-alienating values toward a deeper sense of community, experience wholeness. Janie is both humiliated and angered by the attempts of her first two husbands to win her with materialistic gifts and to make her subservient to them. Thus the dramatic tension of the novel takes place on two levels: Janie has to resist both male domination and the empty materialism of white culture in order to get to the horizon.

Janie (née Crawford) Killicks Starks Woods is one of the few—and certainly the earliest—heroic black women in the Afro-American literary tradition. Critic Robert Stepto says that the primary voice in a literary tradition is ''the personal, heroic voice, delineating the dimensions of heroism by aspiring to a heroic posture ... or expressing an awareness of that which they ought to be.''[29] Janie assumes this heroic stature by her struggles for self-definition, for autonomy, for liberation from the illusions that others have tried to make her live by or that she herself has submitted to. Moreover, she is always the aware voice, consciously undergoing the most severe tests of that autonomy.

In *Their Eyes Were Watching God*, Hurston the creative artist and Hurston the folklorist were perfectly united. Zora Neale Hurston went on to publish two more books in the next two years—*Tell My Horse* (1938), a book of folklore from her experiences in Haiti, and another novel, *Moses, Man of the Mountain* (1939), a re-creation of the Moses myth with black folk characters. By the end of the thirties, she deserved her title: the best and most prolific black woman writer in America.

If the thirties were Hurston's meridian, they were also the beginning of a ground swell of criticism that would become the intellectual lynching of Zora Neale Hurston. The 1936 review of *Mules and Men* written by educator and critic Sterling Brown praised *Mules* for its dramatic appeal but was extremely critical of the book's failure to reveal the exploitation and terrorism in southern black life. This was criticism of Hurston that became commonplace, though undeserved. Brown felt that southern black life was rendered ''pastorally'' in *Mules*, the characters made to appear easygoing and carefree in a land ''shadowed by squalor, poverty, disease, violence, enforced ignorance, and exploitation.''[30] It was not a bitter enough book for Brown, especially considering that 1935, the year of the Scottsboro trial, was a very bitter time for blacks. Brown was expressing an honest concern; Hurston's point of view *is* open to misinterpretation because her views on race, true to her personality, were unpredictable, ambivalent, sometimes contradictory, but certainly never conventional.

In the twenties, thirties, and forties, there were tremendous pressures on black writers. Militant organizations, like the National Association for the Advancement of Colored People, expected them to be "race" people, defending black people, protesting against racism and oppression; while the advocates of the genteel school of literature wanted black writers to create respectable characters that would be "a credit to the race." Many black writers chafed under these restrictions, including Hurston, who chose to write about the positive side of the black experience and to ignore the brutal side. She saw black lives as psychologically integral—not mutilated half-lives, stunted by the effects of racism and poverty. She simply could not depict blacks as defeated, humiliated, degraded, or victimized, because she did not experience black people or herself that way. In her now famous and somewhat controversial essay, "How It Feels to Be Colored Me," she boldly asserts:

But I am not tragically colored. There is no great sorrow dammed up in my soul, nor lurking behind my eyes. I do not mind at all. I do not belong to the sobbing school of Negrohood who hold that nature somehow has given them a lowdown dirty deal and whose feelings are hurt about it. . . . No, I do not weep at the world—I am too busy sharpening my oyster knife.[31]

Sadly for Zora Hurston's career, "tragically colored" was in vogue in the forties. Richard Wright's bestsellers, *Uncle Tom's Children* (1937); *Native Son* (1940); and *Black Boy* (1945), were clearly in the mode of radical racial protest literature. Wright's black characters, in contrast to Hurston's, are victimized, hunted people who, in Hurston's view, created the impression that black lives were nothing more than the sum total of their oppression. They were "a problem," economically deprived and psychologically crippled. Hurston was determined to write about black life as it existed apart from racism, injustice, Jim Crow—where black people laughed, celebrated, loved, sorrowed, struggled—unconcerned about white people and completely unaware of being "a problem." Wright said Hurston's characters were nothing but minstrels. In a niggling review of *Their Eyes Were Watching God*, in 1937, he says the novel "carries no theme, no message, no thought''; it is just a "minstrel technique" to make white folks laugh.[32] Richard Wright, it must be noted, brooded aloud in *Black Boy* about "the strange absence of real kindness in Negroes, how unstable was our tenderness, how lacking in genuine passion we were, how void of great hope, how timid our joy, how bare our traditions. . . . ''[33]

The great power of Wright lay in his ability to depict the violence and brutality of oppression and the resulting tensions in black life; but these preoccupations were also restrictions. Being black was such grimly serious business to Wright that he was incapable of judging Hurston's characters, who laugh and tease as well as suffer and who do not hate themselves or their blackness. But Wright was one of the big names of the forties. He set the model for the period, while Zora Hurston "suffered through devastating critical and popular neglect, inspired no imitators [her work being out of print] and finally died with not even a marker to identify her grave.''[34]

The controversy over Hurston's work and her political views, which surfaced after the publication of *Mules and Men* in 1935, mushroomed and spread in the forties and fifties as Hurston, typically erratic, continued to make unorthodox and paradoxical assertions on racial issues. She was quoted in one newspaper interview as saying that the Jim Crow system worked, and that blacks were better off in the South because, although there was no social intermingling, blacks had the "equivalent" of everything whites had.[35] Roy Wilkins of the NAACP wrote a scathing rebuke of Hurston in New York's black newspaper, *The Amsterdam News,* accusing her of being a publicity hound and selling out her people in order to promote her books.[36] Wilkins obviously did not question the accuracy of the quote, and Hurston insisted she had been misquoted, which was probably true, given that she had few illusions about Jim Crow or the South. She hated, however, the hypocritical notion that intolerance was located in the South, and that, by comparison, the North was a haven of equality.

They [northern whites] use the Negro vote up there to get power, and then bar us from jobs and decent living quarters, and if there is any protests, [they] riot, and terrify Negro workers away from town and jobs, and then laugh up their sleeves while they brush it off with folk-lore about the south the Sout [sic] is certainly doing its bit toward discrimination down here, but they are not pulling off that up there. That is a monstrous insult to our intelligence, or is it?[37]

In another news article, entitled "Author Plans to Upbraid Own Race," Hurston was quoted as saying she was planning a book "that would give her own people 'an awful going over,' particularly the ones who talk about the tragedy of being Negroes." In typical Hurston fashion, she emphasized that what she deplored even more than prejudice was the "appalling waste of young genius" while prosperous Negroes, who could help these young black boys and girls, complain that they "can't go to tea at the Ritz."[38]

Hurston's most highly controversial stand was her opposition to the 1954 Supreme Court desegregation decision, which she criticized because she thought it implied the inferiority of black teachers, black students, and black schools in the South. She resented any suggestion that whites were superior and that blacks could learn better if they went to school with them. This was consistent with her cultural philosophy that blacks had adorned a rather pallid American culture with colorful, dramatic, and dynamic contributions. In every art form, she saw truly original expression rooted in black culture. In language, for example, Hurston claimed that

whatever the Negro does of his own volition he embellishes. His religious service is for the greater part excellent prose poetry. Both prayers and sermons are tooled and polished until they are true works of art. . . . The prayer of the white man is considered humorous in its bleakness. The beauty of the Old Testament does not exceed that of a Negro prayer.[39]

Little wonder, then, that she, as well as many other southern blacks, feared that they would be the losers in the integration plan. It is both ironic and sad to realize that Hurston would not have been denounced for any of these views in the sixties or seventies. She might even have been considered militant.

For Zora Hurston, the forties were "Hell's Basement." In his biography of Hurston, Hemenway calls this chapter in her life, "The Pots in Sorrow's Kitchen," after the old Gulla proverb, "Ah done been in sorrow's kitchen and ah licked de pots clean." Almost like an augur of what the coming years held in store for her, Zora began the decade with a bitter divorce from her second husband,[40] a twenty-three-year-old man named Albert Price III, who claimed in his counter suit that Zora was practicing hoodoo on him.[41] In 1942, her autobiography, *Dust Tracks on a Road*, was published—a strangely disoriented book which Alice Walker calls "oddly false-sounding."[42] Zora used all sorts of manipulative and diversionary tactics in the autobiography to avoid any real self-disclosure. The sections on her adult life are a study in the art of subterfuge. The chapter on "Love" begins,

What do I really know about love? I have had some experiences and feel fluent enough for my own satisfaction. Love, I find is like singing. Everybody can do enough to satisfy themselves, though it may not impress the neighbors as being very much. That is the way it is with me, but whether I know anything unusual, I couldn't say. Don't look for me to call a string of names and point out chapter and verse. Ladies do not kiss and tell any more than gentlemen do. . . .

But pay no attention to what I say about love. . . . Just because my mouth opens like a prayer book, it does not have to flap like a Bible. And then again, anybody whose mouth is cut cross-ways is given to lying, unconsciously as well as knowingly.[43]

The autobiography provides a fairly clear view of Hurston as a child, and it is especially useful for detailing her relationships with her mother, father, and Eatonville, but the rest of it rambles on from one pose to another, sometimes boasting about her achievements and at all times deftly avoiding self-revelation. She was later to admit that she did not want to write the book at all because "it is too hard to reveal one's inner self."[44] The mask Hurston assumed in *Dust Tracks* was a sign of the growing evisceration of her work. After *Dust Tracks,* which was a commercial success, "her mission to celebrate black folkways lost its public intensity."[45] Although she still collected folklore for her own use, she did not write about it after 1942.

The 1940s continued their spiraling trend downward for Zora Hurston. In 1945, she was stricken with a gall bladder and colon infection, a condition which became chronic and seriously impaired her ability to support herself. That same year, her publisher, Lippincott, rejected her proposal for a book on the lives of upper-class blacks. In the essay "What White Publishers Won't Print," written in 1950 for *Negro Digest,* Hurston indicated her belief that the racist American publishing industry was uninterested in the "average struggling non-morbid Negro," because there was more money to be made exploiting the race problem with stereotyped stories of simple, oppressed sharecroppers. Zora spent part of 1947 and 1948 in British

Honduras, where she wrote the major portion of her worst novel, *Seraph on the Suwanee* (1948). All of the main characters in *Seraph* are white, and, apparently, Zora wrote this strange book to prove that she was capable of writing about white people. The intent may have been admirable, but all the white characters in *Seraph* sound exactly like the Eatonville folks sitting on Joe Clarke's front porch. The result is an awkward and contrived novel, as vacuous as a soap opera. It was as though, in abandoning the source of her unique esthetic—the black cultural tradition—she also submerged her power and creativity.

Hurston sailed home from Honduras to take her turn in sorrow's kitchen. On September 13, 1948, she was arrested in New York and charged, along with two other adults she had never met, with sodomizing a young boy, the son of a woman who had rented her a room during the winter of 1946–47. The evidence presented was so flimsy and so contradictory—Hurston was out of the country during the time of the alleged crime, and the boy was found to be psychologically disturbed—that the district attorney, convinced of Zora's innocence, ordered the case dismissed. A court employee leaked the story to a national black newspaper. The October 23, 1948, issue of the *New York Age* featured these headlines: "NOTED NOVELIST DENIES SHE 'ABUSED' 10-YEAR-OLD BOY: ZORA NEALE HURSTON RELEASED ON BAIL." *The Afro-American,* a black Baltimore newspaper, released an even more sensationalized account, using this quote from the novel *The Seraph on the Suwanee:* "I'm just as hungry as a dog for a knowing and doing love," intimating that this quote might represent the author's own desperate need for love.[46] The papers accurately described Hurston as "hysterical and almost prostrate." She was terribly demoralized and even contemplated suicide: "I care nothing for anything anymore. My country has failed me utterly. My race has seen fit to destroy me without reason, and with the vilest tools conceived of by man so far. . . . I have resolved to die."[47]

This tragedy did not kill Zora. Nor, as it has been popularly recounted, did she retire immediately to obscurity, eccentricity, and penury. But the last decade of her life—the fifties—was a difficult time, mainly because she had very little money and few means of self-support other than her writing, which was not going well. She did a few journalistic pieces for the *Saturday Evening Post* and an anti-Communist article for the *American Legion Magazine* which documents a developing political conservatism. She supported the

Republican Taft in the 1952 presidential primary and denounced
communism during the rabid McCarthy era. This growing conservatism, which was interpreted as antiblack, is difficult to explain.
Hurston always saw herself as a self-made success, and she had the
kind of individualism and egoism that generally accompanies that
belief. Moreover, her very positive experiences in Eatonville encouraged
her to believe that brilliance and talent will out, regardless of political
conditions. Thus, she was able to dismiss slavery as an anachronism,
which no longer concerned her, since all the slaveholders were long
since dead and she was too busy getting on with the future to care.[48]
It was a naïve and dangerous viewpoint, and one that led directly to
her right-wing politics.

With the one thousand dollars she received from the *Saturday
Evening Post* article, Hurston moved to a one-room cabin in Eau
Gallie, Florida, where she lived quite peacefully for five years,

digging in my garden, painting my house, planting seeds . . . I have planted
pink verbena, and around the palms and the park-like ground west of the
stones, I have scattered bright colored poppies. Going to let them run
wild . . .
   Living the kind of life for which I was made, strenuous and close to the soil,
I am happier than I have been for at least ten years.[49]

Still, there was the problem of money and the recurring stomach ailment. Scribner's rejected a manuscript in 1955, and she was forced to
work as a librarian at Patrick Air Force Base in Florida in 1956 for
$1.88 per hour, hating every minute of it. In 1956, her landlord sold
the little cabin where she had lived modestly but happily for five
years. She moved to Fort Pierce and worked briefly as a substitute
teacher. In 1959, weighing over two hundred pounds and having suffered a stroke, Zora Neale Hurston, penniless, entered the Saint Lucie
county welfare home, and, three months later, on January 28, 1960,
she died. Contrary to rumor, Hurston did not die in total obscurity.
More than a hundred people attended the funeral services, testament
to the fact that she was well known and loved by the people who
perhaps knew her best.[50]
   Robert Hemenway has a term for the genius of Zora Hurston. He
calls it her "autonomous imagination." Partly that just means that

Hurston did as she pleased. More importantly, it means that she insisted on a medium, however unorthodox, that would satisfy her need to be both folklorist and creative artist. She succeeded magnificently in *Their Eyes Were Watching God.* When Langston Hughes urged the young black writers of the Harlem Renaissance to create a truly racial art based on the rich cultural heritage of black people and to stop trying to ape white writers and artists, in all probability, he did not realize how prophetically he spoke of Hurston:

[The common folks] furnish a wealth of colorful, distinctive material for any artist because they still hold their own individuality in the face of American standardizations. *And perhaps these common people will give to the world its truly great Negro artist, the one who is not afraid to be himself* [emphasis mine].[51]

Change *himself* to read *herself,* and this is a perfect description of Hurston. She believed wholeheartedly in the beauty of black expression and traditions and in the psychological wholeness of black life. With little to guide her, except fidelity to her own experience, she documented the survival of love, loyalty, joy, humor, and affirmation, as well as tragedy, in black life.

Who can help wondering what would have been the difference in Zora Hurston's life and career if there had been a large black reading public, and if she had been able to earn enough money to be self-supporting? Behind those deceptively simple "ifs," and the conditions they allude to, are the very severe complications in Zora's career that would have destroyed a weaker person—that did, in fact, diminish her powers so that we will never know the full potential of this pioneer artist.

"What did it mean for a black woman to be an artist in our grandmother's time? It is a question with an answer cruel enough to stop the blood."[52] The answer is shown in the life of Zora Neale Hurston. It meant that the black woman who chose to work as artist, as creator, would be subjected to the same kind of violence that a black domestic worker had to face. It meant the kind of economic oppression that reduced Hurston to beg her publishers to look at her work—even after she was an established writer. It meant that, besides the struggle every writer faces to find her own voice, to combat loneliness, she would have to work with little hope of triumph.

And yet, she did work. In poverty and ill health, dogged by an undeserved scandal, and without the support of any academic or intellectual community, Zora Neale Hurston worked as writer and scholar for thirty years. She worked without the freedom and peace, without the time to contemplate, that Virginia Woolf insisted were essential for any woman to write. She worked consistently without the necessary five hundred pounds a year, without a room of her own with lock and key. Indeed, she worked most of the time without a door of her own on which to put a lock. What she left us is only a fraction of what she might have accomplished. We should be grateful for the work she did.

We should be grateful for her survival.

Notes

1. Fannie Hurst, "Zora Neale Hurston: A Personality Sketch," *Yale University Library Gazette* 35 (July, 1960): 17.

2. Theodore Pratt, "A Memoir: Zora Neale Hurston: Florida's First Distinguished Author," *Negro Digest* (February, 1962): 54.

3. Telephone interview with Mrs. Alzeda Hacker, October 19, 1977. Mrs. Hacker's description most closely corresponds with photographs of Hurston and other eyewitness reports.

4. Robert E. Hemenway, *Zora Neale Hurston: A Literary Biography* (Urbana: University of Illinois Press, 1977).

5. Zora Neale Hurston, *Their Eyes Were Watching God* (Urbana: University of Illinois Press, 1978). Originally published in 1937 by J.B. Lippincott Company.

6. Hemenway, p. 13. There are no surviving birth records, and Hemenway reports that Hurston was purposely inconsistent about her age, dispensing fictitious birth dates when she was trying to impress someone with either her youth or her age.

7. Zora Neale Hurston, *Dust Tracks on a Road* (Philadelphia: J. B. Lippincott Company, 1942, 1971), p. 3.

8. Zora Neale Hurston, *Dust Tracks*, p. 151.

9. Hemenway, p. 18.

10. Randy Discon, "Author Found Masquerading as Maid for 'change of pace,'" *Philadelphia Daily News*, March 30, 1950, p. 6.

11. Langston Hughes, *The Big Sea* (New York: Hill and Wang, 1963), p. 239.

12. Hemenway, p. 146–147.

13. Nathan Huggins, *Harlem Renaissance* (New York: Oxford University Press, 1971), p. 75.

14. Darwin Turner, *In a Minor Chord* (Carbondale: Southern Illinois University Press, 1971), p. 98.

15. Turner, p. 35.

16. Contract between Mrs. R. Osgood Mason and Zora Neale Hurston, Alain Locke Papers, Moorland-Spingarn Research Center, Howard University Library, Washington, D.C.

17. Hemenway, p. 105.

18. Zora Neale Hurston, Letter to Alain

Locke, June 14, 1928, Alain Locke Papers.

19. Zora Neale Hurston, Letter to Mrs. Mason, Sunday morning, 1931, Alain Locke Papers.

20. Zora Neale Hurston to Mrs. Mason, April 27, 1937.

21. Zora Neale Hurston to Mrs. Mason, September 25, 1931.

22. Zora Neale Hurston to Mrs. Mason, November 25, 1930.

23. *Dust Tracks,* p. 177.

24. *Jonah's Gourd Vine* (Philadelphia: J. B. Lippincott Company, 1934, 1971), p. 206.

25. Hemenway, p. 162.

26. Mary Helen Washington, "Zora Neale Hurston: The Black Woman's Search for Identity," *Black World* 21 (August, 1972). This idea, which I am expanding here, was first developed in the *Black World* Essay.

27. *Their Eyes,* p. 18.

28. The main character, born Janie Crawford, is married three times—to Logan Killicks, Jody Starks, and Vergible (Tea Cake) Woods.

29. Robert B. Stepto, "I Thought I Knew These People: Richard Wright and the Afro-American Literary Tradition," *The Massachusetts Review* 28, No. 3 (Autumn, 1977): 528.

30. Sterling Brown, "Old Time Tales," review of *Mules and Men,* 1936. Unidentified clipping, James Weldon Johnson Collection, Yale University Library, New Haven, Connecticut.

31. Zora Neale Hurston, "How It Feels to Be Colored Me," *The World Tomorrow* 11 (May, 1928): 216.

32. Richard Wright, "Between Laughter and Tears," review of *Their Eyes Were Watching God,* in *New Masses* (October 5, 1937): 23.

33. Richard Wright, *Black Boy* (New York: Harper and Brothers Publishers, 1945), p. 33.

34. June Jordan, "On Richard Wright and Zora Neale Hurston: Notes Toward a Balancing of Love and Hatred," *Black World* 23 (August, 1974): 5.

35. Zora Neale Hurston, in *New York World-Telegram,* article by Douglas Gilbert, "When Negro Succeeds, South is Proud, Zora Hurston Says," February 1, 1943.

36. Roy Wilkins, *The Amsterdam News,* February 27, 1943.

37. Zora Neale Hurston, Letter to Alain Locke, July 23, 1943, Alain Locke Papers.

38. Zora Neale Hurston, *New York World-Telegram,* February 6, 1943.

39. Zora Neale Hurston, "Characteristics of Negro Expression," in *Negro: An Anthology,* ed. Nancy Cunard (London: Wishart, 1934), p. 26.

40. Hurston was at least thirty-eight. She had been married previously to Herbert Sheen, a fellow student at Howard University. They were separated after eight months and divorced a few years later. Zora said in her autobiography that her love affairs always conflicted with her work, and her work took precedence.

41. Hemenway, p. 274.

42. Alice Walker, "In Search of Our Mothers' Gardens: The Creativity of Black Women in the South," *Ms.* (May, 1974): 67.

43. *Dust Tracks,* pp. 249, 265.

44. Hemenway, p. 278.

45. Hemenway, p. 288.

46. Hemenway, pp. 319–323. Hemenway's notes give the most accurate examination of the story of the morals change. This summary is based on his findings and conclusions.

47. Hemenway, pp. 321–322.

48. *Dust Tracks,* p. 282.

49. Hemenway, p. 340.

50. Alice Walker, "In Search of Zora Neale Hurston," *Ms.* 3 (March, 1975): 87.

51. Langston Hughes, "The Negro Artist and the Racial Mountain" in *The Negro Renaissance: An Anthology,* eds. Michael W. Peplow and Arthur P. David (New York: Holt, Rinehart, and Winston, Inc., 1975), p. 472. This essay first appeared in *The Nation* in 1926.

52. Alice Walker, "In Search of Our Mothers' Gardens," p. 60.

ONE

Autobiography, Folklore and Reportage

Dust Tracks on a Road (1942) was Zora Neale Hurston's most commercially successful book. It is also, as Mary Helen Washington points out, filled with evasion, posturing, all kinds of self-concealment, though it is ostensibly an autobiography. The following selections deal mainly with Hurston's childhood. Like many writers, including and prototypically Tolstoy, Hurston's fiction is often autobiographical. The chapter below on her mother's death should be compared with the dying mother's scene in *Jonah's Gourd Vine* in the Fiction section of this anthology. The last selection from the autobiography, on "Love," is frustrating in its generalities. However, we have far too few records—even evasive ones—of what black women have thought about the two most important human drives: the need to work and the need to love.

Mules and Men (1935) is a classic among folklore collections primarily because of Hurston's approach and style. She does not divorce herself from the people she is studying, as traditional folklorists do, nor does she attempt to make people something other than what they are. If the folks are colorist, that is shown; if they harbor self-hatred as well as self-love, that is left clear. At all times Hurston is "the folk," a character in the tales or privy to them, just as the people who tell the tales are.

Zora Neale Hurston spent most of the period from 1936 to 1938 in Jamaica and Haiti. *Tell My Horse* (1938) suffers overall from the inclusion of too much undigested Haitian political history. The selections below, however, give a sense of Hurston's adventuresome nature, as well as insight into Jamaican and Haitian folk culture.

FROM
Dust Tracks on a Road

My Birthplace

LIKE THE DEAD-SEEMING, cold rocks, I have memories within that came out of the material that went to make me. Time and place have had their say.

So you will have to know something about the time and place where I came from, in order that you may interpret the incidents and directions of my life.

I was born in a Negro town. I do not mean by that the black back-side of an average town. Eatonville, Florida, is, and was at the time of my birth, a pure Negro town—charter, mayor, council, town marshal and all. It was not the first Negro community in America, but it was the first to be incorporated, the first attempt at organized self-government on the part of Negroes in America.

My Folks

INTO THIS BURLY, boiling, hard-hitting, rugged-individualistic setting walked one day a tall, heavy-muscled mulatto who resolved to put down roots.

John Hurston, in his late twenties, had left Macon County, Alabama, because the ordeal of share-cropping on a southern Alabama cotton plantation was crushing to his ambition. There was no rise to the thing.

He had been born near Notasulga, Alabama, in an outlying district of landless Negroes, and whites not too much better off. It was ''over the creek,'' which was just like saying on the wrong side of the railroad tracks. John Hurston had learned to read and write somehow between cotton-choppings and cotton-picking, and it might have satisfied him in a way. But somehow he took to going to Macedonia Baptist Church on the right side of the creek. He went one time, and met up with dark-brown Lucy Ann Potts, of the land-owning Richard Potts, which might have given him the going habit.

He was nearly twenty years old then, and she was fourteen. My mother used to claim with a smile that she saw him looking and looking at her up there in the choir and wondered what he was looking at her for. She wasn't studying about *him*. However, when the service was over and he kept standing around, never far from her, she asked somebody, "Who is dat bee-stung yaller nigger?"

"Oh, dat's one of dem niggers from over de creek, one of dem Hurstons—call him John I believe."

That was supposed to settle that. Over-the-creek niggers lived from one white man's plantation to the other. Regular hand-to-mouth folks. Didn't own pots to pee in, nor beds to push 'em under. Didn't have no more pride than to let themselves be hired by poor-white trash. No more to 'em than the stuffings out of a zero. The inference was that Lucy Ann Potts had asked about nothing and had been told.

Mama thought no more about him, she said. Of course, she couldn't help noticing that his gray-green eyes and light skin stood out sharply from the black-skinned, black-eyed crowd he was in. Then, too, he had a build on him that made you look. A stud-looking buck like that would have brought a big price in slavery time. Then, if he had not kept on hanging around where she couldn't help from seeing him, she would never have remembered that she had seen him two or three times before around the cotton-gin in Notasulga, and once in a store. She had wondered then who he was, handling bales of cotton like suitcases.

After that Sunday, he got right worrisome. Slipping her notes between the leaves of hymn-books and things like that. It got so bad that a few months later she made up her mind to marry him just to get rid of him. So she did, in spite of the most violent opposition of her family. She put on the little silk dress which she had made with her own hands, out of goods bought from egg-money she had saved. Her ninety pounds of fortitude set out on her wedding night alone, since none of the family except her brother Jim could bear the sight of her great come-down in the world. She who was considered the prettiest and the smartest black girl was throwing herself away and disgracing the Pottses by marrying an over-the-creek nigger, and a bastard at that. Folks said he was a certain white man's son. But here she was, setting out to walk two miles at night by herself, to keep her pledge to him at the church. Her father, more tolerant than her mother, decided that his daughter was not going alone, nor was she going to walk to her wedding. So he hitched up the buggy and went with her. Nobody much was there. Her brother Jim slipped in just before she stood on the floor.

So she said her words and took her stand for life, and went off to a cabin on a plantation with him. She never forgot how the late moon shone that night as his two hundred pounds of bone and muscle shoved open the door and lifted her in his arms over the doorsill.

That cabin on a white man's plantation had to be all for the present. She had been pointedly made to know that the Potts plantation was nothing to her any more. Her father soon softened and was satisfied to an extent, but her mother, never. To her dying day her daughter's husband was never John Hurston to her. He was always ''dat yaller bastard.'' Four years after my mother's marriage, and during her third pregnancy, she got to thinking of the five acres of cling-stone peaches on her father's place, and the yearning was so strong that she walked three miles to get a few. She was holding the corners of her apron with one hand and picking peaches with the other when her mother spied her, and ordered her off the place.

It was after his marriage that my father began to want things. Plantation life began to irk and bind him. His over-the-creek existence was finished. What else was there for a man like him? He left his wife and three children behind and went out to seek and see.

Months later he pitched into the hurly-burly of South Florida. So he heard about folks building a town all out of colored people. It seemed like a good place to go. Later on, he was to be elected Mayor of Eatonville for three terms, and to write the local laws. The village of Eatonville is still governed by the laws formulated by my father. The town clerk still consults a copy of the original printing which seems to be the only one in existence now. I have tried every way I know how to get this copy for my library, but so far it has not been possible. I had it once, but the town clerk came and took it back.

When my mother joined Papa a year after he had settled in Eatonville, she brought some quilts, her featherbed and bedstead. That was all they had in the house that night. Two burlap bags were stuffed with Spanish moss for the two older children to sleep on. The youngest child was taken into the bed with them.

So these two began their new life. Both of them swore that things were going to be better, and it came to pass as they said. They bought land, built a roomy house, planted their acres and reaped. Children kept coming—more mouths to feed and more feet for shoes. But neither of them seemed to have minded that. In fact, my father not only boasted among other men about "his house full of young'uns" but he boasted that he had never allowed his wife to go out and hit a lick of work for anybody a day in her life. Of weaknesses, he had his share, and I know that my mother was very unhappy at times, but neither of them ever made any move to call the thing off. In fact, on two occasions, I heard my father threaten to kill my mother if she ever started towards the gate to leave him. He was outraged and angry one day when she said lightly that if he did not want to do for her and his children, there was another man over the fence waiting for his job. That expression is a folk-saying and Papa had heard it used hundreds of times by other women, but he was outraged at hearing it from Mama. She definitely understood, before he got through carrying on, that the saying was not for her lips.

On another occasion Papa got the idea of escorting the wife of one of his best friends, and having the friend escort Mama. But Mama seemed to enjoy it more than Papa thought she ought to—though she had opposed the idea when it was suggested—and it ended up with Papa leaving his friend's wife at the reception and following Mama and his friend home, and marching her into the house with the muzzle of his Winchester rifle in her back. The friend's wife, left alone at the hall, gave both her husband and Papa a good cussing out the next day. Mama dared not laugh, even at that, for fear of stirring Papa up more. It was a month or so before the two families thawed out again. Even after that, the subject could never be mentioned before Papa or the friend's wife, though both of them had been red-hot for the experiment.

My mother rode herd on one woman with a horse-whip about Papa, and "spoke out" another one. This, instead of making Papa angry, seemed to please him ever so much. The woman who got "spoken out" threatened to whip my mother. Mama was very small and the other woman was husky. But when Papa heard of the threats against Mama, he notified the outside woman that if she could not whip him too, she had better not bring the mess up. The woman left the county without ever breaking another breath with Papa. Nobody around there knew what became of her.

So, looking back, I take it that Papa and Mama, in spite of his mean-derings, were really in love. Maybe he was just born before his time.

We lived on a big piece of ground with two big chinaberry trees shading the front gate and Cape jasmine bushes with hundreds of blooms on either side of the walks. I loved the fleshy, white, fragrant blooms as a child but did not make too much of them. They were too common in my neighborhood. When I got to New York and found out that the people called them gardenias, and that the flowers cost a dollar each, I was impressed. The home folks laughed when I went back down there and told them. Some of the folks did not want to believe me. A dollar for a Cape jasmine bloom! Folks up north there must be crazy.

There were plenty of orange, grapefruit, tangerine, guavas and other fruits in our yard. We had a five-acre garden with things to eat growing in it, and so we were never hungry. We had chicken on the table often; home-cured meat, and all the eggs we wanted. It was a common thing for us smaller children to fill the iron tea-kettle full of eggs and boil them, and lay around in the yard and eat them until we were full. Any left-over boiled eggs could always be used for missiles. There was plenty of fish in the lakes around the town, and so we had all that we wanted. But beef stew was something rare. We were all very happy whenever Papa went to Orlando and brought back something delicious like stew-beef. Chicken and fish were too common with us. In the same way, we treasured an apple. We had oranges, tangerines and grapefruit to use as hand-grenades on the neighbors' children. But apples were something rare. They came from way up north.

Our house had eight rooms, and we called it a two-story house; but later on I learned it was really one story and a jump. The big boys all slept up there, and it was a good place to hide and shirk from sweeping off the front porch or raking up the back yard.

Downstairs in the dining-room there was an old "safe," a punched design in its tin doors. Glasses of guava jelly, quart jars of pear, peach and other kinds of preserves. The left-over cooked foods were on the lower shelves.

There were eight children in the family, and our house was noisy from the time school turned out until bedtime. After supper we gathered in Mama's room, and everybody had to get their lessons for the next day. Mama carried us all past long division in arithmetic, and parsing sen-tences in grammar, by diagrams on the blackboard. That was as far as she had gone. Then the younger ones were turned over to my oldest brother, Bob, and Mama sat and saw to it that we paid attention. You had to keep on going over things until you did know. How I hated the multiplication tables—especially the sevens!

We had a big barn, and a stretch of ground well covered with Bermuda grass. So on moonlight nights, two-thirds of the village children from seven to eighteen would be playing hide and whoop, chick-mah-chick, hide and seek, and other boisterous games in our yard. Once or twice a year we might get permission to go and play at some other house. But that was most unusual. Mama contended that we had plenty of space to play in; plenty of things to play with; and, furthermore, plenty of us to keep each other's company. If she had her way, she meant to raise her children to stay at home. She said that there was no need for us to live like no-count Negroes and poor-white trash—too poor to sit in the house—had to come outdoors for any pleasure, or hang around somebody else's house. Any of her children who had any tendencies like that must have got it from the Hurston side. It certainly did not come from the Pottses. Things like that gave me my first glimmering of the universal female gospel that all good traits and leanings come from the mother's side.

Mama exhorted her children at every opportunity to "jump at de sun." We might not land on the sun, but at least we would get off the ground. Papa did not feel so hopeful. Let well enough alone. It did not do for Negroes to have too much spirit. He was always threatening to break mine or kill me in the attempt. My mother was always standing between us. She conceded that I was impudent and given to talking back, but she didn't want to "squinch my spirit" too much for fear that I would turn out to be a mealy-mouthed rag doll by the time I got grown. Papa always flew hot when Mama said that. I do not know whether he feared for my future, with the tendency I had to stand and give battle, or that he felt a personal reference in Mama's observation. He predicted dire things for me. The white folks were not going to stand for it. I was going to be hung before I got grown. Somebody was going to blow me down for my sassy tongue. Mama was going to suck sorrow for not beating my temper out of me before it was too late. Posses with ropes and guns were going to drag me out sooner or later on account of that stiff neck I toted. I was going to tote a hungry belly by reason of my forward ways. My older sister was meek and mild. She would always get along. Why couldn't I be like her? Mama would keep right on with whatever she was doing and remark, "Zora is my young'un, and Sarah is yours. I'll be bound mine will come out more than conquer. You leave her alone. I'll tend to her when I figger she needs it." She meant by that that Sarah had a disposition like Papa's, while mine was like hers.

Behind Mama's rocking-chair was a good place to be in times like that. Papa was not going to hit Mama. He was two hundred pounds of bone and muscle and Mama weighed somewhere in the nineties. When people teased him about Mama being the boss, he would say he could break her of headstrong ways if he wanted to, but she was so little that he couldn't find any place to hit her. My Uncle Jim, Mama's brother, used to always take exception to that. He maintained that if a woman had anything big enough to sit on, she had something big enough to hit on. That was his firm conviction, and he meant to hold on to it as long as the bottom end of his backbone pointed towards the ground—don't care who the woman was or what she looked like, or where she came from. Men like Papa who held to any other notion were just beating around the bush, dodging the issue, and otherwise looking like a fool at a funeral.

Papa used to shake his head at this and say, "What's de use of me taking my fist to a poor weakly thing like a woman? Anyhow, you got to submit yourself to 'em, so there ain't no use in beating on 'em and then have to go back and beg 'em pardon."

But perhaps the real reason that Papa did not take Uncle Jim's advice too seriously was because he saw how it worked out in Uncle Jim's own house. He could tackle Aunt Caroline, all right, but he had his hands full to really beat her. A knockdown didn't convince her that the fight was over at all. She would get up and come right on in, and she was nobody's weakling. It was generally conceded that he might get the edge on her in physical combat if he took a hammer or a trace-chain to her, but in other ways she always won. She would watch his various philandering episodes just so long, and then she would go into action. One time she saw all, and said nothing. But one Saturday afternoon, she watched him rush in with a new shoe-box which he thought that she did not see him take out to the barn and hide until he was ready to go out. Just as the sun went down, he went out, got his box, cut across the orange grove and went on down to the store.

He stopped long enough there to buy a quart of peanuts, two stalks of sugarcane, and then tripped on off to the little house in the woods where lived a certain transient light of love. Aunt Caroline kept right on ironing until he had gotten as far as the store. Then she slipped on her shoes, went out in the yard and got the axe, slung it across her shoulder and went walking very slowly behind him.

The men on the store porch had given Uncle Jim a laughing sendoff. They all knew where he was going and why. The shoes had been bought right there at the store. Now here came "dat Cal'line" with her axe on her shoulder. No chance to warn Uncle Jim at all. Nobody expected murder, but they knew that plenty of trouble was on the way. So they just sat and waited. Cal'line had done so many side-splitting things to Jim's lights of love—all without a single comment from her—that they were on pins to see what happened next.

About an hour later, when it was almost black dark, they saw a furtive figure in white dodging from tree to tree until it hopped over Clark's strawberry-patch fence and headed towards Uncle Jim's house until it disappeared.

"Looked mightily like a man in long drawers and nothing else," Walter Thomas observed. Everybody agreed that it did, but who and what could it be?

By the time the town lamp which stood in front of the store was lighted, Aunt Caroline emerged from the blackness that hid the woods and passed the store. The axe was still over her shoulder, but now it was draped with Uncle Jim's pants, shirt and coat. A new pair of women's oxfords were dangling from the handle by their strings. Two stalks of sugarcane were over her other shoulder. All she said was, "Good-evening, gentlemen," and kept right on walking towards home.

The porch rocked with laughter. They had the answer to everything. Later on when they asked Uncle Jim how Cal'line managed to get into the lady's house, he smiled sourly and said, "Dat axe was her key." When they kept on teasing him, he said, "Oh, dat old stubborn woman I married, you can't teach her nothing. I can't teach her no city ways at all."

On another occasion, she caused another lady who couldn't give the community anything but love, baby, to fall off of the high, steep church steps on her head. Aunt Cal'line might have done that just to satisfy her curiosity, since it was said that the lady felt that anything more than a petticoat under her dresses would be an encumbrance. Maybe Aunt Caroline just wanted to verify the rumor. The way the lady tumbled, it left no doubt about the matter. She was really a free soul. Evidently Aunt Caroline was put out about it, because she had to expectorate at that very moment, and it just happened to land where the lady was bare. Aunt

Caroline evidently tried to correct her error in spitting on her rival, for she took her foot and tried to grind it in. She never said a word as usual, so the lady must have misunderstood Aunt Caroline's curiosity. She left town in a hurry—a speedy hurry—and never was seen in those parts again.

So Papa did not take Uncle Jim's philosophy about handling the lady people too seriously. Every time Mama cornered him about some of his doings, he used to threaten to wring a chair over her head. She never even took enough notice of the threat to answer. She just went right on asking questions about his doings and then answering them herself until Papa slammed out of the house looking like he had been whipped all over with peach hickories. But I had better not let out a giggle at such times, or it would be just too bad.

Our house was a place where people came. Visiting preachers, Sunday school and B.Y.P.U. workers, and just friends. There was fried chicken for visitors, and other such hospitality as the house afforded.

Papa's bedroom was the guest-room. Store-bought towels would be taken out of the old round-topped trunk in Mama's room and draped on the washstand. The pitcher and bowl were scrubbed out before fresh water from the pump was put in for the use of the guest. Sweet soap was company soap. We knew that. Otherwise, Octagon laundry soap was used to keep us clean. Bleached-out meal sacks served the family for bath towels ordinarily, so that the store-bought towels could be nice and clean for visitors.

Company got the preference in toilet paper, too. Old newspapers were put out in the privy house for family use. But when company came, something better was offered them. Fair to middling guests got sheets out of the old Sears, Roebuck catalogue. But Mama would sort over her old dress patterns when really fine company came, and the privy house was well scrubbed, lime thrown in, and the soft tissue paper pattern stuck on a nail inside the place for the comfort and pleasure of our guests.

I Get Born

THIS IS ALL HEAR-SAY. Maybe some of the details of my birth as told me might be a little inaccurate, but it is pretty well established that I really did get born.

The saying goes like this. My mother's time had come and my father was not there. Being a carpenter, successful enough to have other helpers on some jobs, he was away often on building business, as well as preaching. It seems that my father was away from home for months this time. I have never been told why. But I did hear that he threatened to cut his throat when he got the news. It seems that one daughter was all that he figured he could stand. My sister, Sarah, was his favorite child, but that one girl was enough. Plenty more sons, but no more girl babies to wear out shoes and bring in nothing. I don't think he ever got over the trick he felt that I played on him by getting born a girl, and while he was off from home at that. A little of my sugar used to sweeten his coffee right now. That is a Negro way of saying his patience was short with me. Let me change a few words with him—and I am of the word-changing kind—and he was ready to change ends. Still and all, I looked more like him than any child in the house. Of course, by the time I got born, it was too late to make any suggestions, so the old man had to put up with me. He was nice about it in a way. He didn't tie me in a sack and drop me in the lake, as he probably felt like doing.

People were digging sweet potatoes, and then it was hog-killing time. Not at our house, but it was going on in general over the country like, being January and a bit cool. Most people were either butchering for themselves, or off helping other folks do their butchering, which was almost just as good. It is a gay time. A big pot of hasslits cooking with plenty of seasoning, lean slabs of fresh-killed pork frying for the helpers to refresh themselves after the work is done. Over and above being neighborly and giving aid, there is the food, the drinks and the fun of getting together.

So there was no grown folks close around when Mama's water broke. She sent one of the smaller children to fetch Aunt Judy, the mid-wife, but she was gone to Woodbridge, a mile and a half away, to eat at a hog-killing. The child was told to go over there and tell Aunt Judy to come. But nature, being indifferent to human arrangements, was impatient. My mother had to make it alone. She was too weak after I rushed out to do anything for herself, so she just was lying there, sick in the body, and worried in mind, wondering what would become of her, as well as me. She was so weak, she couldn't even reach down to where I was. She had one consolation. She knew I wasn't dead, because I was crying strong.

Help came from where she never would have thought to look for it.

A white man of many acres and things, who knew the family well, had butchered the day before. Knowing that Papa was not at home, and that consequently there would be no fresh meat in our house, he decided to drive the five miles and bring a half of a shoat, sweet potatoes, and other garden stuff along. He was there a few minutes after I was born. Seeing the front door standing open, he came on in, and hollered, "Hello, there! Call your dogs!" That is the regular way to call in the country because nearly everybody who has anything to watch has biting dogs.

Nobody answered, but he claimed later that he heard me spreading my lungs all over Orange County, so he shoved the door open and bolted on into the house.

He followed the noise and then he saw how things were, and, being the kind of a man he was, he took out his Barlow Knife and cut the navel cord, then he did the best he could about other things. When the mid-wife, locally known as a granny, arrived about an hour later, there was a fire in the stove and plenty of hot water on. I had been sponged off in some sort of a way, and Mama was holding me in her arms.

As soon as the old woman got there, the white man unloaded what he had brought, and drove off cussing about some blankety-blank people never being where you could put your hands on them when they were needed.

He got no thanks from Aunt Judy. She grumbled for years about it. She complained that the cord had not been cut just right, and the belly-band had not been put on tight enough. She was mighty scared I was going to have a weak back, and that I would have trouble holding my water until I reached puberty. I did.

The next day or so a Mrs. Neale, a friend of Mama's, came in and re-minded her that she had promised to let her name the baby in case it was a girl. She had picked up a name somewhere which she thought was very pretty. Perhaps she had read it somewhere, or somebody back in those woods was smoking Turkish cigarettes. So I became Zora Neale Hurston.

There is nothing to make you like other human beings so much as doing things for them. Therefore, the man who grannied me was back next day to see how I was coming along. Maybe it was a pride in his own handiwork, and his resourcefulness in a pinch, that made him want to see it through. He remarked that I was a God-damned fine baby, fat and plenty of lung-power. As time went on, he came infrequently, but some-how kept a pinch of interest in my welfare. It seemed that I was spying noble, growing like a gourd vine, and yelling bass like a gator. He was the kind of man that had no use for puny things, so I was all to the good with him. He thought my mother was justified in keeping me.

But nine months rolled around, and I just would not get on with the walking business. I was strong, crawling well, but showed no inclination to use my feet. I might remark in passing, that I still don't like to walk. Then I was over a year old, but still I would not walk. They made allowances for my weight, but yet, that was no real reason for my not trying.

They tell me that an old sow-hog taught me how to walk. That is, she didn't instruct me in detail, but she convinced me that I really ought to try.

It was like this. My mother was going to have collard greens for dinner, so she took the dishpan and went down to the spring to wash the greens. She left me sitting on the floor, and gave me a hunk of cornbread to keep me quiet. Everything was going along all right, until the sow with her litter of pigs in convoy came abreast of the door. She must have smelled the cornbread I was messing with and scattering crumbs about the floor. So, she came right on in, and began to nuzzle around.

My mother heard my screams and came running. Her heart must have stood still when she saw the sow in there, because hogs have been known to eat human flesh.

But I was not taking this thing sitting down. I had been placed by a chair, and when my mother got inside the door, I had pulled myself up by that chair and was getting around it right smart.

As for the sow, poor misunderstood lady, she had no interest in me except my bread. I lost that in scrambling to my feet and she was eating it. She had much less intention of eating Mama's baby, than Mama had of eating hers.

With no more suggestions from the sow or anybody else, it seems that I just took to walking and kept the thing a-going. The strangest thing about it was that once I found the use of my feet, they took to wandering. I always wanted to go. I would wander off in the woods all alone, following some inside urge to go places. This alarmed my mother a great deal. She used to say that she believed a woman who was an enemy of hers had sprinkled "travel dust" around the doorstep the day I was born. That was the only explanation she could find. I don't know why it never occurred to her to connect my tendency with my father, who didn't have a thing on his mind but this town and the next one. That should have given her a sort of hint. Some children are just bound to take after their fathers in spite of women's prayers.

The Inside Search

IN CONTRAST TO EVERYBODY about me, I was not afraid of snakes. They fascinated me in a way which I still cannot explain. I got no pleasure from their death.

I do not know when the visions began. Certainly I was not more than seven years old, but I remember the first coming very distinctly. My brother Joel and I had made a hen take an egg back and been caught as we turned the hen loose. We knew we were in for it and decided to scatter until things cooled off a bit. He hid out in the barn, but I combined discretion with pleasure, and ran clear off the place. Mr. Linsay's house was vacant for a spell. He was a neighbor who was off working somewhere at the time. I had not thought of stopping there when I set out, but I saw a big raisin lying on the porch and stopped to eat it. There was some cool shade on the porch, so I sat down, and soon I was asleep in a strange way. Like clearcut stereopticon slides, I saw twelve scenes flash before me, each one held until I had seen it well in every detail, and then be replaced by another. There was no continuity as in an average dream. Just disconnected scene after scene with blank spaces in between. I knew that they were all true, a preview of things to come, and my soul writhed in agony and shrunk away. But I knew that there was no shrinking. These things had to be. I did not wake up when the last one flickered and vanished, I merely sat up and saw the Methodist Church, the line of moss-draped oaks, and our strawberry patch stretching off to the left.

So when I left the porch, I left a great deal behind me. I was weighed down with a power I did not want. I had knowledge before its time. I knew my fate. I knew that I would be an orphan and homeless. I knew that while I was still helpless, that the comforting circle of my family would be broken, and that I would have to wander cold and friendless until I had served my time. I would stand beside a dark pool of water and see a huge fish move slowly away at a time when I would be somehow in the depth of despair. I would hurry to catch a train, with doubts and fears driving me and seek solace in a place and fail to find it when I arrived, then cross many tracks to board the train again. I knew that a house, a shotgun-built house that needed a new coat of white paint, held torture for me, but I must go. I saw deep love betrayed, but I must feel and know it. There was no turning back. And last of all, I would come to a big house. Two women waited there for me. I could not see their faces, but I knew one to be young and one to be old. One of them was arranging some queer-shaped flowers such as I had never seen. When I had come to see these women, then I would be at the end of my pilgrimage, but not the end of my life. Then I would know peace and love and what goes with those things, and not before.

These visions would return at irregular intervals. Sometimes two or three nights running. Sometimes weeks and months apart. I had no warning. I went to bed and they came. The details were always the same, except in the last picture. Once or twice I saw the old faceless woman standing outdoors beside a tall plant with that same off-shape white flower. She turned suddenly from it to welcome me. I knew what was going on in the house without going in, it was all so familiar to me.

I never told anyone around me about these strange things. It was too different. They would laugh me off as a story-teller. Besides, I had a feeling of difference from my fellow men, and I did not want it to be found out. Oh, how I cried out to be just as everybody else! But the voice said No. I must go where I was sent. The weight of the commandment laid heavy and made me moody at times. When I was an ordinary child, with no knowledge of things but the life about me, I was reasonably happy. I would hope that the call would never come again. But even as I hoped I knew that the cup meant for my lips would not pass. I must drink the bitter drink. I studied people all around me, searching for someone to fend it off. But I was told inside myself that there was no one. It gave me a feeling of terrible aloneness. I stood in a world of vanished communion with my kind, which is worse than if it had never been. Nothing is so desolate as a place where life has been and gone. I stood on a soundless island in a tideless sea.

Time was to prove the truth of my visions, for one by one they came to pass. As soon as one was fulfilled, it ceased to come. As this happened, I counted them off one by one and took consolation in the fact that one more station was past, thus bringing me nearer the end of my trials, and nearer to the big white house, with the kind women and the strange white flowers.

Years later, after the last one had come and gone, I read a sentence or a paragraph now and then in the columns of O. O. McIntyre which perhaps held no special meaning for the millions who read him, but in which I could see through those slight revelations that he had had similar experiences. Kipling knew the feeling for himself, for he wrote of it very definitely in his Plain Tales From the Hills. So I took comfort in knowing that they were fellow pilgrims on my strange road.

I consider that my real childhood ended with the coming of the pronouncements. True, I played, fought and studied with other children, but always I stood apart within. Often I was in some lonesome wilderness, suffering strange things and agonies while other children in the same yard played without a care. I asked myself why me? Why? Why? A cosmic loneliness was my shadow. Nothing and nobody around me really touched me. It is one of the blessings of this world that few people see visions and dream dreams.

Wandering

I KNEW THAT MAMA WAS SICK. She kept getting thinner and thinner and her chest cold never got any better. Finally, she took to bed.

She had come home from Alabama that way. She had gone back to her old home to be with her sister during her sister's last illness. Aunt Dinky had lasted on for two months after Mama got there, and so Mama had stayed on till the last.

It seems that there had been other things there that worried her. Down underneath, it appeared that Grandma had never quite forgiven her for the move she had made twenty-one years before in marrying Papa. So that when Mama suggested that the old Potts place be sold so that she could bring her share back with her to Florida, her mother, urged on by Uncle Bud, Mama's oldest brother, refused. Not until Grandma's head was cold, was an acre of the place to be sold. She had long since quit living on it, and it was pretty well run down, but she wouldn't, that was all. Mama could just go on back to that yaller rascal she had married like she came. I do not think that the money part worried Mama as much as the injustice and spitefulness of the thing.

Then Cousin Jimmie's death seemed to come back on Mama during her visit. He went to a party and started home. The next morning his headless body was found beside the railroad track. There was no blood, so the train couldn't have killed him. This had happened before I was born. He was said to have been a very handsome young man, and very popular with the girls. He was my mother's favorite nephew and she took it hard.

She had probably numbed over her misery, but going back there seemed to freshen up her grief. Some said that he had been waylaid by three other young fellows and killed in a jealous rage. But nothing could be proved. It was whispered that he had been shot in the head by a white man unintentionally, and then beheaded to hide the wound. He had been shot from ambush, because his assailant mistook him for a certain white man. It was night. The attacker expected the white man to pass that way, but not Jimmie. When he found out his mistake, he had forced a certain Negro to help him move the body to the railroad track without the head, so that it would look as if he had been run over by the train. Anyway, that is what the Negro wrote back after he had moved to Texas years later. There was never any move to prove the charge, for obvious reasons. Mama took the whole thing very hard.

It was not long after Mama came home that she began to be less active. Then she took to bed. I knew she was ailing but she was always frail, so I did not take it too much to heart. I was nine years old, and even though she had talked to me very earnestly one night, I could not conceive of Mama actually dying. She had talked of it many times.

That day, September 18th, she had called me and given me certain instructions. I was not to let them take the pillow from under her head until she was dead. The clock was not to be covered, nor the looking-glass. She trusted me to see to it that these things were not done. I promised her as solemnly as nine years could do, that I would see to it.

What years of agony that promise gave me! In the first place, I had no idea that it would be soon. But that same day near sundown I was called upon to set my will against my father, the village dames and village custom. I know now that I could not have succeeded.

I had left Mama and was playing outside for a little while when I noted a number of women going inside Mama's room and staying. It looked strange. So I went on in. Papa was standing at the foot of the bed looking down on my mother, who was breathing hard. As I crowded in, they lifted up the bed and turned it around so that Mama's eyes would face the east. I thought that she looked to me as the head of the bed was reversed. Her mouth was slightly open, but her breathing took up so much of her strength that she could not talk. But she looked at me, or so I felt, to speak for her. She depended on me for a voice.

The Master-Maker in His making had made Old Death. Made him with big, soft feet and square toes. Made him with a face that reflects the face of all things, but neither changes itself, nor is mirrored anywhere.

Made the body of Death out of infinite hunger. Made a weapon for his hand to satisfy his needs. This was the morning of the day of the beginning of things.

But Death had no home and he knew it at once.

"And where shall I dwell in my dwelling?" Old Death asked, for he was already old when he was made.

"You shall build you a place close to the living, get far out of the sight of eyes. Wherever there is a building, there you have your platform that comprehends the four roads of the winds. For your hunger, I give you the first and last taste of all things."

We had been born, so Death had had his first taste of us. We had built things, so he had his platform in our yard.

And now, Death stirred from his platform in his secret place in our yard, and came inside the house.

Somebody reached for the clock, while Mrs. Mattie Clarke put her hand to the pillow to take it away.

"Don't!" I cried out. "Don't take the pillow from under Mama's head! She said she didn't want it moved!"

I made to stop Mrs. Mattie, but Papa pulled me away. Others were trying to silence me. I could see the huge drop of sweat collected in the hollow at Mama's elbow and it hurt me so. They were covering the clock and the mirror.

"Don't cover up that clock! Leave that looking-glass like it is! Lemme put Mama's pillow back where it was!"

But Papa held me tight and the others frowned me down. Mama was still rasping out the last morsel of her life. I think she was trying to say something, and I think she was trying to speak to me. What was she trying to tell me? What wouldn't I give to know! Perhaps she was telling me that it was better for the pillow to be moved so that she could die easy, as they said. Perhaps she was accusing me of weakness and failure in carrying out her last wish. I do not know. I shall never know.

Just then, Death finished his prowling through the house on his padded feet and entered the room. He bowed to Mama in his way, and she made her manners and left us to act out our ceremonies over unimportant things.

I was to agonize over that moment for years to come. In the midst of play, in wakeful moments after midnight, on the way home from parties, and even in the classroom during lectures. My thoughts would escape occasionally from their confines and stare me down.

Now, I know that I could not have had my way against the world. The world we lived in required those acts. Anything else would have been sacrilege, and no nine-year-old voice was going to thwart them. My father was with the mores. He had restrained me physically from outraging the ceremonies established for the dying. If there is any consciousness after death, I hope that Mama knows that I did my best. She must know how I have suffered for my failure.

But life picked me up from the foot of Mama's bed, grief, self-despisement and all, and set my feet in strange ways. That moment was the end of a phase in my life. I was old before my time with grief of loss, of failure, and of remorse. No matter what the others did, my mother had put her trust in me. She had felt that I could and would carry out her wishes, and I had not. And then in that sunset time, I failed her. It seemed as she died that the sun went down on purpose to flee away from me.

That hour began my wanderings. Not so much in geography, but in time. Then not so much in time as in spirit.

Mama died at sundown and changed a world. That is, the world which had been built out of her body and her heart. Even the physical aspects fell apart with a suddenness that was startling.

My oldest brother was up in Jacksonville in school, and he arrived home after Mama had passed. By then, she had been washed and dressed and laid out on the ironing-board in the parlor.

Practically all of the village was in the front yard and on the porch, talking in low tones and waiting. They were not especially waiting for my brother Bob. They were doing that kind of waiting that people do around death. It is a kind of sipping up the drama of the thing. However, if they were asked, they would say it was the sadness of the occasion which drew them. In reality it is a kind of feast of the Passover.

Bob's grief was awful when he realized that he was too late. He could not conceive at first that nothing could be done to straighten things out. There was no ear for his excuse nor explanation—no way to ease what was in him. Finally it must have come to him that what he had inside, he must take with him wherever he went. Mama was there on the cooling board with the sheet draped over her blowing gently in the wind. Nothing there seemed to hear him at all.

There was my sister Sarah in the kitchen crying and trying to quiet Everett, who was just past two years old. She was crying and trying to make him hush at the same time. He was crying because he sensed the grief around him. And then, Sarah, who was fifteen, had been his nurse and he would respond to her mood, whatever it was. We were all grubby bales of misery, huddled about lamps.

I have often wished I had been old enough at the time to look into Papa's heart that night. If I could know what that moment meant to him, I could have set my compass towards him and been sure. I know that I did love him in a way, and that I admired many things about him. He had a poetry about him that I loved. That had made him a successful preacher. He could hit ninety-seven out of a hundred with a gun. He could swim Lake Maitland from Maitland to Winter Park, and no man in the village could put my father's shoulders to the ground. We were so certain of Papa's invincibility in combat that when a village woman scolded Everett for some misdemeanor, and told him that God would punish him, Everett, just two years old, reared back and told her, "He better not bother me. Papa will shoot Him down." He found out better later on, but that goes to show you how big our Papa looked to us. We had seen him bring down bears and panthers with his gun, and chin the bar more times than any man in competing distance. He had to our knowledge licked two men who Mama told him had to be licked. All that part was just fine with me. But I was Mama's child. I knew that she had not always been happy, and I wanted to know just how sad he was that night.

I have repeatedly called up that picture and questioned it. Papa cried some too, as he moved in his awkward way about the place. From the kitchen to the front porch and back again. He kept saying, "Poor thing! She suffered so much." I do not know what he meant by that. It could have been love and pity for her suffering ending at last. It could have been remorse mixed with relief. The hard-driving force was no longer opposed to his easy-going pace. He could put his potentialities to sleep and be happy in the laugh of the day. He could do next year or never, what Mama would have insisted must be done today. Rome, the eternal city, meant two different things to my parents. To Mama, it meant, you must build it today so it could last through eternity. To Papa, it meant that you had to lay some bricks today and you have the rest of eternity to finish it. With all time, why hurry? God had made more time than anything else, anyway. Why act so stingy about it?

Then too, I used to notice how Mama used to snatch Papa. That is, he would start to put up an argument that would have been terrific on the store porch, but Mama would pitch in with a single word or a sentence and mess it all up. You could tell he was mad as fire with no words to blow it out with. He would sit over in the corner and cut his eyes at her real hard. He was used to being a hero on the store porch and in church affairs, and I can see how he must have felt to be always outdone around home. I know now that that is a griping thing to a man—not to be able to whip his woman mentally. Some women know how to give their man that conquesting feeling. My mother took her over-the-creek man and bare-knuckled him from brogans to broadcloth, and I am certain that he was proud of the change, in public. But in the house, he might have always felt over-the-creek, and because that was not the statue he had made for himself to look at, he resented it. But then, you cannot blame my mother too much if she did not see him as his entranced congregations did. The one who makes the idols never worships them, however tenderly he might have molded the clay. You cannot have knowledge and worship at the same time. Mystery is the essence of divinity. Gods must keep their distances from men.

Anyway, the next day, Sam Moseley's span of fine horses, hitched to our wagon, carried my mother to Macedonia Baptist Church for the last time. The finality of the thing came to me fully when the earth began to thud on the coffin.

That night, all of Mama's children were assembled together for the last time on earth. The next day, Bob and Sarah went back to Jacksonville to school. Papa was away from home a great deal, so two weeks later I was on my way to Jacksonville, too. I was under age, but the school had agreed to take me in under the circumstances. My sister was to look after me, in a way.

The midnight train had to be waved down at Maitland for me. That would put me into Jacksonville in the daytime.

As my brother Dick drove the mile with me that night, we approached the curve in the road that skirts Lake Catherine, and suddenly I saw the first picture of my visions. I had seen myself upon that curve at night leaving the village home, bowed down with grief that was more than common. As it all flashed back to me, I started violently for a minute, then I moved closer beside Dick as if he could shield me from those others that were to come. He asked me what was the matter, and I said I thought I heard something moving down by the lake. He laughed at that, and we rode on, the lantern showing the roadway, and me keeping as close to Dick as I could. A little, humped-up, shabby-backed trunk was behind us in the buckboard. I was on my way from the village, never to return to it as a real part of the town.

Jacksonville made me know that I was a little colored girl. Things were all about the town to point this out to me. Streetcars and stores and then talk I heard around the school. I was no longer among the white people whose homes I could barge into with a sure sense of welcome. These white people had funny ways. I could tell that even from a distance. I didn't get a piece of candy or a bag of crackers just for going into a store in Jacksonville as I did when I went into Galloway's or Hill's at Maitland, or Joe Clarke's in Eatonville.

Around the school I was an awful bother. The girls complained that they didn't get a chance to talk without me turning up somewhere to be in the way. I broke up many good "He said" conferences just by showing up. It was not my intention to do so. What I wanted was for it to go full steam ahead and let me listen. But that didn't seem to please. I was not in the "he said" class, and they wished I would kindly please stay out of the way. My underskirt was hanging, for instance. Why didn't I go some place and fix it? My head looked like a hoo-raw's nest. Why didn't I go comb it? If I took time enough to match my stockings, I wouldn't have time to be trying to listen in on grown folk's business. These venerable old ladies were anywhere from fifteen to eighteen.

In the classroom I got along splendidly. The only difficulty was that I was rated as sassy. I just had to talk back at established authority and that established authority hated backtalk worse than barbed-wire pie. My brother was asked to speak to me in addition to a licking or two. But on the whole, things went along all right. My immediate teachers were enthusiastic about me. It was the guardians of study-hour and prayer meetings who felt that their burden was extra hard to bear.

School in Jacksonville was one of those twilight things. It was not dark, but it lacked the bold sunlight that I craved. I worshipped two of my teachers and loved gingersnaps with cheese, and sour pickles. But I was deprived of the loving pine, the lakes, the wild violets in the woods and the animals I used to know. No more holding down first base on the team with my brothers and their friends. Just a jagged hole where my home used to be.

At times, the girls of the school were lined up two and two and taken for a walk. On one of these occasions, I had an experience that set my heart to fluttering. I saw a woman sitting on a porch who looked at a distance like Mama. Maybe it *was* Mama! Maybe she was not dead at all. They had made some mistake. Mama had gone off to Jacksonville and they thought that she was dead. The woman was sitting in a rocking-chair just like Mama always did. It must be Mama! But before I came abreast of the porch in my rigid place in line, the woman got up and went inside. I wanted to stop and go in. But I didn't even breathe my hope to anyone. I made up my mind to run away someday and find the house and let Mama know where I was. But before I did, the hope that the woman really was my mother passed. I accepted my bereavement.

Research

RESEARCH IS FORMALIZED CURIOSITY. It is poking and prying with purpose. It is a seeking that he who wishes may know the cosmic secrets of the world and they that dwell therein.

I was extremely proud that Papa Franz felt like sending me on that folklore search. As is well known, Dr. Franz Boas of the Department of Anthropology of Columbia University, is the greatest anthropologist alive, for two reasons. The first is his insatiable hunger for knowledge and then more knowledge; and the second is his genius for pure objectivity. He has no pet wishes to prove. His instructions are to go out and find what is there. He outlines his theory, but if the facts do not agree with it, he would not warp a jot or dot of the findings to save his theory. So knowing all this, I was proud that he trusted me. I went off in a vehicle made out of corona stuff.

My first six months were disappointing. I found out later that it was not because I had no talents for research, but because I did not have the right approach. The glamor of Barnard College was still upon me. I dwelt in marble halls. I knew where the material was all right. But, I went about asking, in carefully accented Barnardese, "Pardon me, but do you know any folk-tales or folk-songs?" The men and women who had whole treasuries of material just seeping through their pores looked at me and shook their heads. No, they had never heard of anything like that around there. Maybe it was over in the next county. Why didn't I try over there? I did, and got the selfsame answer. Oh, I got a few little items. But compared with what I did later, not enough to make a flea a waltzing jacket. Considering the mood of my going south, I went back to New York with my heart beneath my knees and my knees in some lonesome valley.

I stood before Papa Franz and cried salty tears. He gave me a good going over, but later I found that he was not as disappointed as he let me think. He knew I was green and feeling my oats, and that only bitter disappointment was going to purge me. It did.

What I learned from him then and later, stood me in good stead when Godmother, Mrs. R. Osgood Mason, set aside two hundred dollars a month for a two-year period for me to work.

My relations with Godmother were curious. Laugh if you will, but there was and is a psychic bond between us. She could read my mind, not only when I was in her presence, but thousands of miles away. Both Max Eastman and Richmond Barthe have told me that she could do the same with them. But, the thing that delighted her was the fact that I was her only Godchild who could read her thoughts at a distance. Her old fingers were cramped and she could not write, but in her friend Cornelia Chapin's exact script, a letter would find me in Alabama, or Florida, or in the Bahama Islands and lay me by the heels for what I was *thinking*. "You have broken the law," it would accuse sternly. "You are dissipating your powers in things that have no real meaning," and go on to lacerate me. "Keep silent. Does a child in the womb speak?"

She was just as pagan as I. She had lived for years among the Plains Indians and had collected a beautiful book of Indian lore. Often when she wished to impress upon me my garrulity, she would take this book from the shelf and read me something of Indian beauty and restraint. Sometimes, I would feel like a rabbit at a dog convention. She would invite me to dinner at her apartment, 399 Park Avenue, and then she, Cornelia Chapin, and Miss Chapin's sister, Mrs. Katherine Garrison Biddle, would all hem me up and give me what for. When they had given me a proper straightening, and they felt that I saw the light, all the sternness would vanish, and I would be wrapped in love. A present of money from Godmother, a coat from Miss Chapin, a dress from Mrs. Biddle. We had a great deal to talk about because Cornelia Chapin was a sculptor, Katherine Biddle, a poet, and Godmother, an earnest patron of the arts.

Then too, she was Godmother to Miguel Covarrubias and Langston Hughes. Sometimes all of us were there. She has several paintings by Covarrubias on her walls. She summoned us when one or the other of us returned from our labors. Miguel and I would exhibit our movies, and Godmother and the Chapin family, including brother Paul Chapin, would praise us and pan us, according as we had done. Godmother could be as tender as mother-love when she felt that you had been right spiritually. But anything in you, however clever, that felt like insincerity to her, called forth her well-known "That is nothing! It has no soul in it. You have broken the law!" Her tongue was a knout, cutting off your outer pretenses, and bleeding your vanity like a rusty nail. She was merciless to a lie, spoken, acted or insinuated.

She was extremely human. There she was sitting up there at the table over capon, caviar and gleaming silver, eager to hear every word on every phase of life on a saw-mill "job." I must tell the tales, sing the songs, do the dances, and repeat the raucous sayings and doings of the Negro farthest down. She is altogether in sympathy with them, because she says truthfully they are utterly sincere in living.

My search for knowledge of things took me into many strange places and adventures. My life was in danger several times. If I had not learned how to take care of myself in these circumstances, I could have been maimed or killed on most any day of the several years of my research work. Primitive minds are quick to sunshine and quick to anger. Some little word, look or gesture can move them either to love or to sticking a knife between your ribs. You just have to sense the delicate balance and maintain it.

In some instances, there is nothing personal in the killing. The killer wishes to establish a reputation as a killer, and you'll do as a sample. Some of them go around, making their announcements in singing:

> I'm going to make me a graveyard of my own,
> I'm going to make me a graveyard of my own,
> Oh, carried me down on de smoky road,
> Brought me back on de coolin' board,
> But I'm going to make me a graveyard of my own.

And since the law is lax on these big saw-mill, turpentine and railroad "jobs," there is a good chance that they never will be jailed for it. All of these places have plenty of men and women who are fugitives from justice. The management asks no questions. They need help and they can't be bothered looking for a bug under every chip. In some places, the "law" is forbidden to come on the premises to hunt for malefactors who did their malefacting elsewhere. The wheels of industry must move, and if these men don't do the work, who is there to do it?

So if a man, or a woman, has been on the gang for petty-thieving and mere mayhem, and is green with jealousy of the others who did the same amount of time for a killing and had something to brag about, why not look around for an easy victim and become a hero, too? I was nominated like that once in Polk County, Florida, and the only reason that I was not elected, was because a friend got in there and staved off old club-footed Death.

Polk County! Ah!
Where the water tastes like cherry wine.
Where they fell great trees with axe and muscle.

These poets of the swinging blade! The brief, but infinitely graceful, dance of body and axe-head as it lifts over the head in a fluid arc, dances in air and rushes down to bite into the tree, all in beauty. Where the logs march into the mill with its smokestacks disputing with the elements, its boiler room reddening the sky, and its great circular saw screaming arrogantly as it attacks the tree like a lion making its kill. The log on the carriage coming to the saw. A growling grumble. Then contact. Yeelld-u-u-ow! And a board is laid shining and new on a pile. All day, all night. Rumble, thunder and grumble. Yee-ee-ow! Sweating black bodies, muscled like gods, working to feed the hunger of the great tooth. Polk County!

Polk County. Black men laughing and singing. They go down in the phosphate mines and bring up the wet dust of the bones of pre-historic monsters, to make rich land in far places, so that people can eat. But, all of it is not dust. Huge ribs, twenty feet from belly to backbone. Some old-time sea monster caught in the shallows in that morning when God said, ''Let's make some more dry land. Stay there, great Leviathan! Stay there as a memory and a monument to Time.'' Shark-teeth as wide as the hand of a working man. Joints of backbone three feet high, bearing witness to the mighty monster of the deep when the Painted Land rose up and did her first dance with the morning sun. Gazing on these relics, forty thousand years old and more, one visualizes the great surrender to chance and change when these creatures were rocked to sleep and slumber by the birth of land.

Polk County. Black men from tree to tree among the lordly pines, a swift, slanting stroke to bleed the trees for gum. Paint, explosives, marine stores, flavors, perfumes, tone for a violin bow, and many other things which the black men who bleed the trees never heard about.

Polk County. The clang of nine-pound hammers on railroad steel. The world must ride.

Hah! A rhythmic swing of the body, hammer falls, and another spike driven to the head in the tie.

Oh, Mobile! Hank!
Oh, Alabama! Hank!
Oh, Fort Myers! Hank!
Oh, in Florida! Hank!
Oh, let's shake it! Hank!
Oh, let's break it! Hank!
Oh, let's shake it! Hank!
Oh, just a hair! Hank!

The singing-liner cuts short his chant. The straw-boss relaxes with a gesture of his hand. Another rail spiked down. Another offering to the soul of civilization whose other name is travel.

Polk County. Black men scrambling up ladders into orange trees. Singing, laughing, cursing, boasting of last night's love, and looking forward to the darkness again. They do not say embrace when they mean that they slept with a woman. A behind is a behind and not a form. Nobody says anything about incompatibility when they mean it does not suit. No bones are made about being fed up.

I got up this morning, and I knowed I didn't want it,
Yea! Polk County!
You don't know Polk County like I do
Anybody been there, tell you the same thing, too.
Eh, rider, rider!
Polk County, where the water tastes like cherry wine.

Polk County. After dark, the jooks. Songs are born out of feelings with an old beat-up piano, or a guitar for a mid-wife. Love made and unmade. Who put out dat lie, it was supposed to last forever? Love is when it is. No more here? Plenty more down the road. Take you where I'm going, woman? Hell no! Let every town furnish its own. Yeah, I'm going. Who care anything about no train fare? The railroad track is there, ain't it? I can count tires just like I been doing. I can ride de blind, can't I ?

Got on de train didn't have no fare
But I rode some
Yes I rode some.
Got on de train didn't have no fare
Conductor ast me what I'm doing there
But I rode some
Yes I rode some.

Well, he grabbed me by de collar and he led me to de door
But I rode some
Yes I rode some.
Well, he grabbed me by de collar and he led me to de door
He rapped me over de head with a forty-four
But I rode some
Yes I rode some.

Polk County in the jooks. Dancing the square dance. Dancing the scronch. Dancing the belly-rub. Knocking the right hat off the wrong head, and backing it up with a switch-blade.

"Fan-foot, what you doing with my man's hat cocked on *your* nappy head? I know you want to see your Jesus. Who's a whore? Yeah I sleeps with my mens, but they pays me. I wouldn't be a fan-foot like you—just on de road somewhere. Runs up and down de road from job to job making pay-days. Don't nobody hold her! Let her jump on me! She pay her way on me, and I'll pay it off. Make time in old Bartow jail for her."

Maybe somebody stops the fight before the two switch-blades go together. Maybe nobody can. A short, swift dash in. A lucky jab by one opponent and the other one is dead. Maybe one gets a chill in the feet and leaps out of the door. Maybe both get cut badly and back off. Anyhow, the fun of the place goes on. More dancing and singing and buying of drinks, parched peanuts, fried rabbit. Full drummy bass from the piano with weepy, intricate right-hand stuff. Singing the memories of Ella Wall, the Queen of love in the jooks of Polk County. Ella Wall, Planchita, Trottin' Liza.

It is a sad, parting song. Each verse ends up with:

Quarters Boss! High Sheriff? Lemme git gone from here!
Cold, rainy day, some old cold, rainy day
I'll be back, some old cold, rainy day.

Oh, de rocks may be my pillow, Lawd!
De sand may be my bed
I'll be back some old cold, rainy day.

"Who run? What you running from the man for, nigger? Me, I don't aim to run a step. I ain't going to run unless they run me. I'm going to live anyhow until I die. Play me some music so I can dance! Aw, spank dat box, man!! Them white folks don't care nothing bout no nigger getting cut and kilt, nohow. They ain't coming in here. I done kilt me four and they ain't hung me yet. Beat dat box!"

"Yeah, but you ain't kilt no women, yet. They's mighty particular 'bout you killing up women."

"And I ain't killing none neither. I ain't crazy in de head. Nigger woman can kill all us men she wants to and they don't care. Leave us kill a woman and they'll run you just as long as you can find something to step on. I got good sense. I know I ain't got no show. De white mens and de nigger women is running this thing. Sing about old Georgy Buck and let's dance off of it. Hit dat box!"

Old Georgy Buck is dead
Last word he said
I don't want no shortening in my bread.
Rabbit on de log
Ain't got no dog
Shoot him wid my rifle, bam! bam!

And the night, the pay night rocks on with music and gambling and laughter and dancing and fights. The big pile of cross-ties burning out in front simmers down to low ashes before sun-up, so then it is time to throw up all the likker you can't keep down and go somewhere and sleep the rest off, whether your knife has blood on it or not. That is, unless some strange, low member of your own race has gone and pimped to the white folks about something getting hurt. Very few of those kind are to be found.

That is the primeval flavor of the place, and as I said before, out of this primitive approach to things, I all but lost my life.

It was in a saw-mill jook in Polk County that I almost got cut to death.

Lucy really wanted to kill me. I didn't mean any harm. All I was doing was collecting songs from Slim, who used to be her man back up in
West Florida before he ran off from her. It is true that she found out
where he was after nearly a year, and followed him to Polk County and he
paid her some slight attention. He was knocking the pad with women, all
around, and he seemed to want to sort of free-lance at it. But what he
seemed to care most about was picking his guitar, and singing.

He was a valuable source of material to me, so I built him up a bit by
buying him drinks and letting him ride in my car.

I figure that Lucy took a pick at me for three reasons. The first one
was, her vanity was rubbed sore at not being able to hold her man. That
was hard to own up to in a community where so much stress was laid on
suiting. Nobody else had offered to shack up with her either. She was getting a very limited retail trade and Slim was ignoring the whole business.
I had store-bought clothes, a lighter skin, and a shiny car, so she saw
wherein she could use me for an alibi. So in spite of public knowledge of
the situation for a year or more before I came, she was telling it around
that I came and broke them up. She was going to cut everything off of me
but "quit it."

Her second reason was, because of my research methods I had dug in
with the male community. Most of the women liked me, too. Especially
her sworn enemy, Big Sweet. She was scared of Big Sweet, but she probably reasoned that if she cut Big Sweet's protégée it would be a slam on
Big Sweet and build up her own reputation. She was fighting Big Sweet
through me.

Her third reason was, she had been in little scraps and been to jail off
and on, but she could not swear that she had ever killed anybody. She
was small potatoes and nobody was paying her any mind. I was easy. I
had no gun, knife or any sort of weapon. I did not even know how to do
that kind of fighting.

Lucky for me, I had friended with Big Sweet. She came to my notice
within the first week that I arrived on location. I heard somebody, a woman's voice "specifying" up this line of houses from where I lived and
asked who it was.

"Dat's Big Sweet" my landlady told me. "She got her foot up on
somebody. Ain't she specifying?"

She was really giving the particulars. She was giving a "reading," a
word borrowed from the fortune-tellers. She was giving her opponent
lurid data and bringing him up to date on his ancestry, his looks, smell,

gait, clothes, and his route through Hell in the hereafter. My landlady went outside where nearly everybody else of the four or five hundred people on the "job" were to listen to the reading. Big Sweet broke the news to him, in one of her mildest bulletins that his pa was a double-humpted camel and his ma was a grass-gut cow, but even so, he tore her wide open in the act of getting born, and so on and so forth. He was a bitch's baby out of a buzzard egg.

My landlady explained to me what was meant by "putting your foot up" on a person. If you are sufficiently armed—enough to stand off a panzer division—and know what to do with your weapons after you get 'em, it is all right to go to the house of your enemy, put one foot up on his steps, rest one elbow on your knee and play in the family. That is another way of saying play the dozens, which is also a way of saying low-rate your enemy's ancestors and him, down to the present moment for reference, and then go into his future as far as your imagination leads you. But if you have no faith in your personal courage and confidence in your arsenal, don't try it. It is a risky pleasure. So then I had a measure of this Big Sweet.

"Hurt who?" Mrs. Bertha snorted at my fears. "Big Sweet? Humph! Tain't a man, woman nor child on this job going to tackle Big Sweet. If God send her a pistol she'll send him a man. She can handle a knife with anybody. She'll join hands and cut a duel. Dat Cracker Quarters Boss wears two pistols round his waist and goes for bad, but he won't break a breath with Big Sweet lessen he got his pistol in his hand. Cause if he start anything with her, he won't never get a chance to draw it. She ain't mean. She don't bother nobody. She just don't stand for no foolishness, dat's all."

Right away, I decided that Big Sweet was going to be my friend. From what I had seen and heard in the short time I had been there, I felt as timid as an egg without a shell. So the next afternoon when she was pointed out to me, I waited until she was well up the sawdust road to the Commissary, then I got in my car and went that way as if by accident. When I pulled up beside her and offered her a ride, she frowned at me first, then looked puzzled, but finally broke into a smile and got in.

By the time we got to the Commissary post office we were getting along fine. She told everybody I was her friend. We did not go back to the Quarters at once. She carried me around to several places and showed me off. We made a date to go down to Lakeland come Saturday, which we did. By the time we sighted the Quarters on the way back from Lake-

land, she had told me, "You sho is crazy!" Which is a way of saying I was
witty. "I loves to friend with somebody like you. I aims to look out for
you, too. Do your fighting for you. Nobody better start nothing with
you, do I'll get my switch-blade and go round de ham-bone looking for
meat."

We shook hands and I gave her one of my bracelets. After that
everything went well for me. Big Sweet helped me to collect material in a
big way. She had no idea what I wanted with it, but if I wanted it, she
meant to see to it that I got it. She pointed out people who knew songs
and stories. She wouldn't stand for balkiness on their part. We held two
lying contests, story-telling contests to you, and Big Sweet passed on who
rated the prizes. In that way, there was no argument about it.

So when the word came to Big Sweet that Lucy was threatening me,
she put her foot up on Lucy in a most particular manner and warned her
against the try. I suggested buying a knife for defense, but she said I
would certainly be killed that way.

"You don't know how to handle no knife. You ain't got dat kind of
a sense. You wouldn't even know how to hold it to de best advantage.
You would draw your arm way back to stop her, and whilst you was doing
all dat, Lucy would run in under your arm and be done; cut you to death
before you could touch her. And then again, when you sure 'nough
fighting, it ain't enough to just stick 'em wid your knife. You got to ram
it in to de hilt, then you pull *down*. They ain't no more trouble after dat.
They's *dead*. But don't you bother 'bout no fighting. You ain't like me.
You don't even sleep with no mens. I wanted to be a virgin one time, but
I couldn't keep it up. I needed the money too bad. But I think it's nice
for you to be like that. You just keep on writing down them lies. I'll take
care of all de fighting. Dat'll make it more better, since we done made
friends."

She warned me that Lucy might try to "steal" me. That is, ambush
me, or otherwise attack me without warning. So I was careful. I went nowhere on foot without Big Sweet.

Several weeks went by, then I ventured to the jook alone. Big Sweet
let it be known that she was not going. But later she came in and went
over to the coon-can game in the corner. Thinking I was alone, Lucy
waited till things were in full swing and then came in with the very man
to whom Big Sweet had given the "reading." There was only one door. I
was far from it. I saw no escape for me when Lucy strode in, knife in

hand. I saw sudden death very near that moment. I was paralyzed with fear. Big Sweet was in a crowd over in the corner, and did not see Lucy come in. But the sudden quiet of the place made her look around as Lucy charged. My friend was large and portly, but extremely light on her feet. She sprang like a lioness and I think the very surprise of Big Sweet being there when Lucy thought she was over at another party at Pine Mill unnerved Lucy. She stopped abruptly as Big Sweet charged. The next moment, it was too late for Lucy to start again. The man who came in with Lucy tried to help her out, but two other men joined Big Sweet in the battle. It took on amazingly. It seemed that anybody who had any fighting to do, decided to settle-up then and there. Switch-blades, ice-picks and old-fashioned razors were out. One or two razors had already been bent back and thrown across the room, but our fight was the main attraction. Big Sweet yelled to me to run. I really ran, too. I ran out of the place, ran to my room, threw my things in the car and left the place. When the sun came up I was a hundred miles up the road, headed for New Orleans.

In New Orleans, I delved into Hoodoo, or sympathetic magic. I studied with the Frizzly Rooster, and all of the other noted "doctors." I learned the routines for making and breaking marriages; driving off and punishing enemies; influencing the minds of judges and juries in favor of clients; killing by remote control and other things. In order to work with these "two-headed" doctors, I had to go through an initiation with each. The routine varied with each doctor.

In one case it was not only elaborate, it was impressive. I lay naked for three days and nights on a couch, with my navel to a rattlesnake skin which had been dressed and dedicated to the ceremony. I ate no food in all that time. Only a pitcher of water was on a little table at the head of the couch so that my soul would not wander off in search of water and be attacked by evil influences and not return to me. On the second day, I began to dream strange exalted dreams. On the third night, I had dreams that seemed real for weeks. In one, I strode across the heavens with lightning flashing from under my feet, and grumbling thunder following in my wake.

In this particular ceremony, my finger was cut and I became blood brother to the rattlesnake. We were to aid each other forever. I was to walk with the storm and hold my power, and get my answers to life and things in storms. The symbol of lightning was painted on my back. This was to be mine forever.

In another ceremony, I had to sit at the crossroads at midnight in complete darkness and meet the Devil, and make a compact. That was a long, long hour as I sat flat on the ground there alone and invited the King of Hell.

The most terrifying was going to a lonely glade in the swamp to get the black cat bone. The magic circle was made and all of the participants were inside. I was told that anything outside that circle was in deadly peril. The fire was built inside, the pot prepared and the black cat was thrown in with the proper ceremony and boiled until his bones fell apart. Strange and terrible monsters seemed to thunder up to that ring while this was going on. It took months for me to doubt it afterwards.

When I left Louisiana, I went to South Florida again, and from what I heard around Miami, I decided to go to the Bahamas. I had heard some Bahaman music and seen a Jumping Dance out in Liberty City and I was entranced.

This music of the Bahaman Negroes was more original, dynamic and African, than American Negro songs. I just had to know more. So without giving Godmother a chance to object, I sailed for Nassau.

I loved the place the moment I landed. Then, that first night as I lay in bed, listening to the rustle of a cocoanut palm just outside my window, a song accompanied by string and drum broke out in full harmony. I got up and peeped out and saw four young men and they were singing Bellamina, led by Ned Isaacs. I did not know him then, but I met him the next day. The song has a beautiful air, and the oddest rhythm.

Bellamina, Bellamina!
She come back in the harbor
Bellamina, Bellamina
She come back in the harbor
Put Bellamina on the dock
And paint Bellamina black! Black!
Oh, put the Bellamina on the dock
And paint Bellamina, black! Black!

I found out later that it was a song about a rum-running boat that had been gleaming white, but after it had been captured by the United

States Coast Guard and released, it was painted black for obvious reasons.

That was my welcome to Nassau, and it was a beautiful one. The next day I got an idea of what prolific song-makers the Bahamans are. In that West African accent grafted on the English of the uneducated Bahaman, I was told, "You do anything, we put you in sing." I walked carefully to keep out of "sing."

This visit to Nassau was to have far-reaching effects. I stayed on, ran to every Jumping Dance that I heard of, learned to "jump," collected more than a hundred tunes and resolved to make them known to the world.

On my return to New York in 1932, after trying vainly to interest others, I introduced Bahaman songs and dances to a New York audience at the John Golden Theater, and both the songs and the dances took on. The concert achieved its purpose. I aimed to show what beauty and appeal there was in genuine Negro material, as against the Broadway concept, and it went over.

Since then, there has been a sharp trend towards genuine Negro material. The dances aroused a tremendous interest in primitive Negro dancing. Hall Johnson took my group to appear with his singers at the Lewisohn Stadium that summer and built his "Run Lil' Chillun" around them and the religious scene from my concert, "From Sun to Sin." That was not all, the dramatized presentation of Negro work-songs in that same concert aroused interest in them and they have been exploited by singers ever since.

I had no intention of making concert my field. I wanted to show the wealth and beauty of the material to those who were in the field and therefore I felt that my job was well done when it took on.

My group was invited to perform at the New School of Social Research; in the folk-dance carnival at the Vanderbilt Hotel in New York; at Nyack; at St. Louis; Chicago; Rollins College in Winter Park, Florida; Lake Wales; Sanford; Orlando; Constitution Hall, Washington, D.C.; and Daytona Beach, Florida.

Besides the finding of the dances and the music, two other important things happened to me in Nassau. One was, I lived through that terrible five-day hurricane of 1929. It was horrible in its intensity and duration. I saw dead people washing around on the streets when it was over. You could smell the stench from dead animals as well. More than three hundred houses were blown down in the city of Nassau alone.

Then I saw something else out there. I met Leon Walton Young. He is a grizzly, stocky black man, who is a legislator in the House. He represented the first district in the Bahamas and had done so for more than twenty years when I met him.

Leon Walton Young was either a great hero, or a black bounder, according to who was doing the talking. He was a great champion and a hero in the mouths of the lowly blacks of the islands and to a somewhat lesser degree to the native-born whites. He was a Bahaman for the Bahaman man and a stout fellow along those lines. To the English, who had been sent out to take the jobs of the natives, white and black, he was a cheeky dastard of a black colonial who needed to be put in his place. He was also too much for the mixed-blood Negroes of education and property, who were as prejudiced against his color as the English. What was more, Leon Walton Young had no formal education, though I found him like George Schuyler of New York to be better read than most people with college degrees. But did he, because of his lack of schooling, defer to the Negroes who had journeyed to London and Edinburgh? He most certainly did not, and what was more, he more than held his own in the hustings.

There was a much felt need for him to be put down, but those who put on the white armor of St. George to go out and slay the dragon always came back—not honorably dead on their shields—but splattered all over with mud and the seat of their pants torn and missing. A peasant mounted on a mule had unhorsed a cavalier and took his pants. The dance drums of Grantstown and Baintown would throb and his humbled opponents would be "put in sing."

He so humbled a governor, who tried to overawe Young by reminding him that he was "His Majesty's representative in these Islands" that the governor was recalled and sent to some peaceful spot in West Africa. Young had replied to that pompous statement with, "Yes, but if you continue your tactics out here you will make me forget it."

That was one of his gentlest thumps on the Governor's pride and prestige. His Majesty's Representative accused Young of having said publicly that he, the Governor, was a bum out of the streets of London, and to his eternal rage, Young more than admitted the statement. The English appointees and the high yellows shuddered at such temerity, but the local whites and the working blacks gloried in his spunk.

The humble Negroes of America are great song-makers, but the Bahaman is greater. He is more prolific and his tunes are better. Nothing is too big, or little, to be "put in sing." They only need discovery. They are much more original than the Calypso singers of Trinidad, as will be found the moment you put it to the proof.

I hear that now the Duke of Windsor is their great hero. To them, he is "Our King." I would love to hear how he and his Duchess have been put in sing.

I enjoyed collecting the folk-tales and I believe the people from whom I collected them enjoyed the telling of them, just as much as I did the hearing. Once they got started, the "lies" just rolled and story-tellers fought for a chance to talk. It was the same with the songs. The one thing to be guarded against, in the interest of truth, was over-enthusiasm. For instance, if a song was going good, and the material ran out, the singer was apt to interpolate pieces of other songs into it. The only way you can know when that happens, is to know your material so well that you can sense the violation. Even if you do not know the song that is being used for padding, you can tell the change in rhythm and tempo. The words do not count. The subject matter in Negro folk-songs can be anything and go from love to work, to travel, to food, to weather, to fight, to demanding the return of a wig by a woman who has turned unfaithful. The tune is the unity of the thing. And you have to know what you are doing when you begin to pass on that, because Negroes can fit in more words and leave out more and still keep the tune better than anyone I can think of.

One bit of research I did jointly for the Journal of Negro History and Columbia University, was in Mobile, Alabama. There I went to talk to Cudjo Lewis. That is the American version of his name. His African name was Kossola-O-Lo-Loo-Ay.

He arrived on the last load of slaves run into the United States and was the only Negro alive that came over on a slave ship. It happened in 1859 just when the fight between the South and the Abolitionists was moving toward the Civil War. He has died since I saw him.

I found him a cheerful, poetical old gentleman in his late nineties, who could tell a good story. His interpretation of the story of Jonah was marvelous.

He was a good Christian and so he pretended to have forgotten all of his African religion. He turned me off with the statement that his Nigerian religion was the same as Christianity. "We know it a God, you unner'stand, but we don't know He got a Son."

He told me in detail of the circumstances in Africa that brought about his slavery here. How the powerful Kingdom of Dahomey, finding the slave trade so profitable, had abandoned farming, hunting and all else to capture slaves to stock the barracoons on the beach at Dmydah to sell to the slavers who came from across the ocean. How quarrels were manufactured by the King of Dahomey with more peaceful agricultural nations in striking distance of Dahomey in Nigeria and Gold Coast; how they were assaulted, completely wiped off the map, their names never to appear again, except when they were named in boastful chant before the King at one of his "customs" when his glory was being sung. The able-bodied who were captured were marched to Abomey, the capital city of Dahomey and displayed to the King, then put into the barracoons to await a buyer. The too old, the too young, the injured in battle were instantly beheaded and their heads smoked and carried back to the King. He paid off on heads, dead or alive. The skulls of the slaughtered were not wasted either. The King had his famous Palace of Skulls. The Palace grounds had a massive gate of skull-heads. The wall surrounding the grounds were built of skulls. You see, the Kings of Dahomey were truly great and mighty and a lot of skulls were bound to come out of their ambitions. While it looked awesome and splendid to him and his warriors, the sight must have been most grewsome and crude to Western eyes.

One thing impressed me strongly from this three months of association with Cudjo Lewis. The white people had held my people in slavery here in America. They had bought us, it is true and exploited us. But the inescapable fact that stuck in my craw, was: my people had *sold* me and the white people had bought me. That did away with the folklore I had been brought up on—that the white people had gone to Africa, waved a red handkerchief at the Africans and lured them aboard ship and sailed away. I know that civilized money stirred up African greed. That wars between tribes were often stirred up by white traders to provide more slaves in the barracoons and all that. But, if the African princes had been as pure and as innocent as I would like to think, it could not have happened. No, my own people had butchered and killed, exterminated whole nations and torn families apart, for a profit before the strangers got their chance at a cut. It was a sobering thought. What is more, all that this Cudjo told me was verified from other historical sources. It impressed upon me the universal nature of greed and glory. Lack of power and opportunity passes off too often for virtue. If I were King, let us say, over the Western Hemisphere tomorrow, instead of who I am, what would I consider right and just? Would I put the cloak of Justice on my ambition and send her out a-whoring after conquests? It is something to ponder over with fear.

Cudjo's eyes were full of tears and memory of fear when he told me of the assault on his city and its capture. He said that his nation, the Takkoi, lived "three sleeps" from Dahomey. The attack came at dawn as the Takkoi were getting out of bed to go to their fields outside the city. A whooping horde of the famed Dahoman women warriors burst through the main gate, seized people as they fled from their houses and beheaded victims with one stroke of their big swords.

"Oh, oh! I runnee this way to that gate, but they there. I runnee to another one, but they there, too. All eight gates they there. Them women, they very strong. I nineteen years old, but they too strong for me. They take me and tie me. I don't know where my people at. I never see them no more."

He described the awful slaughter as the Amazons sacked the city. The clusters of human heads at their belts. The plight of those who fled through the gates to fall into the hands of the male warriors outside. How his King was finally captured and carried before the King of Dahomey, who had broken his rule and come on this expedition in person because of a grudge against the King of Takkoi, and how the vanquished monarch was led before him, bound.

"Now, that you have dared to send impudent words to me," the King of Dahomey said, "your country is conquered and you are before me in chains. I shall take you to Abomey."

"No," the King of Takkoi answered. "I am King in Takkoi. I will not go to Dahomey." He knew that he would be killed for a spectacle in Dahomey. He chose to die at home.

So two Dahoman warriors held each of his hands and an Amazon struck off his head.

Later, two representatives of a European power attended the customs of the King at Abomey, and told of seeing the highly polished skull of the King of Takkoi mounted in a beautiful ship-model. His name and his nation were mentioned in the chant to the glory of Dahomey. The skull was treated with the utmost respect, as the King of Dahomey would expect his to be treated in case he fell in battle. That was the custom in West Africa. For the same reason, no one of royal blood was sold into slavery. They were killed. There are no descendants of royal African blood among American Negroes for that reason. The Negroes who claim that they are descendants of royal African blood have taken a leaf out of the book of the white ancestor-hounds in America, whose folks went to England with William the Conqueror, got restless and caught the *Mayflower* for Boston, then feeling a romantic lack, rushed down the coast and descended from Pocahontas. From the number of her children, one is forced to the conclusion that that Pocahontas wasn't so poky, after all.

Kossola told me of the March to Abomey after the fall of Takkoi. How they were yoked by forked sticks and tied in a chain. How the Dahomans halted the march the second day in order to smoke the heads of the victims because they were spoiling. The prisoners had to watch the heads of their friends and relatives turning on long poles in the smoke. Abomey and the palace of the King and then the march to the coast and the barracoons. They were there sometime before a ship came to trade. Many, many tribes were there, each in a separate barracoon, lest they war among themselves. The traders could choose which tribe they wanted. When the tribe was decided upon, he was carried into the barracoon where that tribe was confined, the women were lined up on one side and the men on the other. He walked down between the lines and selected the individuals he wanted. They usually took an equal number.

He described the embarcation and the trip across the ocean in the *Chlotilde,* a fast sailing vessel built by the Maher brothers of Maine, who had moved to Alabama. They were chased by a British man-of-war on the lookout for slavers, but the *Chlotilde* showed her heels. Finally the cargo arrived in Mobile. They were unloaded up the river, but the boat sunk, and the hundred-odd Africans began a four-year life of slavery.

"We so surprised to see mule and plow. We so surprised to see man pushee and mule pullee."

After the war, these Africans made a settlement of their own at Plateau, Alabama, three miles up the river from Mobile. They farmed and worked in the lumber mills and bought property. The descendants of these people are still there.

Kossola's great sorrow in America was the death of his favorite son, David, killed by a train. He refused to believe it was his David when he saw the body. He refused to let the bell be tolled for him.

"If dat my boy, where his head? No, dat not my David. Dat not my boy. My boy gone to Mobile. No, No! Don't ringee de bell for David. Dat not him.''

But, finally his wife persuaded him that the headless body on the window blind was their son. He cried hard for several minutes and then said, ''Ringee de bell.''

His other great sorrow was that he had lost track of his folks in Africa. ''They don't know what became of Kossola. When you go there, you tellee where I at.'' He begged me. He did not know that his tribe was no more upon this earth, except for those who reached the barracoon at Dmydah. None of his family was in the barracoon. He had missed seeing their heads in the smoke, no doubt. It is easy to see how few would have looked on that sight too closely.

''I lonely for my folks. They don't know. Maybe they ask everybody go there where Kossola. I know they hunt for me.'' There was a tragic catch in his voice like the whimper of a lost dog.

After seventy-five years, he still had that tragic sense of loss. That yearning for blood and cultural ties. That sense of mutilation. It gave me something to feel about.

Of my research in the British West Indies and Haiti, my greatest thrill was coming face to face with a Zombie and photographing her. This act had never happened before in the history of man. I mean the taking of the picture. I have said all that I know on the subject in the book, ''Tell My Horse,'' which has been published also in England under the title ''Voodoo Gods.'' I have spoken over the air on We the People on the subject, and the matter has been so publicized that I will not go into details here. But, it was a tremendous thrill, though utterly macabre.

I went Canzo in Voodoo ceremonies in Haiti and the ceremonies were both beautiful and terrifying.

I did not find them any more invalid than any other religion. Rather, I hold that any religion that satisfies the individual urge is valid for that person. It does satisfy millions, so it is true for its believers. The Sect Rouge, also known as the Cochon Gris (gray pig) and Ving Bra-Drig (from the sound of the small drum), a cannibalistic society there, has taken cover under the name of Voodoo, but the two things are in no wise the same. What is more, if science ever gets to the bottom of Voodoo in Haiti and Africa, it will be found that some important medical secrets, still unknown to medical science, give it its power, rather than the gestures of ceremony.

Books and Things

WHILE I WAS IN THE RESEARCH FIELD in 1929, the idea of "Jonah's Gourd Vine" came to me. I had written a few short stories, but the idea of attempting a book seemed so big, that I gazed at it in the quiet of the night, but hid it away from even myself in the daylight.

For one thing, it seemed off-key. What I wanted to tell was a story about a man, and from what I had read and heard, Negroes were supposed to write about the Race Problem. I was and am thoroughly sick of the subject. My interest lies in what makes a man or a woman do such-and-so, regardless of his color. It seemed to me that the human beings I met reacted pretty much the same to the same stimuli. Different idioms, yes. Circumstances and conditions having power to influence, yes. Inherent difference, no. But I said to myself that that was not what was expected of me, so I was afraid to tell a story the way I wanted, or rather the way the story told itself to me. So I went on that way for three years.

Something else held my attention for a while. As I told you before, I had been pitched head-foremost into the Baptist Church when I was born. I had heard the singing, the preaching and the prayers. They were a part of me. But on the concert stage, I always heard songs called spirituals sung and applauded as Negro music, and I wondered what would happen if a white audience ever heard a real spiritual. To me, what the Negroes did in Macedonia Baptist Church was finer than anything that any trained composer had done to the folk-songs.

I had collected a mass of work-songs, blues and spirituals in the course of my years of research. After offering them to two Negro composers and having them refused on the ground that white audiences would not listen to anything but highly arranged spirituals, I decided to see if that was true. I doubted it because I had seen groups of white people in my father's church as early as I could remember. They had come to hear the singing, and certainly there was no distinguished composer in Zion Hope Baptist Church. The congregation just got hold of the tune and arranged as they went along as the spirit moved them. And any musician, I don't care if he stayed at a conservatory until his teeth were gone and he smelled like old-folks, could never even aproach what those untrained singers could do. LET THE PEOPLE SING, was and is my motto, and finally I resolved to see what would happen.

So on money I had borrowed, I put on a show at the John Golden Theater on January 10, 1932, and tried out my theory. The performance was well received by both the audience and the critics. Because I know that music without motion is not natural with my people, I did not have the singers stand in a stiff group and reach for the high note. I told them to just imagine that they were in Macedonia and go ahead. I had dramatized a working day on a railroad camp, from the shack-rouser waking up the camp at dawn until the primitive dance in the deep woods at night.

While I did not lose any money, I did not make much. But I am satisfied that I proved my point. I have seen the effects of that concert in all the Negro singing groups since then. Primitive Negro dancing has been given tremendous impetus. Work-songs have taken on. In that performance I introduced West Indian songs and dances and they have come to take an important place in America. I am not upset by the fact that others have made something out of the things I pointed out. Rather I am glad if I have called any beauty to the attention of those who can use it.

In May, 1932, the depression did away with money for research so far as I was concerned. So I took my nerve in my hand and decided to try to write the story I had been carrying around in me. Back in my native village, I wrote first "Mules and Men." That is, I edited the huge mass of material I had, arranged it in some sequence and laid it aside. It was published after my first novel. Mr. Robert Wunsch and Dr. John Rice were both on the faculty at Rollins College, at Winter Park, which is three miles from Eatonville. Dr. Edwin Osgood Grover, Dr. Hamilton Holt, President of Rollins, together with Rice and Wunsch, were interested in me. I gave three folk concerts at the college under their urging.

Then I wrote a short story, "The Gilded Six-Bits," which Bob Wunsch read to his class in creative writing before he sent it off to *Story Magazine*. Thus I came to know Martha Foley and her husband, Whit Burnett, the editors of *Story*. They bought the story and it was published in the August issue, 1933. They never told me, but it is my belief that they did some missionary work among publishers in my behalf, because four publishers wrote me and asked if I had anything of book-length. One of the editors of the J. B. Lippincott Company, was among these. He wrote a gentle-like letter and so I was not afraid of him. Exposing my efforts did not seem so rash to me after reading his letter. I wrote him and said that I was writing a book. Mind you, not the first word was on paper when I wrote him that letter. But the very next week I moved up to Sanford where I was not so much at home as at Eatonville, and could concentrate more and sat down to write "Jonah's Gourd Vine.

I rented a house with a bed and stove in it for $1.50 a week. I paid two weeks and then my money ran out. My cousin, Willie Lee Hurston, was working and making $3.50 per week, and she always gave me the fifty cents to buy groceries with. In about three months, I finished the book. The problem of getting it typed was then upon me. Municipal Judge S. A. B. Wilkinson asked his secretary, Mildred Knight, if she would not do it for me and wait on the money. I explained to her that the book might not even be taken by Lippincott. I had been working on a hope. She took the manuscript home with her and read it. Then she offered to type it for me. She said, "It is going to be accepted, all right. I'll type it. Even if the first publisher does not take it, somebody will." So between them, they bought the paper and carbon and the book was typed.

I took it down to the American Express office to mail it and found that it cost $1.83 cents to mail, and I did not have it. So I went to see Mrs. John Leonardi, a most capable woman lawyer, and wife of the County Prosecutor. She did not have the money at the moment, but she was the treasurer of the local Daughter Elks. She "borrowed" $2.00 from the treasury and gave it to me to mail my book. That was on October 3, 1933. On October 16th, I had an acceptance by wire.

But it did not come so simply as that. I had been hired by the Seminole County Chamber of Commerce to entertain the business district of Sanford with my concert group for that day. I was very glad to get the work, because my landlord was pressing me for the back rent. I now owed $18. I was to receive $25 for the day, so I saw my way clear to pay up my rent, and have a little over. It was not to be that way, however. At eight o'clock of October 16th, my landlady came and told me to get out. I told her that I could pay her that day, but she said she didn't believe that I would ever have that much money. No, she preferred the house. So I took my card table and my clothes up to my Uncle Isaiah's house and went off to entertain the city at eleven o'clock. The sound truck went up and down the streets and my boys sang. That afternoon while I was still on the sound truck, a Western Union messenger handed me a wire. Naturally I did not open it there. We were through at three o'clock. The Chamber of Commerce not only paid us, we were all given an order which we could take to any store we wanted and get what we chose. I needed shoes, so I took mine to a shoe store. My heart was weighing as much as cord-wood, and so I forgot the wire until I was having the shoes fitted. When I opened it and read that "Jonah's Gourd Vine" was accepted and that Lippincott was offering me $200 advance, I tore out of that place with one old shoe and one new one on and ran to the Western Union office. Lippincott had asked for an answer by wire and they got it! Terms accepted. I never expect to have a greater thrill than that wire gave me. You know the feeling when you found your first pubic hair. Greater than that. When Producer Arthur Hornblow took me to lunch at Lucey's and hired me at Paramount, it was nice—very nice. I was most elated. But I had had five books accepted then, been a Guggenheim Fellow twice, spoken at three book fairs with all the literary greats of America and some from abroad, and so I was a little more used to things. So you see why that editor is *Colonel* to me. When the Negroes in the South name a white man a colonel, it means CLASS. Something like a monarch, only bigger and better. And when the colored population in the South confer a title, the white people recognize it because the Negroes are never wrong. They may flatter an ordinary bossman by calling him "Cap'n" but when they say "Colonel," "General" and "Governor" they are recognizing something internal. It is there, and it is accepted because it can be seen.

I wrote "Their Eyes Were Watching God" in Haiti. It was damned up in me, and I wrote it under internal pressure in seven weeks. I wish that I could write it again. In fact, I regret all of my books. It is one of the tragedies of life that one cannot have all the wisdom one is ever to possess in the beginning. Perhaps, it is just as well to be rash and foolish for a while. If writers were too wise, perhaps no books would be written at all. It might be better to ask yourself "Why?" afterwards than before. Anyway, the force from somewhere in Space which commands you to write in the first place, gives you no choice. You take up the pen when you are told, and write what is commanded. There is no agony like bearing an untold story inside you. You have all heard of the Spartan youth with the fox under his cloak.

"Dust Tracks on a Road" is being written in California where I did not expect to be at this time. . . .

Love

WHAT DO I REALLY know about love? I have had some experiences and feel fluent enough for my own satisfaction. Love, I find is like singing.

Everybody can do enough to satisfy themselves, though it may not impress the neighbors as being very much. That is the way it is with me, but whether I know anything unusual, I couldn't say. Don't look for me to call a string of names and point out chapter and verse. Ladies do not kiss and tell any more than gentlemen do.

I have read many books where the heroine was in love for a long time without knowing it. I have talked with people and they have told me the same thing. So maybe that is the way it ought to be. That is not the way it is with me at all. I have been *out* of love with people for a long time, perhaps without finding it out. But when I fall *in,* I can feel the bump. That is a fact and I would not try to fool you. Love may be a sleepy, creeping thing with some others, but it is a mighty wakening thing with me. I feel the jar, and I know it from my head on down.

Though I started falling in love before I was seven years old, I never had a fellow until I was nearly grown. I was such a poor picker. I would have had better luck if I had stuck to boys around my own age, but that wouldn't do me. I wanted somebody with long pants on, and they acted as if they didn't know I was even born. The heartless wretches would walk right past my gate with grown women and pay me no attention at all, other than to say hello or something like that. Then I would have to look around for another future husband, only to have the same thing happen all over again.

Of course, in high school I received mushy notes and wrote them. A day or two, a week or month at most would see the end of the affair. Gone without a trace. I was in my Freshman year in college when I first got excited, really.

He could stomp a piano out of this world, sing a fair baritone and dance beautifully. He noticed me, too, and I was carried away. For the first time since my mother's death, there was someone who felt really close and warm to me.

This affair went on all through my college life, with the exception of two fallings-out. We got married immediately after I finished my work at Barnard College, which should have been the happiest day of my life. St. Augustine, Florida, is a beautiful setting for such a thing.

But, it was not my happiest day. I was assailed by doubts. For the first time since I met him, I asked myself if I really were in love, or if this had been a habit. I had an uncomfortable feeling of unreality. The day and the occasion did not underscore any features of nature or circumstance, and I wondered why. Who had canceled the well-advertised tour of the moon? Somebody had turned a hose on the sun. What I had taken for eternity turned out to be a moment walking in its sleep.

After our last falling-out, he asked me please to forgive him, and I said that I did. But now, had I really? A wind full of memories blew out of the past and brought a chilling fog. This was not the expected bright dawn. Rather, some vagrant ray had played a trick on the night. I could not bring myself to tell him my thoughts. I just couldn't, no matter how hard I tried, but there they were crowding me from pillar to post.

Back in New York, I met Mrs. Mason and she offered me a chance to return to my research work, and I accepted it. It seemed a way out without saying anything very much. Let nature take its course. I did not tell him about the arrangement. Rather, I urged him to return to Chicago to continue his medical work. Then I stretched my shivering insides out and went back to work. I have seen him only once since then. He has married again, and I hope that he is happy.

Having made such a mess, I did not rush at any serious affair right away. I set to work and really worked in earnest. Work was to be all of me, so I said. Three years went by. I had finished that phase of research and was considering writing my first book, when I met the man who was really to lay me by the heels. I met A.W.P.

He was tall, dark brown, magnificently built, with a beautifully modeled back head. His profile was strong and good. The nose and lips were especially good front and side. But his looks only drew my eyes in the beginning. I did not fall in love with him just for that. He had a fine mind and that intrigued me. When a man keeps beating me to the draw mentally, he begins to get glamorous.

I did not just fall in love. I made a parachute jump. No matter which way I probed him, I found something more to admire. We fitted each other like a glove. His intellect got me first for I am the kind of a woman that likes to move on mentally from point to point, and I like for my man to be there way ahead of me. Then if he is strong and honest, it goes on from there. Good looks are not essential, just extra added attraction. He had all of those things and more. It seems to me that God must have put in extra time making him up. He stood on his own feet so firmly that he reared back.

To illustrate the point, I got into trouble with him for trying to loan him a quarter. It came about this way.

I lived in the Graham Court at 116th Street and Seventh Avenue. He lived down in 64th Street, Columbus Hill. He came to call one night and everything went off sweetly until he got ready to leave. At the door he told me to let him go because he was going to walk home. He had spent the only nickel he had that night to come to see me. That upset me, and I ran to get a quarter to loan him until his pay day. What did I do that for? He flew hot. In fact he was the hottest man in the five boroughs. Why did I insult him like that? The responsibility was all his. He had known that he did not have his return fare when he left home, but he had wanted to come, and so he had come. Let him take the consequences for his own acts. What kind of coward did I take him for? How could he deserve my respect if he behaved like a cream puff? He was a *man!* No woman on earth could either lend him or give him a cent. If a man could not do for a woman, what good was he on earth? His great desire was to do for me. *Please* let him be a *man!*

For a minute I was hurt and then I saw his point. He had done a beautiful thing and I was killing it off in my blindness. If it pleased him to walk all of that distance for my sake, it pleased him as evidence of his devotion. Then too, he wanted to do all the doing, and keep me on the receiving end. He soared in my respect from that moment on. Nor did he ever change. He meant to be the head, *so help him over the fence!*

That very manliness, sweet as it was, made us both suffer. My career balked the completeness of his ideal. I really wanted to conform, but it was impossible. To me there was no conflict. My work was one thing, and he was all of the rest. But, I could not make him see that. Nothing must be in my life but himself.

But, I am ahead of my story. I was interested in him for nearly two years before he knew it. A great deal happened between the time we met and the time we had any serious talk.

As I said, I loved, but I did not say so, because nobody asked me. I made up my mind to keep my feelings to myself since they did not seem to matter to anyone else but me.

I went South, did some more concert work and wrote "Jonah's Gourd Vine" and "Mules and Men," then came back to New York.

He began to make shy overtures to me. I pretended not to notice for a while so that I could be sure and not be hurt. Then he gave me the extreme pleasure of telling me right out loud about it. It seems that he had been in love with me just as long as I had been with him, but he was afraid that I didn't mean him any good, as the saying goes. He had been trying to make me tell him something. He began by complimenting me on my clothes. Then one night we had attended the Alpha Phi Alpha fraternity dance—yes, he is an Alpha man—he told me that the white dress I was wearing was beautiful, but I did not have on an evening wrap rich enough to suit him. He had in mind just the kind he wanted to see me in, and when he made the kind of money he expected to, the first thing he meant to do was to buy me a gorgeous evening wrap and everything to go with it. He wanted *his* wife to look swell. He looked at me from under his eyelashes to see how I was taking it. I smiled and so he went on.

"You know, Zora, you've got a real man on your hands. You've got somebody to do for you. I'm tired of seeing you work so hard. I wouldn't want *my* wife to do anything but look after me. Be home looking like Skookums when I got there."

He always said I reminded him of the Indian on the Skookum Apples, so I knew he meant me to understand that he wanted to be coming home to me, and with those words he endowed me with Radio City, the General Motors Corporation, the United States, Europe, Asia and some outlying continents. I had everything!

So actively began the real love affair of my life. He was then a graduate of City College, and was working for his Master's degree at Columbia. He had no money. He was born of West Indian parents in the Columbus Hill district of New York City, and had nothing to offer but what it takes—a bright soul, a fine mind in a fine body, and courage. He is so modest that I do not think that he yet knows his assets. That was to make trouble for us later on.

It was a curious situation. He was so extraordinary that I lived in terrible fear lest women camp on his doorstep in droves and take him away from me. I found out later on that he could not believe that I wanted just him. So there began an agonizing tug of war. Looking at a very serious photograph of me that Carl Van Vechten had made, he told me one night in a voice full of feeling that that was the way he wanted me to look all the time unless I was with him. I almost laughed out loud. That was just the way I felt. I hated to think of him smiling unless he was smiling at me. His grins were too precious to be wasted on ordinary mortals, especially women.

If he could only have realized what a lot he had to offer, he need not have suffered so much through doubting that he could hold me. I was hog-tied and branded, but he didn't realize it. He could make me fetch and carry, but he wouldn't believe it. So when I had to meet people on business, or went to literary parties and things like that, it would drive him into a sulk, and then he would make me unhappy. I, too, failed to see how deeply he felt. I would interpret his moods as indifference and die, and die, and die.

He begged me to give up my career, marry him and live outside of New York City. I really wanted to do anything he wanted me to do, but that one thing I could not do. It was not just my contract with my publishers, it was that I had things clawing inside of me that must be said. I could not see that my work should make any difference in marriage. He was all and everything else to me but that. One did not conflict with the other in my mind. But it was different with him. He felt that he did not matter to me enough. He was the master kind. All, or nothing, for him.

The terrible thing was that we could neither leave each other alone, nor compromise. Let me seem too cordial with any male and something was going to happen. Just let him smile too broad at any woman, and no sooner did we get inside my door than the war was on! One night (I didn't decide this) something primitive inside me tore past the barriers and before I realized it I had slapped his face. That was a mistake. He was still smoldering from an incident a week old. A fellow had met us on Seventh Avenue and kissed me on my cheek. Just one of those casual things, but it had burned up A.W.P. So I had unknowingly given him an opening he had been praying for. He paid me off then and there with interest. No broken bones, you understand, and no black eyes. I realized afterwards that my hot head could tell me to beat him, but it would cost me something. I would have to bring head to get head. I couldn't get his and leave mine locked up in the dresser-drawer.

Then I knew I was too deeply in love to be my old self. For always a blow to my body had infuriated me beyond measure. Even with my parents, that was true. But somehow, I didn't hate him at all. We sat down on the floor and each one of us tried to take all the blame. He went out and bought some pie and I made a pot of hot chocolate and we were more affectionate than ever. The next day he made me a bookcase that I needed and you couldn't get a pin between us.

But fate was watching us and laughing. About a month later when he was with me, the telephone rang. Would I please come down to an apartment in the Fifties and meet an out-of-town celebrity? He was in town for only two days and he wanted to meet me before he left. When I turned from the phone, A.W.P. was changed. He begged me not to go. I reminded him that I had promised, and begged him to come along. He refused and walked out. I went, but I was most unhappy.

This sort of thing kept up time after time. He would not be reconciled to the thing. We were alternately the happiest people in the world, and the most miserable. I suddenly decided to go away to see if I could live without him. I did not even tell him that I was going. But I wired him from some town in Virginia.

Miss Barnicle of New York University asked me to join her and Alan Lomax on a short bit of research. I was to select the area and contact the subjects. Alan Lomax was joining us with a recording machine. So because I was delirious with joy and pain, I suddenly decided to leave New York and see if I could come to some decision. I knew no more at the end than I did when I went South. Six weeks later I was back in New York and just as much his slave as ever.

Really, I never had occasion to doubt his sincerity, but I used to drag my heart over hot coals by supposing. I did not know that I could suffer so. Then all of my careless words came to haunt me. For theatrical effect, I had uttered sacred words and oaths to others before him. How I hated myself for the sacrilege now! It would have seemed so wonderful never to have uttered them before.

But no matter how soaked we were in ecstasy, the telephone or the doorbell would ring, and there would be my career again. A charge had been laid upon me and I must follow the call. He said once with pathos in his voice, that at times he could not feel my presence. My real self had escaped him. I could tell from both his face and his voice that it hurt him terribly. It hurt me just as much to see him hurt. He really had nothing to worry about, but I could not make him see it. So there we were. Caught in a fiendish trap. We could not leave each other alone, and we could not shield each other from hurt. Our bitterest enemies could not have contrived more exquisite torture for us.

Another phase troubled me. As soon as he took his second degree, he was in line for bigger and better jobs. I began to feel that our love was slowing down his efforts. He had brains and character. He ought to go a long way. I grew terribly afraid that later on he would feel that I had thwarted him in a way and come to resent me. That was a scorching thought. Even if I married him, what about five years from now, the way we were going?

In the midst of this, I received my Guggenheim Fellowship. This was my chance to release him, and fight myself free from my obsession. He would get over me in a few months and go on to be a very big man. So I sailed off to Jamaica. But I freely admit that everywhere I set my feet down, there were tracks of blood. Blood from the very middle of my heart. I did not write because if I had written and he answered my letter, everything would have broken down.

So I pitched in to work hard on my research to smother my feelings. But the thing would not down. The plot was far from the circumstances, but I tried to embalm all the tenderness of my passion for him in ''Their Eyes Were Watching God.''

When I returned to America after nearly two years in the Caribbean, I found that he had left his telephone number with my publishers. For some time, I did not use it. Not because I did not want to, but because the moment when I should hear his voice something would be in wait for me. It might be warm and eager. It might be cool and impersonal, just with overtones from the grave of things. So I went South and stayed several months before I ventured to use it. Even when I returned to New York it took me nearly two months to get up my courage. When I did make the call, I cursed myself for the delay. Here was the shy, warm man I had left.

Then we met and talked. We both were stunned by the revelation that all along we had both thought and acted desperately in exile, and all to no purpose. We were still in the toils and after all my agony, I found out that he was a sucker for me, and he found out that I was in his bag. And I had a triumph that only a woman could understand. He had not turned into a tramp in my absence, but neither had he flamed like a newborn star in his profession. He confessed that he needed my aggravating presence to push him. He had settled down to a plodding desk job and reconciled himself. He had let his waistline go a bit and that bespoke his inside feeling. That made me happy no end. No woman wants a man all finished and perfect. You have to have something to work on and prod. That waistline went down in a jiffy and he began to discuss work-plans with enthusiasm. He could see something ahead of him besides time. I was happy. If he had been crippled in both legs, it would have suited me even better.

What will be the end? That is not for me to know. Life poses questions and that two-headed spirit that rules the beginning and the end of things called Death, has all the answers. And even if I did know all, I am supposed to have some private business to myself. Whatever I do know, I have no intention of putting but so much in the public ears.

Perhaps the oath of Hercules shall always defeat me in love. Once when I was small and first coming upon the story of The Choice of Hercules, I was so impressed that I swore an oath to leave all pleasure and take the hard road of labor. Perhaps God heard me and wrote down my words in His book. I have thought so at times. Be that as it may, I have the satisfaction of knowing that I have loved and been loved by the perfect man. If I never hear of love again, I have known the real thing.

So much for what I know about the major courses in love. However, there are some minor courses which I have not grasped so well, and would be thankful for some coaching and advice.

First is the number of men who pant in my ear on short acquaintance, "You passionate thing! I can see you are just *burning* up! Most men would be disappointing to you. It takes a man like me for you. Ahhh! I know that you will just wreck me! Your eyes and your lips tell me a lot. You are a walking furnace!" This amazes me sometimes. Often when this is whispered gustily into my ear, I am feeling no more amorous than a charter member of the Union League Club. I may be thinking of turnip greens with dumplings, or more royalty checks, and here is a man who visualizes me on a divan sending the world up in smoke. It has happened so often that I have come to expect it. There must be something about me that looks sort of couchy. Maybe it is a birthmark. My mother could have been frightened by a bed. There is nothing to be done about it, I suppose. But, I must say about these mirages that seem to rise around me, that the timing is way off on occasion.

Number two is, a man may lose interest in me and go where his fancy leads him, and we can still meet as friends. But if I get tired and let on about it, he is certain to become an enemy of mine. That forces me to lie like the cross-ties from New York to Key West. I have learned to frame it so that I can claim to be deserted and devastated by him. Then he goes off with a sort of twilight tenderness for me, wondering what it is that he's got that brings so many women down! I do not even have to show real tears. All I need to do is show my stricken face and dash away from him to hide my supposed heartbreak and renunciation. He understands that I am fleeing before his allure so that I can be firm in my resolution to save the pieces. He knew all along that he was a hard man to resist, so he visualized my dampened pillow. It is a good thing that some of them have sent roses as a poultice and stayed away. Otherwise, they might have found the poor, heartbroken wreck of a thing all dressed to kill and gone out for a high-heel time with the new interest, who has the new interesting things to say and do. Now, how to break off without acting deceitful and still keep a friend?

Number three is kin to Number two, in a way. Under the spell of moonlight, music, flowers, or the cut and smell of good tweeds, I sometimes feel the divine urge for an hour, a day or maybe a week. Then it is gone and my interest returns to corn pone and mustard greens, or rubbing a paragraph with a soft cloth. Then my ex-sharer of a mood calls up in a fevered voice and reminds me of every silly thing I said, and eggs me on to say them all over again. It is the third presentation of turkey hash after Christmas. It is asking me to be a seven-sided liar. Accuses me of being faithless and inconsistent if I don't. There is no inconsistency there. I was sincere for the moment in which I said the things. It is strictly a matter of time. It was true for the moment, but the next day or the next week, is not that moment. No two moments are any more alike than two snowflakes. Like snowflakes, they get that same look from being so plentiful and falling so close together. But examine them closely and see the multiple differences between them. Each moment has its own task and capacity; doesn't melt down like snow and form again. It keeps its character forever. So the great difficulty lies in trying to transpose last night's moment to a day which has no knowledge of it. That look, that tender touch, was issued by the mint of the richest of all kingdoms. That same expression of today is utter counterfeit, or at best the wildest of inflation. What could be more zestless than passing out canceled checks? It is wrong to be called faithless under circumstances like that. What to do?

I have a strong suspicion, but I can't be sure, that much that passes for constant love is a golded-up moment walking in its sleep. Some people know that it is the walk of the dead, but in desperation and desolation, they have staked everything on life after death and the resurrecton, so they haunt the graveyard. They build an altar on the tomb and wait there like faithful Mary for the stone to roll away. So the moment has authority over all of their lives. They pray constantly for the miracle of the moment to burst its bonds and spread out over time.

But pay no attention to what I say about love, for as I said before, it may not mean a thing. It is my own bathtub singing. Just because my mouth opens up like a prayer book, it does not have to flap like a Bible.

And then again, anybody whose mouth is cut cross-ways is given to lying, unconsciously as well as knowingly. So pay my few scattering remarks no mind as to love in general. I know only my part.

Anyway, it seems to be the unknown country from which no traveler ever returns. What seems to be a returning pilgrim is another person born in the strange country with the same-looking ears and hands. He is a stranger to the person who fared forth, and a stranger to family and old friends. He is clothed in mystery henceforth and forever. So, perhaps nobody knows, or can tell, any more than I. Maybe the old Negro folk rhyme tells all there is to know:

Love is a funny thing; Love is a blossom;
If you want your finger bit, poke it at a possum.

FROM
Mules and Men

I WAS GLAD WHEN SOMEBODY TOLD ME, "You may go and collect Negro folk-lore."

In a way it would not be a new experience for me. When I pitched headforemost into the world I landed in the crib of negroism. From the earliest rocking of my cradle, I had known about the capers Brer Rabbit is apt to cut and what the Squinch Owl says from the house top. But it was fitting me like a tight chemise. I couldn't see it for wearing it. It was only when I was off in college, away from my native surroundings, that I could see myself like somebody else and stand off and look at my garment. Then I had to have the spy-glass of Anthropology to look through at that.

Dr. Boas asked me where I wanted to work and I said, "Florida," and gave, as my big reason, that "Florida is a place that draws people— white people from all over the world, and Negroes from every Southern state surely and some from the North and West." So I knew that it was possible for me to get a cross section of the Negro South in the one state. And then I realized that I was new myself, so it looked sensible for me to choose familiar ground.

First place I aimed to stop to collect material was Eatonville, Florida.

And now, I'm going to tell you why I decided to go to my native village first. I didn't go back there so that the home folks could make admiration over me because I had been up North to college and come back with a diploma and a Chevrolet. I knew they were not going to pay either one of these items too much mind. I was just Lucy Hurston's daughter, Zora, and even if I had—to use one of our down-home expressions—had a Kaiser baby*, and that's something that hasn't been done in this Country yet, I'd still be just Zora to the neighbors. If I had exalted myself to impress the town, somebody would have sent me word in a match-box that I had been up North there and had rubbed the hair off of my head against some college wall, and then come back there with a lot of form and fashion and outside show to the world. But they'd stand

*Have a child by the Kaiser.

flat-footed and tell me that they didn't have me, neither my sham-polish, to study 'bout. And that would have been that.

I hurried back to Eatonville because I knew that the town was full of material and that I could get it without hurt, harm or danger. As early as I could remember it was the habit of the men folks particularly to gather on the store porch of evenings and swap stories. Even the women folks would stop and break a breath with them at times. As a child when I was sent down to Joe Clarke's store, I'd drag out my leaving as long as possible in order to hear more.

Folk-lore is not as easy to collect as it sounds. The best source is where there are the least outside influences and these people, being usually underprivileged, are the shyest. They are most reluctant at times to reveal that which the soul lives by. And the Negro, in spite of his open-faced laughter, his seeming acquiescence, is particularly evasive. You see we are a polite people and we do not say to our questioner, "Get out of here!" We smile and tell him or her something that satisfies the white person because, knowing so little about us, he doesn't know what he is missing. The Indian resists curiosity by a stony silence. The Negro offers a feather-bed resistance. That is, we let the probe enter, but it never comes out. It gets smothered under a lot of laughter and pleasantries.

The theory behind our tactics: "The white man is always trying to know into somebody else's business. All right, I'll set something outside the door of my mind for him to play with and handle. He can read my writing but he sho' can't read my mind. I'll put this play toy in his hand, and he will seize it and go away. Then I'll say my say and sing my song."

I knew that even *I* was going to have some hindrance among strangers. But here in Eatonville I knew everybody was going to help me. So below Palatka I began to feel eager to be there and I kicked the little Chevrolet right along.

I thought about the tales I had heard as a child. How even the Bible was made over to suit our vivid imagination. How the devil always out-smarted God and how that over-noble hero Jack or John—not *John Henry,* who occupies the same place in Negro folk-lore that Casey Jones does in white lore and if anything is more recent—outsmarted the devil. Brer Fox, Brer Deer, Brer 'Gator, Brer Dawg, Brer Rabbit, Ole Massa and his wife were walking the earth like natural men way back in the days when God himself was on the ground and men could talk with him. Way back there before God weighed up the dirt to make the mountains. When I was rounding Lily Lake I was remembering how God had made the world and the elements and people. He made souls for people, but he didn't give them out because he said:

"Folks ain't ready for souls yet. De clay ain't dry. It's de strongest thing Ah ever made. Don't aim to waste none thru loose cracks. And then men got to grow strong enough to stand it. De way things is now, if Ah give it out it would tear them shackly bodies to pieces. Bimeby, Ah give it out."

So folks went round thousands of years without no souls. All de time de soul-piece, it was setting 'round covered up wid God's loose raiment. Every now and then de wind would blow and hist up de cover and then de elements would be full of lightning and de winds would talk. So people told one 'nother that God was talking in de mountains.

De white man passed by it way off and he looked but he wouldn't go close enough to touch. De Indian and de Negro, they tipped by cautious too, and all of 'em seen de light of diamonds when de winds shook de cover, and de wind dat passed over it sung songs. De Jew come past and heard de song from de soul-piece then he kept on passin' and all of a sudden he grabbd up de soul-piece and hid it under his clothes, and run off down de road. It burnt him and tore him and throwed him down and lifted him up and toted him across de mountain and he tried to break loose but he couldn't do it. He kept on hollerin' for help but de rest of 'em run hid 'way from him. Way after while they come out of holes and corners and picked up little chips and pieces that fell back on de ground. So God mixed it up wid feelings and give it out to 'em. 'Way after while when He ketch dat Jew, He's goin' to 'vide things up more ekal'.

So I rounded Park Lake and came speeding down the straight stretch into Eatonville, the city of five lakes, three croquet courts, three hundred brown skins, three hundred good swimmers, plenty guavas, two schools, and no jail-house.

Before I enter the township, I wish to make acknowledgments to Mrs. R. Osgood Mason of New York City. She backed my falling in a hearty way, in a spiritual way, and in addition, financed the whole expedition in the manner of the Great Soul that she is. The world's most gallant woman.

AS I CROSSED the Maitland-Eatonville township line I could see a group on the store porch. I was delighted. The town had not changed. Same love of talk and song. So I drove on down there before I stopped. Yes, there was George Thomas, Calvin Daniels, Jack and Charlie Jones, Gene Brazzle, B. Moseley and "Seaboard." Deep in a game of Florida-flip. All of those who were not actually playing were giving advice—"bet straightening" they call it.

"Hello, boys," I hailed them as I went into neutral.

They looked up from the game and for a moment it looked as if they had forgotten me. Then B. Moseley said, "Well, if it ain't Zora Hurston!" Then everybody crowded around the car to help greet me.

"You gointer stay awhile, Zora?"

"Yep. Several months."

"Where you gointer stay, Zora?"

"With Mett and Ellis, I reckon."

"Mett" was Mrs. Armetta Jones, an intimate friend of mine since childhood and Ellis was her husband. Their house stands under the huge camphor tree on the front street.

"Hello, heart-string," Mayor Hiram Lester yelled as he hurried up the street. "We heard all about you up North. You back home for good, I hope."

"Nope, Ah come to collect some old stories and tales and Ah know y'all know a plenty of 'em and that's why Ah headed straight for home."

"What you mean, Zora, them big old lies we tell when we're jus' sittin' around here on the store porch doin' nothin'?" asked B. Moseley.

"Yeah, those same ones about Ole Massa, and colored folks in heaven, and—oh, y'all know the kind I mean."

"Aw shucks," exclaimed George Thomas doubtfully. "Zora, don't you come here and tell de biggest lie first thing. Who you reckon want to read all them old-time tales about Brer Rabbit and Brer Bear?"

"Plenty of people, George. They are a lot more valuable than you might think. We want to set them down before it's too late."

"Too late for what?"

"Before everybody forgets all of 'em."

"No danger of that. That's all some people is good for—set 'round and lie and murder groceries."

"Ah know one right now," Calvin Daniels announced cheerfully. "It's a tale 'bout John and de frog."

"Wait till she gets out her car, Calvin. Let her get settled at 'Met's' and cook a pan of ginger bread then we'll all go down and tell lies and eat ginger bread. Dat's de way to do. She's tired now from all dat drivin'.''

"All right, boys," I agreed. "But Ah'll be rested by night. Be lookin' for everybody."

So I unloaded the car and crowded it into Ellis' garage and got settled. Armetta made me lie down and rest while she cooked a big pan of ginger bread for the company we expected.

Calvin Daniels and James Moseley were the first to show up.

"Calvin, Ah sure am glad that you got here. Ah'm crazy to hear about John and dat frog," I said.

"That's why Ah come so early so Ah could tell it to you and go. Ah got to go over to Wood Bridge a little later on."

"Ah'm glad you remembered me first, Calvin."

"Ah always like to be good as my word, and Ah just heard about a toe-party over to Wood Bridge tonight and Ah decided to make it."

"A toe-party! What on earth is that?"

"Come go with me and James and you'll see!"

"But, everybody will be here lookin' for me. They'll think Ah'm crazy—tellin' them to come and then gettin' out and goin' to Wood Bridge myself. But Ah certainly would like to go to that toe-party."

"Aw, come on. They kin come back another night. You gointer like this party."

"Well, you tell me the story first, and by that time, Ah'll know what to do."

"Ah, come on, Zora," James urged. "Git de car out. Calvin kin tell you dat one while we're on de way. Come on, let's go to de toe-party."

"No, let 'im tell me this one first, then, if Ah go he can tell me some more on de way over."

James motioned to his friend. "Hurry up and tell it, Calvin, so we kin go before somebody else come."

"Aw, most of 'em ain't comin' nohow. They all 'bout goin' to Wood Bridge, too. Lemme tell you 'bout John and dis frog:

It was night and Ole Massa sent John, his favorite slave, down to the spring to get him a cool drink of water. He called John to him.

"John!"

"What you want, Massa?"

"John, I'm thirsty. Ah wants a cool drink of water, and Ah wants you to go down to de spring and dip me up a nice cool pitcher of water."

John didn't like to be sent nowhere at night, but he always tried to do everything Ole Massa told him to do, so he said, "Yessuh, Massa, Ah'll go git you some!"

Ole Massa said: "Hurry up, John, Ah'm mighty thirsty."

John took de pitcher and went on down to de spring. There was a great big ole bull frog settin' right on de edge of de spring, and when John dipped up de water de noise skeered de frog and he hollered and jumped over in de spring.

John dropped de water pitcher and tore out for de big house, hollerin' "Massa! Massa! A big ole booger* done got after me!"

Ole Massa told him, "Why, John, there's no such thing as a booger."

"Oh, yes it is, Massa. He down at dat Spring."

Don't tell me, John. Youse just excited. Furthermore, you go git me dat water Ah sent you after."

"No, indeed, Massa, you and nobody else can't send me back there so dat booger kin git me."

Ole Massa begin to figger dat John musta seen somethin' sho nuff because John never had disobeyed him before, so he ast: "John, you say you seen a booger. What did it look like?"

John tole him, "Massa, he had two great big eyes lak balls of fire, and when he was standin' up he was sittin' down and when he moved, he moved by jerks, and he had most no tail."

Long before Calvin had ended his story James had lost his air of impatience.

"Now, Ah'll tell one," he said. "That is, if you so desire."

"Sure, Ah want to hear you tell 'em till daybreak if you will," I said eagerly.

"But where's the ginger bread?" James stopped to ask.

"It's out in the kitchen," I said. "Ah'm waiting for de others to come."

"Aw, naw, give us ours now. Them others may not get here before forty o'clock and Ah'll be done et mine and be in Wood Bridge. Anyhow Ah want a corner piece and some of them others will beat me to it."

So I served them with ginger bread and buttermilk.

"You sure going to Wood Bridge with us after Ah git thru tellin' this one?" James asked.

*A bogey man

"Yeah, if the others don't show up by then," I conceded.

So James told the story about the man who went to Heaven from Johnstown.

You know, when it lightnings, de angels is peepin' in de lookin' glass; when it thunders, they's rollin' out de rain-barrels; and when it rains, somebody done dropped a barrel or two and bust it.

One time, you know, there was going to be big doin's in Glory and all de angels had brand new clothes to wear and so they was all peepin' in the lookin' glasses, and therefore it got to lightning all over de sky. God tole some of de angels to roll in all de full rain barrels and they was in such a hurry that it was thunderin' from the east to the west and the zigzag lightning went to join the mutterin' thunder and, next thing you know, some of them angels got careless and dropped a whole heap of them rain barrels, and didn't it rain!

In one place they call Johnstown they had a great flood. And so many folks got drownded that it jus' look like Judgment day.

So some of de folks that got drownded in that flood went one place and some went another. You know, everything that happen, they got to be a nigger in it—and so one of de brothers in black went up to Heben from de flood.

When he got to the gate, Ole Peter let 'im in and made 'im welcome. De colored man was named John, so John ast Peter, says, "Is it dry in dere?"

Ole Peter tole 'im, "Why, yes it's dry in here. How come you ast that?"

"Well, you know Ah jus' come out of one flood, and Ah don't want to run into no mo'. Ooh, man! You ain't *seen* no water. You just oughter seen dat flood we had at Johnstown."

Peter says, "Yeah, we know all about it. Jus' go wid Gabriel and let him give you some new clothes."

So John went on off wid Gabriel and come back all dressed up in brand new clothes and all de time he was changin' his clothes he was tellin' Ole Gabriel all about dat flood, jus' like he didn't know already.

So when he come back from changin' his clothes, they give him a brand new gold harp and handed him to a gold bench and made him welcome. They was so tired of hearing about dat flood they was glad to see him wid his harp 'cause they figgered he'd get to playin' and forget all about it. So Peter tole him, "Now you jus' make yo'self at home and play all de music you please."

John went and took a seat on de bench and commenced to tune up his harp. By dat time, two angels come walkin' by where John was settin' so he throwed down his harp and tackled 'em.

"Say," he hollered, "Y'all want to hear 'bout de big flood Ah was in down on earth? Lawd, Lawd! It sho rained, and talkin' 'bout water!"

Dem two angels hurried on off from 'im jus' as quick as they could. He started to tellin' another one and he took to flyin'. Gab'ull went over to 'im and tried to get 'im to take it easy, but John kept right on stoppin' every angel dat he could find to tell 'im about dat flood of water.

Way after while he went over to Ole Peter and said: "Thought you said everybody would be nice and polite?"

Peter said, "Yeah, Ah said it. Ain't everybody treatin' you right?"

John said, "Naw. Ah jus' walked up to a man as nice and friendly as Ah could and started to tell 'im 'bout all dat water Ah left back there in Johnstown and instead of him turnin' me a friendly answer he said, 'Shucks! You ain't seen no water!' and walked off and left me standin' by myself."

"Was he a *ole* man wid a crooked walkin' stick?" Peter ast John.

"Yeah."

"Did he have whiskers down to here?" Peter measured down to his waist.

"He sho did," John tol' 'im.

"Aw shucks," Peter tol' im. "Dat was Ole Nora.* You can't tell *him* nothin' 'bout no flood."

There was a lot of horn-honking outside and I went to the door. The crowd drew up under the mothering camphor tree in four old cars. Everybody in boisterous spirits.

"Come on, Zora! Le's go to Wood Bridge. Great toe-party goin' on. All kinds of 'freshments. We kin tell you some lies most any ole time. We never run outer lies and lovin'. Tell 'em tomorrow night. Come on if you comin'—le's go if you gwine."

So I loaded up my car with neighbors and we all went to Wood Bridge. It is a Negro community joining Maitland on the north as Eatonville does on the west, but no enterprising souls have ever organized it. They have no schoolhouse, no post office, no mayor. It is lacking in Eatonville's feeling of unity. In fact, a white woman lives there.

While we rolled along Florida No. 3, I asked Armetta where was the shindig going to be in Wood Bridge. "At Edna Pitts' house," she told me. "But she ain't givin' it by herself; it's for the lodge."

"Think it's gointer be lively?"

*Noah.

"Oh, yeah. Ah heard that a lot of folks from Altamonte and Longwood is comin'. Maybe from Winter Park too."

We were the tail end of the line and as we turned off the highway we could hear the boys in the first car doing what Ellis Jones called bookooing* before they even hit the ground. Charlie Jones was woofing† louder than anybody else. "Don't y'all sell off dem pretty li'l pink toes befo' Ah git dere."

Peter Stagg: "Save me de best one!"

Soddy Sewell: "Hey, you mullet heads! Get out de way there and let a real man smoke them toes over."

Gene Brazzle: "Come to my pick, gimme a vaseline brown!"

Big Willie Sewell: "Gimme any kind so long as you gimme more'n one."

Babe Brown, riding a running-board, guitar in hand, said, "Ah want a toe, but if it ain't got a good looking face on to it, don't bring de mess up."

When we got there the party was young. The house was swept and garnished, the refreshments on display, several people sitting around; but the spot needed some social juices to mix the ingredients. In other words, they had the carcass of a party lying around up until the minute Eatonville burst in on it. Then it woke up.

"Y'all done sold off any toes yet?" George Brown wanted to know.

Willie Mae Clarke gave him a certain look and asked him, "What's dat got to do with you, George Brown?" And he shut up. Everybody knows that Willie Mae's got the business with George Brown.

"Nope. We ain't had enough crowd, but I reckon we kin start now," Edna said. Edna and a sort of committee went inside and hung up a sheet across one end of the room. Then she came outside and called all of the young women inside. She had to coax and drag some of the girls.

"Oh, Ah'm shame-face-ted!" some of them said.

"Nobody don't want to buy *mah* ole rusty toe." Others fished around for denials from the male side.

I went on in with the rest and was herded behind the curtain.

"Say, what *is* this toe-party business?" I asked one of the girls. "Good gracious, Zora! Ain't you ever been to a toe-party before?"

---

*Loud talking, bullying, woofing. From French *beaucoup*.
†Aimless talking.

"Nope. They don't have 'em up North where Ah been and Ah just got back today."

"Well, they hides all de girls behind a curtain and you stick out yo' toe. Some places you take off yo' shoes and some places you keep 'em on, but most all de time you keep 'em on. When all de toes is in a line, sticking out from behind de sheet they let de men folks in and they looks over all de toes and buys de ones they want for a dime. Then they got to treat de lady dat owns dat toe to everything she want. Sometime they play it so's you keep de same partner for de whole thing and sometime they fix it so they put de girls back every hour or so and sell de toes agin."

Well, my toe went on the line with the rest and it was sold five times during the party. Everytime a toe was sold there was a great flurry before the curtain. Each man eager to see what he had got, and whether the other men would envy him or ridicule him. One or two fellows ungallantly ran out of the door rather than treat the girls whose toe they had bought sight unseen.

Babe Brown got off on his guitar and the dancing was hilarious. There was plenty of chicken perleau and baked chicken and fried chicken and rabbit. Pig feet and chitterlings and hot peanuts and drinkables. Everybody was treating wildly.

"Come on, Zora, and have a treat on me!" Charlie Jones insisted. "You done et chicken-ham and chicken-bosom wid every shag-leg in Orange County *but* me. Come on and spend some of *my* money."

"Thanks, Charlie, but Ah got five helpin's of chicken inside already. Ah either got to get another stomach or quit eatin'."

"Quit eatin' then and go to thinking. Quit thinkin' and start to drinkin'. What you want?"

"Coca-Cola right off de ice, Charlie, and put some salt in it. Ah got a slight headache."

Aw now, my money don't buy no sweet slop. Choose some coon dick."

"What is coon dick?"

"Aw, Zora, jus' somethin' to make de drunk come. Made out uh grape fruit juice, corn meal mash, beef bones and a few mo' things. Come on le's git some together. It might make our love come down."

As soon as we started over into the next yard where coon dick was to be had, Charlie yelled to the barkeep, "Hey, Seymore! fix up another quart of dat low wine—here come de boom!"

It was handed to us in a quart fruit jar and we went outside to try it.

The raw likker known locally as coon dick was too much. The minute it touched my lips, the top of my head flew off. I spat it out and "choosed" some peanuts. Big Willie Sewell said, "Come on, heart-string, and have some gospel-bird* on me. My money spends too." His Honor Hiram Lester, the Mayor, heard him and said, "There's no mo' chicken left, Willie. Why don't you offer her something she can get?"

"Well there *was* some chicken there when Ah passed the table a little while ago."

"Oh, so you offerin' her some chicken *was*. She can't eat that. What she want is some chicken *is*."

"Aw shut up, Hiram. Come on, Zora, le's go inside and make out we dancin'." We went on inside but it wasn't a party any more. Just some people herded together. The high spirits were simmering down and nobody had a dime left to cry so the toe-business suffered a slump. The heaped-up tables of refreshments had become shambles of chicken bones and empty platters anyway so that there was no longer any point in getting your toe sold, so when Columbus Montgomery said, "Le's go to Eatonville," Soddy Sewell jumped up and grabbed his hat and said, "I heard you buddy."

Eatonville began to move back home right then. Nearly everybody was packed in one of the five cars when the delegation from Altamonte arrived. Johnnie Barton and Georgia Burke. Everybody piled out again.

"Got yo' guitar wid you, Johnnie?"

"Man, you know Ah don't go nowhere unless Ah take my box wid me," said Johnnie in his starched blue shirt, collar pin with heart bangles hanging on each end and his cream pants with the black stripe. "And what make it so cool, Ah don't go nowhere unless I play it."

"And when you git to strowin' yo' mess and Georgy gits to singin' her alto, man it's hot as seven hells. Man, play dat 'Palm Beach'."

Babe Brown took the guitar and Johnnie Barton grabbed the piano stool. He sung. Georgia Burke and George Thomas singing about Polk County where the water taste like wine.

My heart struck sorrow, tears come running down.

At about the thirty-seventh verse, something about:

*Chicken. Preachers are supposed to be fond of them.

Ah'd ruther be in Tampa with the Whip-poor-will,
Ruther be in Tampa with the Whip-poor-will,
Than to be 'round here—
Honey with a hundred dollar bill,

I staggered sleepily forth to the little Chevrolet for Eatonville. The car was overflowing with passengers but I was so dull from lack of sleep that I didn't know who they were. All I knew is they belonged in Eatonville.

Somebody was woofing in my car about love and I asked him about his buddy—I don't know why now. He said, "Ah ain't got no buddy. They kilt my buddy so they could raise me. Jus' so Ah be yo' man Ah don't want no damn buddy. Ah hope they kill every man dat ever cried, 'titty-mamma' but me. Lemme be yo' kid."

Some voice from somewhere else in the car commented, "You sho' Lawd is gointer have a lot of hindrance."

Then somehow I got home and to bed and Armetta had Georgia syrup and waffles for breakfast.

THE VERY NEXT AFTERNOON, as usual, the gregarious part of the town's population gathered on the store porch. All the Florida-flip players, all the eleven-card layers.* But they yelled over to me they'd be over that night in full. And they were.

"Zora," George Thomas informed me, "you come to de right place if lies is what you want. Ah'm gointer lie up a nation."

Charlie Jones said, "Yeah, man. Me and my sworn buddy Gene Brazzle is here. Big Moose done come down from de mountain."†

"Now, you gointer hear lies above suspicion," Gene added.

It was a hilarious night with a pinch of everything social mixed with the story-telling. Everybody ate ginger bread; some drank the buttermilk provided and some provided coon dick for themselves. Nobody guzzled it —just took it in social sips.

But they told stories enough for a volume by itself. Some of the stories were the familiar drummer-type of tale about two Irishmen, Pat and Mike, or two Jews as the case might be. Some were the European folk-tales undiluted, like Jack and the Beanstalk. Others had slight local variations, but Negro imagination is so facile that there was little need for

---

*Coon-can players. A two-handed card game popular among Southern Negroes.
†Important things are about to happen.

outside help. A'nt Hagar's son, like Joseph, put on his many-colored coat an paraded before his brethren and every man there was a Joseph.

Steve Nixon was holding class meeting across the way at St. Lawrence Church and we could hear the testimony and the songs. So we began to talk about church and preachers.

"Aw, Ah don't pay all dese ole preachers no rabbit-foot,"* said Ellis Jones. "Some of 'em is all right but everybody dats up in de pulpit whoopin' and hollerin' ain't called to preach."

"They ain't no different from nobody else," added B. Moseley. "They mouth is cut cross ways, ain't it? Well, long as you don't see no man wid they mouth cut up and down, you know they'll all lie jus' like de rest of us."

"Yeah; and hard work in de hot sun done called a many a man to preach," said a woman called Gold, for no evident reason. "Ah heard about one man out clearin' off some new ground. De sun was so hot till a grindstone melted and run off in de shade to cool off. De man was so tired till he went and sit down on a log. 'Work, work, work! Everywhere Ah go de boss say hurry, de cap' say run. Ah got a durn good notion not to do nary one. Wisht Ah was one of dese preachers wid a whole lot of folks makin' my support for me.' He looked back over his shoulder and seen a narrer li'l strip of shade along side of de log, so he got over dere and laid down right close up to de log in de shade and said, 'Now, Lawd, if you don't pick me up and chunk me on de other side of dis log, Ah know you done called me to preach.'

"You know God never picked 'im up, so he went off and tol' everybody dat he was called to preach."

"There's many a one been called just lak dat," Ellis corroborated. "Ah knowed a man dat was called by a mule."

"A mule, Ellis? All dem b'lieve dat, stand on they head," said Little Ida.

"Yeah, a mule did call a man to preach. Ah'll show you how it was done, if you'll stand a straightenin'."

"Now, Ellis, don't mislay de truth. Sense us into dis mule-callin' business."

Ellis: These was two brothers and one of 'em was a big preacher and had good collections every Sunday. He didn't pastor nothin' but big charges. De other

*I ignore these preachers.

brother decided he wanted to preach so he went way down in de swamp behind a big plantation to de place they call de prayin' ground, and got down on his knees.

"O Lawd, Ah wants to preach. Ah feel lak Ah got a message. If you done called me to preach, gimme a sign."

Just 'bout dat time he heard a voice, "Wanh, uh wanh! Go preach, go preach, go preach!"

He went and tol' everybody, but look lak he never could git no big charge. All he ever got called was on some sawmill, half-pint church or some turpentine still. He knocked around lak dat for ten years and then he seen his brother. De big preacher says, "Brother, you don't look like you gittin' holt of much."

"You tellin' dat right, brother. Groceries is scarce. Ah ain't dirtied a plate today."

"Whut's de matter? Don't you git no support from your church?"

"Yeah, Ah gits it such as it is, but Ah ain't never pastored no big church. Ah don't git called to nothin' but saw-mill camps and turpentine stills."

De big preacher reared back and thought a while, then he ast de other one, "Is you sure you was called to preach? Maybe you ain't cut out for no preacher."

"Oh, yeah," he told him. "Ah *know* Ah been called to de ministry. A voice spoke and tol' me so."

"Well, seem lak if God called you He is mighty slow in puttin' yo' foot on de ladder. If Ah was you Ah'd go back and ast 'im agin."

So de po' man went on back to de prayin' ground agin and got down on his knees. But there wasn't no big woods like it used to be. It has been all cleared off. He prayed and said, "Oh, Lawd, right here on dis spot ten years ago Ah ast you if Ah was called to preach and a voice tole me to go preach. Since dat time Ah been strugglin' in Yo' moral vineyard, but Ah ain't gathered no grapes. Now, if you really called me to preach Christ and Him crucified, please gimme another sign."

Sho nuff, jus' as soon as he said dat, de voice said "Wanh-uh! Go preach! Go preach! Go preach!"

De man jumped up and says, "Ah knowed Ah been called. Dat's de same voice. Dis time Ah'm goin ter ast Him where *must* Ah go preach."

By dat time de voice come agin and looked 'way off and seen a mule in de plantation lot wid his head all stuck out to bray agin, and he said, "Unh hunh, youse de very son of a gun dat called me to preach befo'."

So he went on off and got a job plowin'. Dat's what he was called to do in de first place.

Armetta said, "A many one been called to de plough and they run off and got up in de pulpit. Ah wish dese mules knowed how to take a pair of plow-lines and go to de church and ketch some of 'em like they go to de lot with a bridle and ketch mules.''

Ellis: Ah knowed one preacher dat was called to preach at one of dese split-off cnurches. De members had done split off from a big church because they was all mean and couldn't git along wid nobody.

Dis preacher was a good man, but de congregation was so tough he couldn't make a convert in a whole year. So he sent and invited another preacher to come and conduct a revival meeting for him. De man he ast to come was a powerful hard preacher wid a good strainin' voice. He was known to get converts.

Well, he come and preached at dis split-off for two whole weeks. De people would all turn out to church and jus' set dere and look at de man up dere strainin' his lungs out and nobody would give de man no encouragement by sayin' ''Amen,'' and not a soul bowed down.

It was a narrer church wid one winder and dat was in de pulpit and de door was in de front end. Dey had a mean ole sexton wid a wooden leg. So de last night of de protracted meetin' de preacher come to church wid his grip-sack in his hand and went on up in de pulpit. When he got up to preach he says, ''Brother Sexton, dis bein' de last night of de meetin' Ah wants you to lock de do' and bring me de key. Ah want everybody to stay and hear whut Ah got to say.''

De sexton brought him de key and he took his tex and went to preachin'. He preached and he reared and pitched, but nobody said ''Amen'' and nobody bowed down. So 'way after while he stooped down and opened his suit-satchel and out wid his .44 Special. ''Now,'' he said, ''you rounders and brick-bats— yeah, you women, Ah'm talkin' to you. If you ain't a whole brick, den you must be a bat—and gamblers and 'leven-card layers. Ah done preached to you for two whole weeks and not one of you has said 'Amen,' and nobody has bowed down.''

He thowed de gun on 'em. ''And now Ah say bow down!'' And they beginned to bow all over dat church.

De sexton looked at his wooden leg and figgered he couldn't bow because his leg was cut off above de knee. So he ast, ''Me too, Elder?''

''Yeah, you too, you peg-leg son of a gun. You bow down too.''

Therefo' dat sexton bent dat wooden leg and bowed down. De preacher fired a couple of shots over they heads and stepped out de window and went on 'bout his business. But he skeered dem people so bad till they all rushed to one side of de church tryin' to git out and carried dat church buildin' twenty-eight miles befo' they thought to turn it loose.

·"Now Ellis," chided Gold when she was thru her laughter, "You know dat's a lie. Folks over there in St. Lawrence holdin' class meetin' and you over here lyin' like de crossties from Jacksonville to Key West."

"Now, dat ain't no lie!" Ellis contended, still laughing himself.

"Aw, yes it 'tis," Gold said. "Dat's all you men is good for—settin' 'round and lyin'. Some of you done quit lyin' and gone to flyin'."

Gene Brazzle said, "Get off of us mens now. We *is* some good. Plenty good too if you git de right one. De trouble is you women ain't good for nothin' exceptin' readin' Sears and Roebuck's bible and hollerin' ' bout, 'gimme dis and gimme dat' as soon as we draw our pay."

Shug* said, "Well, we don't git it by astin' you mens for it. If we work for it we kin git it. You mens don't draw no pay. You don't do nothin' but stand around and draw lightnin'."

"Ah don't say Ah'm detrimental," Gene said dryly, "but if Gold and Shug don't stop crackin' us, Ah'm gointer get 'em to go."

Gold: "Man, if you want me any, some or none, do whut you gointer do and stop cryin'."

Gene: "You ain't seen me cryin'. See me cryin', it's sign of a funeral. If Ah even look cross somebody gointer bleed."

Gold: "Aw, shut up, Gene, you ain't no big hen's biddy if you do lay gobbler eggs. You tryin' to talk like big wood when you ain't nothin' but brush."

Armetta sensed a hard anger creepin' into the teasing so she laughed to make Gene and Gold laugh and asked, "Did y'all have any words before you fell out?"

"We ain't mad wid one 'nother," Gene defended. "We jus' jokin'."

"Well, stop blowin' it and let de lyin' go on," said Charlie Jones. "Zora's gittin' restless. She think she ain't gointer hear no more."

"Oh, no Ah ain't," I lied. After a short spell of quiet, good humor was restored to the porch. In the pause we could hear Pa Henry over in the church house sending up a prayer:

. . . You have been with me from the earliest rocking of
my cradle up until this present moment.

*Short for sugar.

You know our hearts, our Father,
And all de range of our deceitful minds,
And if you find anything like sin lurking
In and around our hearts,
Ah ast you, My Father, and my Wonder-workin' God
To pluck it out
And cast it into de sea of Fuhgitfulness
Where it will never rise to harm us in dis world
Nor condemn us in de judgment.
You heard me when Ah laid at hell's dark door
With no weapon in my hand
And no God in my heart,
And cried for three long days and nights.
You heard me, Lawd,
And stooped so low
And snatched me from the hell
Of eternal death and damnation.
You cut loose my stammerin' tongue;
You established my feet on de rock of Salvation
And yo' voice was heard in rumblin' judgment.
I thank Thee that my last night's sleepin' couch
Was not my coolin' board
And my cover
Was not my windin' sheet.
Speak to de sinner-man and bless 'im.
Touch all those
Who have been down to de doors of degradation.
Ketch de man dat's layin' in danger of consumin' fire;
And Lawd,
When Ah kin pray no mo';
When Ah done drunk down de last cup of sorrow
Look on me, yo' weak servant who feels de least of all;
'Point my soul a restin' place
Where Ah kin set down and praise yo' name forever
Is my prayer for Jesus sake
Amen and thank God.

As the prayer ended the bell of Macedonia, the Baptist church, began to ring.

"Prayer meetin' night at Macedony," George Thomas said.

"It's too bad that it must be two churches in Eatonville," I commented. "De town's too little. Everybody ought to go to one."

"Dey wouldn't do dat, Zora, and you know better. Fack is, de Christian churches nowhere don't stick together," this from Charlie.

Everybody agreed that this was true. So Charlie went on. "Look at all de kind of denominations we got. But de people can't help dat 'cause de church wasn't built on no solid foundation to start wid."

"Oh yes, it 'twas!" Johnnie Mae disputed him. "It was built on solid rock. Didn't Jesus say 'On dis rock Ah build my church?'"

"Yeah," chimed in Antie Hoyt. "And de songs says, 'On Christ de solid rock I stand' and 'Rock of Ages.'"

Charlie was calm and patient. "Yeah, he built it on a rock, but it wasn't solid. It was a pieced-up rock and that's how come de church split up now. Here's de very way it was:

Christ was walkin' long one day wid all his disciples and he said, "We're goin' for a walk today. Everybody pick up a rock and come along." So everybody got their selves a nice big rock 'ceptin' Peter. He was lazy so he picked up a li'l bit of a pebble and dropped it in his side pocket and come along.

Well, they walked all day long and de other 'leven disciples changed them rocks from one arm to de other but they kept on totin' 'em. Long towards sundown they come 'long by de Sea of Galilee and Jesus tole 'em, "Well, le's fish awhile. Cast in yo' nets right here." They done like he tole 'em and caught a great big mess of fish. Then they cooked 'em and Christ said, "Now, all y'all bring up yo' rocks." So they all brought they rocks and Christ turned 'em into bread and they all had a plenty to eat wid they fish exceptin' Peter. He couldn't hardly make a moufful offa de li'l bread he had and he didn't like dat a bit.

Two or three days after dat Christ went out doors and looked up at de sky and says, "Well, we're goin' for another walk today. Everybody git yo'self a rock and come along."

They all picked up a rock apiece and was ready to go. All but Peter. He went and tore down half a mountain. It was so big he couldn't move it wid his hands. He had to take a pinch-bar to move it. All day long Christ walked and talked to his disciples and Peter sweated and strained wid dat rock of his'n.

Way long in de evenin' Christ went up under a great big ole tree and set down and called all of his disciples around 'im and said, "Now everybody bring up yo' rocks."

So everybody brought theirs but Peter. Peter was about a mile down de road punchin' dat half a mountain he was bringin'. So Christ waited till he got dere. He looked at de rocks dat de other 'leven disciples had, den he seen dis great big mountain dat Peter had and so he got up and walked over to it and put one foot up on it and said "Why Peter, dis is a fine rock you got here! It's a noble rock! And Peter, on dis rock Ah'm gointer build my church.''

Peter says, ''Naw you ain't neither. You won't build no church house on *dis* rock. You gointer turn dis rock into bread.''

Christ knowed dat Peter meant dat thing so he turnt de hillside into bread and dat mountain is de bread he fed de 5,000 wid. Den he took dem 'leven other rocks and glued 'em together and built his church on it.

And that's how come de Christian churches is split up into so many different kinds—cause it's built on pieced-up rock.

There was a storm of laughter following Charlie's tale. "Zora, you come talkin' bout puttin' de two churches together and not havin' but one in dis town,'' Armetta said chidingly, ''You know better'n dat. Baptis' and Methdis' always got a pick out at one 'nother. One time two preachers—one Methdis' an de other one Baptis' wuz on uh train and de engine blowed up and bein' in de colored coach right back of de engine they got blowed up too. When they saw theyself startin' up in de air de Baptis' preacher hollered, ''Ah bet Ah go higher than you!''

Then Gold spoke up and said, ''Now, lemme tell one. Ah know one about a man as black as Gene.''

''Whut you always crackin' me for?'' Gene wanted to know. ''Ah ain't a bit blacker than you.''

''Oh, yes you is, Gene. Youse a whole heap blacker than Ah is.''

''Aw, go head on, Gold. Youse blacker than me. You jus' look my color cause youse fat. If you wasn't no fatter than me you'd be so black till lightnin' bugs would follow you at twelve o'clock in de day, thinkin' it's midnight.''

''Dat's a lie, youse blacker than Ah ever dared to be. Youse lam' black. Youse so black till they have to throw a sheet over yo' head so de sun kin rise every mornin'. Ah know yo' ma cried when she seen *you*.''

''Well, anyhow, Gold, youse blacker than me. If Ah was as fat as you Ah'd be a yaller man.''

''Youse a liar. Youse as yaller as you ever gointer git. When a person is poor he look bright and de fatter you git de darker you look.''

''Is dat yo' excuse for being so black, Gold?''

Armetta soothed Gold's feelings and stopped the war. When the air cleared Gold asked, "Do y'all know how come we are black?"

"Yeah," said Ellis. "It's because two black niggers got together."

"Aw, naw," Gold disputed petulantly. "Well, since you so smart, tell me where dem two black niggers come from in de first beginnin'."

"They musta come from Zar, and dat's on de other side of far."

"Uh, hunh!" Gold gloated. "Ah knowed you didn't know whut you was talkin' about. Now Ah'm goin' ter tell you how come we so black:

Long before they got thru makin' de Atlantic Ocean and haulin' de rocks for de mountains, God was makin' up de people. But He didn't finish 'em all at one time. Ah'm compelled to say dat some folks is walkin' 'round dis town right now ain't finished yet and never will be.

Well, He give out eyes one day. All de nations come up and got they eyes. Then He give out teeth and so on. Then He set a day to give out color. So seven o'clock dat mornin' everybody was due to git they color except de niggers. So God give everybody they color and they went on off. Then He set there for three hours and one-half and no niggers. It was gettin' hot and God wanted to git His work done and go set in de cool. So He sent de angels. Rayfield and Gab'ull to go git 'em so He could 'tend some mo' business.

They hunted all over Heben till dey found de colored folks. All stretched out sleep on de grass under de tree of life. So Rayfield woke 'em up and tole 'em God wanted 'em.

They all jumped up and run on up to de th'one and they was so skeered they might miss sumpin' they begin to push and shove one 'nother, bumpin' against all de angels and turnin' over foot-stools. They even had de th'one all pushed one-sided.

So God hollered "Git back! Git back!" And they misunderstood Him and thought He said, "Git black," and they been black ever since.

Gene rolled his eyeballs into one corner of his head.

"Now Gold call herself gettin' even wid me—tellin' dat lie. 'Tain't no such story nowhere. She jus' made dat one up herself."

"Naw, she didn't," Armetta defended. "Ah *been* knowin' dat ole tale."

"Me too," said Shoo-pie.

"Don't you know you can't git de best of no woman in de talkin' game? Her tongue is all de weapon a woman got," George Thomas chided Gene. "She could have had mo' sense, but she told God no, she'd ruther take it out in hips. So God give her her ruthers. She got plenty hips, plenty mouf and no brains."

"Oh, yes, womens is got sense too," Mathilda Moseley jumped in. "But they got too much sense to go 'round braggin' about it like y'all do. De lady people always got de advantage of mens because God fixed it dat way."

"Whut ole black advantage is y'all got?" B. Moseley asked indignantly. "We got all de strength and all de law and all de money and you can't git a thing but whut we jes' take pity on you and give you."

"And dat's jus' de point," said Mathilda triumphantly. "You *do* give it to us, but how come you do it?" And without waiting for an answer Mathilda began to tell why women always take advantage of men.

You see in de very first days, God made a man and a woman and put 'em in a house together to live. 'Way back in them days de woman was just as strong as de man and both of 'em did de same things. They useter get to fussin' 'bout who gointer do this and that and sometime they'd fight, but they was even balanced and neither one could whip de other one.

One day de man said to hisself, "B'lieve Ah'm gointer go see God and ast Him for a li'l mo' strength so Ah kin whip dis 'oman and make her mind. Ah'm tired of de way things is." So he went on up to God.

"Good mawnin', Ole Father."

"Howdy man. Whut you doin' 'round my throne so soon dis mawnin'?"

"Ah'm troubled in mind, and nobody can't ease mah spirit 'ceptin' you."

God said: "Put yo' plea in de right form and Ah'll hear and answer."

"Ole Maker, wid de mawnin' stars glitterin' in yo' shinin' crown, wid de dust from yo' footsteps makin' worlds upon worlds, wid de blazin' bird we call de sun flyin' out of yo' right hand in de mawnin' and consumin' all day de flesh and blood of stump-black darkness, and comes flyin' home every evenin' to rest on yo' left hand, and never once in all yo' eternal years, mistook de left hand for de right, Ah ast you *please* to give me mo' strength than dat woman you give me, so Ah kin make her mind. Ah know you don't want to be always comin' down way past de moon and stars to be straightenin' her out and its got to be done. So give me a li'l mo' strength, Ole Maker and Ah'll do it."

"All right, Man, you got mo' strength than woman."

So de man run all de way down de stairs from Heben till he got home. He was so anxious to try his strength on de woman dat he couldn't take his time.

Soon's he got in de house he hollered "Woman! Here's yo' boss. God done tole me to handle you in which ever way Ah please. Ah'm yo' boss."

De woman flew to fightin' 'im right off. She fought 'im frightenin' but he beat her. She got her wind and tried 'im agin but he whipped her agin. She got herself together and made de third try on him vigorous but he beat her every time. He was so proud he could whip 'er at last, dat he just crowed over her and made her do a lot of things she didn't like. He told her, "Long as you obey me, Ah'll be good to yuh, but every time yuh rear up Ah'm gointer put plenty wood on yo' back and plenty water in yo' eyes."

De woman was so mad she went straight up to Heben and stood befo' de Lawd. She didn't waste no words. She said, "Lawd, Ah come befo' you mighty mad t'day. Ah want back my strength and power Ah useter have."

"Woman, you got de same power you had since de beginnin'."

"Why is it then, dat de man kin beat me now and he useter couldn't do it?"

"He got mo' strength than he useter have. He come and ast me for it and Ah give it to 'im. Ah gives to them that ast, and you ain't never ast me for no mo' power."

"Please suh, God, Ah'm astin' you for it now. Jus' gimme de same as you give him."

God shook his head. "It's too late now, woman. Whut Ah give, Ah never take back. Ah give him mo' strength than you and no matter how much Ah give you, he'll have mo'."

De woman was so mad she wheeled around and went on off. She went straight to de devil and told him what had happened.

He said, "Don't be dis-incouraged, woman. You listen to me and you'll come out mo' than conqueror. Take dem frowns out yo' face and turn round and go right on back to Heben and ast God to give you dat bunch of keys hangin' by de mantel-piece. Then you bring 'em to me and Ah'll show you what to do wid 'em."

So de woman climbed back up to Heben agin. She was mighty tired but she was more out-done that she was tired so she climbed all night long and got back up to Heben agin. When she got befo' de throne, butter wouldn't melt in her mouf.

"O Lawd and Master of de rainbow, Ah know yo' power. You never make two mountains without you put a valley in between. Ah know you kin hit a straight lick wid a crooked stick."

"Ast for whut you want, woman."

"God, gimme dat bunch of keys hangin' by yo' mantel-piece."

"Take 'em."

So de woman took de keys and hurried on back to de devil wid 'em. There was three keys on de bunch. Devil say, ''See dese three keys? They got mo' power in 'em than all de strength de man kin ever git if you handle 'em right. Now dis first big key is to de do' of de kitchen, and you know a man always favors his stomach. Dis second one is de key to de bedroom and he don't like to be shut out from dat neither and dis last key is de key to de cradle and he don't want to be cut off from his generations at all. So now you take dese keys and go lock up everything and wait till he come to you. Then don't you unlock nothin' until he use his strength for yo' benefit and yo' desires.''

De woman thanked 'im and tole 'im, ''If it wasn't for you, Lawd knows whut us po' women folks would do.''

She started off but de devil halted her. ''Jus' one mo' thing: don't go home braggin' 'bout yo' keys. Jus' lock up everything and say nothin' until you git asked. And then don't talk too much.''

De woman went on home and did like de devil tole her. When de man come home from work she was settin' on de porch singin' some song 'bout ''Peck on de wood make de bed go good.''

When de man found de three doors fastened what useter stand wide open he swelled up like pine lumber after a rain. First thing he tried to break in cause he figgered his strength would overcome all obstacles. When he saw he couldn't do it, he ast de woman, ''Who locked dis do'?''

She tole 'im, ''Me.''

''Where did you git de key from?''

''God give it to me.''

He run up to God and said, ''God, woman got me locked 'way from my vittles, my bed and my generations, and she say you give her the keys.''

God said, ''I did, Man, Ah give her de keys, but de devil showed her how to use 'em!''

''Well, Ole Maker, please gimme some keys jus' lak 'em so she can't git de full control.''

''No, Man, what Ah give Ah give. Woman got de key.''

''How kin Ah know 'bout my generations?''

''Ast de woman.''

So de man come on back and submitted hisself to de woman and she opened de doors.

He wasn't satisfied but he had to give in. 'Way after while he said to de woman, ''Le's us divide up. Ah'll give you half of my strength if you lemme hold de keys in my hands.''

De woman thought dat over so de devil popped and told her, ''Tell 'im, naw. Let 'im keep his strength and you keep yo' keys.''

So de woman wouldn't trade wid 'im and de man had to mortgage his strength to her to live. And dat's why de man makes and de woman takes. You men is still braggin' 'bout yo' strength and de women is sittin' on de keys and lettin' you blow off till she git ready to put de bridle on you.

B. Moseley looked over at Mathilda and said, "You just like a hen in de barnyard. You cackle so much you give de rooster de blues.''

Mathilda looked over at him archly and quoted:

Stepped on a pin, de pin bent
And dat's de way de story went.

"Y'all lady people ain't smarter *than* all men folks. You got plow lines on some of us, but some of us is too smart for you. We go past you jus' like lightnin' thru de trees," Willie Sewell boasted. "And what make it so cool, we close enough to you to have a scronchous time, but never no halter on our necks. Ah know they won't git none on dis last neck of mine.''

"Oh, you kin be had," Gold retorted. "Ah mean dat abstifically.''

"Yeah? But not wid de trace chains. Never no shack up. Ah want dis tip-in love and tip yo' hat and walk out. Ah don't want nobody to have dis dyin' love for me.''

Richard Jones said: "Yeah, man. Love is a funny thing; love is a blossom. If you want yo' finger bit poke it at a possum.''

Jack Oscar Jones, who had been quiet for some time, slumped way down in his chair, straightened up and said, "Ah know a speech about love.''

Ruth Marshall laughed doubtfully. "Now, Jack, you can't make me b'lieve you know de first thing about no love.''

"Yeah he do, too," Clara, Jack's wife defended.

"Whut do he know, then?" Ruth persisted.

"Aw, Lawd," Clara wagged her head knowingly. "You ain't got no business knowing dat. Dat's *us* business. But he know jus' as much about love as de nex' man.''

"You don't say!" Johnnie Mae twitted her sister-in-law. "Blow it out, then, Jack, and tell a blind man somethin'.''

"Ah'm gointer say it, then me and Zora's goin' out to Montgomery and git up a cool watermelon, ain't we, Zora?''

"If you got de price," I came back. "Ah got de car so all we need is a strong determination and we'll have melon."

"No, Zora ain't goin' nowhere wid my husband," Clara announced. "If he got anything to tell her—it's gointer be right here in front of me."

Jack laughed at Clara's feigned jealousy and recited:

Song Poem

When the clock struck one I had just begun. Begun with Sue, begun with Sal, begun with that pretty Johnson gal.

When the clock struck two, I was through, I was through with Sue, through with Sal, through with that pretty Johnson gal.

When the clock struck three I was free, free with Sue, free with Sal, free with that pretty Johnson gal.

When the clock struck four I was at the door, at the door with Sue, at the door with Sal, at the door with that pretty Johnson gal.

When the clock struck five I was alive, alive with Sue, alive with Sal, alive with that pretty Johnson gal.

When the clock struck six I was fixed, fixed with Sue, fixed with Sal, fixed with that pretty Johnson gal.

When the clock struck seven I was even, even with Sue, even with Sal, even with that pretty Johnson gal.

When the clock struck eight I was at your gate, gate with Sue, gate with Sal, gate with that pretty Johnson gal.

When the clock struck nine I was behind, behind with Sue, behind with Sal, behind with that pretty Johnson gal.

When the clock struck ten I was in the bin, in the bin with Sue, in the bin with Sal, in the bin with that pretty Johnson gal.

When the clock struck eleven, I was in heaven, in heaven with Sue, in heaven with Sal, in heaven with that pretty Johnson gal.

When the clock struck twelve I was in hell, in hell with Sue, in hell with Sal, in hell with that pretty Johnson gal.

"Who was all dis Sue and dis Sal and dat pretty Johnson gal?" Clara demanded of Jack.

"Dat ain't for you to know. My name is West, and Ah'm so different from de rest."

"You sound like one man courtin' three gals, but Ah know a story 'bout three mens courtin' one gal," Shug commented.

"Dat's bogish,"* cried Bennie Lee thickly.

"What's bogish?" Shug demanded. She and Bennie were step-brother and sister and they had had a lawsuit over the property of his late father and her late mother, so a very little of Bennie's sugar would sweeten Shug's tea and vice versa.

"Ah don't want to lissen to no ole talk 'bout three mens after no one 'oman. It's always more'n three womens after every man."

"Well, de way Ah know de story, there was three mens after de same girl," Shug insisted. "You drunk, Bennie Lee. You done drunk so much of dis ole coon dick till you full of monkies."

"Whut you gointer do?" Bennie demanded. "Whut you gointer do?" No answer was expected to this question. It was just Bennie Lee's favorite retort. "De monkies got me, now whut you gointer do?"

"Ah ain't got you to study about, Bennie Lee. If God ain't payin' you no mo' mind than Ah is, youse in hell right now. Ah ain't talkin' to you nohow. Zora, you wanter hear dis story?"

"Sure, Shug. That's what Ah'm here for."

"Somebody's gointer bleed," Bennie Lee threatened. Nobody paid him any mind.

"God knows Ah don't wanter hear Shug tell nothin'," Bennie Lee complained.

"Ah wish yo' monkies would tell you to go hide in de hammock and forgit to tell you de way home." Shug was getting peeved.

"You better shut up befo' Ah whip yo' head to de red. Ah wish Ah was God. Ah'd turn you into a blamed hawg, and then Ah'd concrete de whole world over so you wouldn't have not one nary place to root."

"Dat's dat two-bits in change you got in yo' pocket now dat's talkin' for you. But befo' de summer's over *you'll* be rootin' lak a hawg. You already lookin' over-plus lak one now. Don't you worry 'bout me."

Bennie Lee tried to ask his well-known question but the coon dick was too strong. He mumbled down into his shirt bosom and went to sleep.

YOUSE IN DE MAJORITY, NOW SHUG," B. Moseley said, seeing Bennie asleep. "Le's hear 'bout dat man wid three women."

Shug said:

*Bogus.

Naw, it was three mens went to court a girl, Ah told you. Dis was a real pretty girl wid shiny black hair and coal black eyes. And all dese men wanted to marry her, so they all went and ast her pa if they could have her. He looked 'em all over, but he couldn't decide which one of 'em would make de best husband and de girl, she couldn't make up her mind, so one Sunday night when he walked into de parlor where they was all sittin' and said to 'em, "Well, all y'all want to marry my daughter and youse all good men and Ah can't decide which one will make her de best husband. So y'all be here tomorrow mornin' at daybreak and we'll have a contest and de one dat can do de quickest trick kin have de girl."

Nex' mornin' de first one got up seen it wasn't no water in de bucket to cook breakfas' wid. So he tole de girl's mama to give him de water bucket and he would go to the spring and git her some.

He took de bucket in his hand and then he found out dat de spring was ten miles off. But he said he didn't mind dat. He went on and dipped up de water and hurried on back wid it. When he got to de five-mile post he looked down into de bucket and seen dat de bottom had done dropped out. Then he recollected dat he heard somethin' fall when he dipped up de water so he turned round and run back to de spring and clapped in dat bottom before de water had time to spill.

De ole man thought dat was a pretty quick trick, but de second man says, "Wait a minute. Ah want a grubbin' hoe and a axe and a plow and a harrow." So he got everything he ast for. There was ten acres of wood lot right nex' to de house. He went out dere and chopped down all de trees, grubbed up de roots, ploughed de field, harrowed it, planted it in cow-peas, and had green peas for dinner.

De ole man says "Dat's de quickest trick. Can't nobody beat dat. No use in tryin'. He done won de girl."

De last man said, "You ain't even givin' me a chance to win de girl."

So he took his high-powered rifle and went out into de woods about seben or eight miles until he spied a deer. He took aim and fired. Then he run home, run round behind de house and set his gun down and then run back out in de woods and caught de deer and held 'im till de bullet hit 'im.

So he won de girl.

Robert Williams said:

Ah know another man wid a daughter.

The man sent his daughter off to school for seben years, den she come home all finished up. So he said to her, "Daughter, git yo' things and write me a letter to my brother!" So she did.

He says, "Head it up," and she done so.

"Now tell 'im, 'Dear Brother, our chile is done come home from school and all finished up and we is very proud of her.' "

Then he ast de girl "Is you got dat?"

She tole 'im "yeah."

"Now tell him some mo'. 'Our mule is dead but Ah got another mule and when Ah say (clucking sound of tongue and teeth) he moved from de word.' "

"Is you got dat?" he ast de girl.

"Naw suh," she tole 'im.

He waited a while and he ast her again, "You got dat down yet?"

"Naw suh, Ah ain't got it yet."

"How come you ain't got it?"

"Cause Ah can't spell (clucking sound)."

"You mean to tell me you been off to school seben years and can't spell (clucking sound)? Why Ah could spell dat myself and Ah ain't been to school a day in mah life. Well jes' say (clucking sound) he'll know what yo' mean and go on wid de letter."

Henry "Nigger" Byrd said:

I know one about a letter too.

My father owned a fas' horse—I mean a *fast* horse. We was livin' in Ocala then. Mah mother took sick and mah father come and said, "Skeet,"—he uster call me Skeet—"You oughter wire yo' sister in St. Petersburg."

"I jus' wired her," I tole him.

"Whut did you put in it?"

I tole 'im.

He says, "Dat ain't right. I'm goin' ketch it." He went out in de pasture and caught de horse and shod 'im and curried 'im and brushed 'im off good, put de saddle on 'im and got on 'im, and caught dat telegram and read it and took it on to mah sister.

Soon as he left de house, mama said, "You chillun make a fire in de stove and fix somethin' for de ole man to eat."

Befo' she could git de word out her mouf, him and mah sister rode up to de do' and said "Whoa!"

By dat time a flea ast me for a shoe-shine so I left.

Armetta said: "Nigger, I didn't know you could lie like that."

"I ain't lyin', Armetta. We had dat horse. We had a cow too and she was so sway-backed that she could use de bushy part of her tail for a umbrella over her head.''

''Shet up, Nig!'' ''Seaboard'' Hamilton pretended to be outraged. ''Ah knowed you could sing barytone but Ah wouldn't a b'lieved de lyin' was in you if Ah didn't hear you myself. Whut makes you bore wid such a great big augur?''

Little Julius Henry, who should have been home in bed spoke up. ''Mah brother John had a horse 'way back dere in slavery time.''

''Let de dollars hush whilst de nickel speak,'' Charlie Jones derided Julius' youth. ''Julius, whut make you wanta jump in a hogshead when a kag* will hold yuh? You hear dese hard ole coons lyin' up a nation and you stick in yo' bill.''

''If his mouf is cut cross ways and he's two years ole, he kin lie good as anybody else,'' John French defended. ''Blow it, Julius.''

Julius spat out into the yard, trying to give the impression that he was skeeting tobacco juice like a man.

De rooster chew t'backer, de hen dip snuff
De biddy can't do it, but he struts his stuff.

Ole John, he was workin' for Massa and Massa had two hawses and he lakted John, so he give John one of his hawses.

When John git to workin' 'em he'd haul off and beat Massa's hawse, but he never would hit his'n. So then some white folks tole ole Massa 'bout John beatin' his hawse and never beatin' his own. So Massa tole John if he ever heard tell of him layin' a whip on his hawse agin he was gointer take and kill John's hawse dead as a nit.

John tole 'im, ''Massa, if you kill my hawse, Ah'll beatcher makin' money.''

One day John hit ole Massa's hawse agin. Dey went and tole Massa' bout it. He come down dere where John was haulin' trash, wid a great big ole knife and cut John's hawse's th'oat and he fell dead.

John jumped down off de wagon and skint his hawse, and tied de hide up on a stick and throwed it cross his shoulder, and went on down town.

Ole John was a fortune teller hisself, but nobody 'round dere didn't know it. He met a man and de man ast John, ''What's dat you got over yo' shoulder dere, John?''

''It's a fortune teller, boss.''

*Keg.

"Make it talk some, John, and I'll give you a sack of money and a hawse and saddle, and five head of cattle."

John put de hide on de ground and pulled out de stick and hit 'cross de hawse hide and hold his head down dere to lissen.

"Dere's a man in yo' bed-room behind de bed talkin' to yo' wife."

De man went inside his house to see. When he come back out he said, "Yeah, John, you sho tellin' de truth. Make him talk some mo'."

John went to puttin' de stick back in de hide. "Naw, Massa, he's tired now."

De white man says, "Ah'll give you six head of sheeps and fo' hawses and fo' sacks of money."

John pulled out de stick and hit down on de hide and hold down his head to lissen.

"It's a man in yo' kitchen openin' yo' stove." De man went back into his house and come out agin and tole John, "Yo' fortune-teller sho is right. Here's de things Ah promised you."

John rode on past Ole Massa's house wid all his sacks of money and drivin' his sheeps and cattle, whoopin' and crackin' his whip. "Yee, whoo-pee, yee!" Crack!

Massa said, "John, where did you git all dat?"

John said, "Ah tole you if you kilt mah hawse Ah'd beatcher makin' money."

Massa said to 'im, "Reckon if Ah kilt mah hawse Ah'd make dat much money?"

"Yeah, Massa, Ah reckon so."

So ole Massa went out and kilt his hawse and went to town hollerin', "Hawse hide for sale! Hawse hide for sale!"

One man said, "Hold on dere. Ah'll give you two-bits for it to bottom some chears."

Ole Massa tole 'im, "Youse crazy!" and went on hollerin' "Hawse hide for sale!"

"Ah'll gi' you twenty cents for it to cover some chears," another man said.

"You must be stone crazy! Why, dis hide is worth five thousand dollars."

De people all laughed at 'im so he took his hawse hide and he throwed it away and went and bought hisself another hawse.

Ole John, he already rich, he didn't have to work but he jus' love to fool 'round hawses so he went to drivin' hawse and buggy for Massa. And when nobody wasn't wid him, John would let his grandma ride in Massa's buggy. Dey tole ole Massa 'bout it and he said, "John, Ah hear you been had yo' grandma ridin' in mah buggy. De first time Ah ketch her in it, Ah'm gointer kill 'er."

John tole 'im, "If you kill my grandma, Ah'll beatcher makin' money."

Pretty soon some white folks tole Massa dat John was takin' his gran'ma to town in his buggy and was hittin' his hawse and showin' off. So ole Massa come out dere and cut John's gran'ma's th'oat.

So John buried his gran'ma in secret and went and got his same ole hawse hide and keered it up town agin and went 'round talkin' 'bout, "Fortune-teller, fortune-teller!"

One man tole 'im, "Why, John, make it talk some for me. Ah'll give you six head of goats, six sheeps, and a hawse and saddle to ride 'im wid."

So John made it talk and de man was pleased so he give John more'n he promised 'im, and John went on back past Massa's house wid his stuff so ole Massa could see 'im.

Ole Massa run out and ast, "Oh, John, where did you git all dat?"

John said, "Ah tole you if you kill mah gran'ma Ah'd beatcher makin' money."

Massa said, "You reckon if Ah kill mine, Ah'll make all dat?"

"Yeah, Ah reckon so."

So Massa runned and cut his gran'ma's th'oat and went up town hollerin' "gran'ma for sale! gran'ma for sale!"

Wouldn't nobody break a breath wid him. Dey thought he was crazy. He went on back home and grabbed John and tole 'im, "You made me kill my gran'ma and my good hawse and Ah'm gointer throw you in de river."

John tole 'im, "If you throw me in de river, Ah'll beatcher makin' money."

"Naw you won't neither," Massa tole 'im. "You done made yo' last money and done yo' las' do."

He got ole John in de sack and keered 'im down to de river, but he done forgot his weights, so he went back home to git some.

While he was gone after de weights a toad frog come by dere and John seen 'im. So he hollered and said, "Mr. Hoptoad, if you open dis sack and let me out Ah'll give you a dollar."

Toad frog let 'im out, so he got a soft-shell turtle and put it in de sack wid two big ole bricks. Then ole Massa got his weights and come tied 'em on de sack and throwed it in de river.

Whilst Massa was down to de water foolin' wid dat sack, John had done got out his hawse hide and went on up town agin hollerin', "Fortune-teller! fortune-teller!"

One rich man said "Make it talk for me, John."

John pulled out de stick and hit on de hide, and put his ear down. "Uh man is in yo' smoke-house stealin' meat and another one is in yo' money-safe."

De man went inside to see and when he come back he said, "You sho kin tell de truth."

So John went by Massa's house on a new hawse, wid a sack of money tied on each side of de saddle. Ole Massa seen 'im and ast, "Oh, John, where'd you git all dat?"

"Ah tole you if you throw me in de river Ah'd beatcher makin' money."

Massa ast, "Reckon if Ah let you throw me in de river, Ah'd make all dat?"

"Yeah, Massa, Ah *know* so."

John got ole Massa in de sack and keered 'im down to de river. John didn't forgit *his* weights. He put de weights on ole Massa and jus' befo' he throwed 'im out he said, "Goodbye, Massa, Ah hope you find all you lookin' for."

And dat wuz de las' of ole Massa.

"Dat wuz a long tale for a li'l boy lak you," George Thomas praised Julius.

"Ah knows a heap uh tales," Julius retorted.

Whut is de workinest pill you ever seen? Lemme tell you whut kind of a pill it was and how much it worked.

It wuz a ole man one time and he had de rheumatism so bad he didn't know what to do. Ah tole 'im to go to town and git some of dem conthartic pills.

He went and got de pills lak Ah tole 'im, but on his way back he opened up de box and went to lookin' at de pills. He wuz comin' cross some new ground where dey hadn't even started to clear up de land. He drop one of de pills but he didn't bother to pick it up—skeered he might hurt his back stoopin' over.

He got to de house and say, "Ole lady, look down yonder whut a big smoke! Whut is dat, nohow?"

She say, "Ah don't know."

"Well," he say. "Guess Ah better walk down dere and see what dat big smoke *is* down dere."

He come back. "Guess whut it is, ole lady? One of dem conthartic pills done worked all dem roots out de ground and got 'em burning!"

"Julius, you little but you loud. Dat's a over average lie you tole," Shug laughed. "Lak de wind Ah seen on de East Coast. It blowed a crooked road straight and blowed a well up out de ground and blowed and blowed until it scattered de days of de week so bad till Sunday didn't come till late Tuesday evenin'.''

"Shug, whuss yuh gonna do?'' Bennie Lee tried to rise to the surface but failed and slumped back into slumber.

"A good boy, but a po' boy,'' somebody commented as John French made his mind up.

"Zora, Ah'm gointer tell one, but you be sho and tell de folks Ah tole it. Don't say Seymore said it because he took you on de all-day fishin' trip to Titusville. Don't say Seaboard Hamilton tole it 'cause he always give you a big hunk of barbecue when you go for a sandwich. Give ole John French whut's comin' to 'im.''

"You gointer tell it or you gointer spend de night tellin' us you gointer tell it?'' I asked.

Ah got to say a piece of litery (literary) fust to git mah wind on.

Well Ah went up on dat meat-skin
And Ah come down on dat bone
And Ah grabbed dat piece of corn-bread
And Ah made dat biscuit moan.

Once a man had two sons. One was name Jim and de other one dey call him Jack for short. Dey papa was a most rich man, so he called de boys to 'im one night and tole 'em, "Ah don't want y'all settin' 'round waitin' for me tuh die tuh git whut Ah'm gointer give yuh. Here's five hundred dollars apiece. Dat's yo' sheer of de proppity. Go put yo'selves on de ladder. Take and make men out of yourselves.''

Jim took his and bought a big farm and a pair of mules and settled down.

Jack took his money and went on down de road skinnin' and winnin'. He won from so many mens till he had threbbled his money. Den he met a man says, "Come on, le's skin some.'' De man says "Money on de wood'' and he laid down a hundred dollars.

Jack looked at de hund'ud dollars and put down five hund'ud and says, "Man, Ah ain't for no spuddin'.* You playin' wid yo' stuff out de winder.† You fat 'round de heart.‡ Bet some money.''

---

*Playing for small change.
†Risking nothing, i.e. hat, coat and shoes out the window so that the owner can run if he loses.
‡Scared.

De man covered Jack's money and dey went to skinnin'. Jack was dealin' and he thought he seen de other man on de turn so he said, "Five hund'ud mo' my ten spot is de bes'."

De other man covered 'im and Jack slapped down another five hund'ud and said, "Five hund'ud mo' you fall dis time."

De other man never said a word. He put down five hund'ud mo'.

Jack got to singin':

"When yo' card git-uh lucky, oh pardner
You oughter be in a rollin' game."

He flipped de card and bless God it wuz de ten spot! Jack had done fell hisself instead of de other man. He was all put out.

Says, "Nell, Ah done los' all mah money so de game is through."

De other man say, "We kin still play on. Ah'll bet you all de money on de table against yo' life."

Jack agreed to play 'cause he figgered he could out-shoot and out-cut any man on de road and if de man tried to kill *him* he'd git kilt hisself. So dey shuffled agin and Jack pulled a card and it fell third in hand.

Den de man got up and he was twelve foot tall and Jack was so skeered he didn't know whut to do. De man looked down on 'im and tole 'im says, "De Devil is mah name and Ah live across de deep blue sea. Ah could kill you right now, but Ah'll give yuh another chance. If you git to my house befo' de sun sets and rise agin Ah won't kill yuh, but if you don't Ah'll be compelled to take yo' life."

Den he vanished.

Jack went on down de road jus' a cryin' till he met uh ole man.

Says, "Whuss de matter, Jack?"

"Ah played skin wid de Devil for mah life and he winned and tole me if Ah ain't to his house by de time de sun sets and rise agin he's gointer take mah life, and he live way across de ocean."

De ole man says, "You sho is in a bad fix, Jack. Dere ain't but one thing dat kin cross de ocean in dat time."

"Whut is dat?"

"It's uh bald eagle. She come down to de edge of de ocean every mornin' and dip herself in de sea and pick off all de dead feathers. When she dip herself de third time and pick herself she rocks herself and spread her wings and mount de sky and go straight across de deep blue sea. And every time she holler, you giver her piece uh dat yearlin' or she'll eat you.

"Now if you could be dere wid a yearlin' bull and when she git thru dippin' and pick herself and rock to mount de sky and jump straddle of her back wid dat bull yearlin' you could make it.''

Jack wuz dere wid de yearlin' waitin' for dat eagle to come. He wuz watchin' her from behind de bushes and seen her when she come out de water and picked off de dead feather and rocked to go on high.

He jumped on de eagle's back wid his yearlin' and de eagle was out flyin' de sun. After while she turned her head from side to side and her blazin' eyes lit up first de north den de south and she hollered, ''Ah-h-h, Ah, ah! One quarter cross de ocean! Don't see nothin' but blue water, uh!''

Jack was so skeered dat instead of him givin' de eagle uh quarter of de meat, he give her de whole bull. After while she say, ''Ah-h-h, ah, ah! One half way cross de ocean! Don't see nothin' but blue water!''

Jack didn't have no mo' meat so he tore off one leg and give it to her. She swallowed dat and flew on. She hollered agin, ''Ah-h-h, Ah, ha! Mighty nigh cross de ocean! Don't see nothin' but blue water! Uh!''

Jack tore off one arm and give it to her and she et dat and pretty soon she lit on land and Jack jumped off and de eagle flew on off to her nest.

Jack didn't know which way de Devil lived so he ast. ''Dat first big white house 'round de bend in de road,'' they tole 'im.

Jack walked to de Devil's house and knocked on de do'.

''Who's dat?''

''One of de Devil's friends. One widout uh arm and widout uh leg.''

Devil tole his wife, says: ''Look behind de do' and hand dat man uh arm and leg.'' She gave Jack de arm and leg and Jack put 'em on.

Devil says, ''See you got here in time for breakfas'. But Ah got uh job for yuh befo' you eat. Ah got uh hund'ud acres uh new ground ain't never had uh brush cut on it. Ah want you to go out dere and cut down all de trees and brushes, grub up all de roots and pile 'em and burn 'em befo' dinner time. If you don't, Ah'll have to take yo' life.''

Jus' 'bout dat time de Devil's chillen come out to look at Jack and he seen he had one real pretty daughter, but Jack wuz too worried to think 'bout no girls. So he took de tools and went on out to de wood lot and went to work.

By de time he chopped down one tree he wuz tired and he knowed it would take 'im ten years to clear dat ground right, so Jack set down and went to cryin'. 'Bout dat time de Devil's pretty daughter come wid his breakfas'. ''Whuss de matter, Jack?''

''Yo papa done gimme uh job he know Ah can't git through wid, and he's gonna take mah life and Ah don't wanna die.''

"Eat yo' breakfas' Jack, and put yo' head in mah lap and go to sleep."

Jack done lak she tole 'im and went to sleep and when he woke up every tree was down, every bush—and de roots grubbed up and burnt. Look lak never had been a blade uh grass dere.

De Devil come out to see how Jack wuz makin' out and seen dat hundred acres cleaned off so nice and said, "Uh, huh, Ah see youse uh wise man, 'most wise as me. Now Ah got another job for yuh. Ah got uh well, uh hundred feet deep and Ah want yuh to dip it dry. Ah mean dry, Ah want it so dry till Ah kin see dust from it and den Ah want you to bring me whut you find at de bottom."

Jack took de bucket and went to de well and went to work but he seen dat de water wuz comin' in faster dan he could draw it out. So he sat down and begin to cry.

De Devil's daughter come praipsin long wid Jack's dinner and seen Jack settin' down cryin'. "Whuss de matter, Jack? Don't cry lak dat lessen you wanta make me cry too."

"Yo' pa done put me to doin' somethin' he know Ah can't never finish and if Ah don't git thru he is gonna take mah life."

"Eat yo' dinner, Jack and put yo' head in mah lap and go to sleep."

Jack done lak she tole 'im and when he woke up de well wuz so dry till red dust wuz boilin' out of it lak smoke. De girl handed 'im a ring and tole 'im "Give papa dis ring. Dat's whut he wanted. It's mama's ring and she lost it in de well de other day."

When de devil come to see whut Jack wuz doin', Jack give 'im de ring and de devil looked and seen all dat dust pourin' out de well. He say, "Ah see youse uh very smart man. Almos' as wise as me. All right, Ah got just one mo' job for you and if you do dat Ah'll spare yo' life and let you marry mah daughter to boot. You take dese two geeses and go up dat cocoanut palm tree and pick 'em, and bring me de geeses when you git 'em picked and bring me every feather dat come off 'em. If you lose one Ah'll have to take yo life."

Jack took de two geeses and clammed up de cocoanut palm tree and tried to pick dem geeses. But he was more'n uh hundred feet off de ground and every time he'd pull uh feather offen one of dem birds, de wind would blow it away. So Jack began to cry agin. By dat time Beatrice Devil come up wid his supper. "Whuss de matter, Jack?"

"Yo' papa is bound tuh kill me. He know Ah can't pick no geeses up no palm tree, and save de feathers."

"Eat yo' supper Jack and lay down in mah lap."

When Jack woke up all both de geeses wuz picked and de girl had all de feathers even; she had done caught dem out de air dat got away from Jack. De Devil said "Well, now you done everything Ah tole you, you kin have mah daughter. Y'all take dat ole house down de road apiece. Dat's where me and her ma got our start."

Way in de night, Beatrice woke up and shook Jack. "Jack! Jack! Wake up! Papa's comin' here to kill you. Git up and go to de barn. He got two horses dat kin jump a thousand miles at every jump. One is named Hallowed-be-thy-name and de other, Thy-kingdom-come. Go hitch 'em to dat buck board and head 'em dis way and le's go."

Jack run to de barn and harnessed de hawses and headed towards de house where his wife wuz at. When he got to de do' she jumped in and hollered, "Le's go, Jack. Papa's comin' after us!"

When de Devil got to de house to kill Jack and found out Jack wuz gone, he run to de barn to hitch up his fas' hawses. When he seen dat dey wuz gone, he hitched up his jumpin' bull dat could jump five hundred miles at every jump, and down de road, baby!

De Devil wuz drivin' dat bull! Wid every jump he'd holler, "Oh! Hallowed-be-thy-name! Thy-kingdom-come!" And every time de hawses would hear 'im call 'em they'd fall to they knees and de bull would gain on 'em.

De girl say, "Jack, he's 'bout to ketch us! Git out and drag yo' feet backwards nine steps, throw some sand over yo' shoulders and le's go!"

Jack done dat and de hawses got up and off they went, but every time they hear they master's voice they'd stop till de girl told Jack to drag his foot three times nine times and he did it and they gained so fast on de Devil dat de hawses couldn't hear 'im no mo', and dey got away.

De Devil passed uh man and he say, "Is you seen uh man in uh buck board wid uh pretty girl wid coal black hair and red eyes behind two fas' hawses?"

De man said, "No, Ah speck dey done made it to de mountain and if dey gone to de mountain you can't overtake 'em."

"Jack and his wife wuz right dere den listenin' to de Devil. When de daughter saw her pa comin' she turned herself and de hawses into goats and they wuz croppin' grass. Jack wuz so tough though she couldn't turn him into nothin' so she saw a holler log and she tole 'im to go hide in it, which he did. De Devil looked all around and he seen dat log and his mind jus' tole 'im to go look in it and he went and picked de log up and said, "Ah, ha! Ah gotcher!"

Jack wuz so skeered inside dat log he begin to call on de Lawd and he said, "O Lawd, have mercy."

You know de Devil don't lak tuh hear de name uh de Lawd so he throwed down dat log and said "Damn it! If Ah had of knowed dat God wuz in dat log Ah never would a picked it up."

So he got back in and picked up de reins and hollered to de bull, "Turn, bull, turn! Turn clean roh-hound. Turn bull tu-urn, turn clee-ean round!"

De jumpin' bull turnt so fast till he fell and broke his own neck and throwed de Devil out on his head and kilt 'im. So dat's why dey say Jack beat de Devil.

"Boy, how kin you hold all dat in yo' head?" Jack Jones asked John. "Bet if dat lie was somethin' to do yuh some good yuh couldn't remember it."

Johnnie Mae yawned wide open and Ernest seeing her called out, "Hey, Johnnie Mae, throw mah trunk out befo' you shet up dat place!"

This reflection upon the size of her mouth peeved Johnnie Mae no end and she and Ernest left in a red hot family argument. Then everybody else found out that they were sleepy. So in the local term everybody went to the "pad."

Lee Robinson over in the church was leading an ole spiritual, "When I come to Die," to which I listened with one ear, while I heard the parting quips of the story-tellers with the other.

Though it was after ten the street lights were still on. B. Moseley had not put out the lights because the service in the church was not over yet, so I sat on the porch for a while looking towards the heaven-rasping oaks on the back street, towards the glassy sliver of Lake Sabelia. Over in the church I could hear Mrs. Laura Henderson finishing her testimony . . . "to make Heben mah home when Ah come to die. Oh, Ah'll never forget dat day when de mornin' star bust in mah heart! Ah'll never turn back! O evenin' sun, when you git on de other side, tell mah Lawd Ah'm here prayin'."

The next afternoon I sat on the porch again. The young'uns had the grassy lane that ran past the left side of the house playing the same games that I had played in the same lane years before. With the camphor tree as a base, they played "Going 'Round de Mountain." Little Hubert Alexander was in the ring. The others danced rhythmically 'round him and sang:

Going around de mountain two by two
Going around de mountain two by two
Tell me who love sugar and candy.

Now, show me your motion, two by two
Show me your motion two by two
Tell me who love sugar and candy.

I tried to write a letter but the games were too exciting.

"Little Sally Walker," "Draw a bucket of water," "Sissy in de barn," and at last that most raucous, popular and most African of games, "Chick, mah Chick, mah Craney crow." Little Harriet Staggers, the smallest girl in the game, was contending for the place of mama hen. She fought hard, but the larger girls promptly overruled her and she had to take her place in line behind the other little biddies, two-year-old Donnie Brown, being a year younger than Harriet, was the hindmost chick.

During the hilarious uproar of the game, Charlie Jones and Buber Mimms came up and sat on the porch with me.

"Good Lawd, Zora! How kin you stand all dat racket? Why don't you run dem chaps 'way from here?" Seeing his nieces, Laura and Melinda and his nephew, Judson, he started to chase them off home but I made him see that it was a happy accident that they had chosen the lane as a playground. That I was enjoying it more than the chaps.

That settled, Charlie asked, "Well, Zora, did we lie enough for you las' night?"

"You lied good but not enough," I answered.

"Course, Zora, you ain't at de right place to git de bes' lies. Why don't you go down 'round Bartow and Lakeland and 'round in dere— Polk County? Dat's where they really lies up a mess and dats where dey makes up all de songs and things lak dat. Ain't you never hea'd dat in Polk County de water drink lak cherry wine?"

"Seems like when Ah was a child 'round here Ah heard de folks pickin' de guitar and singin' songs to dat effect."

"Dat's right. If Ah was you, Ah'd drop down dere and see. It's liable to do you a lot uh good."

"If Ah wuz in power* Ah'd go 'long wid you, Zora," Bubber added wistfully. "Ah learnt all Ah know 'bout pickin' de box† in Polk County. But Ah ain't even got money essence. 'Tain't no mo' hawgs 'round here. Ah cain't buy no chickens. Guess Ah have tuh eat gopher."‡

---

*Funds.
†Playing the guitar.
‡Dry land tortoise.

"Where you gointer git yo' gophers, Bubber?" Charlie asked. "Doc Biddy and his pa done 'bout cleaned out dis part of de State."

"Oh, Ah got a new improvement dat's gointer be a lot of help to me and Doc Biddy and all of us po' folks."

"What is it, Bubber?"

"Ah'm gointer prune a gang of soft-shells (turtles) and grow me some gophers."

The sun slid lower and lower and at last lost its grip on the western slant of the sky and dipped three times into the bloody sea—sending up crimson spray with each plunge. At last it sunk and night roosted on the tree-tops and houses.

Bubber picked the box and Charlie sang me songs of the railroad camps. Among others, he taught me verses of JOHN HENRY, the king of railroad track-laying songs which runs as follows:

John Henry driving on the right hand side,
Steam drill driving on the left,
Says, 'fore I'll let your steam drill beat me down
I'll hammer my fool self to death,
Hammer my fool self to death.

John Henry told his Captain,
When you go to town
Please bring me back a nine pound hammer
And I'll drive your steel on down,
And I'll drive your steel on down.

John Henry told his Captain,
Man ain't nothing but a man,
And 'fore I'll let that steam drill beat me down
I'll die with this hammer in my hand,
Die with this hammer in my hand.

Captain ast John Henry,
What is that storm I hear?
He says Cap'n that ain't no storm,
'Tain't nothing but my hammer in the air,
Nothing but my hammer in the air.

John Henry told his Captain,
Bury me under the sills of the floor,

So when they get to playing good old Georgy skin,
Bet 'em fifty to a dollar more,
Fifty to a dollar more.

John Henry had a little woman,
The dress she wore was red,
Says I'm going down the track,
And she never looked back.
I'm going where John Henry fell dead,
Going where John Henry fell dead.

Who's going to shoe your pretty lil feet?
And who's going to glove your hand?
Who's going to kiss your dimpled cheek?
And who's going to be your man?
Who's going to be your man?

My father's going to shoe my pretty lil feet;
My brother's going to glove my hand;
My sister's going to kiss my dimpled cheek;
John Henry's going to be my man,
John Henry's going to be my man.

Where did you get your pretty lil dress?
The shoes you wear so fine?
I got my shoes from a railroad man,
My dress from a man in the mine,
My dress from a man in the mine.

They talked and told strong stories of Ella, Wall, East Coast Mary,
Planchita and lesser jook* lights around whom the glory of Polk County
surged. Saw-mill and turpentine bosses and prison camp "cap'ns" set to
music passed over the guitar strings and Charlie's mouth and I knew I
had to visit Polk County right now.

A hasty good-bye to Eatonville's oaks and oleanders and the wheels
of the Chevvie split Orlando wide open—headed southwest for corn
(likker) and song.

---

*A fun house. Where they sing, dance, gamble, love, and compose "blues" songs
incidentally.

FROM
Tell My Horse

The Rooster's Nest

JAMAICA, BRITISH WEST INDIES, has something else besides its mountains of majesty and its quick, green valleys. Jamaica has its moments when the land, as in St. Mary's, thrusts out its sensuous bosom to the sea. Jamaica has its "bush." That is, the island has more usable plants for medicinal and edible purposes than any other spot on earth. Jamaica has its Norman W. Manley, that brilliant young barrister who looks like the younger Pitt in yellow skin, and who can do as much with a jury as Darrow or Liebowitz ever did. The island has its craze among the peasants known as Pocomania, which looks as if it might be translated into "a little crazy." But Brother Levi says it means "something out of nothing." It is important to a great number of people in Jamaica, so perhaps we ought to peep in on it a while.

The two greatest leaders of the cult in Jamaica are Mother Saul, who is the most regal woman since Sheba went to see Solomon, and Brother Levi, who is a scrontous-looking man himself.

Brother Levi said that this cult all started in a joke but worked on into something important. It was "dry" Pocomania when it began. Then it got "spirit" in it and "wet." What with the music and the barbaric rituals, I became interested and took up around the place. I witnessed a wonderful ceremony with candles. I asked Brother Levi why this ceremony and he said, "We hold candle march after Joseph. Joseph came from cave where Christ was born in the manger with a candle. He was walking before Mary and her baby. You know Christ was not born in the manger. Mary and Joseph were too afraid for that. He was born in a cave and He never came out until He was six months old. The three wise men see the star but they can't find Him because He is hid in cave. When they can't find Him after six months, they make a magic ceremony and the angel come tell Joseph the men wanted to see Him. That day was called 'Christ must day' because it means 'Christ must find today,' so we have Christmas day, but the majority of people are ignorant. They think Him born that day."

I went to the various "tables" set in Pocomania, which boils down to a mixture of African obeah and christianity enlivened by very beautiful singing. I went to a "Sun Dial"—that is a ceremony around the clock (24 hours long). The place was decorated from the gate in, with braided palm fronds and quacca bush. Inside the temple, the wall behind the altar was papered with newspapers.

There, the ceremony was in the open air. A long table covered with white. Under this table, on the ground, lighted candles to attract the spirits. There was a mysterious bottle which guaranteed "the spirit come." The Shepherd entered followed by the Sword Boy with a cross, chanting. Then came the Unter Boy with a supple jack, a switch very much like a rattan cane in his hand. During the ceremony he flogged those who were "not in spirit" that is, those who sat still. They are said to "cramp" the others who are in spirit. The Governess followed the Unter Boy. She has charge of all the women, but otherwise she functions something like the Mambo of Haiti. She aids the Shepherd and generally fires the meeting by leading the songs and whipping up the crowd. There followed then the Shepherd Boy who is the "armor-bearer" to the Shepherd.

Their ceremony is exciting at times with singing, marching, baptisms at sacred pools in the yard. Miraculous "cures" (Mother Saul actually sat down upon a screaming Chinese boy to cure him of insanity); and the dancing about the tables with that tremendous exhalation of the breath to set the rhythm. That is the most characteristic thing of the whole ceremony. That dancing about the lighted candle pattern on the ground and that way of making a rhythmic instrument and of the breathing apparatus—such is Pocomania, but what I have discussed certainly is not all of it.

These "Balm yards" are deep in the lives of the Jamaican peasants. A Balm Yard is a place where they give baths, and the people who operate these yards are to their followers both doctor and priest. Sometimes he or she diagnoses a case as a natural ailment, and a bath or series of baths in infusions of secret plants is prescribed. More often the diagnosis is that the patient has been "hurt" by a duppy, and the bath is given to drive the spirit off. The Balm Yard with a reputation is never lacking for business. These anonymous rulers of the common people have decreed certain rules and regulations for events in life that are rigidly adhered to. For instance the customs about birth and death. The childbed and the person of the newborn baby must be protected from the dead by marks made

·with bluing. When it is moved from this room, the open Bible must precede it to keep off the duppies, and so on.

Tables are usually set because something for which a ceremony has been performed is accomplished. The grateful recipient of favor from the gods then sets a table of thanksgiving. No one except the heads of the Balm Yard and the supplicants are told what it is for. Most of the country products are served with plenty of raw rum. The first and most important thing is a small piece of bread in a small glass of water as a symbol of plenty.

And then Jamaica has its social viewpoints and stratifications which influence so seriously its economic direction.

Jamaica is the land where the rooster lays an egg. Jamaica is two per cent white and the other ninety-eight per cent all degrees of mixture between white and black, and that is where the rooster's nest comes in. Being an English colony, it is very British. Colonies always do imitate the mother country more or less. For instance some Americans are still aping the English as best they can even though they have had one hundred and fifty years in which to recover.

So in Jamaica it is the aim of everybody to talk English, act English and *look* English. And that last specification is where the greatest difficulties arise. It is not so difficult to put a coat of European culture over African culture, but it is next to impossible to lay a European face over an African face in the same generation. So everybody who has any hope at all is looking out for the next generation and so on. The color line in Jamaica between the white Englishman and the blacks is not as sharply drawn as between the mulattoes and the blacks. To avoid the consequences of posterity the mulattoes give the blacks a first class letting alone. There is a frantic stampede white-ward to escape from Jamaica's black mass. Under ordinary circumstances the trend would be towards the majority group, of course. But one must remember that Jamaica has slavery in her past and it takes many generations for the slave derivatives to get over their awe for the master-kind. Then there is the colonial attitude. Add to that the Negro's natural aptitude for imitation and you have Jamaica.

In some cases the parents of these mulattoes have been properly married, but most often that is not the case. The mixed-blood bears the name with the bar sinister. However, the mulatto has prestige, no matter how he happened to come by his light skin. And the system of honoring or esteeming his approach to the Caucasian state is so elaborate that first, second, third and fourth degrees of illegitimacy are honored in order of their nearness to the source of whiteness. Sometimes it is so far fetched, that one is reminded of that line from "Of Thee I Sing," where the French Ambassador boasts, "She is the illegitimate daughter of the illegitimate son of the illegitimate nephew of the great Napoleon." In Jamaica just substitute the word Englishman for Napoleon and you have the situation.

Perhaps the Jamaican mixed bloods are logical and right, perhaps the only answer to the question of what is to become of the Negro in the Western world is that he must be absorbed by the whites. Frederick Douglass thought so. If he was right, then the strategy of the American Negro is all wrong, that is, the attempt to achieve a position equal to the white population in every way but each race to maintain its separate identity. Perhaps we should strike our camps and make use of the cover of night and execute a masterly retreat under white skins. If that is what must be, then any way at all of getting more whiteness among us is a step in the right direction. I do not pretend to know what is wise and best. The situation presents a curious spectacle to the eyes of an American Negro. It is as if one stepped back to the days of slavery or the generation immediately after surrender when Negroes had little else to boast of except a left-hand kinship with the master, and the privileges that usually went with it of being house servants instead of field hands. Then, as in Jamaica at present, no shame was attached to a child born "in a carriage with no top." But the pendulum has swung away over to the other side of our American clock. Even in His Majesty's colony it may work out to everybody's satisfaction in a few hundred years, if the majority of the population, which is black, can be persuaded to cease reproduction. That is the weak place in the scheme. The blacks keep on being black and reminding folks where mulattoes come from, thus conjuring up tragi-comic dramas that bedevil security of the Jamaican mixed bloods.

Everywhere else a person is white or black by birth, but it is so arranged in Jamaica that a person may be black by birth but white by proclamation. That is, he gets himself declared legally white. When I used the word black I mean in the American sense where anyone who has any colored blood at all, no matter how white the appearance, speaks of himself as black. I was told that the late John Hope, late President of Atlanta University, precipitated a panic in Kingston on his visit there in 1935, a few months before his death. He was quite white in appearance and when he landed and visited the Rockefeller Institute in Kingston and was so honored by them, the "census white" Jamaicans assumed that he was of pure white blood. A great banquet was given him at the Myrtle Bank Hotel, which is the last word in swank in Jamaica. All went well until John Hope was called upon to respond to a toast. He began his reply with, "We Negroes—." Several people all but collapsed. John Hope was whiter than any of the mulattoes there who had had themselves ruled white. So that if a man as white as that called himself a Negro, what about them? Consternation struck the banquet like a blight. Of course, there were real white English and American people there too, and I would have loved to have read their minds at that moment. I certainly would.

The joke about being white on the census records and colored otherwise has its curious angles. The English seem to feel that "If it makes a few of you happy and better colonials to be officially white, very well. You are white on the census rolls." The Englishman keeps on being very polite and cordial to the legal whites in public, but ignores them utterly in private and social life. And the darker Negroes do not forget how they came to be white. So I wonder what really is gained by it. George Bernard Shaw on his recent tour observed this class of Jamaicans and called them "those pink people" of Jamaica.

That brings us to the matter of the rooster's nest again. When a Jamaican is born of a black woman and some English or Scotsman, the black mother is literally and figuratively kept out of sight as far as possible, but no one is allowed to forget that white father, however questionable the circumstances of birth. You hear about "My father this and my father that, and my father who was English, you know," until you get the impression that he or she *had* no mother. Black skin is so utterly condemned that the black mother is not going to be mentioned nor exhibited. You get the impression that these virile Englishmen do not require women to reproduce. They just come out to Jamaica, scratch out a nest and lay eggs that hatch out into "pink" Jamaicans.

But a new day is in sight for Jamaica. The black people of Jamaica are beginning to respect themselves. They are beginning to love their own things like their songs, their Anansi stories and proverbs and dances. Jamaican proverbs are particularly rich in philosophy, irony and humor. The following are a few in common use:

1. Rockatone at ribber bottom no know sun hot. (The person in easy circumstances cannot appreciate the sufferings of the poor.)

2. Seven year no 'nough to wash speckle off guinea hen back. (Human nature never changes.)

3. Sharp spur mek maugre horse cut caper. (The pinch of circumstances forces people to do what they thought impossible.)

4. Sickness ride horse come, take foot go away. (It is easier to get sick than it is to get well.)

5. Table napkin want to turn table cloth. (Referring to social climbing.)

6. Bull horn nebber too heavy for him head. (We always see ourselves in a favorable light.)

7. Cock roach nebber in de right befo' fowl. (The oppressor always justifies his oppression of the weak.)

8. If you want fo' lick old woman pot, you scratch him back. (The masculine pronoun is always used for female. Use flattery and you will succeed.)

9. Do fe do make guinea nigger come a' Jamaica. (Fighting among themselves in Africa caused the Negroes to be sold into slavery in America.)

10. Dog run for him character; hog run for him life. (It means nothing to you, but everything to me.)

11. Finger nebber say, "look here," him say "look dere." (People always point out the shortcomings of others but never their own.)

12. Cutacoo on man back no yerry what kim massa yerry. (The basket on a man's back does not hear what he hears.)

Up until three years ago these proverbs and everything else Jamaican have been lumped with black skins and utterly condemned.

There is Mrs. Norman W. Manley, a real Englishwoman who is capturing Jamaican form in her sculpture. Her work has strength of conception and a delicate skill in execution. Because she used native models, she has been cried down by the "census whites" who know nothing about art but know that they do not like anything dark, however great the art may be. Mrs. Manley's work belongs in New York and London and Paris. It is wasted on Kingston for the most part, but the *West Indian Review*, which is the voice of thinking Jamaica, has found her. That is a very hopeful sign. And there is the yeast of the Bailey Sisters and the Meikle Brothers and their leagues, and influences like the Quill and Ink Club which is actively inviting Jamaica's soul to come out from its hiding place. The Rooster's Nest is bound to be less glamorous in the future.

Curry Goat

THE VERY BEST PLACE to be in all the world is St. Mary's parish, Jamaica. And the best spot in St. Mary's is Port Maria, though all of St. Mary's is fine. Old Maker put himself to a lot of trouble to make that part of the island of Jamaica, for everything there is perfect. The sea is the one true celestial blue, and the shore, the promontories, the rocks and the grass are the models for the rest of the world to take pattern after. If Jamaica is the first island of the West Indies in culture, then St. Mary's is the first parish of Jamaica. The people there are alert, keen, well-read and hospitable.

They did something for me there that has never been done for another woman. They gave me a curry goat feed. That is something utterly masculine in every detail. Even a man takes the part of a woman in the "shay shay" singing and dancing that goes on after the feed.

It was held on a Wednesday night at the house of C. I. Magnus. His bachelor quarters sat upon a hill that overlooked his large banana plantation. I heard that Dr. Leslie, Claude Bell, Rupert Meikle and his two big, handsome brothers and Larry Coke and some others bought up all those goats that were curried for the feed. I have no way of knowing who all chipped in to buy things, but the affair was lavish.

We set out from Port Maria in Claude Bell's car, containing Claude, Dr. Leslie and I. Then Larry Coke overtook us and we ambled along until we ran into something exciting. Just around a bend in the road we came to an arch woven of palm fronds before a gate. There were other arches of the same leading back to a booth constructed in the same manner. It was not quite finished. Men were seated in the yard braiding more palm fronds. A great many people were in the yard, under the palm booth and in the house. Three women with elaborate cakes upon their heads were dancing under the arch at the gate. The cakes were of many layers and one of the cakes was decorated with a veil. The cake-bearers danced and turned under the arch, and turned and danced and sang with the others something about "Let the stranger in." This kept up until an elderly woman touched one of the dancers. Then the one who was touched whirled around gently, went inside the yard and on into the house. Another was touched and turned and she went in and then the third.

"What is going on here?" I asked Claude Bell, and he told me that this was a country wedding. That is, it was the preparation for one. Claude Bell is the Superintendent of Public Works in St. Mary's, so that everybody knows him. He went over and said that we wished to come in and the groom-to-be made us welcome. I asked how was it that they all knew at once who the groom was and they said that he would always be found out front being very proud and expansive and doing all the greeting and accepting all the compliments.

We went inside the house and saw the cakes arranged to keep their vigil for the night. A lighted candle was placed beside the main cake, and it was kept burning all that night. It did add something to the weight of the occasion to drape that bride's cake in a white lace veil and surround it with lights for a night. It made one spectator at least feel solemn about marriage. After being introduced to the shy little bride and shaking hands with the proud groom we went off after promising to come back to the wedding next day.

So on to the Magnus plantation and the curry goat feed. It was after sundown when we arrived. Already some of the others were there before us. Around a fire under a clump of mango trees, two or three Hindoos were preparing the food. Magnus was setting out several dozen quarts of the famous T.T.L. rum, considered the best in Jamaica. They told me that a feed without T.T.L. was just nothing at all. It must be served or it is no proper curry goat feed. The moon rose full and tropical white and under it I could see the musicians huddled under another clump of trees waiting until they should be told to perform.

Finally there were about thirty guests in all including some very pretty half-Chinese girls. The cooks announced and we went inside to eat. Before that everybody had found congenial companions and had wandered around the grounds warming themselves by the moonlight.

It appeared that there must be a presiding officer at a curry goat. Some wanted the very popular Larry Coke, but it seemed that more wanted the more popular Dr. Leslie, so it went that way. He sat at the head of the table and directed the fun. There was a story-telling contest, bits of song, reminiscences that were side splitting and humorous pokes and jibes at each other. All of this came along with the cock soup. This feast is so masculine that chicken soup would not be allowed. It must be soup from roosters. After the cock soup comes ram goat and rice. No nanny goat in this meal either. It is ram goat or nothing. The third spread was banana dumpling with dip-and-flash. That is, you dip your boiled banana in the suruwa sauce, flash off the surplus and take a bite. By that time the place was on fire with life. Every course was being washed down with T.T.L. Wits were marvelously sharpened; that very pretty Lucille

Woung was eating out of the same spoon with J. T. Robertson; Reginald Beckford kept on trying to introduce somebody and the others always howled him down because he always got wound up and couldn't find his way out. Finally Dr. Leslie asked him why he never finished and he said "Being a banana man, I have to go around the corner before I get my target." The award for the best story-teller went to Rupert Meikle, but his brother H. O. S. Meikle ran him a close second.

The band began playing outside there in the moonlight and we ran away from the table to see it. You have to see those native Jamaica bands to hear them. They are doing almost as much dancing with the playing as they are playing. As I said before no woman appears with the players, though there is a woman's part in the dancing. That part is taken by a man especially trained for that. The whole thing is strong meat, but compelling. There is some barbaric dancing to magnificent rhythms. They played that famous Jamaican air, "Ten Pound Ten," "Donkey Want Water," "Salaam," and "Sally Brown." All strong and raw, but magnificent music and dancing. It is to be remembered that curry goat is a strong feed, so they could not have femalish music around there.

We got home in time to sleep a little before going on to the wedding the next afternoon.

The wedding was at the church and the guests all finally got there by sending one car back and forth several times. The bride came in the last load. There were many, many delays, but finally the couple were married and everybody went back to the house for the reception.

At the house it came to me what a lot of trouble these country people were taking to create the atmosphere of romance and mystery. Here was a couple who were in late middle life, who had lived together so long that they had grown children and were just getting married. Seemingly it all should have been rather drab and matter of fact. Surely there could be no mystery and glamor left for them to find in each other. But the couple and all the district were making believe that there was. It was like sewing ruffles on fence rails. The will to make life beautiful was strong. It happens this way frequently in Jamaica. That is, many couples live together as husband and wife for a generation and then marry. They explain that they always intended to marry, but never had the money. They do not mean by that that they did not have the price of the marriage license. They mean that they did not have the money for the big wedding and all that it means. So they go on raising their children on the understanding that if and when they can afford it they will have the wedding. Sometimes, as in this case, the couple is along in years and with grown children before the money can be spared. In the meanwhile, they live and work together like any two people who have been married by the preacher.

Back at the house everything was very gay with cake and wine and banter. There was a master of ceremonies. The bride's face was covered with her veil. In fact it had never been uncovered. She was made to stand like that and the master of ceremonies received bids on who was to lift her veil first. The highest bidder got the first peep. The first man to peep had bid six shillings. I thought that that was very high for a poor man until I found that on such occasions it was agreed that the word shilling is substituted for pence. It would sound too poor to say pence. He paid his sixpence amid great applause and lifted the bride's veil and peeped and put it back in place. Then the bidding began again and kept up until the master of ceremonies put a stop to it. The bidding had gone on for some time and everyone pretended a curiosity about the youth and glamor they imagined to be hidden under the veil.

After the unveiling of the bride we left. The groom made us promise that we would be present at the "turn thanks." That is a ceremony held at the church on the Sunday after the eighth day after the wedding. Again everybody goes to the church to see the bride again in her finery. The pastor and the Justice of the Peace are there and give the happy couple a lecture on how to live together. But the bride does not wear her veil this time, she is resplendent in her "turn-thanks" hat. The couple are turning thanks for the blessing of getting married.

But we did not go to the turn-thanks. Something happened in Claude Bell's summer house that rushed me off in another direction.

The next morning after the wedding I was lounging in the summer house and looking at the sea when a young man of St. Mary's dropped in. I do not remember how we got around to it, but the subject of love came up somehow. He let it be known that he thought that women who went in for careers were just so much wasted material. American women, he contended, were destroyed by their brains. But they were only a step or two worse off than the rest of the women of the western world. He felt it was a great tragedy to look at American women whom he thought the most beautiful and vivacious women on earth, and then to think what little use they were as women. I had been reclining on my shoulderblades in a deck chair, but this statement brought me up straight. I assured him that he was talking about what he didn't know.

"Oh, yes, I do," he countered, "I was not born yesterday and my light has not been kept under a bushel, whatever that is."

"You are blaspheming, of course, but go ahead and let me see what you are driving at."

"Oh, these wisdom-wise western women, afraid of their function in life, are so tiresomely useless! We men do not need your puny brains to settle the affairs of the world. The truth is, it is yet to be proved that you have any. But some of you are clever enough to run mental pawnshops, that is you loan out a certain amount of entertainment and hospitality on some masculine tricks and phrases and later pass them off as your own. Being a woman is the only thing that you can do with any real genius and you refuse to do that."

I tried to name some women of genius but I was cut short. The man was vehement.

"You self-blinded women are like the hen who lived by a sea-wall. She could hear the roar of the breakers but she never flew to the top of the wall to see what it was that made the sound. She said to herself and to all who would listen to her, 'The world is something that makes a big noise.' Having arrived at that conclusion, she thought that she had found a great truth and was satisfied for the rest of her life. She died without ever hopping upon the sea-wall to look and see if there was anything to the world besides noise. She had lived beside the biggest thing in the world and never saw it."

"So you really feel that all women are dumb, I see."

"No, not all women. Just those who think that they are the most intelligent, as a rule. And the occidental men are stupid for letting you ruin yourselves and the men along with you."

Of course I did not agree with him and so I gave him my most aggravating grunt. I succeeded in snorting a bit of scorn into it. I went on to remark that western men, especially American men, probably knew as much about love as the next one.

Then *he* snorted scornfully. He went on to say that the men of the west and American men particularly knew nothing about the function of love in the scheme of life. I cut in to mention Bernarr McFadden. He snorted again and went on. Even if a few did have some inkling, they did not know how to go about it. He was very vehement about it. He said we insulted God's intentions so grossly that it was a wonder that western women had not given up the idea of mating and marriage altogether. But many men, and consequently women, in Jamaica were better informed. I wanted to know how it was that these Jamaicans had been blessed beyond all others on this side of the big waters, and he replied that there were oriental influences in Jamaica that had been at work for generations, so that Jamaica was prepared to teach continental America something about love. Saying this, he left the summer house and strode towards his car which was parked in the drive. But he could not say all that to me and then walk off like that. I caught him on the running board of his car and carried him back. When I showed a disposition to listen instead of scoffing, we had a very long talk. That is, he talked and I listened most respectfully.

Before he drove away he had told me about the specialists who prepare young girls for love. This practise is not universal in Jamaica, but it is common enough to speak of here. I asked to be shown, and he promised to use his influence in certain quarters that I might study the matter at close range. It was arranged for me to spend two weeks with one of the practitioners and learn what I could in that time. There are several of these advisors scattered about that section of Jamaica, but people not inside the circle know nothing about what is going on.

These specialists are always women. They are old women who have lived with a great deal of subtlety themselves. Having passed through the active period and become widows, or otherwise removed from active service, they are re-inducted in an advisory capacity.

The young girl who is to be married shortly or about to become the mistress of an influential man is turned over to the old woman for preparation. The wish is to bring complete innocence and complete competence together in the same girl. She is being educated for her life work under experts.

For a few days the old woman does not touch her. She is taking her pupil through the lecture stages of instruction. Among other things she is told that the consummation of love cannot properly take place in bed. Soft beds are not for love. They are comforts for the old and lack-a-daisical. Also she is told that her very position must be an invitation. When her lord and master enters the chamber she must be on the floor with only her shoulders and the soles of her feet touching the floor. It is *so* that he must find her. Not lying sluggishly in bed like an old cow, and hiding under the covers like a thief who has snatched a bit of beef from the market stall. The exact posture is demonstrated over and over again. The girl must keep on trying until she can assume it easily. In addition she is instructed at length on muscular control inside her body and out, and this also was rehearsed again and again, until it was certain that the young candidate had grasped all that was meant.

The last day has arrived. This is the day of the wedding. The old woman gives her first a "balm bath," that is a hot herb bath. Only these old women know the secret of which herbs to use to steep a virgin for marriage. It is intended, this bath is, to remove everything mental, spiritual and physical that might work against a happy mating. No soap is used at this point. It is a medicinal sweating tub to open the pores and stimulate the candidate generally. Immediately that the virgin leaves the bath she is covered and sweated for a long time. Then she is bathed again in soapy water.

Now the subtleties begin. Jamaica has a grass called khus khus. The sweet scent from its roots is the very odor of seduction. Days before the old woman has prepared an extract from these roots in oil and it is at hand in a bowl. She begins and massages the girl from head to foot with this fragrant unction. The toes, the fingers, the thighs, and there is a special motional treatment for every part of the body. It seemed to me that the breasts alone were ignored. But when the body massage is over, she returns to the breasts. These are bathed several times in warm water in which something special had been steeped. After that they are massaged ever so lightly with the very tips of the fingers dipped in khus khus. This fingertip motion is circular and moves ever towards the nipple. Arriving there, it begins over and over again. Finally the breasts are cupped and the nipples flicked with a warm feather back and forth, back and forth until there was a reaction to stimulation. The breasts stiffened and pouted, while the rest of the body relaxed.

But the old woman is not through. She carries this same light-fingered manipulation down the body and the girl swoons. She is revived by a mere sip of rum in which a single leaf of ganga has been steeped. Ganga is that "wisdom weed" which has been brought from the banks of the sacred Ganges to Jamaica. The girl revives and the massage continues. She swoons again and is revived. But she is not aware of the work-a-day world. She is in a twilight state of awareness, cushioned on a cloud of love thoughts.

Now the old woman talks to her again. It is a brief summation of all that has been said and done for the past week.

"You feel that you are sick now but that is because the reason for which you were made has not been fulfilled. You cannot be happy nor complete until that has happened. But the success of everything is with you. You have the happiest duty of any creature on earth and you must perform it well. The whole duty of a woman is love and comfort. You were never intended for anything else. You are made for love and comfort. Think of yourself in that way and no other. If you do as I teach you, heaven is with you and the man who is taking you to his house to love and comfort him. He is taking you there for that reason and for no other. That is all that men ever want women for, love and softness and peace, and you must not fail him.''

The old instructor ran over physical points briefly again. She stressed the point that there must be no fear. If the girl experienced any pain, then she had failed to learn what she had been taught with so much comfort and repetition. *There was nothing to fear.* Love killed no one. Rather it made them beautiful and happy. She said this over and over again.

Still stressing relaxed muscles, the old woman took a broad white band of cloth and wound it tightly about the loins of the girl well below the navel. She circled the body with the band perhaps four times and then secured it with safety pins. It was wound very tightly and seemed useless at first. All the time that this was being done the girl was crying to be taken to her future husband. The old woman seemingly ignored her and massaged her here and there briefly.

They began to put her wedding clothes upon the girl. The old woman was almost whispering to her that she was the most important part of all creation, and that she must accept her role gladly. She must not make war on her destiny and creation. The impatient girl was finally robed for her wedding and she was led out of the room to face the public and her man. But here went no frightened, shaking figure under a veil. No nerve-racked female behaving as if she approached her doom. This young, young thing went forth with the assurance of infinity. And she had such eagerness in her as she went!

Hunting the Wild Hog

IF YOU GO TO JAMAICA you are going to want to visit the Maroons at Accompong. They are under the present rule of Colonel Rowe, who is an intelligent, cheerful man. But I warn you in advance not to ride his wall-eyed, pot-bellied mule. He sent her to meet me at the end of the railroad line so that I would not have to climb that last high peak on foot. That was very kind of Colonel Rowe, and I appreciate his hospitality, but that mule of his just did not fall in with the scheme somehow. The only thing that kept her from throwing me, was the fact that I fell off first. And the only thing that kept her from kicking me, biting me and trampling me under foot after I fell off was the speed with which I got out of the way after the fall. I think she meant to chase me straight up that mountain afterwards, but one of Colonel Rowe's boys grabbed her bridle and held her while I withdrew. She was so provoked when she saw me escaping, that she reared and pitched till the saddle and everything else fell off except the halter. Maybe it was that snappy orange-colored four-in-hand tie that I was wearing that put her against me. I hate to think it was my face. Whatever it was, she started to rolling her pop-eyes at me as soon as I approached her. One thing I will say for her, she was not deceitful. She never pretended to like me. I got upon her back without the least bit of co-operation from her. She was against it from the start and let me know. I was the one who felt we might be sisters under the skin. She corrected all of that about a half mile down the trail and so I had to climb that mountain into Accompong on my own two legs.

The thing that struck me forcefully was the feeling of great age about the place. Standing on that old parade ground, which is now a cricket field, I could feel the dead generations crowding me. Here was the oldest settlement of freedmen in the Western world, no doubt. Men who had thrown off the bands of slavery by their own courage and ingenuity. The courage and daring of the Maroons strike like a purple beam across the history of Jamaica. And yet as I stood there looking into the sea beyond Black river from the mountains of St. Catherine, and looking at the thatched huts close at hand, I could not help remembering that a whole civilization and the mightiest nation on earth had grown up on the mainland since the first runaway slave had taken refuge in these mountains. They were here before the Pilgrims landed on the bleak shores of Massachusetts. Now, Massachusetts had stretched from the Atlantic to the Pacific and Accompong had remained itself.

I settled down at the house of Colonel Rowe to stay a while. I knew that he wondered about me—why I had come there and what I wanted. I never told him. He told me how Dr. Herskovits had been there and passed a night with him; how some one else had spent three weeks to study their dances and how much money they had spent in doing this. I kept on day by day saying nothing as to why I had come. He offered to stage a dance for me also. I thanked him, but declined. I did not tell him that I was too old a hand at collecting to fall for staged-dance affairs. If I do not see a dance or a ceremony in its natural setting and sequence, I do not bother. Self-experience has taught me that those staged affairs are never the same as the real thing. I had been told by some of the Maroons that their big dance, and only real one, came on January 6th. That was when they went out to the wooded peaks the day before and came back with individual masques and costumes upon them. They are summoned from their night-long retreat by the Abeng, or Conk-shell. Then there is a day of Afro-Karamante' dancing and singing, and feasting on jerked pork.

What I was actually doing was making general observations. I wanted to see what the Maroons were like, really. Since they are a self-governing body, I wanted to see how they felt about education, transportation, public health and democracy. I wanted to see their culture and art expressions and knew that if I asked for anything especially, I would get something out of context. I had heard a great deal about their primitive medicines and wanted to know about that. I was interested in vegetable poisons and their antidote. So I just sat around and waited.

There are other Maroon settlements besides Accompong, but England made treaty with Accompong only. There are now about a thousand people there and Colonel Rowe governs the town according to Maroon law and custom. The whole thing is very primitive, but he told me he wished to bring things up to date. There is a great deal of lethargy, however, and utter unconsciousness of what is going on in the world outside.

For instance, there was not a stove in all Accompong. The cooking, ironing and whatever else is done, is done over an open fire with the women squatting on their haunches inhaling the smoke. I told Rowe that he ought to buy a stove himself to show the others what to do. He said he could not afford one. Stoves are not customary in Jamaica outside of good homes in the cities anyway. They are imported luxuries. I recognized that and took another tack. We would build one! I designed an affair to be made of rock and cement and Colonel Rowe and some men he gathered undertook to make it. We sent out to the city and bought some sheet tin for the stove pipe and the pot-holes. I measured the bottoms of the pots and designed a hole to fit each of the three. The center hole was for the great iron pot, and then there were two other holes of different sizes. Colonel Rowe had some lime there, and he sent his son and grandchildren out to collect more rocks. His son-in-law-to-be mixed the clay and lime and in a day the furnace-like stove was built. The kitchen house lacking a floor anyway, the stove was built clear across one side of the room so that there was room on top of it for pots and pans not in use. The pot-holes were lined with tin so that the pots would not break the mortar. Then we left it a day to dry. We were really joyful when we fired it the next day and found out that it worked. Many of the Maroons came down to look at the miracle. There were pots boiling on the fire; no smoke in the room, but a great column of black smoke shooting out of the stove pipe which stuck out of the side of the house.

In the building of the stove I came to know little Tom, the Colonel's grandson. He is a most lovable and pathetic little figure. He is built very sturdy and is over strong for his age. He lives at the house of his grand-father because he has no mother and his father will not work for himself, let alone for his son. He is not only lazy and shiftless, he is disloyal to Colonel Rowe who has wasted a great deal of money on him. Little Tom is there among more favored grandchildren and his life is wretched. The others may strike him, kick him, I even saw one of them burn him with-out being punished for it. He is fed last and least and is punished severely for showing any resentment towards the treatment he gets from his cousins. They are the children of the Colonel's favorite child, his youngest daughter, and she is there to watch and see that her three darlings are not in any way annoyed by Tom. He was so warmed by the little comfort he got out of me that I wished very much to adopt him. He is just full of love and goodwill and nowhere to use it. It was most pointedly scorned when he offered it. When I asked why all this cruelty to such a small child, they answered with that excuse of all cruel people, ''He is a very bad child. He has criminal tendencies. If we do not treat him harshly he will grow up to be nothing but a brute.'' So they abuse him and beat him and scorn him for his future good.

It was not long before I noticed people who were not Maroons climbing the mountain road past the Colonel's gate. I found that they were coming to Accompong for treatment. Colonel Rowe began to tell me about it and soon after that I met the chief medicine man. Colonel Rowe told me he was a liar and over ambitious politically, but that he really knew his business as a primitive doctor. Later I found that to be true. He was a wonderful doctor, but he wanted to be the chief. At one time he had seized the treaty that was signed long ago between England and the Maroons and attempted to make himself the chief. This had failed and he was still not too sincere in his dealings with Colonel Rowe, but their outward relations were friendly enough. So he took to coming around to talk with me.

First we talked about things that are generally talked about in Jamaica. Brother Anansi, the Spider, that great culture hero of West Africa who is personated in Haiti by Ti Malice and in the United States by Brer Rabbit. About duppies and how and where they existed, and how to detect them. I learned that they lived mostly in silk-cotton trees and in almond trees. One should never plant either of those trees too close to the house because the duppies will live in them and "throw heat" on the people as they come and go about the house. One can tell when a duppy is near by the feeling of heat and the swelling of the head. A duppy can swell one's head to a huge thing just by being near. But if one drinks tea from that branch of the snake weed family known as Spirit Weed, duppies can't touch you. You can walk into a room where all kinds of evil and duppies are and be perfectly safe.

The Whooping Boy came up. Some say that the Whooping Boy is the great ghost of a "penner." (a Cow-herd). He can be seen and heard only in August. Then he can be heard at a great distance whooping, cracking his whip and "penning" his ghost cows. He frightens real cows when he "pauses" (cracks) his whip.

The Three-leg-Horse manifests himself just before Christmas, a woman said that "him drag hearse when him was alive." (He was used to pull a hearse when he was alive) and that he did not appear until one in the morning. From then until four o'clock he ranged the highways and might attack a wayfarer if he chanced to meet one. If he chases you, you can only escape by running under a fence. If you climb over it, he will jump the fence after you.

But the men all looked at each other and laughed. They denied that the Three-leg-Horse ever hurt any one. Girls they said, were afraid of it, but it was not dangerous. He appeared around Christmas time to enjoy himself. When the country people masque with the horse head and cow head for the parades, the Three-legged-Horse wrapped himself up in a sheet and went along with them in disguise. But if one looked close he could be distinguished from the people in masques, because he was two legs in front and one behind. His gait is a jump and a leap that sounds "Te-coom-tum! Te-coom-tum!" In some parts of Jamaica he is called "The Three-legged Aurelia," and they, the people, dance in the road with the expectation that the spirit horse will come before seven o'clock at night, and pass the night revelling in masquerade. Two main singers and dancers lead the rest in this outdoor ceremony and it is all quite happy.

All in all from what I heard, I have the strong belief that the Three-legged-Horse is a sex symbol and that the celebration of it is a fragment of some West African puberty ceremony for boys. All the women feared it. They had all been told to fear it. But none of the men were afraid at all. Perhaps under those masques and robes of the male revellers is some culture secret worth knowing. But it was quite certain that my sex barred me from getting anything more than the other women knew. (I found the "Société Trois-jambe" in Haiti also but could learn nothing definite of its inner meaning.)

But the Rolling-Calf is the most celebrated of all the apparitions in Jamaica. His two great eyes are balls of fire, he moves like lightning and "he has no abiding city." He wanders all over Jamaica. The Rolling-Calf is a plague put upon the earth to trouble people, and he will always be here. He keeps chiefly to the country parts and comes whirling down hills to the terror of the wayfarer. But the biggest harm that he does is to spoil the shape of the female dog. He harms the dog; she squeals and the owner goes into the yard and sees nothing but a flame of fire vanishing in the distance. The dog's shape is ruined, and she will never have puppies again. Rolling-Calf can be seen most any moonlight night roving the lanes of the countryside.

After a night or two of talk, the medicine man began to talk about his profession and soon I was a spectator while he practised his arts. I learned of the terrors and benefits of Cow-itch and of that potent plant known as Madame Fate. "It is a cruel weed." He told me, and I found he had understated its powers. I saw him working with the Cassada bean, the Sleep-and-Wake, Horse Bath and Marjo Bitters. Boil five leaves of Horse Bath and drink it with a pinch of salt and your kidneys are cleaned out magnificently. Boil six leaves and drink it and you will die. Marjo Bitter is a vine that grows on rocks. Take a length from your elbow to your wrist and make a tea and it is a most excellent medicine. Boil a length to the palm of your hand and you are violently poisoned. He used the bark of a tree called Jessamy, well boiled for a purgative. Twelve minutes after drinking the wine glass of medicine the purge begins and keeps up for five days without weakening the patient or griping.

I went with him to visit the "God wood" tree (Birch Gum). It is called "God Wood" because it is the first tree that ever was made. It is the original tree of good and evil. He had a convenant with that tree on the sunny side. We went there more than once. One day we went there to prevent the enemies of the medicine man from harming him. He took a strong nail and a hammer with him and drove the nail into the tree up to the head with three strokes; dropped the hammer and walked away rapidly without looking back. Later on, he sent me back to fetch the hammer to him.

He proved to me that all you need to do to poison a person and leave them horribly swollen was to touch a chip of this tree to their skin while they were sweating. It was uncanny.

We went to see a girl sick in bed. The medicine man was not in high favor with the mother; but Accompong is self-sufficient. They keep to their primitive medicine particularly. He went in and looked down on the sick girl and said that it was a desperate case, but he could cure her. But first the mother must chop down the papaya tree that was growing just outside the bed-room window. The mother objected. That was the only tree that she had and that she needed the fruit for food. The medicine man said that she *must* cut it down. It was too close to the house to begin with. It sapped the strength of the inmates. And it was a tall tree, taller than the house and she ought to know that if a paw-paw or papaya tree were allowed to grow taller than the house, that somebody would die. The mother hooted that off. That tree had nothing to do with the sickness of her daughter. If he did not know what to do for her, let him say so and go on about his business and she would call in someone else. If he knew what to do, get busy and stop wasting time on the paw paw tree.

Day by day the young woman grew weaker in spite of all that was done for her. Finally she called her mother to the bed and said, "Mama, cut the tree for me, please."

"I will do anything to make you well again, daughter, but cutting that tree is so unnecessary. It is nothing but a belief of ignorant people. Why must I cut down the tree that gives us so much food?"

Several times a day, now the girl begged her mother to cut the tree. She said if she were strong enough she would find the machete and chop it down herself. She cried all the time and followed her mother with her eyes pleading.

"Mama, I am weaker today than I was yesterday. Mama, please chop down the tree. Since I was a baby I have heard that the paw paw was an unlucky tree."

"And ever since you were a baby you have been eating the fruit," the mother retorted. "I spend every ha' penny I can find to make you well, and now you want me to do a foolish thing like killing my tree. No!''

"Mama if it is cut I will live. If you don't cut it I will die.''

The girl grew weaker and finally died. The grief stricken mother rushed outside with the machete and chopped down the tree. It was lying in the yard full of withered leaves and fruit when the girl was buried. But even then the woman was not completely convinced. She thinks often that it might have been coincidence. I passed her house on my way to visit the daughter of Esau Rowe, who is the brother of the Colonel. The mourning mother was looking down at the great mass of withered fruit when I spoke to her. She did not exactly ask me for a little money, but she opened the way for me to offer it. I gave her three shillings with the utmost joy because I knew she needed it.

"Thank you,'' she said half choked with tears. "My girl is dead. I-I don't know—'' she looked down at the tree, "I don't know if it was I who could have saved her. I wish I could know. Have you noticed how hungry a person can be the next day after a funeral? But I don't suppose you could know about such things at all.''

One night Colonel Rowe, Medicine Man and I sat on what is going to be a porch when the Colonel finds enough money to finish it, looking down on the world and talking. The tree frogs on the mountainside opposite were keeping up a fearful din. Colonel Rowe said it was a sign of rain. I said I hoped not, for then all Accompong would become a sea of sticky mud. I expressed the wish that the frogs would shut up. Colonel Rowe said that Medicine Man could make them hush but that would have no effect upon the weather.

"He can stop those frogs over on that other peak?'' I asked.

"Yes, he can stop them at will. I have seen him do it, many times.''

"Can you really?'' I turned to Medicine Man.

"That is very easy to do.''

"Do it for me, then. I'd like to see that done.''

He stood up and turned his face toward the mountain peak opposite and made a quick motion with one hand and seemed to inhale deeply from his waist up. He held this pose stiffly for a moment, then relaxed. The millions of frogs in the trees on that uninhabited peak opposite us ceased chirping as suddenly as a lightning flash. Medicine Man sat back down and would have gone on telling me the terrible things that the milk from the stalk of the paw paw tree does to male virility, but I stopped him. I had to listen to this sudden silence for a while.

"Oh they will not sing again until I permit them," Medicine Man assured me. "They will not sing again until I pass the house of Esau on my way home. When I get there I will whistle so that you will know that I am there. Then they will commence again."

We talked on awhile about the poisonous effect of Dumb Cane and of bissy (Kola nut) as an antidote, and how to kill with horse hair and bamboo dust. I was glad, however, when Medicine Man rose to go.

"Oh you need not worry," Colonel Rowe told me, "he can do what he says."

He walked out of Colonel's tumbledown gate and began to climb the mountain in that easy way that Maroons have from a life time of mountain climbing, and grew dim in the darkness. After a few minutes we heard the whistle way up on the path and like an orchestra under the conductor's baton, the frog symphony broke out. And it was certainly going on when I finally dropped off to sleep.

I kept on worrying the Colonel about jerked pig. I wanted to eat some of it. The jerked pig of the Maroons is famous beyond the seas. He explained to me that the Maroons did not jerk domestic pork. It was the flesh of the wild hog that they dressed that way. Why not kill a wild hog then, and jerk it, I wanted to know.

"Mama! That is much harder than you think. Wild hog is a very sensible creature. He does not let you kill him so easily. Besides, he lives in the Cock-Pit country and that is hard travelling even for us here who are accustomed to rocks and mountains."

"And there are not so many now as there use to be. We have killed many and then the mongoose also kill some," Medicine Man added.

"A mongoose kill a wild hog? I cannot believe it!" I exclaimed.

"Oh that mongoose, he a terrible insect," Medicine Man said. "He is very destroyfull, Mama! If the pig is on her feet she will tear that mongoose to pieces, Mama! But when she is giving birth the mongoose run there and seize the little pig as it is born and eat it. So we do not have so many wild pig now."

But I kept on talking and begging and coaxing until a hunting party was organized. A hunting party usually consists of four hunters, the dogs and the baggage boy, but this one was augmented because few of the men had much work to do at the moment, and then I was going, and women do not go on hog hunts in Accompong. If I had had more sense I would not have gone either, but you live and learn. The party was made up of Colonel Rowe, his brother Esau, Tom Colly, his two sons-in-law, his prospective son-in-law, his son who acted as baggage boy and your humble servant.

The day before, old machetes were filed down to spear heads and made razor sharp. Then they were attached to long handles and thus became spears. All of this *had* to be done the day before, especially the sharpening of all blades. If you sharpen your cutting weapons on the day of the hunt, your dogs will be killed by the hog.

We were up before dawn the day of the hunt, and with all equipment, food for several days, cooking utensils, weapons, and the like, we found our way by stealth to the graveyard. Medicine Man was to meet us there and he was true to his word. There the ancestors of all the hunters were invoked to strengthen their arms. The graves are never marked in Accompong for certain reasons, and thus if a person does not himself know the graves of his relatives there is no way of finding out. One of the men had been away in Cuba for several years and could not find his father's grave. That was considered not so good, but not too bad either. No attempt was made to guess at it for fear of waking up the wrong duppy who might do him harm. So the ceremony over, it was necessary for us to be out and gone before anyone in Accompong should speak to us. That would be the worst of luck. In fact, we were all prepared to turn back in case it happened to us. Some of us would be expected to be killed before we returned.

The baggage-boy was carrying our food which was not very heavy for the Maroons are splendid human engines. Not a fat person in all Maroon town. That comes, I suppose, from climbing mountains and a simple diet. They are lean, tough and durable. They can march, fight or work for hours on a small amount of food. The food on the hunt was corn pone, Cassada-by-me (Cassava bread), green plantain, salt, pimento and other spices to cure the hog when and if we caught him, *and* coffee. The baggage boy carried the iron skillet and coffee pot also. The hunters carried their own guns and blades. I stumbled along with my camera and note book and a few womanish things like comb and tooth brush and a towel.

We struck out back of the cemetery and by full sun-up we were in the Cock-Pit country. There is no need for me to try to describe the Cock-Pits. They are great gaping funnel-shaped holes in the earth that cover miles and miles of territory in this part of Jamaica. They are monstrous things that have never been explored. The rock formations are hardly believable. Mr. Astly Clerk is all for exploiting them as a tourist lure. But very few tourists have the stamina necessary to visit even one of them let alone descend into these curious, deep openings. They are monstrous.

By the time we reached the first of the Cock-Pits I was tired but I did not let on to the men. I thought that they would soon be tired too and I could get a rest without complaining. But they marched on and on. The dogs ran here and there but no hog sign. As the country became more rocky and full of holes and jags and points and loose looking boulders, I thought more and more how nice it would be to be back in Accompong.

Around noon, we halted briefly, ate and marched on. I suggested to Colonel Rowe that perhaps all the hogs had been killed already and we might be wasting our time. I let him know that I would not hold the party responsible if they killed no hogs. We had tried and now we could return with colors flying. He just looked at me and laughed. "Why," he said, "this is too soon to expect to find hog sign. Sometimes we are out four days before we even pick up the sign. If we pick up the hog sign tomorrow before night, we will have a luck."

And four more hours till sun-down!

We picked up no hog sign that day, but the men found a nest of wild bees in a tree growing out of the wall down inside a Cock-Pit. Everybody was delighted over the find. I asked them how would they get it. They tried several times to climb down to it but the wall was too sheer and the tree leaned too far out to climb into it. So Colly let himself be swung head foremost over the precipice by his heels and he was pulled up with the dripping honey combs. I had to look away. It was too much for my nerves, but no one else seemed to think anything of the feat.

While they were eating the honey, I sprawled out on a big hot rock to rest and the Colonel noticed it and ordered the men to build a hut for the night. It was near sun-down anyway.

The men took their machetes and chopped down enough branches to make a small shack and inside of an hour it was ready for use.

We found no hog sign the second day and I lost my Kodak somewhere. Maybe I threw it away. My riding boots were chafing my heels and I was sore all over. But those Maroons were fresh as daisies and swinging along singing their Karamante' songs. The favorite one means "We we are coming, oh." It says in Karamanti, "Blue Yerry, ai! Blue Yerry Gallo, Blue Yerry!"

It was near dark on the third day the dogs picked up the hog sign. No sight of him, you understand. They struck a scent and began to dash about like ferrets hungry for blood. But it was too late for even a Maroon to do anything about it. The men built the hut dead on the trail and we settled down for the night. Esau explained that they built the hut on the trail for a purpose. He said that the wild hog is an enchanted beast. He has his habits and does not change them. He has several hiding places along one trail and works from one to the other. When he reaches the limit of his range, he is bound to double back on his trail, seeking one of his other hideaways. He can go a long time without food but he must have water. When there is little rain and the waterholes are dried up, he will climb the rocks and drink the water from Wild Pines (a species of orchid). But it takes time for him to find these plants. He cannot do it with dogs at his heels. The hunters must not sleep too soundly during the night as the hog will repass and they will not know it. He is very shrewd. When he gets near the camp and smells the smoke he will climb higher and pass the camp higher up the mountain and be lost before morning.

We did not sleep much that night. And I suppose it was mostly my fault that we didn't. I was inside the hut by myself for one thing and I was a little scared because the men had told me scary things about hogs. They had said that when a wild boar, harassed by the dogs and hunter turns back down the trail, you must be prepared to give him the trail or kill him. His hide was tough and unless the bullet struck squarely and in a vital spot, it might be deflected. Then the men had to go in with their knives and spears and kill or be killed. I was afraid that the men would go to sleep and the boar be upon us before we knew it. So I kept awake and kept the others awake by talking and asking questions. We could hear the dogs at a distance, barking and charging and parrying. So the night passed.

The next day the chase was really hot. About noon the party divided. Colonel Rowe with three men went ahead to catch up with the dogs and see if the hog had made a stand. Esau, Colly and Tom stayed with me. That is, they stayed back to tackle the brute in case he doubled back on his track. We heard a great deal of noise far ahead, but no sound of shots nor anything conclusive. By three o'clock, however, the sounds were coming nearer, and the men looked after their guns. Then we heard a terrific and prolonged battle and the barking of the dogs ceased.

"Sounds like he has killed the dogs," said Esau.

"Killed five dogs?" I asked.

"If he is a big one, that would not be hard for him to do," Esau said. "When he gets desperate he will kill anything that stands in his way. But he will not kill the dogs if he can get at the hunter. He knows that the hunter is his real enemy. Sometimes he will charge the dogs and swerve so fast that the hunter is caught off guard, and attack. A man is in real danger there.''

It was not long after that, that we heard deep panting. It was a long way off but it seemed upon us. There was a huge boulder over to the right and I moved nearer to it so that I might hide behind it if necessary after seeing the wild boar approach and pass. The panting came nearer. Now we could hear him trotting and dislodging small stones. The men got ready to meet the charge. The boar with his huge, curving tusks dripping with dogs' blood came charging down upon us. I had never pictured anything so huge, so fierce nor so fast. Everybody cleared the way. He had come too fast for Esau to get good aim on a vital spot.

Just around a huge rock he whirled about. He made two complete circles faster than thought and backed into a small opening in the rock. He had made his stand and resolved to fight. Only his snout was visible from where we were. The men crept closer and Esau chanced a shot. The bullet nicked his nose and the shocking power of it knocked the hog to his knees. We rushed forward, the men expecting to finish him off with the knives. At that moment he leaped up and charged the crowd. I raced back to the big rock and scrambled up. What was going on behind my back I did not know until I got on top of the rock and looked back. Tom had scurried to safety also. Colly had not quite made it. The hog had cut the muscle in the calf of his leg and he was down. But Esau rushed in and almost pressed the muzzle of his rifle against the head of the boar and fired. The hog made a half turn and fell. Esau shot him again to make sure and he scarcely twitched after that.

While we were doing the best we could for Colly, the others came. They had heard the shooting. As soon as Colly was made as comfortable as possible, the men supported him and all made a circle around the fallen boar. They shook each other's hand most solemnly across the body of the hog and kissed each other for dangers past. All this was done with the utmost gravity. Finally Colonel Rowe said, ''Well, we got him. We have a luck.''

Then all of the men began to cut dry wood for a big fire. When the fire began to be lively, they cut green bush of a certain kind. They put the pig into the fire on his side and covered him with green bush to sweat him so that they could scrape off the hair. When one side was thoroughly cleaned, they scraped the other side and then washed the whole to a snowy white and gutted the hog. Everything was now done in high good humor. No effort was made to save the chitterlings and hasslets which were referred to as "the fifth quarter," because there was no way to handle it on the march. All of the bones were removed, seasoned and dried over the fire so that they could be taken home. The meat was then seasoned with salt, pepper and spices and put over the fire to cook. It was such a big hog that it took nearly all night to finish cooking. It required two men to turn it over when necessary. While it was being cooked and giving off delicious odors, the men talked and told stories and sang songs. One told the story of Paul Bogle, the Jamaican hero of the war of 1797 who made such a noble fight against the British. Unable to stop the fighting until they could capture the leader, they finally appealed to their new allies, the Maroons, who some say betrayed Bogle into the hands of the English. Paul Bogle never knew how it was that he was surprised by the English in a cave and taken. He was hanged with his whole family and the war stopped.

Towards morning we ate our fill of jerked pork. It is more delicious than our barbecue. It is hard to imagine anything better than pork the way the Maroons jerk it. When we had eaten all that we could hold, the rest was packed up with the bones and we started the long trek back to Accompong. My blistered feet told me time and time again that we would never get there, but we finally did. What was left of the wild pig was given to the families and friends of the hunters. They never sell it because they say they hunt for fun. We came marching in singing the Karamante' songs.

Blue yerry, ai
Blue yerry
Blue yerry, gallo
Blue yerry!

TWO
Essays and Articles

"How It Feels to Be Colored Me" is an excellent example of Zora Neale Hurston at her most exasperating. Published in 1928, near the beginning of Hurston's career, this essay presents two stereotypes: the "happy darky" who sings and dances for white folks, for money and for joy; and the educated black person who is, underneath the thin veneer of civilization, still a "heathen." And Hurston actually says, "Slavery is the price I paid for civilization." We can assume this was not an uncommon sentiment during the early part of this century, among black and white; read today, however, it makes one's flesh crawl.

One wonders, though, if white people's stereotypes of the "happy darky" and the "civilized heathen" did not exist—and had not caused black people enormous suffering—would we see these self-descriptions Hurston gives us differently? Would we see, instead, what she was undoubtedly endeavoring to project: a cheerful, supremely confident and extroverted little girl who assumed anyone and everyone would be delighted with her; and a passionate, nationalistic adult who exulted in her color, her "Africanism," and her ability to *feel?* In "What White Publishers Won't Print," published in *The Negro Digest* some twenty years later in 1950, Hurston shows a definite awareness of white people's use of stereotype to keep blacks, Asians, and Indians in their "place." In one of the two "Negro" stereotypes dear to white publishers, a black person, she writes, "is seated on a stump picking away on his banjo and singing and laughing." She knows there is nothing inherently wrong with a black person sitting on a stump singing and laughing and picking his banjo. What is wrong is the insistence of the powerful—who can make their version of life stick—that that is all the person does.

Hurston also, interestingly enough considering her own statements twenty years earlier, discusses the "ridiculous notion" of "reversion to type." She writes: "One has only to examine the huge literature on it to be convinced. No matter how high we may climb, put us under strain and we revert to type, that is, to the bush. Under a superficial layer of Western culture, the jungle drums throb in our veins." She understands the damaging effects of this "curious folklore doctrine."

In "Crazy for This Democracy" (1945), "The 'Pet' Negro System" (1943), and "My Most Humiliating Jim Crow Experience" (1944), it is clear that Hurston grew to understand the weight that racism lays on the whole world, and to know that though slavery *was* sixty years or more behind black people at the time she wrote, the "operation" was not the success she had previously assumed it was, and "the patient," far from "doing well, thank you," must struggle every minute of life to affirm black people's right to a healthy existence.

How It Feels to Be Colored Me

I AM COLORED but I offer nothing in the way of extenuating circumstances except the fact that I am the only Negro in the United States whose grandfather on the mother's side was *not* an Indian chief.

I remember the very day that I became colored. Up to my thirteenth year I lived in the little Negro town of Eatonville, Florida. It is exclusively a colored town. The only white people I knew passed through the town going to or coming from Orlando. The native whites rode dusty horses, the Northern tourists chugged down the sandy village road in automobiles. The town knew the Southerners and never stopped cane chewing when they passed. But the Northerners were something else again. They were peered at cautiously from behind curtains by the timid. The more venturesome would come out on the porch to watch them go past and got just as much pleasure out of the tourists as the tourists got out of the village.

The front porch might seem a daring place for the rest of the town, but it was a gallery seat for me. My favorite place was atop the gate-post. Proscenium box for a born first-nighter. Not only did I enjoy the show, but I didn't mind the actors knowing that I liked it. I usually spoke to them in passing. I'd wave at them and when they returned my salute, I would say something like this: "Howdy-do-well-I-thank-you-where-you-goin'?" Usually automobile or the horse paused at this, and after a queer exchange of compliments, I would probably "go a piece of the way" with them, as we say in farthest Florida. If one of my family happened to come to the front in time to see me, of course negotiations would be rudely broken off. But even so, it is clear that I was the first "welcome-to-our-state" Floridian, and I hope the Miami Chamber of Commerce will please take notice.

During this period, white people differed from colored to me only in that they rode through town and never lived there. They liked to hear me "speak pieces" and sing and wanted to see me dance the parse-me-la, and gave me generously of their small silver for doing these things, which seemed strange to me for I wanted to do them so much that I needed bribing to stop. Only they didn't know it. The colored people gave no dimes. They deplored any joyful tendencies in me, but I was their Zora nevertheless. I belonged to them, to the nearby hotels, to the county—everybody's Zora.

But changes came in the family when I was thirteen, and I was sent to school in Jacksonville. I left Eatonville, the town of the oleanders, as Zora. When I disembarked from the river-boat at Jacksonville, she was no more. It seemed that I had suffered a sea change. I was not Zora of Orange County any more, I was now a little colored girl. I found it out in certain ways. In my heart as well as in the mirror, I became a fast brown—warranted not to rub nor run.

BUT I AM NOT tragically colored. There is no great sorrow dammed up in my soul, nor lurking behind my eyes. I do not mind at all. I do not belong to the sobbing school of Negrohood who hold that nature somehow has given them a lowdown dirty deal and whose feelings are all hurt about it. Even in the helter-skelter skirmish that is my life, I have seen that the world is to the strong regardless of a little pigmentation more or less. No, I do not weep at the world—I am too busy sharpening my oyster knife.

Someone is always at my elbow reminding me that I am the grand-daughter of slaves. It fails to register depression with me. Slavery is sixty years in the past. The operation was successful and the patient is doing well, thank you. The terrible struggle that made me an American out of a potential slave said "On the line!" The Reconstruction said "Get set!"; and the generation before said "Go!" I am off to a flying start and I must not halt in the stretch to look behind and weep. Slavery is the price I paid for civilization, and the choice was not with me. It is a bully adventure and worth all that I have paid through my ancestors for it. No one on earth ever had a greater chance for glory. The world to be won and nothing to be lost. It is thrilling to think—to know that for any act of mine, I shall get twice as much praise or twice as much blame. It is quite exciting to hold the center of the national stage, with the spectators not knowing whether to laugh or to weep.

The position of my white neighbor is much more difficult. No brown specter pulls up a chair beside me when I sit down to eat. No dark ghost thrusts its leg against mine in bed. The game of keeping what one has is never so exciting as the game of getting.

I do not always feel colored. Even now I often achieve the unconscious Zora of Eatonville before the Hegira. I feel most colored when I am thrown against a sharp white background.

For instance at Barnard. "Beside the waters of the Hudson" I feel my race. Among the thousand white persons, I am a dark rock surged upon, and overswept, but through it all, I remain myself. When covered by the waters, I am; and the ebb but reveals me again.

SOMETIMES IT IS the other way around. A white person is set down in our midst, but the contrast is just as sharp for me. For instance, when I sit in the drafty basement that is The New World Cabaret with a white person, my color comes. We enter chatting about any little nothing that we have in common and are seated by the jazz waiters. In the abrupt way that jazz orchestras have, this one plunges into a number. It loses no time in circumlocutions, but gets right down to business. It constricts the thorax and splits the heart with its tempo and narcotic harmonies. This orchestra grows rambunctious, rears on its hind legs and attacks the tonal veil with primitive fury, rending it, clawing it until it breaks through to the jungle beyond. I follow those heathen—follow them exultingly. I dance wildly inside myself; I yell within, I whoop; I shake my assegai above my head, I hurl it true to the mark *yeeeeooww!* I am in the jungle and living in the jungle way. My face is painted red and yellow and my body is painted blue. My pulse is throbbing like a war drum. I want to slaughter something—give pain, give death to what, I do not know. But the piece ends. The men of the orchestra wipe their lips and rest their fingers. I creep back slowly to the veneer we call civilization with the last tone and find the white friend sitting motionless in his seat, smoking calmly.

"Good music they have here," he remarks, drumming the table with his fingertips.

Music. The great blobs of purple and red emotion have not touched him. He has only heard what I felt. He is far away and I see him but dimly across the ocean and the continent that have fallen between us. He is so pale with his whiteness then and I am *so* colored.

AT CERTAIN TIMES I have no race, I am *me*. When I set my hat at a certain angle and saunter down Seventh Avenue, Harlem City, feeling as snooty as the lions in front of the Forty-Second Street Library, for instance. So far as my feelings are concerned, Peggy Hopkins Joyce on the Boule Mich with her gorgeous raiment, stately carriage, knees knocking together in a most aristocratic manner, has nothing on me. The cosmic Zora emerges. I belong to no race nor time. I am the eternal feminine with its string of beads.

I have no separate feeling about being an American citizen and colored. I am merely a fragment of the Great Soul that surges within the boundaries. My country, right or wrong.

Sometimes, I feel discriminated against, but it does not make me angry. It merely astonishes me. How *can* any deny themselves the pleasure of my company? It's beyond me.

But in the main, I feel like a brown bag of miscellany propped against a wall. Against a wall in company with other bags, white, red and yellow. Pour out the contents, and there is discovered a jumble of small things priceless and worthless. A first-water diamond, an empty spool, bits of broken glass, lengths of string, a key to a door long since crumbled away, a rusty knife-blade, old shoes saved for a road that never was and never will be, a nail bent under the weight of things too heavy for any nail, a dried flower or two still a little fragrant. In your hand is the brown bag. On the ground before you is the jumble it held—so much like the jumble in the bags, could they be emptied, that all might be dumped in a single heap and the bags refilled without altering the content of any greatly. A bit of colored glass more or less would not matter. Perhaps that is how the Great Stuffer of Bags filled them in the first place—who knows?

The "Pet" Negro System

BROTHERS AND SISTERS, I take my text this morning from the Book of Dixie. I take my text and I take my time.

Now it says here, "And every white man shall be allowed to pet himself a Negro. Yea, he shall take a black man unto himself to pet and to cherish, and this same Negro shall be perfect in his sight. Nor shall hatred among the races of men, nor conditions of strife in the walled cities, cause his pride and pleasure in his own Negro to wane."

Now, beloved Brothers and Sisters, I see you have all woke up and you can't wait till the service is over to ask me how come? So I will read you further from the sacred word which says here:

"Thus spake the Prophet of Dixie when slavery was yet a young thing, for he saw the yearning in the hearts of men. And the dwellers in the bleak North, they who pass old-made phrases through their mouths, shall cry out and say, 'What are these strange utterances? Is it not written that the hand of every white man in the South is raised against his black brother? Do not the sons of Japheth drive the Hammites before them like beasts? Do they not lodge them in shacks and hovels and force them to share the crops? Is not the condition of black men in the South most horrible? Then how doth this scribe named Hurston speak of pet Negroes? Perchance she hath drunk of new wine, and it has stung her like an adder?' "

Now, my belov-ed, before you explode in fury you might look to see if you know your facts or if you merely know your phrases. It happens that there are more angles to this race-adjustment business than are ever pointed out to the public, white, black or in-between. Well-meaning outsiders make plans that look perfect from where they sit, possibly in some New York office. But these plans get wrecked on hidden snags. John Brown at Harpers Ferry is a notable instance. The simple race-agin-race pattern of those articles and speeches on the subject is not that simple at all. The actual conditions do not jibe with the fulminations of the so-called spokesmen of the white South, nor with the rhetoric of the champions of the Negro cause either.

II.   BIG MEN LIKE BILBO, HEFLIN AND TILLMAN bellow threats which they know they couldn't carry out even in their own districts. The orators at both extremes may glint and glitter in generalities, but the South lives and thinks in individuals. The North has no interest in the particular Negro, but talks of justice for the whole. The South has no interest, and pretends none, in the mass of Negroes but is very much concerned about the individual. So that brings us to the pet Negro, because to me at least it symbolizes the web of feelings and mutual dependencies spun by generations and generations of living together and natural adjustment. It isn't half as pretty as the ideal adjustment of theorizers, but it's a lot more real and durable, and a lot of black folk, I'm afraid, find it mighty cosy.

The pet Negro, belov-ed, is someone whom a particular white person or persons wants to have and to do all the things forbidden to other Negroes. It can be Aunt Sue, Uncle Stump, or the black man at the head of some Negro organization. Let us call him John Harper. John Harper is the pet of Colonel Cary and his lady, and Colonel Cary swings a lot of weight in his community.

The Colonel will tell you that he opposes higher education for Negroes. It makes them mean and cunning. Bad stuff for Negroes. He is against having lovely, simple blacks turned into rascals by too much schooling. But there are exceptions. Take John, for instance. Worked hard, saved up his money and went up there to Howard University and got his degree in education. Smart as a whip! Seeing that John had such a fine head, of course he helped John out when necessary. Not that he would do such a thing for the average darky, no sir! He is no nigger lover. Strictly unconstructed Southerner, willing to battle for white supremacy! But his John is different.

So naturally when John finished college and came home, Colonel Cary knew he was the very man to be principal of the Negro high school, and John got the post even though someone else had to be eased out. And making a fine job of it. Decent, self-respecting fellow. Built himself a nice home and bought himself a nice car. John's wife is county nurse; the Colonel spoke to a few people about it and she got the job. John's children are smart and have good manners. If all the Negroes were like them he wouldn't mind what advancement they made. But the rest of them, of course, lie like the cross-ties from New York to Key West. They steal things and get drunk. Too bad, but Negroes are like that.

Now there are some prominent white folk who don't see eye to eye with Colonel Cary about this John Harper. They each have a Negro in mind who is far superior to John. They listen to eulogies about John only because they wish to be listened to about their own pets. They pull strings for the Colonel's favorites knowing that they will get the same thing done for theirs.

Now, how can the Colonel make his attitude towards John Harper jibe with his general attitude towards Negroes? Easy enough. He got his general attitude by tradition, and he has no quarrel with it. But he found John truthful and honest, clean, reliable and a faithful friend. He *likes* John and so considers him as white inside as anyone else. The treatment made and provided for Negroes generally is suspended, restrained and done away with. He knows that John is able to learn what white people of similar opportunities learn. Colonel Cary's affection and respect for John, however, in no way extend to black folk in general.

When you understand that, you can see why it is so difficult to change certain things in the South. His particular Negroes are not suffering from the strictures, and the rest are no concern of the Colonel's. Let their own white friends do for them. If they are worth the powder and lead it would take to kill them, they have white friends; if not, then they belong in the "stray nigger" class and nobody gives a damn about them. If John should happen to get arrested for anything except assault and murder upon the person of a white man, or rape, the Colonel is going to stand by him and get him out. It would be a hard-up Negro who would work for a man who couldn't get his black friends out of jail.

And mind you, the Negroes have their pet whites, so to speak. It works both ways. Class-consciousness of Negroes is an angle to be reckoned with in the South. They love to be associated with "the quality" and consequently are ashamed to admit that they are working for "strainers." It is amusing to see a Negro servant chasing the madam or the boss back on his or her pedestal when they behave in an unbecoming manner. Thereby he is to a certain extent preserving his own prestige, derived from association with that family.

If ever it came to the kind of violent showdown the orators hint at, you could count on all the Colonel Carys tipping off and protecting their John Harpers; and you could count on all the John Harpers and Aunt Sues to exempt their special white folk. And that means that pretty nearly everybody on both sides would be exempt, except the "pore white trash" and the "stray niggers," and not all of them.

III.   AN OUTSIDER DRIVING THROUGH a street of well-off Negro homes, seeing the great number of high-priced cars, will wonder why he has never heard of this side of Negro life in the South. He has heard about the shacks and the sharecroppers. He has had them before him in literature and editorials and crusading journals. But the other side isn't talked about by the champions of white supremacy, because it makes their stand, and their stated reasons for keeping the Negro down, look a bit foolish. The Negro crusaders and their white adherents can't talk about it because it is obviously bad strategy. The worst aspects must be kept before the public to force action.

It has been so generally accepted that all Negroes in the South are living under horrible conditions that many friends of the Negro up North actually take offense if you don't tell them a tale of horror and suffering. They stroll up to you, cocktail glass in hand, and say, "I am a friend of the Negro, you know, and feel awful about the terrible conditions down there." That's your cue to launch into atrocities amidst murmurs of sympathy. If, on the other hand, just to find out if they really have done some research down there, you ask "What conditions do you refer to?" you get an injured, and sometimes a malicious, look. Why ask foolish questions? Why drag in the many Negroes of opulence and education? Yet these comfortable, contented Negroes are as real as the sharecroppers.

There is, in normal times, a regular stream of high-powered cars driven by Negroes headed North each summer for a few weeks' vacation. These people go, have their fling, and hurry back home. Doctors, teachers, lawyers, businessmen, they are living and working in the South because that is where they want to be. And why not? Economically, they are at ease and more. The professional men do not suffer from the competition of their white colleagues to anything like they do up North. Personal vanity, too, is served. The South makes a sharp distinction between the upper-class and lower-class Negro. Businessmen cater to him. His word is *good* downtown. There is some Mr. Big in the background who is interested in him and will back his fall. All the plums that a Negro can get are dropped in his mouth. He wants no part of the cold, impersonal North. He notes that there is segregation and discrimination up there, too, with none of the human touches of the South.

As I have said, belov-ed, these Negroes who are petted by white friends think just as much of their friends across the line. There is a personal attachment that will ride over practically anything that is liable to happen to either. They have their fingers crossed, too, when they say they don't like white people. "White people" does not mean their particular friends, any more than niggers means John Harper to the Colonel. This is important. For anyone, or any group, counting on a solid black South, or a solid white South in opposition to each other will run into a hornet's nest if he discounts these personal relations. Both sides admit the general principle of opposition, but when it comes to putting it into practice, behold what happens. There is a quibbling, a stalling, a backing and filling that nullifies all the purple oratory.

So well is this underground hookup established, that it is not possible to keep a secret from either side. Nearly everybody spills the beans to his favorite on the other side of the color line—in strictest confidence, of course. That's how the "petting system" works in the South.

Is it a good thing or a bad thing? Who am I to pass judgment? I am not defending the system, belov-ed, but trying to explain it. The low-down fact is that it weaves a kind of basic fabric that tends to stabilize relations and give something to work from in adjustments. It works to prevent hasty explosions. There are some people in every community who can always talk things over. It may be the proof that this race situation in America is not entirely hopeless and may even be worked out eventually.

There are dangers in the system. Too much depends on the integrity of the Negro so trusted. It cannot be denied that this trust has been abused at times. What was meant for the whole community has been turned to personal profit by the pet. Negroes have long groaned because of this frequent diversion of general factors into the channels of private benefits. Why do we not go to Mr. Big and expose the Negro in question? Sometimes it is because we do not like to let white people know that we have folks of that ilk. Sometimes we make a bad face and console ourselves, "At least one Negro has gotten himself a sinecure not usually dealt out to us." We curse him for a yellow-bellied sea-buzzard, a ground-mole and a woods-pussy, call him a white-folkses nigger, an Uncle Tom, and a handkerchief-head and let it go at that. In all fairness, it must be said that these terms are often flung around out of jealousy: somebody else would like the very cinch that the accused has grabbed himself.

But when everything is discounted, it still remains true that white people North and South have promoted Negroes—usually in the capacity of "representing the Negro"—with little thought of the ability of the person promoted but in line with the "pet system." In the South it can be pointed to scornfully as a residue of feudalism; in the North no one says *what* it is. And that, too, is part of the illogical, indefensible but somehow useful "pet system."

IV.   THE MOST POWERFUL REASON why Negroes do not do more about false "representation" by pets is that they know from experience that the thing is too deep-rooted to be budged. The appointer has his reasons, personal or political. He can always point to the beneficiary and say, "Look, Negroes, you have been taken care of. Didn't I give a member of your group a big job?" White officials assume that the Negro element is satisfied and they do not know what to make of it when later they find that so large a body of Negroes charge indifference and double-dealing. The white friend of the Negroes mumbles about ingratitude and decides that you simply can't understand Negroes . . . just like children.

A case in point is Dr. James E. Sheppard, President of the North Carolina State College for Negroes. He has a degree in pharmacy, and no other. For years he ran a one-horse religious school of his own at Durham, North Carolina. But he has always been in politics and has some good friends in power at Raleigh. So the funds for the State College for Negroes were turned over to him, and his little church school became the Negro college so far as that State is concerned. A fine set of new buildings has been erected. With a host of Negro men highly trained as educators within the State, not to mention others who could be brought in, a pharmacist heads up higher education for Negroes in North Carolina. North Carolina can't grasp why Negroes aren't perfectly happy and grateful.

In every community there is some Negro strong man or woman whose word is going to go. In Jacksonville, Florida, for instance, there is Eartha White. You better see Eartha if you want anything from the white powers-that-be. She happens to be tremendously interested in helping the unfortunates of her city and she does get many things for them from the whites.

I have white friends with whom I would, and do, stand when they have need of me, race counting for nothing at all. Just friendship. All the well-known Negroes could honestly make the same statement. I mean that they all have strong attachments across the line whether they intended them in the beginning or not. Carl Van Vechten and Henry Allen Moe could ask little of me that would be refused. Walter White, the best known race champion of our time, is hand and glove with Supreme Court Justice Black, a native of Alabama and an ex-Klansman. So you see how this friendship business makes a sorry mess of all the rules made and provided. James Weldon Johnson, the crusader for Negro rights, was bogged to his neck in white friends whom he loved and who loved him. Dr. William E. Burkhardt DuBois, the bitterest opponent of the white race that America has ever known, loved Joel Spingarn and was certainly loved in turn by him. The thing doesn't make sense. It just makes beauty.

Friendship, however it comes about, is a beautiful thing. The Negro who loves a white friend is shy in admitting it because he dreads the epithet "white folks' nigger!" The white man is wary of showing too much warmth for his black friends for fear of being called "nigger-lover," so he explains his attachment by extolling the extraordinary merits of his black friend to gain tolerance for it.

This is the inside picture of things, as I see it. Whether you like it or not, is no concern of mine. But it is an important thing to know if you have any plans for racial manipulations in Dixie. You cannot batter in doors down there, and you can save time and trouble, and I do mean trouble, by hunting up the community keys.

In a way, it is a great and heartening tribute to human nature. It will be bound by nothing. The South frankly acknowledged them long ago in its laws against marriage between blacks and whites. If the Southern lawmakers were so sure that racial antipathy would take care of racial purity, there would have been no need for the laws.

"And no man shall seek to deprive a man of his Pet Negro. It shall be unwritten-lawful for any to seek to prevent him in his pleasure thereof. Thus spoke the Prophet of Dixie." *Selah.*

My Most Humiliating
Jim Crow Experience

MY MOST HUMILIATING Jim Crow experience came in New York instead of the South as one would have expected. It was in 1931 when Mrs. R. Osgood Mason was financing my researches in anthropology. I returned to New York from the Bahama Islands ill with some disturbances of the digestive tract.

Godmother (Mrs. Mason liked for me to call her Godmother) became concerned about my condition and suggested a certain white specialist at her expense. His office was in Brooklyn.

Mr. Paul Chapin called up and made the appointment for me. The doctor told the wealthy and prominent Paul Chapin that I would get the best of care.

So two days later I journeyed to Brooklyn to submit myself to the care of the great specialist.

His reception room was more than swanky, with a magnificent hammered copper door and other decor on the same plane as the door.

But his receptionist was obviously embarrassed when I showed up. I mentioned the appointment and got inside the door. She went into the private office and stayed a few minutes, then the doctor appeared in the door all in white, looking very important, and also very unhappy from behind his rotund stomach.

He did not approach me at all, but told one of his nurses to take me into a private examination room.

The room was private all right, but I would not rate it highly as an examination room. Under any other circumstances, I would have sworn it was a closet where the soiled towels and uniforms were tossed until called for by the laundry. But I will say this for it, there was a chair in there wedged in between the wall and the pile of soiled linen.

The nurse took me in there, closed the door quickly and disappeared. The doctor came in immediately and began in a desultory manner to ask me about symptoms. It was evident he meant to get me off the premises as quickly as possible. Being the sort of objective person I am, I did not get up and sweep out angrily as I was first disposed to do. I stayed to see just what would happen, and further to torture him more. He went through some motions, stuck a tube down my throat to extract some bile from my gall bladder, wrote a prescription and asked for twenty dollars as a fee.

I got up, set my hat at a reckless angle and walked out, telling him that I would send him a check, which I never did. I went away feeling the pathos of Anglo-Saxon civilization.

And I still mean pathos, for I know that anything with such a false foundation cannot last. Whom the gods would destroy, they first made mad.

Crazy for
This Democracy

THEY TELL ME THIS DEMOCRACY form of government is a wonderful thing. It has freedom, equality, justice, in short, everything! Since 1937 nobody has talked about anything else.

The late Franklin D. Roosevelt sort of re-decorated it, and called these United States the boastful name of "The Arsenal of Democracy."

The radio, the newspapers, and the columnists inside the newspapers, have said how lovely it was.

And this talk and praise-giving has got me in the notion to try some of the stuff. All I want to do is to get hold of a sample of the thing, and I declare, I sure will try it. I don't know for myself, but I have been told that it is really wonderful.

Like the late Will Rogers, all I know is what I see by the papers. It seems like now, I do not know geography as well as I ought to, or I would not get the wrong idea about so many things. I heard so much about "global" "world-freedom" and things like that, that I must have gotten mixed up about oceans.

I thought that when they said Atlantic Charter, that meant me and everybody in Africa and Asia and everywhere. But it seems like the Atlantic is an ocean that does not touch anywhere but North America and Europe.

Just the other day, seeing how things were going in Asia, I went out and bought myself an atlas and found out how narrow this Atlantic ocean was. No wonder that those Four Freedoms couldn't get no further than they did! Why, that poor little ocean can't even wash up some things right here in America, let alone places like India, Burma, Indo-China, and the Netherlands East Indies. We need two more whole oceans for that.

Maybe, I need to go out and buy me a dictionary, too. Or perhaps a spelling-book would help me out a lot. Or it could be that I just mistook the words. Maybe I mistook a British pronunciation for a plain American word. Did F.D.R., aristocrat from Groton and Harvard, using the British language say "arse-and-all" of Democracy when I thought he said plain arsenal? Maybe he did, and I have been mistaken all this time. From what is going on, I think that is what he must have said.

That must be what he said, for from what is happening over on that other, unmentioned ocean, we look like the Ass-and-All of Democracy. Our weapons, money, and the blood of millions of our men have been used to carry the English, French and Dutch and lead them back on the millions of unwilling Asiatics. The Ass-and-all-he-has has been very useful.

The Indo-Chinese are fighting the French now in Indo-China to keep the freedom that they have enjoyed for five or six years now. The Indonesians are trying to stay free from the Dutch, and the Burmese and Malayans from the British.

But American soldiers and sailors are fighting along with the French, Dutch and English to rivet these chains back on their former slaves. How can we so admire the fire and determination of Toussaint Louverture to resist the orders of Napoleon to "Rip the gold braids off those Haitian slaves and put them back to work" after four years of freedom, and be indifferent to these Asiatics for the same feelings under the same circumstances?

Have we not noted that not one word has been uttered about the freedom of the Africans? On the contrary, there have been mutterings in undertones about being fair and giving different nations sources of raw materials there? The Ass-and-All of Democracy has shouldered the load of subjugating the dark world completely.

The only Asiatic power able to offer any effective resistance has been double-teened by the combined powers of the Occident and rendered incapable of offering or encouraging resistance, and likewise removed as an example to the dark people of the world.

The inference is, that God has restated the superiority of the West. God always does like that when a thousand white people surround one dark one. Dark people are always "bad" when they do not admit the Divine Plan like that. A certain Javanese man who sticks up for Indonesian Independence is very lowdown by the papers, and suspected of being a Japanese puppet. Wanting the Dutch to go back to Holland and go to work for themselves! The very idea! A very, very bad man, that Javanese.

As for me, I am just as sceptical as this contrary Javanese. I accept this idea of Democracy. I am all for trying it out. It must be a good thing if everybody praises it like that. If our government has been willing to go to war and to sacrifice billions of dollars and millions of men for the idea, I think that I ought to give the thing a trial.

The only thing that keeps me from pitching headlong into the thing is the presence of numerous Jim Crow laws on the statute books of the nation. I am crazy about the idea of this Democracy. I want to see how it feels. Therefore, I am all for the repeal of every Jim Crow law in the nation here and now. Not in another generation or so. The Hurstons have already been waiting eighty years for that. I want it here and now.

And why not? A lot of people in these United States have been saying all this time that things ought to be equal. Numerous instances of inequality have been pointed out, and fought over in the courts and in the newspapers. That seems like a waste of time to me.

The patient has the small-pox. Segregation and things like that are the bumps and blisters on the skin, and not the disease, but evidence and symptoms of the sickness. The doctors around the bedside of the patient are desperately picking bumps. Some assume that the opening of one blister will cure the case. Some strangely assert that a change of climate is all that is needed to kill the virus in the blood!

But why this sentimental over-simplification in diagnosis? Do the doctors not know anything about the widespread occurrence of this disease? It is NOT peculiar to the South. Canada, once the refuge of escaping slaves, has now its denomination of second-class citizens, and they are the Japanese and other non-Caucasians. The war cannot explain it, because enemy Germans are not put in that second class.

Jim Crow is the rule in South Africa, and is even more extensive than in America. More rigid and grinding. No East Indian may ride first-class in the trains of British-held India. Jim Crow is common in all colonial Africa, Asia and the Netherlands East Indies. There, too, a Javanese male is punished for flirting back at a white female. So why this stupid assumption that "moving North" will do away with social smallpox? Events in northern cities do not bear out this juvenile contention.

So why the waste of good time and energy, and further delay the recovery of the patient by picking him over bump by bump and blister to blister? Why not the shot of serum that will kill the thing in the blood? The bumps are symptoms. The symptoms cannot disappear until the cause is cured.

These Jim Crow laws have been put on the books for a purpose, and that purpose is psychological. It has two edges to the thing. By physical evidence, back seats in trains, back-doors of houses, exclusion from certain places and activities, to promote in the mind of the smallest white child the conviction of First by Birth, eternal and irrevocable like the place assigned to the Levites by Moses over the other tribes of the Hebrews. Talent, capabilities, nothing has anything to do with the case. Just FIRST BY BIRTH.

No one of darker skin can ever be considered an equal. Seeing the daily humiliations of the darker people confirms the child in its superiority, so that it comes to feel it the arrangement of God. By the same means, the smallest dark child is to be convinced of its inferiority, so that it is to be convinced that competition is out of the question, and against all nature and God.

All physical and emotional things flow from this premise. It perpetuates itself. The unnatural exaltation of one ego, and the equally unnatural grinding down of the other. The business of some whites to help pick a bump or so is even part of the pattern. Not a human right, but a concession from the throne has been made. Otherwise why do they not take the attitude of Robert Ingersoll that all of it is wrong? Why the necessity for the little concession? Why not go for the underskin injection? Is it a bargaining with a detail to save the whole intact? It is something to think about.

As for me, I am committed to the hypodermic and the serum. I see no point in the picking of a bump. Others can erupt too easily. That same one can burst out again. Witness the easy scrapping of FEPC. No, I give my hand, my heart and my head to the total struggle. I am for complete repeal of All Jim Crow Laws in the United States once and for all, and right now. For the benefit of this nation and as a precedent to the world.

I have been made to believe in this democracy thing, and I am all for tasting this democracy out. The flavor must be good. If the Occident is so intent in keeping the taste out of darker mouths that it spends all those billions and expends all those millions of lives, colored ones too, to keep it among themselves, then it must be something good. I crave to sample this gorgeous thing. So I cannot say anything different from repeal of all Jim Crow laws! Not in some future generation, but repeal *now* and forever!!

What White Publishers Won't Print

I HAVE BEEN AMAZED by the Anglo-Saxon's lack of curiosity about the internal lives and emotions of the Negroes, and for that matter, any non-Anglo-Saxon peoples within our borders, above the class of unskilled labor.

This lack of interest is much more important than it seems at first glance. It is even more important at this time than it was in the past. The internal affairs of the nation have bearings on the international stress and strain, and this gap in the national literature now has tremendous weight in world affairs. National coherence and solidarity is implicit in a thorough understanding of the various groups within a nation, and this lack of knowledge about the internal emotions and behavior of the minorities cannot fail to bar out understanding. Man, like all the other animals fears and is repelled by that which he does not understand, and mere difference is apt to connote something malign.

The fact that there is no demand for incisive and full-dress stories around Negroes above the servant class is indicative of something of vast importance to this nation. This blank is NOT filled by the fiction built around upper-class Negroes exploiting the race problem. Rather, it tends to point it up. A college-bred Negro still is not a person like other folks, but an interesting problem, more or less. It calls to mind a story of slavery time. In this story, a master with more intellectual curiosity than usual, set out to see how much he could teach a particularly bright slave of his. When he had gotten him up to higher mathematics and to be a fluent reader of Latin, he called in a neighbor to show off his brilliant slave, and to argue that Negroes had brains just like the slave-owners had, and given the same opportunities, would turn out the same.

The visiting master of slaves looked and listened, tried to trap the literate slave in Algebra and Latin, and failing to do so in both, turned to his neighbor and said:

"Yes, he certainly knows his higher mathematics, and he can read Latin better than many white men I know, but I cannot bring myself to believe that he understands a thing that he is doing. It is all an aping of our culture. All on the outside. You are crazy if you think that it has changed him inside in the least. Turn him loose, and he will revert at once to the jungle. He is still a savage, and no amount of translating Virgil and Ovid is going to change him. In fact, all you have done is to turn a useful savage into a dangerous beast.''

That was in slavery time, yes, and we have come a long, long way since then, but the troubling thing is that there are still too many who refuse to believe in the ingestion and digestion of western culture as yet. Hence the lack of literature about the higher emotions and love life of upper-class Negroes and the minorities in general.

Publishers and producers are cool to the idea. Now, do not leap to the conclusion that editors and producers constitute a special class of un-believers. That is far from true. Publishing houses and theatrical promo-ters are in business to make money. They will sponsor anything that they believe will sell. They shy away from romantic stories about Negroes and Jews because they feel that they know the public indifference to such works, unless the story or play involves racial tension. It can then be offered as a study in Sociology, with the romantic side subdued. They know the scepticism in general about the complicated emotions in the minorities. The average American just cannot conceive of it, and would be apt to reject the notion, and publishers and producers take the stand that they are not in business to educate, but to make money. Sympathetic as they might be, they cannot afford to be crusaders.

In proof of this, you can note various publishers and producers edging forward a little, and ready to go even further when the trial balloons show that the public is ready for it. This public lack of interest is the nut of the matter.

The question naturally arises as to the why of this indifference, not to say scepticism, to the internal life of educated minorities.

The answer lies in what we may call THE AMERICAN MUSEUM OF UN-NATURAL HISTORY. This is an intangible built on folk belief. It is assumed that all non-Anglo-Saxons are uncomplicated stereotypes. Everybody knows all about them. They are lay figures mounted in the museum where all may take them in at a glance. They are made of bent wires with-out insides at all. So how could anybody write a book about the non-existent?

The American Indian is a contraption of copper wires in an eternal war-bonnet, with no equipment for laughter, expressionless face and that says ''How'' when spoken to. His only activity is treachery leading us to massacres. Who is so dumb as not to know all about Indians, even if they have never seen one, nor talked with anyone who ever knew one?

The American Negro exhibit is a group of two. Both of these mechanical toys are built so that their feet eternally shuffle, and their eyes pop and roll. Shuffling feet and those popping, rolling eyes denote the Negro and no characterization is genuine without this monotony. One is seated on a stump picking away on his banjo and singing and laughing. The other is a most amoral character before a share-cropper's shack mumbling about injustice. Doing this makes him out to be a Negro "intellectual." It is as simple as all that.

The whole museum is dedicated to the convenient "typical." In there is the "typical" Oriental, Jew, Yankee, Westerner, Southerner, Latin, and even out-of-favor Nordics like the German. The Englishman "I say old chappie," and the gesticulating Frenchman. The least observant American can know all at a glance. However, the public willingly accepts the untypical in Nordics, but feels cheated if the untypical is portrayed in others. The author of *Scarlet Sister Mary* complained to me that her neighbors objected to her book on the grounds that she had the characters thinking, "and everybody know that Nigras don't think."

But for the national welfare, it is urgent to realize that the minorities do think, and think about something other than the race problem. That they are very human and internally, according to natural endowment, are just like everybody else. So long as this is not conceived, there must remain that feeling of unsurmountable difference, and difference to the average man means something bad. If people were made right, they would be just like him.

The trouble with the purely problem arguments is that they leave too much unknown. Argue all you will or may about injustice, but as long as the majority cannot conceive of a Negro or a Jew feeling and reacting inside just as they do, the majority will keep right on believing that people who do not feel like them cannot possibly feel as they do, and conform to the established pattern. It is well known that there must be a body of waived matter, let us say, things accepted and taken for granted by all in a community before there can be that commonality of feeling. The usual phrase is having things in common. Until this is thoroughly established in respect to Negroes in America, as well as of other minorities, it will remain impossible for the majority to conceive of a Negro experiencing a deep and abiding love and not just the passion of sex. That a great mass of Negroes can be stirred by the pageants of Spring and Fall; the extravaganza of summer, and the majesty of winter. That they can and do experience discovery of the numerous subtle faces as a foundation for a great and selfless love, and the diverse nuances that go to destroy that love as with others. As it is now, this capacity, this evidence of high and complicated emotions, is ruled out. Hence the lack of interest in a romance uncomplicated by the race struggle has so little appeal.

This insistence on defeat in a story where upperclass Negroes are portrayed, perhaps says something from the subconscious of the majority. Involved in western culture, the hero or the heroine, or both, must appear frustrated and go down to defeat, somehow. Our literature reeks with it. Is it the same as saying, "You can translate Virgil, and fumble with the differential calculus, but can you really comprehend it? Can you cope with our subtleties?"

That brings us to the folklore of "reversion to type." This curious doctrine has such wide acceptance that it is tragic. One has only to examine the huge literature on it to be convinced. No matter how high we may *seem* to climb, put us under strain and we revert to type, that is, to the bush. Under a superficial layer of western culture, the jungle drums throb in our veins.

This ridiculous notion makes it possible for that majority who accept it to conceive of even a man like the suave and scholarly Dr. Charles S. Johnson to hide a black cat's bone on his person, and indulge in a midnight voodoo ceremony, complete with leopard skin and drums if threatened with the loss of the presidency of Fisk University, or the love of his wife. "Under the skin . . . better to deal with them in business, etc., but otherwise keep them at a safe distance and under control. I tell you, Carl Van Vechten, think as you like, but they are just not like us."

The extent and extravagance of this notion reaches the ultimate in nonsense in the widespread belief that the Chinese have bizarre genitals, because of that eye-fold that makes their eyes seem to slant. In spite of the fact that no biology has ever mentioned any such difference in reproductive organs makes no matter. Millions of people believe it. "Did you know that a Chinese has . . ." Consequently, their quiet contemplative manner is interpreted as a sign of slyness and a treacherous inclination.

But the opening wedge for better understanding has been thrust into the crack. Though many Negroes denounced Carl Van Vechten's *Nigger Heaven* because of the title, and without ever reading it, the book, written in the deepest sincerity, revealed Negroes of wealth and culture to the white public. It created curiosity even when it aroused scepticism. It made folks want to know. Worth Tuttle Hedden's *The Other Room* has definitely widened the opening. Neither of these well-written works take a romance of upper-class Negro life as the central theme, but the atmosphere and the background is there. These works should be followed up by some incisive and intimate stories from the inside.

The realistic story around a Negro insurance official, dentist, general practitioner, undertaker and the like would be most revealing. Thinly disguised fiction around the well known Negro names is not the answer, either. The "exceptional" as well as the Ol' Man Rivers has been exploited all out of context already. Everybody is already resigned to the "exceptional" Negro, and willing to be entertained by the "quaint." To grasp the penetration of western civilization in a minority, it is necessary to know how the average behaves and lives. Books that deal with people like in Sinclair Lewis' *Main Street* is the necessary metier. For various reasons, the average, struggling, non-morbid Negro is the best-kept secret in America. His revelation to the public is the thing needed to do away with that feeling of difference which inspires fear and which ever expresses itself in dislike.

It is inevitable that this knowledge will destroy many illusions and romantic traditions which America probably likes to have around. But then, we have no record of anybody sinking into a lingering death on finding out that there was no Santa Claus. The old world will take it in its stride. The realization that Negroes are no better nor no worse, and at times just as boring as everybody else, will hardly kill off the population of the nation.

Outside of racial attitudes, there is still another reason why this literature should exist. Literature and other arts are supposed to hold up the mirror to nature. With only the fractional "exceptional" and the "quaint" portrayed, a true picture of Negro life in America cannot be. A great principle of national art has been violated.

These are the things that publishers and producers, as the accredited representatives of the American people, have not as yet taken into consideration sufficiently. Let there be light!

THREE
Fiction

"The Eatonville Anthology," published in 1926 and apparently the written version of stories Hurston told to entertain at parties during the Harlem Renaissance, proves how much *Their Eyes Were Watching God*, Hurston's masterpiece, was influenced by the ambience and the actual people and experiences of Eatonville.

It is something of a shock to read:

> Mrs. Clarke is Joe Clarke's wife....
> She waits on the store sometimes and
> cries every time he yells at her....
> They say he used to beat her in the
> store when he was a young man....
> She shouts in church every Sunday....

and to realize this was published over ten years before the novel. It is a revelation to see how Hurston changed "Mrs. Clarke's" ending. Instead of finding comfort in religion—a conventional choice for unhappily married women—in *Their Eyes Were Watching God*, Janie Crawford Starks's taste runs to baseball, checkers, and the love of a younger man who knows how to love and enjoy life.

The selections from *Jonah's Gourd Vine* (1934), Hurston's first novel, reveal themes that remained in her fiction and her life: the use of "supernatural" power—hoo-doo—to aid or kill; the inequality between men and women in traditional marriage; and the impact of death on individual members of a community and on the community itself.

"Sweat," a short story Hurston published in 1926, is about a marriage that is torn apart by economic inequality between the partners. Whites are a peripheral force, but even their absence is felt, as it is in "The Gilded Six-Bits."

"The Gilded Six-Bits" (1933) gives us a woman so convinced that her entire being is defined through her role of wife, that she says, "If you was to burn me you wouldn't get nothing but wife ashes." Being a wife means what it has traditionally meant: washing the clothes, cooking the food, providing sex, having children (preferably boys), and loving it. Precisely the kind of existence one can not imagine Zora Neale Hurston choosing for herself. Missy May is, even so, not completely different from Janie Crawford, Hurston's liberated heroine in *Their Eyes Were Watching God*: what ties her to conventional duties is not coercion but love. Of course, should the love ever cease, Missy May will find herself in the same miserable prison other women, unloved and unloving, have found in conventional marriage. Proving once again that stereotypes—to work harmlessly—require, at the least, perpetual good will.

It is in ''The Gilded Six-Bits'' that Hurston was able to make a literary statement about the use of stereotypes by whites to denigrate blacks; people quite different in themselves and to themselves from what white people apparently saw.

Moses, Man of the Mountain (1939) is one of the rarest, most important books in black literature and should be required reading for all black children. It successfully blends the Biblical story of Moses's struggle to lead the Hebrews out of Egypt and the twentieth-century black personality—post-slavery but pre-liberation—obsessed with the same kind of monumental endeavor. It presents Moses as a harrassed, Afro-Egyptian naturalist, revolutionary, and master of hoo-doo, who sounds at times like Martin Luther King (speaking off the record), Malcolm X, and Fannie Lou Hamer. The language is early twentieth-century rural black, for the most part (a veritable thicket of similes, proverbs, and metaphors), and is a brilliant elaboration of the traditional Sunday morning sermon on Moses that all black people born before 1965 have heard at least once. In the selection from *Moses, Man of the Mountain* that follows, we see how Hurston ''invents'' a legend to demonstrate how the traditional legend of Moses might have been created.

In a sense, everything Zora Neale Hurston wrote came out of her experience of Eatonville, a town she left for good—except for visits and research—when she was a teenager. And everything she experienced in Eatonville she eventually put into her books. Indeed, one gets the feeling that she tried over and over again with the same material until she felt she had gotten it right. She got it perfectly right in *Their Eyes Were Watching God*, in 1937. The novelist, the folklorist, and the teenager combine to present the indelible story of one woman, Janie Crawford Killicks Starks Woods, seeking freedom to be herself—heroic, beautiful, full of feeling and needful of love, in the prime of life.

The Eatonville Anthology

I. The Pleading Woman

MRS. TONY ROBERTS is the pleading woman. She just loves to ask for things. Her husband gives her all he can rake and scrape, which is considerably more than most wives get for their housekeeping, but she goes from door to door begging for things.

She starts at the store. "Mist' Clarke," she sing-songs in a high keening voice, "gimme lil' piece uh meat tuh boil a pot uh greens wid. Lawd knows me an' mah chillen is SO hongry! Hits uh SHAME! Tony don't fee-ee-eee-ed me!"

Mr. Clarke knows that she has money and that her larder is well stocked, for Tony Roberts is the best provider on his list. But her keening annoys him and he rises heavily. The pleader at his elbow shows all the joy of a starving man being seated at a feast.

"Thass right Mist' Clarke. De Lawd loveth de cheerful giver. Gimme jes' a lil' piece 'bout dis big (indicating the width of her hand) an' de Lawd'll bless yuh."

She follows this angel-on-earth to his meat tub and superintends the cutting, crying out in pain when he refuses to move the knife over just a teeny bit mo'.

Finally, meat in hand, she departs, remarking on the meanness of some people who give a piece of salt meat only two-fingers wide when they were plainly asked for a hand-wide piece. Clarke puts it down to Tony's account and resumes his reading.

With the slab of salt pork as a foundation, she visits various homes until she has collected all she wants for the day. At the Piersons, for instance: "Sister Pierson, plee-ee-ease gimme uh han'ful uh collard greens fuh me an' mah po' chillen! 'Deed, me an' mah chillen is SO hongry. Tony doan' fee-ee-eed me!"

Mrs. Pierson picks a bunch of greens for her, but she springs away from them as if they were poison. "Lawd a mussy, Mis' Pierson, you ain't gonna gimme dat lil' eye-full uh greens fuh me an' mah chillen, is you? Don't be so graspin'; Gawd won't bless yuh. Gimme uh han'full mo'. Lawd, some folks is got everything, an' theys jes' as gripin' an stingy!"

Mrs. Pierson raises the ante, and the pleading woman moves on to the next place, and on and on. The next day, it commences all over.

II. Turpentine Love

JIM MERCHANT is always in good humor—even with his wife. He says he fell in love with her at first sight. That was some years ago. She has had all her teeth pulled out, but they still get along splendidly.

He says the first time he called on her he found out that she was subject to fits. This didn't cool his love, however. She had several in his presence.

One Sunday, while he was there, she had one, and her mother tried to give her a dose of turpentine to stop it. Accidentally, she spilled it in her eye and it cured her. She never had another fit, so they got married and have kept each other in good humor ever since.

III.

BECKY MOORE has eleven children of assorted colors and sizes. She has never been married, but that is not her fault. She has never stopped any of the fathers of her children from proposing, so if she has no father for her children it's not her fault. The men round about are entirely to blame.

The other mothers of the town are afraid that it is catching. They won't let their children play with hers.

IV. Tippy

SYKES JONES' FAMILY all shoot craps. The most interesting member of the family—also fond of bones, but of another kind—is Tippy, the Jones' dog.

He is so thin, that it amazes one that he lives at all. He sneaks into village kitchens if the housewives are careless about the doors and steals meats, even off the stoves. He also sucks eggs.

For these offenses he has been sentenced to death dozens of times, and the sentences executed upon him, only they didn't work. He has been fed bluestone, strychnine, nux vomica, even an entire Peruna bottle beaten up. It didn't fatten him, but it didn't kill him. So Eatonville has resigned itself to the plague of Tippy, reflecting that is has erred in certain matters and is being chastened.

In spite of all the attempts upon his life, Tippy is still willing to be friendly with anyone who will let him.

V. The Way of a Man with a Train

OLD MAN ANDERSON lived seven or eight miles out in the country from Eatonville. Over by Lake Apopka. He raised feed-corn and cassava and went to market with it two or three times a year. He bought all of his victuals wholesale so he wouldn't have to come to town for several months more.

He was different from citybred folks. He had never seen a train. Everybody laughed at him for even the smallest child in Eatonville had either been to Maitland or Orlando and watched a train go by. On Sunday afternoons all of the young people of the village would go over to Maitland, a mile away, to see Number 35 whizz southward on its way to Tampa and wave at the passengers. So we looked down on him a little. Even we children felt superior in the presence of a person so lacking in wordly knowledge.

The grown-ups kept telling him he ought to go see a train. He always said he didn't have time to wait so long. Only two trains a day passed through Maitland. But patronage and ridicule finally had its effect and Old Man Anderson drove in one morning early. Number 78 went north to Jacksonville at 10:20. He drove his light wagon over in the woods beside the railroad below Maitland, and sat down to wait. He began to fear that his horse would get frightened and run away with the wagon. So he took him out and led him deeper into the grove and tied him securely. Then he returned to his wagon and waited some more. Then he remembered that some of the train-wise villagers had said the engine belched fire and smoke. He had better move his wagon out of danger. It might catch fire. He climbed down from the seat and placed himself between the shafts to draw it away. Just then 78 came thundering over the trestle spouting smoke, and suddenly began blowing for Maitland. Old Man Anderson became so frightened he ran away with the wagon through the woods and tore it up worse than the horse ever could have done. He doesn't know yet what a train looks like, and says he doesn't care.

VI. Coon Taylor

COON TAYLOR never did any real stealing. Of course, if he saw a chicken or a watermelon he'd take it. The people used to get mad but they never could catch him. He took so many melons from Joe Clarke that he set up in the melon patch one night with his shotgun loaded with rock salt. He was going to fix Coon. But he was tired. It is hard work being a mayor, postmaster, storekeeper and everything. He dropped asleep sitting on a stump in the middle of the patch. So he didn't see Coon when he came. Coon didn't see him either, that is, not at first. He knew the stump was there, however. He had opened many of Clarke's juicy Florida Favorite on it. He selected his fruit, walked over to the stump and burst the melon on it. That is, he thought is was the stump until it fell over with a yell. Then he knew it was no stump and departed hastily from those parts. He had cleared the fence when Clarke came to, as it were. So the charge of rock-salt was wasted on the desert air.

During the sugar-cane season, he found he couldn't resist Clarke's soft green cane, but Clarke did not go to sleep this time. So after he had cut six of eight stalks by the moonlight, Clarke rose up out of the cane strippings with his shotgun and made Coon sit right down and chew up the last one of them on the spot. And the next day he made Coon leave his town for three months.

VII. Village Fiction

JOE LINDSAY is said by Lum Boger to be the largest manufacturer of prevarications in Eatonville; Brazzle (late owner of the world's leanest and meanest mule) contends that his business is the largest in the state and his wife holds that he is the biggest liar in the world.

Exhibit A—He claims that while he was in Orlando one day he saw a doctor cut open a woman, remove everything—liver, lights and heart included—clean each of them separately; the doctor then washed out the empty woman, dried her out neatly with a towel and replaced the organs so expertly that she was up and about her work in a couple of weeks.

VIII.

SEWELL is a man who lives all to himself. He moves a great deal. So often, that 'Lige Moseley says his chickens are so used to moving that every time he comes out into his backyard the chickens lie down and cross their legs, ready to be tied up again.

He is baldheaded; but he says he doesn't mind that, because he wants as little as possible between him and God.

IX.

MRS. CLARKE is Joe Clarke's wife. She is a soft-looking, middle-aged woman, whose bust and stomach are always holding a get-together.

She waits on the store sometimes and cries every time he yells at her which he does every time she makes a mistake, which is quite often. She calls her husband "Jody." They say he used to beat her in the store when he was a young man, but he is not so impatient now. He can wait until he goes home.

She shouts in Church every Sunday and shakes the hand of fellowship with everybody in the Church with her eyes closed, but somehow always misses her husband.

X.

MRS. MCDUFFY goes to Church every Sunday and always shouts and tells her "determination." Her husband always sits in the back row and beats her as soon as they get home. He says there's no sense in her shouting, as big a devil as she is. She just does it to slur him. Elijah Moseley asked her why she didn't stop shouting, seeing she always got a beating about it. She says she can't "squinch the sperrit." Then Elijah asked Mr. McDuffy to stop beating her, seeing that she was going to shout anyway. he answered that she just did it for spite and that his fist was just as hard as her head. He could last just as long as she. So the village let the matter rest.

XI. Double-Shuffle

BACK IN THE GOOD OLD DAYS before the World War, things were very simple in Eatonville. People didn't fox-trot. When the town wanted to put on its Sunday clothes and wash behind the ears, it put on a "breakdown." The daring younger set would two-step and waltz, but the good church members and the elders stuck to the grand march. By rural canons dancing is wicked, but one is not held to have danced until the feet have been crossed. Feet don't get crossed when one grand marches.

At elaborate affairs the organ from the Methodist church was moved up to the hall and Lizzimore, the blind man presided. When informal gatherings were held, he merely played his guitar assisted by any volunteer with mouth organs or accordions.

Among white people the march is as mild as if it had been passed on by Volstead. But it still has a kick in Eatonville. Everybody happy, shining eyes, gleaming teeth. Feet dragged 'shhlap, shhlap! to beat out the time. No orchestra needed. Round and round! Back again, parse-me-la! shlap! shlap! Strut! Strut! Seaboard! Shlap! Shlap! Tiddy bumm! Mr. Clarke in the lead with Mrs. Moseley.

It's too much for some of the young folks. Double shuffling commences. Buck and wing. Lizzimore about to break his guitar. Accordion doing contortions. People fall back against the walls, and let the soloist have it, shouting as they clap the old, old double shuffle songs.

'Me an' mah honey got two mo' days
Two mo' days tuh do de buck'

Sweating bodies, laughing mouths, grotesque faces, feet drumming fiercely. Deacons clapping as hard as the rest.

"Great big nigger, black as tar
Trying tuh git tuh hebben on uh 'lectric car."

"Some love cabbage, some love kale
But I love a gal wid a short skirt tail."

Long tall angel—steppin' down,
Long white robe an' starry crown.

'Ah would not marry uh black gal (bumm bumm!)
Tell yuh de reason why
Every time she comb her hair
She make de goo-goo eye.

Would not marry a yaller gal (bumm bumm!)
Tell yuh de reason why
Her neck so long an' stringy
Ahm 'fraid she'd never die.

Would not marry uh preacher
Tell yuh de reason why
Every time he comes tuh town
He makes de chicken fly.

When the buck dance was over, the boys would give the floor to the
girls and they would parse-me-la with a slye eye out of the corner to see if
anybody was looking who might "have them up in church" on
conference night. Then there would be more dancing. Then Mr. Clarke
would call for everybody's best attention and announce that *'freshments
was served! Every gent'man would please take his lady by the arm and
scorch her right up to de table fur a treat!*

Then the men would stick their arms out with a flourish and ask their
ladies: "You lak chicken? Well, then, take a wing." And the ladies
would take the proffered "wings" and parade up to the long table and
be served. Of course most of them had brought baskets in which were
heaps of jointed and fried chicken, two or three kinds of pies, cakes,
potato pone and chicken purlo. The hall would separate into happy
groups about the baskets until time for more dancing.

But the boys and girls got scattered about during the war, and now
they dance the fox-trot by a brand new piano. They do waltz and two-
step still, but no one now considers it good form to lock his chin over his
partner's shoulder and stick out behind. One night just for fun and to

humor the old folks, they danced, that is, they grand marched, but everyone picked up their feet. *Bah!!*

XII. The Head of the Nail

DAISY TAYLOR was the town vamp. Not that she was pretty. But sirens were all but non-existent in the town. Perhaps she was forced to it by circumstances. She was quite dark, with little bushy patches of hair squatting over her head. These were held down by shingle-nails often. No one knows whether she did this for artistic effect or for lack of hair-pins, but there they were shining in the little patches of hair when she got all dressed for the afternoon and came up to Clarke's store to see if there was any mail for her.

It was seldom that anyone wrote to Daisy, but she knew that the men of the town would be assembled there by five o'clock, and some one could usually be induced to buy her some soda water or peanuts.

Dasy flirted with married men. There were only two single men in town. Lum Boger, who was engaged to the assistant school-teacher, and Hiram Lester, who had been off to school at Tuskegee and wouldn't look at a person like Daisy. In addition to other drawbacks, she was pigeon-toed and her petticoat was always showing so perhaps he was justified. There was nothing else to do except flirt with married men.

This went on for a long time. First one wife and then another complained of her, or drove her from the preserves by threat.

But the affair with Crooms was the most prolonged and serious. He was even known to have bought her a pair of shoes.

Mrs. Laura Crooms was a meek little woman who took all of her troubles crying, and talked a great deal of leaving things in the hands of God.

The affair came to a head one night in orange picking time. Crooms was over at Oneido picking oranges. Many fruit pickers move from one town to the other during the season.

The *town* was collected at the store-postoffice as is customary on Saturday nights. The *town* has had its bath and with its week's pay in pocket fares forth to be merry. The men tell stories and treat the ladies to soda-water, peanuts and peppermint candy.

Daisy was trying to get treats, but the porch was cold to her that night.

"Ah don't keer if you don't treat me. What's a dirty lil nickel?" She flung this at Walter Thomas. "The everloving Mister Crooms will gimme anything atall Ah wants."

"You better shet up yo' mouf talking 'bout Albert Crooms. Heah his wife comes right now."

Daisy went akimbo. "Who? Me! Ah don't keer whut Laura Crooms think. If she ain't a heavy hip-ted Mama enough to keep him, she don't need to come crying to me."

She stood making goo-goo eyes as Mrs. Crooms walked upon the porch. Daisy laughed loud, made several references to Albert Crooms, and when she saw the mail-bag come in from Maitland she said, "Ah better go in an' see if Ah ain't got a letter from Oneido."

The more Daisy played the game of getting Mrs. Crooms' goat, the better she liked it. She ran in and out of the store laughing until she could scarcely stand. Some of the people present began to talk to Mrs. Crooms—to egg her on to halt Daisy's boasting, but she was for leaving it all in the hands of God. Walter Thomas kept on after Mrs. Crooms until she stiffened and resolved to fight. Daisy was inside when she came to this resolve and never dreamed anything of the kind could happen. She had gotten hold of an envelope and came laughing and shouting, "Oh, Ah can't stand to see Oneido lose!"

There was a box of ax-handles on display on the porch, propped up against the door jamb. As Daisy stepped upon the porch, Mrs. Crooms leaned the heavy end of one of those handles heavily upon her head. She staggered from the porch to the ground and the timid Laura, fearful of a counter-attack, struck again and Daisy toppled into the town ditch. There was not enough water in there to do more than muss her up. Every time she tried to rise, down would come that ax-handle again. Laura was fighting a scared fight. With Daisy thoroughly licked, she retired to the store porch and left her fallen enemy in the ditch. But Elijah Moseley, who was some distance down the street when the trouble began arrived as the victor was withdrawing. He rushed up and picked Daisy out of the mud and began feeling her head.

"Is she hurt much?" Joe Clarke asked from the doorway.

"I don't know," Elijah answered, "I was just looking to see if Laura had been lucky enough to hit one of those nails on the head and drive it in."

Before a week was up, Daisy moved to Orlando. There in a wider sphere, perhaps, her talents as a vamp were appreciated.

XIII. Pants and Cal'line

SISTER CAL'LINE POTTS was a silent woman. Did all of her laughing down inside, but did the thing that kept the town in an uproar of laughter. It was the general opinion of the village that Cal'line would do anything she had a mind to. And she had a mind to do several things.

Mitchell Potts, her husband, had a weakness for women. No one ever believed that she was jealous. She did things to the women, surely. But most any townsman would have said that she did them because she liked the novel situation and the queer things she could bring out of it.

Once he took up with Delphine—called Mis' Pheeny by the town. She lived on the outskirts on the edge of the piney woods. The town winked and talked. People don't make secrets of such things in villages. Cal'line went about her business with her thin black lips pursed tight as ever, and her shiny black eyes unchanged.

"Dat devil of a Cal'line's got somethin' up her sleeve!" The town smiled in anticipation.

"Delphine is too big a cigar for her to smoke. She ain't crazy," said some as the weeks went on and nothing happened. Even Pheeny herself would give an extra flirt to her over-starched petticoats as she rustled into church past her of Sundays.

Mitch Potts said furthermore, that he was tired of Cal'line's foolishness. She had to stay where he put her. His African soup-bone (arm) was too strong to let a woman run over him. 'Nough was 'nough. And he did some fancy cussing, and he was the fanciest cusser in the county.

So the town waited and the longer it waited, the odds changed slowly from the wife to the husband.

One Saturday, Mitch knocked off work at two o'clock and went over to Maitland. He came back with a rectangular box under his arm and kept straight on out to the barn to put it away. He ducked around the corner of the house quickly, but even so, his wife glimpsed the package. Very much like a shoe-box. So!

He put on the kettle and took a bath. She stood in her bare feet at the ironing boad and kept on ironing. He dressed. It was about five o'clock but still very light. He fiddled around outside. She kept on with her ironing. As soon as the sun got red, he sauntered out to the barn, got the parcel and walked away down the road, past the store and out into the piney woods. As soon as he left the house, Cal'line slipped on her shoes without taking time to don stockings, put on one of her husband's old Stetsons, worn and floppy, slung the axe over her shoulder and followed in his wake. He was hailed cheerily as he passed the sitters on the store porch and answered smiling sheepishly and passed on. Two minutes later passed his wife, silently, unsmilingly, and set the porch to giggling and betting.

An hour passed perhaps. It was dark. Clarke had long ago lighted the swinging kerosene lamp inside.

XIV.

ONCE 'WAY BACK YONDER before the stars fell all the animals used to talk just like people. In them days dogs and rabbits was the best of friends—even tho both of them was stuck on the same gal—which was Miss Nancy Coon. She had the sweetest smile and the prettiest striped and bushy tail to be found anywhere.

They both run their legs nigh off trying to win her for themselves—fetching nice ripe persimmons and such. But she never give one or the other no satisfaction.

Finally one night Mr. Dog popped the question right out. "Miss Coon," he says, "Ma'am, also Ma'am which would you ruther be—a lark flyin' or a dove a settin'?"

Course Miss Nancy she blushed and laughed a little and hid her face behind her bushy tail for a spell. The she said sorter shy like, "I does love yo' sweet voice, brother dawg—but—I ain't jes' exactly set my mind yit."

Her and Mr. Dog set on a spell, when up comes hopping Mr. Rabbit wid his tail fresh washed and his whiskers shining. He got right down to business and asked Miss Coon to marry him, too.

"Oh, Miss Nancy," he says, "Ma'am, also Ma'am, if you'd see me settin' straddle of a mud-cat leadin' a minnow, what would you think? Ma'am also Ma'am?" Which is a out and out proposal as everybody knows.

"Youse awful nice, Brother Rabbit and a beautiful dancer, but you cannot sing like Brother Dog. Both you uns come back next week to gimme time for to decide."

They both left arm-in-arm. Finally Mr. Rabbit says to Mr. Dog. "Taint no use in me going back—she ain't gwinter have me. So I mought as well give up. She loves singing, and I ain't got nothing but a squeak.''

"Oh, don't talk that a way," says Mr. Dog, tho' he is glad Mr. Rabbit can't sing none.

"Thass all right, Brer Dog. But if I had a sweet voice like you got, I'd have it worked on and make it sweeter.''

"How! How! How!'' Mr. Dog cried, jumping up and down.

"Lemme fix it for you, like I do for Sister Lark and Sister Mockingbird.''

"When? Where?'' asked Mr. Dog, all excited. He was figuring that if he could sing just a little better Miss Coon would be bound to have him.

"Just you meet me t'morrer in de huckleberry patch," says the rabbit and off they both goes to bed.

The dog is there on time next day and after a while the rabbit comes loping up.

"Mawnin', Brer Dawg," he says kinder chippy like. "Ready to git yo' voice sweetened?''

"Sholy, sholy, Brer Rabbit. Let's we all hurry about it. I wants tuh serenade Miss Nancy from the piney woods tuh night.''

"Well, den, open yo' mouf and poke out yo' tongue," says the rabbit.

No sooner did Mr. Dog poke out his tongue than Mr. Rabbit split it with a knife and ran for all he was worth to a hollow stump and hid hisself.

The dog has been mad at the rabbit ever since.

Anybody who don't believe it happened, just look at the dog's tongue and he can see for himself where the rabbit slit it right up the middle.

Stepped on a tin, mah story ends.

FROM
Jonah's Gourd Vine

AN' DANGIE DEWOE'S HUT squatted low and peered at the road from behind a mass of Palma Christi and elderberry. The little rag-stuffed windows hindered the light and the walls were blackened with ancient smoke.

She had thrown several stalks of dried rabbit tobacco on the fire for power and sat with her wrinkled old face pursed up like a black fist, watching the flames.

Three quick sharp raps on the door.

"Who come?"

"One."

"Come on in, Hattie." As the woman entered An' Dangie threw some salt into the flame without so much as a look at her visitor. "Knowed you'd be back. Set down."

Hattie sat a moment impatiently, then she looked anxiously at An' Dangie and said, "He ain't been."

"He will. Sich things ez dat takes time. Did yuh feed 'im lak Ah tole yuh?"

"Ain't laid eyes on 'im in seben weeks. How Ahm goin' do it?"

"Hm-m-m." She struggled her fatness up from the chair and limped over to an old tin safe in the corner. She fumbled with the screw top of a fruit jar and returned with a light handful of wish-beans. "Stan' over de gate whar he sleeps and eat dese beans and drop de hulls 'round yo' feet. Ah'll do de rest."

"Lawd, An' Dangie, dere' uh yard full uh houn' dawgs and chillun. Eben if none uh dem chillun see me, de dawgs gwine bark. Ah wuz past dere one day 'thout stoppin'."

"G'wan do lak Ah tell yuh. Ahm gwine hold de bitter bone in mah mouf so's you kin walk out de sight uh men. You bound tuh come out more'n conquer. Jes' you pay me what Ah ast and 'tain't nothin' built up dat Ah can't tear down."

"Ah know you got de power."

"Humph! Ah reckon Ah is. Y' ever hear 'bout me boilin' uh wash-pot on uh sail needle?"

"Yas ma'am and mo' besides."

"Well don't come heah doubtin' lak you done jes' now. Aw right, pay me and g'wan do lak Ah tell yuh."

Hattie took the knotted handkerchief out of her stocking and paid. As she reached the door, the old woman called after her, " 'Member now, you done started dis and it's got tuh be kep' up do hit'll turn back on yuh."

"Yas'm."

The door slammed and An' Dangie crept to her altar in the back room and began to dress candles with war water. When the altar had been set, she dressed the coffin in red, lit the inverted candles on the altar, saying as she did so, "Now fight! Fight and fuss 'til you part." When all was done at the altar she rubbed her hands and forehead with war powder, put the cat-bone in her mouth, and laid herself down in the red coffin facing the altar and went into the spirit.

LUCY WAS LYING SICK. The terrible enemy had so gnawed away her lungs that her frame was hardly distinguishable from the bed things.

"Isie?"

"Yes ma'am."

"Come give mama uh dose uh medicine."

"Yes'm."

The skinny-legged child of nine came bringing a cheap glass pitcher of water. "Ah pumped it off so it would be cool and nice fuh yuh."

"Thankee, Isie. Youse mah chile 'bove all de rest. Yo' pa come yet?"

"Yes'm, he out 'round de barn somewhere."

"Tell 'im Ah say tuh step heah uh minute."

John Pearson crossed the back porch slowly and heavily and entered the bedroom with downcast eyes.

"Whut you want wid me, Lucy?"

"Here 'tis Wednesday and you jus' gittin' home from Sanford, and know Ahm at uh mah back too. You know dat Hezekiah and John is uhway in school up tuh Jacksonville, and dese other chillun got tuh make out de bes' dey kin. You ought tuh uh come on home Monday and seen after things.''

He looked sullenly at the floor and said nothing. Lucy used her spit cup and went on.

''Know too Ahm sick and you been home fuh de las' longest and ain't been near me tuh offer me uh cup uh cool water uh ast me how Ah feel.''

''Oh you sick, sick, sick! Ah hates tuh be 'round folks always complainin', and then agin you always doggin' me 'bout sumpin'. Ah gits sick and tired uh hearing it!''

''Well, John, you puts de words in mah mouf. If you'd stay home and look after yo' wife and chillun, Ah wouldn't have nothin' tuh talk uhbout.''

''Aw, yes you would! Always jawin' and complainin'.''

Lucy said, ''If you keep ole Hattie Tyson's letters out dis house where mah chillun kin git holt of 'em and you kin stop folkses mouf by comin' on home instid uh layin' 'round wid her in Oviedo.''

''Shet up! Ahm sick an' tired uh yo' yowin' and jawin'. 'Tain't nothin' Ah hate lak gittin' sin throwed in mah face dat done got cold. Ah do ez Ah please. You jus' uh hold-back tuh me nohow. Always sick and complainin'. Uh man can't utilize hisself.''

He came to the bed and stood glaring down upon her. She seemed not to notice and said calmly after a short pause, ''Ahm glad tuh know dat, John. After all dese years and all dat done went on dat Ah ain't been nothin' but uh stumblin'-stone tuh yuh. Go 'head on, Mister, but remember—youse born but you ain't dead. 'Tain't nobody so slick but whut they kin stand uh 'nother greasin'. Ah done told yuh time and time uhgin dat ignorance is de hawse dat wisdom rides. Don't git miss-put on yo' road. God don't eat okra.''

''Oh you always got uh mouf full uh opinions, but Ah don't need you no mo' nor nothin you got tuh say, Ahm uh man grown. Don't need no guardzeen atall. So shet yo' mouf wid me.''

''Ah ain't goin' tuh hush nothin' uh de kind. Youse livin' dirty and Ahm goin' tuh tell you 'bout it. Me and mah chillun got some rights. Big talk ain't changin' whut you doin'. You can't clean yo' self wid yo' tongue lak uh cat.''

There was a resounding smack. Lucy covered her face with her hand, and John drew back in a sort of horror, and instantly strove to remove the brand from his soul by words, "Ah tole yuh tuh hush." He found himself shaking as he backed towards the door.

"De hidden wedge will come tuh light some day, John. Mark mah words. Youse in de majority now, but God sho don't love ugly."

John shambled out across the back porch, and stood for an unknowing time among the palmetto bushes in a sweating daze feeling like Nebuchadnezer in his exile.

Lucy turned her face to the wall and refused her supper that her older daughter Emmeline cooked and that Isis brought to her.

"But mama, you said special you wanted some batter-cakes."

"You eat 'em, Isie. Mama don't want uh thing. Come on in when you thru wid yo' supper lak you always do and read mama something out yo' reader."

But Isis didn't read. Lucy lay so still that she was frightened. She turned down the lamp by the head of the bed and started to leave, but Lucy stopped her.

"Thought you was sleep, mama."

"Naw, Isie, been watchin' dat great big ole spider."

"Where?"

"Up dere on de wall next tuh de ceilin'. Look lak he done took up uh stand."

"Want me tuh kill 'im wid de broom?"

"Nah, Isie, let 'im be. You didn't put 'im dere. De one dat put 'im dere will move 'im in his own time."

Isis could hear the other children playing in the back room.

"Reckon you wanta go play wid de rest, Isie, but mama wants tuh tell yuh somethin'."

"Whut is it, mama?"

"Isie, Ah ain't goin' tuh be wid yuh much longer, and when Ahm dead Ah wants you tuh have dis bed. Iss mine. Ah sewed fuh uh white woman over in Maitland and she gimme dis bedstead fuh mah work. Ah wants you tuh have it. Dis mah feather tick on here too."

"Yes'm mama, Ah—"

"Stop cryin', Isie, you can't hear whut Ahm sayin', 'member tuh git all de education you kin. Dat's de onliest way you kin keep out from under people's feet. You always strain tuh be de bell cow, never be de tail uh nothin'. Do de best you kin, honey, 'cause neither yo' paw nor dese older chillun is goin' tuh be bothered too much wid yuh, but you goin'

tuh git 'long. Mark mah words. You got de spunk, but mah po' li'l'
sandy-haired chile goin' suffer uh lot 'fo' she git tuh de place she kin
'fend fuh herself. And Isie, honey, stop cryin' and lissen tuh me. Don't
you love nobody better'n you do yo'self. Do, you'll be dying befo' yo'
time is out. And, Isie, uh person kin be killed 'thout being stuck uh
blow. Some uh dese things Ahm tellin' yuh, you wont understand 'em
fuh years tuh come, but de time will come when you'll know. And Isie,
when Ahm dyin' don't you let 'em take de pillow from under mah head,
and be covering up de clock and de lookin' glass and all sich ez dat. Ah
don't want it done, heah? Ahm tellin' you in preference tuh de rest
'cause Ah know you'll see tuh it. Go wash yuh face and turn tuh de
Twenty-Sixth Chapter of de Acts fuh me. Den you go git yo' night rest. If
Ah want yuh, Ah'll call yuh.''

Way in the night Lucy heard John stealthily enter the room and
stand with the lamp in his hand peering down into her face. When she
opened her eyes she saw him start.

''Oh,'' he exclaimed sharply with rising inflection. Lucy searched his
face with her eyes but said nothing.

''Er, er, Ah jus' thought Ah'd come see if you wanted anything,''
John said nervously, ''if you want anything, Lucy, all you got tuh do is
tuh ast me. De favor is in me.''

Lucy looked at her husband in a way that stepped across the ordinary
boundaries of life and said, ''Jus' have patience, John, uh few mo'
days,'' and pulled down her lids over her eyes, and John was glad of that.

John rushed from Lucy's bedside to the road and strode up and down
in the white moonlight. Finally he took his stand beneath the umbrella
tree before the house and watched the dim light in Lucy's room. Nothing
came to him there and he awoke Emmeline at daybreak, ''Go in yo' ma's
room Daught' and come back and tell me how she makin' it.''

''She say she ain't no better,'' Daught' told him.

The spider was lower on the wall and Lucy entertained herself by
watching to see if she could detect it move.

She sent Isis to bed early that Thursday night but she herself lay
awake regarding the spider. She thought that she had not slept a
moment, but when in the morning Isis brought the wash basin and tooth
brush, Lucy noted that the spider was lower and she had not seen it move.

That afternoon Mrs. Mattie Clarke sat with her and sent Isis out to
play.

"Lucy, how is it 'tween you and God?"

"You know Ah ain't never been one to whoop and holler in church, Sister Clarke, but Ah done put on de whole armor uh faith. Ah ain't afraid tuh die."

"Ahm sho glad tuh hear dat, Sister Pearson. Yuh know uh person kin live uh clean life and den dey kin be so fretted on dey dyin' bed 'til dey lose holt of de kingdom."

"Don't worry 'bout me, Sister Clarke. Ah done been in sorrow's kitchen and Ah done licked out all de pots. Ah done died in grief and been buried in de bitter waters, and Ah done rose agin from de dead lak Lazarus. Nothin' kin touch mah soul no mo'. It wuz hard tuh loose de string-holt on mah li'l' chillun." Her voice sank to a whisper, "but Ah reckon Ah done dat too."

"Put whip tuh yo' hawses, honey. Whip 'em up."

Despite Lucy's all-night vigil she never saw the spider when he moved, but at first light she noted that he was at least a foot from the ceiling but as motionless as a painted spider in a picture.

The evening train brought her second son, John, from Jacksonville. Lucy brightened.

"Where's Hezekiah?" she asked eagerly.

"He's comin'. His girl is gointer sing uh solo at de church on Sunday and he wants to hear her. Then he's coming right on. He told me to wire him how you were."

"Don't do it, John. Let 'im enjoy de singin'."

John told her a great deal about the school and the city and she listened brightly but said little.

After that look in the late watches of the night John was afraid to be alone with Lucy. His fear of her kept him from his bed at night. He was afraid lest she should die while he was asleep and he should awake to find her spirit standing over him. He was equally afraid of her reproaches should she live, and he was troubled. More troubled than he had ever been in all his life. In all his struggles of sleep, the large bright eyes looked thru and beyond him and saw too much. He wished those eyes would close and was afraid again because of his wish.

Lucy watched the spider each day as it stood lower. And late Sunday night she cried out, "O Evening Sun, when you git on de o'her side, tell mah Lawd Ahm here waitin'."

And God awoke at last and nodded His head.

In the morning she told Emmeline to fry chicken for dinner. She sent Isis out to play. "You been denyin' yo' pleasure fuh me. G'wan out and play wid de rest. Ah'll call yuh if Ah want yuh. Tell everybody tuh leave me alone. Ah don't want no bother. Shet de door tight."

She never did call Isis. Late in the afternoon she saw people going and coming, coming and going. She was playing ball before the house, but she became alarmed and went in.

The afternoon was bright and a clear light streamed into the room from the bare windows. They had turned Lucy's bed so that her face was to the East. The way from which the sun comes walking in red and white. Great drops of sweat stood out on her forehead and trickled upon the quilt and Isis saw a pool of sweat standing in a hollow at the elbow. She was breathing hard, and Isis saw her set eyes fasten on her as she came into the room. She thought that she tried to say something to her as she stood over her mother's head, weeping with her heart.

"Get her head offa dat pillow!" Mattie Mosely ordered. "Let her head down so she kin die easy."

Hoyt Thomas moved to do it, but Isis objected. "No, no, don't touch her pillow! Mama don't want de pillow from under her head!"

"Hush Isie!" Emmeline chided, "and let mama die easy. You makin' her suffer."

"Naw, naw! she said *not* tuh!" As her father pulled her away from her place above Lucy's head, Isis thought her mother's eyes followed her and she strained her ears to catch her words. But none came.

John stood where he could see his wife's face, but where Lucy's fixed eyes might not rest upon him. They drew the pillow from beneath Lucy's head and she gulped hard once, and was dead. "6:40" someone said looking at a watch.

"Po' thing," John wept. "She don't have tuh hear no mo' hurtin' things." He hurried out to the wood pile and sat there between two feelings until Sam Mosely led him away.

"She's gone!" rang out thru the crowded room and they heard it on the porch and Mattie Mosely ran shouting down the street, "She's gone, she's gone at last!"

And the work of the shrouding began. Little Lucy, somewhat smaller in death than she had been even in life, lay washed and dressed in white beneath a sheet upon the cooling board when her oldest son arrived that evening to break his heart in grief.

That night a wind arose about the house and blew from the kitchen wall to the clump of oleanders that screened the chicken house, from the oleanders to the fence palings and back again to the house wall, and the pack of dogs followed it, rearing against the wall, leaping and pawing the fence, howling, barking and whining until the break of day, and John huddled beneath his bed-covers shaking and afraid.

THEY PUT LUCY In a little coffin next day, the shiny coffin that held the beginning and the ending of so much. And the September woods were ravished by the village to provide tight little bouquets for the funeral. Sam Mosely, tall, black and silent, hitched his bays to his light wagon and he bore Lucy from her house and children and husband and worries to the church, while John, surrounded by his weeping family, walked after the wagon, shaking and crying. The village came behind and filled the little church with weeping and wild-flowers. People were stirred. The vital Lucy was gone. The wife of Moderator Pearson was dead.

"There is rest for the weary" rose and fell like an organ. Harmony soaked in tears.

"She don't need me no mo' nohow," John thought defensively.

"On the other side of Jordan, in the sweet fields of Eden—where the tree of life is blooming—"

And the hot blood in John's veins made him deny kinship with any rider of the pale white horse of death.

"Man born of woman has but a few days."

Clods of damp clay falling hollowly on the box. Out of sight of the world, and dead men heard her secrets.

That night they sat in the little parlor about the organ and the older children sang songs while the smaller ones cried and whimpered on. John sat a little apart and thought. He was free. He was sad, but underneath his sorrow was an exultation like a live coal under gray ashes. There was no longer guilt. But a few days before he had shuddered at the dread of discovery and of Lucy's accusing eye. There was no more sin. Just a free man having his will of women. He was glad in his sadness.

The next day John Pearson and Sam Mosely met on Clarke's porch. Sam remarked, "Funny thing, ain't it John—Lucy come tuh town twelve years uhgo in mah wagon and mah wagon took her uhway."

"Yeah, but she b'longed tuh me, though, all de time," John said and exulted over his friend.

Sweat

IT WAS ELEVEN O'CLOCK of a Spring night in Florida. It was Sunday. Any other night, Delia Jones would have been in bed for two hours by this time. But she was a washwoman, and Monday morning meant a great deal to her. So she collected the soiled clothes on Saturday when she returned the clean things. Sunday night after church, she sorted them and put the white things to soak. It saved her almost a half day's start. A great hamper in the bedroom held the clothes that she brought home. It was so much neater than a number of bundles lying around.

She squatted in the kitchen floor beside the great pile of clothes, sorting them into small heaps according to color, and humming a song in a mournful key, but wondering through it all where Sykes, her husband, had gone with her horse and buckboard.

Just then something long, round, limp and black fell upon her shoulders and slithered to the floor beside her. A great terror took hold of her. It softened her knees and dried her mouth so that it was a full minute before she could cry out or move. Then she saw that it was the big bull whip her husband liked to carry when he drove.

She lifted her eyes to the door and saw him standing there bent over with laughter at her fright. She screamed at him.

"Sykes, what you throw dat whip on me like dat? You know it would skeer me—looks just like a snake, an' you knows how skeered Ah is of snakes."

"Course Ah knowed it! That's how come Ah done it." He slapped his leg with his hand and almost rolled on the ground in his mirth. "If you such a big fool dat you got to have a fit over a earth worm or a string, Ah don't keer how bad Ah skeer you."

"You aint got no business doing it. Gawd knows it's a sin. Some day Ah'm gointuh drop dead from some of yo' foolishness. 'Nother thing, where you been wid mah rig? Ah feeds dat pony. He aint fuh you to be drivin' wid no bull whip."

"You sho is one aggravatin' nigger woman!" he declared and stepped into the room. She resumed her work and did not answer him at once. "Ah done tole you time and again to keep them white folks' clothes outa dis house."

He picked up the whip and glared down at her. Delia went on with her work. She went out into the yard and returned with a galvanized tub and set it on the washbench. She saw that Sykes had kicked all of the clothes together again, and now stood in her way truculently, his whole manner hoping, *praying,* for an argument. But she walked calmly around him and commenced to re-sort the things.

"Next time, Ah'm gointer kick 'em outdoors," he threatened as he struck a match along the leg of his corduroy breeches.

Delia never looked up from her work, and her thin, stooped shoulders sagged further.

"Ah aint for no fuss t'night Sykes. Ah just come from taking sacrament at the church house."

He snorted scornfully. "Yeah, you just come from de church house on a Sunday night, but heah you is gone to work on them clothes. You ain't nothing but a hypocrite. One of them amen-corner Christians— sing, whoop, and shout, then come home and wash white folks clothes on the Sabbath."

He stepped roughly upon the whitest pile of things, kicking them helter-skelter as he crossed the room. His wife gave a little scream of dismay, and quickly gathered them together again.

"Sykes, you quit grindin' dirt into these clothes! How can Ah git through by Sat'day if Ah don't start on Sunday?"

"Ah don't keer if you never git through. Anyhow, Ah done promised Gawd and a couple of other men, Ah aint gointer have it in mah house. Don't gimme no lip neither, else Ah'll throw 'em out and put mah fist up side yo' head to boot."

Delia's habitual meekness seemed to slip from her shoulders like a blown scarf. She was on her feet; her poor little body, her bare knuckly hands bravely defying the strapping hulk before her.

"Looka heah, Sykes, you done gone too fur. Ah been married to you fur fifteen years, and Ah been takin' in washin' fur fifteen years. Sweat, sweat, sweat! Work and sweat, cry and sweat, pray and sweat!"

"What's that got to do with me?" he asked brutally.

"What's it got to do with you, Sykes? Mah tub of suds is filled yo' belly with vittles more times than yo' hands is filled it. Mah sweat is done paid for this house and Ah reckon Ah kin keep on sweatin' in it."

She seized the iron skillet from the stove and struck a defensive pose, which act surprised him greatly, coming from her. It cowed him and he did not strike her as he usually did.

"Naw you won't," she panted, "that ole snaggle-toothed black woman you runnin' with aint comin' heah to pile up on *mah* sweat and blood. You aint paid for nothin' on this place, and Ah'm gointer stay right heah till Ah'm toted out foot foremost."

"Well, you better quit gittin' me riled up, else they'll be totin' you out sooner than you expect. Ah'm so tired of you Ah don't know whut to do. Gawd! how Ah hates skinny wimmen!"

A little awed by this new Delia, he sidled out of the door and slammed the back gate after him. He did not say where he had gone, but she knew too well. She knew very well that he would not return until nearly daybreak also. Her work over, she went on to bed but not to sleep at once. Things had come to a pretty pass!

She lay awake, gazing upon the debris that cluttered their matrimonial trail. Not an image left standing along the way. Anything like flowers had long ago been drowned in the salty stream that had been pressed from her heart. Her tears, her sweat, her blood. She had brought love to the union and he had brought a longing after the flesh. Two months after the wedding, he had given her the first brutal beating. She had the memory of his numerous trips to Orlando with all of his wages when he had returned to her penniless, even before the first year had passed. She was young and soft then, but now she thought of her knotty, muscled limbs, her harsh knuckly hands, and drew herself up into an unhappy little ball in the middle of the big feather bed. Too late now to hope for love, even if it were not Bertha it would be someone else. This case differed from the others only in that she was bolder than the others. Too late for everything except her little home. She had built it for her old days, and planted one by one the trees and flowers there. It was lovely to her, lovely.

Somehow, before sleep came, she found herself saying aloud: "Oh well, whatever goes over the Devil's back, is got to come under his belly. Sometime or ruther, Sykes, like everybody else, is gointer reap his sowing." After that she was able to build a spiritual earthworks against her husband. His shells could no longer reach her. *Amen*. She went to sleep and slept until he announced his presence in bed by kicking her feet and rudely snatching the covers away.

"Gimme some kivah heah, an' git yo' damn foots over on yo' own side! Ah oughter mash you in yo' mouf fuh drawing dat skillet on me."

Delia went clear to the rail without answering him. A triumphant indifference to all that he was or did.

THE WEEK WAS AS FULL of work for Delia as all other weeks, and Saturday found her behind her little pony, collecting and delivering clothes.

It was a hot, hot day near the end of July. The village men on Joe Clarke's porch even chewed cane listlessly. They did not hurl the cane-knots as usual. They let them dribble over the edge of the porch. Even conversation had collapsed under the heat.

"Heah come Delia Jones," Jim Merchant said, as the shaggy pony came 'round the bend of the road toward them. The rusty buckboard was heaped with baskets of crisp, clean laundry.

"Yep," Joe Lindsay agreed. "Hot or col', rain or shine, jes ez reg'lar ez de weeks roll roun' Delia carries 'em an' fetches 'em on Sat'day."

"She better if she wanter eat," said Moss. "Syke Jones aint wuth de shot an' powder hit would tek tuh kill 'em. Not to *huh* he aint."

"He sho' aint," Walter Thomas chimed in. "It's too bad, too, cause she wuz a right pritty lil trick when he got huh. Ah'd uh mah'ied huh mahseff if he hadnter beat me to it."

Delia nodded briefly at the men as she drove past.

"Too much knockin' will ruin *any* 'oman. He done beat huh 'nough tuh kill three women, let 'lone change they looks," said Elijah Moseley. "How Syke kin stommuck dat big black greasy Mogul he's layin' roun' wid, gits me. Ah swear dat eight-rock couldn't kiss a sardine can Ah done thowed out de back do' 'way las' yeah."

"Aw, she's fat, thass how come. He's allus been crazy 'bout fat women," put in Merchant. "He'd a' been tied up wid one long time ago if he could a' found one tuh have him. Did Ah tell yuh 'bout him come sidlin' roun' *mah* wife—bringin' her a basket uh peecans outa his yard fuh a present? Yessir, mah wife! She tol' him tuh take 'em right straight back home, cause Delia works so hard ovah dat washtub she reckon everything on de place taste lak sweat an' soapsuds. Ah jus' wisht Ah'd a' caught 'im 'roun' dere! Ah'd a' made his hips ketch on fiah down dat shell road."

"Ah know he done it, too. Ah sees 'im grinnin' at every 'oman dat passes," Walter Thomas said. "But even so, he useter eat some mighty big hunks uh humble pie tuh git dat lil' 'oman he got. She wuz ez pritty ez a speckled pup! Dat wuz fifteen yeahs ago. He useter be so skeered uh losin' huh, she could make him do some parts of a husband's duty. Dey never wuz de same in de mind.''

"There oughter be a law about him,'' said Lindsay. "He aint fit tuh carry guts tuh a bear.''

Clarke spoke for the first time. "Taint no law on earth dat kin make a man be decent if it aint in 'im. There's plenty men dat takes a wife lak dey do a joint uh sugar-cane. It's round, juicy an' sweet when dey gits it. But dey squeeze an' grind, squeeze an' grind an' wring tell dey wring every drop uh pleasure dat's in 'em out. When dey's satisfied dat dey is wrung dry, dey treats 'em jes lak dey do a cane-chew. Dey thows 'em away. Dey knows whut dey is doin' while dey is at it, an' hates theirselves fuh it but they keeps on hangin' after huh tell she's empty. Den dey hates huh fuh bein' a cane-chew an' in de way.''

"We oughter take Syke an' dat stray 'oman uh his'n down in Lake Howell swamp an' lay on de rawhide till they cain't say Lawd a' mussy.' He allus wuz uh ovahbearin' niggah, but since dat white 'oman from up north done teached 'im how to run a automobile, he done got too biggety to live—an' we oughter kill 'im,'' Old Man Anderson advised.

A grunt of approval went around the porch. But the heat was melting their civic virtue and Elijah Moseley began to bait Joe Clarke.

"Come on, Joe, git a melon outa dere an' slice it up for yo' customers. We'se all sufferin' wid de heat. De bear's done got *me!*''

"Thass right, Joe, a watermelon is jes' whut Ah needs tuh cure de eppizudicks,'' Walter Thomas joined forces with Moseley. "Come on dere, Joe. We all is steady customers an' you aint set us up in a long time. Ah chooses dat long, bowlegged Floridy favorite.''

"A god, an' be dough. You all gimme twenty cents and slice way,'' Clarke retorted. "Ah needs a col' slice m'self. Heah, everybody chip in. Ah'll lend y'll mah meat knife.''

The money was quickly subscribed and the huge melon brought forth. At that moment, Sykes and Bertha arrived. A determined silence fell on the porch and the melon was put away again.

Merchant snapped down the blade of his jackknife and moved toward the store door.

"Come on in, Joe, an' gimme a slab uh sow belly an' uh pound uh coffee—almost fuhgot 'twas Sat'day. Got to git on home.'' Most of the men left also.

Just then Delia drove past on her way home, as Sykes was ordering magnificently for Bertha. It pleased him for Delia to see.

"Git whutsoever yo' heart desires, Honey. Wait a minute, Joe. Give huh two botles uh strawberry soda-water, uh quart uh parched ground-peas, an' a block uh chewin' gum."

With all this they left the store, with Sykes reminding Bertha that this was his town and she could have it if she wanted it.

The men returned soon after they left, and held their watermelon feast.

"Where did Syke Jones git da 'oman from nohow?" Lindsay asked.

"Ovah Apopka. Guess dey musta been cleanin' out de town when she lef'. She don't look lak a thing but a hunk uh liver wid hair on it."

"Well, she sho' kin squall," Dave Carter contributed. "When she gits ready tuh laff, she jes' opens huh mouf an' latches it back tuh de las' notch. No ole grandpa alligator down in Lake Bell ain't got nothin' on huh."

BERTHA HAD BEEN IN TOWN three months now. Sykes was still paying her room rent at Della Lewis'—the only house in town that would have taken her in. Sykes took her frequently to Winter Park to "stomps." He still assured her that he was the swellest man in the state.

"Sho' you kin have dat lil' ole house soon's Ah kin git dat 'oman outa dere. Everything b'longs tuh me an' you sho' kin have it. Ah sho' 'bominates uh skinny 'oman. Lawdy, you sho' is got one portly shape on you! You kin git *anything* you wants. Dis is *mah* town an' you sho' kin have it."

Delia's work-worn knees crawled over the earth in Gethsemane and up the rocks of Calvary many, many times during these months. She avoided the villagers and meeting places in her efforts to be blind and deaf. But Bertha nullified this to a degree, by coming to Delia's house to call Sykes out to her at the gate.

Delia and Sykes fought all the time now with no peaceful interludes. They slept and ate in silence. Two or three times Delia had attempted a timid friendliness, but she was repulsed each time. It was plain that the breaches must remain agape.

The sun had burned July to August. The heat streamed down like a million hot arrows, smiting all things living upon the earth. Grass withered, leaves browned, snakes went blind in shedding and men and dogs went mad. Dog days!

Delia came home one day and found Sykes there before her. She wondered, but started to go on into the house without speaking, even though he was standing in the kitchen door and she must either stoop under his arm or ask him to move. He made no room for her. She noticed a soap box beside the steps, but paid no particular attention to it, knowing that he must have brought it there. As she was stooping to pass under his outstretched arm, he suddenly pushed her backward, laughingly.

"Look in de box dere Delia, Ah done brung yuh somethin'!"

She nearly fell upon the box in her stumbling, and when she saw what it held, she all but fainted outright.

"Syke! Syke, mah Gawd! You take dat rattlesnake 'way from heah! You *gottuh*. Oh, Jesus, have mussy!"

"Ah aint gut tuh do nuthin' uh de kin'—fact is Ah aint got tuh do nothin' but die. Taint no use uh you puttin' on airs makin' out lak you skeered uh dat snake—he's gointer stay right heah tell he die. He wouldn't bite me cause Ah knows how tuh handle 'im. Nohow he wouldn't risk breakin' out his fangs 'gin *yo'* skinny laigs."

"Naw, now Syke, don't keep dat thing 'roun' heah tuh skeer me tuh death. You knows Ah'm even feared uh earth worms. Thass de biggest snake Ah evah did see. Kill 'im Syke, please."

"Doan ast me tuh do nothin' fuh yuh. Goin' 'roun' tryin' tuh be so damn asterperious. Naw, Ah aint gonna kill it. Ah think uh damn sight mo' uh him dan you! Dat's a nice snake an' anybody doan lak 'im kin jes' hit de grit."

The village soon heard that Sykes had the snake, and came to see and ask questions.

"How de hen-fire did you ketch dat six-foot rattler, Syke?" Thomas asked.

"He's full uh frogs so he caint hardly move, thass how Ah eased up on 'm. But Ah'm a snake charmer an' knows how tuh handle 'em. Shux, dat aint nothin'. Ah could ketch one eve'y day if Ah so wanted tuh."

"Whut he needs is a heavy hick'ry club leaned real heavy on his head. Dat's de bes 'way tuh charm a rattlesnake."

"Naw, Walt, y'll jes' don't understand dese diamon' backs lak Ah do," said Sykes in a superior tone of voice.

The village agreed with Walter, but the snake stayed on. His box remained by the kitchen door with its screen wire covering. Two or three days later it had digested its meal of frogs and literally came to life. It rattled at every movement in the kitchen or the yard. One day as Delia came down the kitchen steps she saw his chalky-white fangs curved like scimitars hung in the wire meshes. This time she did not run away with averted eyes as usual. She stood for a long time in the doorway in a red fury that grew bloodier for every second that she regarded the creature that was her torment.

That night she broached the subject as soon as Sykes sat down to the table.

"Syke, Ah wants you tuh take dat snake 'way fum heah. You done starved me an' Ah put up widcher, you done beat me an Ah took dat, but you done kilt all mah insides bringin' dat varmint heah."

Sykes poured out a saucer full of coffee and drank it deliberately before he answered her.

"A whole lot Ah keer 'bout how you feels inside uh out. Dat snake aint goin' no damn wheah till Ah gits ready fuh 'im tuh go. So fur as beatin' is concerned, yuh aint took near all dat you gointer take ef yuh stay 'roun' *me*."

Delia pushed back her plate and got up from the table. "Ah hates you, Sykes," she said calmly. "Ah hates you tuh de same degree dat Ah useter love yuh. Ah done took an' took till mah belly is full up tuh mah neck. Dat's de reason Ah got mah letter fum de church an' moved mah membership tuh Woodbridge—so Ah don't haftuh take no sacrament wid yuh. Ah don't wantuh see yuh 'roun' me atall. Lay 'roun' wid dat 'oman all yuh wants tuh, but gwan 'way fum me an' mah house. Ah hates yuh lak uh suck-egg dog."

Sykes almost let the huge wad of corn bread and collard greens he was chewing fall out of his mouth in amazement. He had a hard time whipping himself up to the proper fury to try to answer Delia.

"Well, Ah'm glad you does hate me. Ah'm sho' tiahed uh you hangin' ontuh me. Ah don't want yuh. Look at yuh stringey ole neck! Yo' rawbony laigs an' arms is enough tuh cut uh man tuh death. You looks jes' lak de devvul's doll-baby tuh *me*. You cain't hate me no worse dan Ah hates you. Ah been hatin' *you* fuh years."

"Yo' ole black hide don't look lak nothin' tuh me, but uh passle uh wrinkled up rubber, wid yo' big ole yeahs flappin' on each side lak uh paih uh buzzard wings. Don't think Ah'm gointuh be run 'way fum mah house neither. Ah'm goin' tuh de white folks bout *you*, mah young man, de very nex' time you lay yo' han's on me. Mah cup is done run ovah."

Delia said this with no signs of fear and Sykes departed from the house, threatening her, but made not the slightest move to carry out any of them.

That night he did not return at all, and the next day being Sunday, Delia was glad she did not have to quarrel before she hitched up her pony and drove the four miles to Woodbridge.

She stayed to the night service—''love feast''—which was very warm and full of spirit. In the emotional winds her domestic trials were borne far and wide so that she sang as she drove homeward,

> ''Jurden water, black an' col'
> Chills de body, not de soul
> An' Ah wantah cross Jurden in uh calm time.''

She came from the barn to the kitchen door and stopped.

''Whut's de mattah, ol' satan, you aint kickin' up yo' racket?'' She addressed the snake's box. Complete silence. She went on into the house with a new hope in its birth struggles. Perhaps her threat to go to the white folks had frightened Sykes! Perhaps he was sorry! Fifteen years of misery and suppression had brought Delia to the place where she would hope *anything* that looked towards a way over or through her wall of inhibitions.

She felt in the match safe behind the stove at once for a match. There was only one there.

''Dat niggah wouldn't fetch nothin' heah tuh save his rotten neck, but he kin run thew whut Ah brings quick enough. Now he done toted off nigh on tuh haff uh box uh matches. He done had dat 'oman heah in mah house, too.''

Nobody but a woman could tell how she knew this even before she struck the match. But she did and it put her into a new fury.

Presently she brought in the tubs to put the white things to soak. This time she decided she need not bring the hamper out of the bedroom; she would go in there and do the sorting. She picked up the pot-bellied lamp and went in. The room was small and the hamper stood hard by the foot of the white iron bed. She could sit and reach through the bedposts—resting as she worked.

''Ah wantah cross Jurden in uh calm time.'' She was singing again. The mood of the ''love feast'' had returned. She threw back the lid of the basket almost gaily. Then, moved by both horror and terror, she sprang back toward the door. *There lay the snake in the basket!* He moved sluggishly at first, but even as she turned round and round, jumped up and down in an insanity of fear, he began to stir vigorously. She saw him pouring his awful beauty from the basket upon the bed, then she seized the lamp and ran as fast as she could to the kitchen. The wind from the open door blew out the light and the darkness added to her terror. She sped to the darkness of the yard, slamming the door after her before she thought to set down the lamp. She did not feel safe even on the ground, so she climbed up in the hay barn.

There for an hour or more she lay sprawled upon the hay a gibbering wreck.

Finally she grew quiet, and after that, coherent thought. With this, stalked through her a cold, bloody rage. Hours of this. A period of introspection, a space of retrospection, then a mixture of both. Out of this an awful calm.

"Well, Ah done de bes' Ah could. If things aint right, Gawd knows taint mah fault."

She went to sleep—a twitch sleep—and woke up to a faint gray sky. There was a loud hollow sound below. She peered out. Sykes was at the wood-pile, demolishing a wire-covered box.

He hurried to the kitchen door, but hung outside there some minutes before he entered, and stood some minutes more inside before he closed it after him.

The gray in the sky was spreading. Delia descended without fear now, and crouched beneath the low bedroom window. The drawn shade shut out the dawn, shut in the night. But the thin walls held back no sound.

"Dat ol' scratch is woke up now!" She mused at the tremendous whirr inside, which every woodsman knows, is one of the sound illusions. The rattler is a ventriloquist. His whirr sounds to the right, to the left, straight ahead, behind, close under foot—everywhere but where it is. Woe to him who guesses wrong unless he is prepared to hold up his end of the argument! Sometimes he strikes without rattling at all.

Inside, Sykes heard nothing until he knocked a pot lid off the stove while trying to reach the match safe in the dark. He had emptied his pockets at Bertha's.

The snake seemed to wake up under the stove and Sykes made a quick leap into the bedroom. In spite of the gin he had had, his head was clearing now.

"Mah Gawd!" he chattered, "ef Ah could on'y strack uh light!"

The rattling ceased for a moment as he stood paralyzed. He waited. It seemed that the snake waited also.

"Oh, fuh de light! Ah thought he'd be too sick"—Sykes was muttering to himself when the whirr began again, closer, right underfoot this time. Long before this, Sykes' ability to think had been flattened down to primitive instinct and he leaped—onto the bed.

Outside Delia heard a cry that might have come from a maddened chimpanzee, a stricken gorilla. All the terror, all the horror, all the rage that man possibly could express, without a recognizable human sound.

A tremendous stir inside there, another series of animal screams, the intermittent whirr of the reptile. The shade torn violently down from the window, letting in the red dawn, a huge brown hand seizing the window stick, great dull blows upon the wooden floor punctuating the gibberish of sound long after the rattle of the snake had abruptly subsided. All this Delia could see and hear from her place beneath the window, and it made her ill. She crept over to the four-o'clocks and stretched herself on the cool earth to recover.

She lay there. "Delia, Delia!" She could hear Sykes calling in a most despairing tone as one who expected no answer. The sun crept on up, and he called. Delia could not move—her legs were gone flabby. She never moved, he called, and the sun kept rising.

"Mah Gawd!" She heard him moan, "Mah Gawd fum Heben!" She heard him stumbling about and got up from her flower-bed. The sun was growing warm. As she approached the door she heard him call out hopefully, "Delia, is dat you Ah heah?"

She saw him on his hands and knees as soon as she reached the door. He crept an inch or two toward her—all that he was able, and she saw his horribly swollen neck and his one open eye shining with hope. A surge of pity too strong to support bore her away from that eye that must, could not, fail to see the tubs. He would see the lamp. Orlando with its doctors was too far. She could scarcely reach the Chinaberry tree, where she waited in the growing heat while inside she knew the cold river was creeping up and up to extinguish that eye which must know by now that she knew.

The Gilded Six-Bits

IT WAS A NEGRO YARD around a Negro house in a Negro settlement that looked to the payroll of the G and G Fertilizer works for its support.

But there was something happy about the place. The front yard was parted in the middle by a sidewalk from gate to door-step, a sidewalk edged on either side by quart bottles driven neck down into the ground on a slant. A mess of homey flowers planted without a plan but blooming cheerily from their helter-skelter places. The fence and house were whitewashed. The porch and steps scrubbed white.

The front door stood open to the sunshine so that the floor of the front room could finish drying after its weekly scouring. It was Saturday. Everything clean from the front gate to the privy house. Yard raked so that the strokes of the rake would make a pattern. Fresh newspaper cut in fancy edge on the kitchen shelves.

Missie May was bathing herself in the galvanized washtub in the bedroom. Her dark-brown skin glistened under the soapsuds that skittered down from her wash rag. Her stiff young breasts thrust forward aggressively like broad-based cones with the tips lacquered in black.

She heard men's voices in the distance and glanced at the dollar clock on the dresser.

"Humph! Ah'm way behind time t'day! Joe gointer be heah 'fore Ah git mah clothes on if Ah don't make haste."

She grabbed the clean meal sack at hand and dried herself hurriedly and began to dress. But before she could tie her slippers, there came the ring of singing metal on wood. Nine times.

Missie May grinned with delight. She had not seen the big tall man come stealing in the gate and creep up the walk grinning happily at the joyful mischief he was about to commit. But she knew that it was her husband throwing silver dollars in the door for her to pick up and pile beside her plate at dinner. It was this way every Saturday afternoon. The nine dollars hurled into the open door, he scurried to a hiding place behind the cape jasmine bush and waited.

Missie May promptly appeared at the door in mock alarm.

"Who dat chunkin' money in mah do'way?" She demanded. No answer from the yard. She leaped off the porch and began to search the shrubbery. She peeped under the porch and hung over the gate to look up and down the road. While she did this, the man behind the jasmine darted to the china berry tree. She spied him and gave chase.

"Nobody ain't gointer be chunkin' money at me and Ah not do 'em nothin'," she shouted in mock anger. He ran around the house with Missie May at his heels. She overtook him at the kitchen door. He ran inside but could not close it after him before she crowded in and locked with him in a rough and tumble. For several minutes the two were a furious mass of male and female energy. Shouting, laughing, twisting, turning, tussling, tickling each other in the ribs; Missie May clutching onto Joe and Joe trying, but not too hard, to get away.

"Missie May, take yo' hand out mah pocket!" Joe shouted out between laughs.

"Ah ain't, Joe, not lessen you gwine gimme whateve' it is good you got in yo' pocket. Turn it go, Joe, do Ah'll tear yo' clothes."

"Go on tear 'em. You de one dat pushes de needles round heah. Move yo' hand Missie May."

"Lemme git dat paper sack out yo' pocket. Ah bet its candy kisses."

"Tain't. Move yo' hand. Woman ain't go no business in a man's clothes nohow. Go way."

Missie May gouged way down and gave an upward jerk and triumphed.

"Unhhunh! Ah got it. It 'tis so candy kisses. Ah knowed you had somethin' for me in yo' clothes. Now Ah got to see whut's in every pocket you got."

Joe smiled indulgently and let his wife go through all of his pockets and take out the things that he had hidden there for her to find. She bore off the chewing gum, the cake of sweet soap, the pocket handkerchief as if she had wrested them from him, as if they had not been bought for the sake of this friendly battle.

"Whew! dat play-fight done got me all warmed up." Joe exclaimed. "Got me some water in de kittle?"

"Yo' water is on de fire and yo' clean things is cross de bed. Hurry up and wash yo'self and git changed so we kin eat. Ah'm hongry." As Missie said this, she bore the steaming kettle into the bedroom.

"You ain't hongry, sugar," Joe contradicted her. "Youse jes' a little empty. Ah'm de one whut's hongry. Ah could eat up camp meetin', back off 'ssociation, and drink Jurdan dry. Have it on de table when Ah git out de tub.''

"Don't you mess wid mah business, man. You git in yo' clothes. Ah'm a real wife, not no dress and breath. Ah might not look lak one, but if you burn me, you won't git a thing but wife ashes.''

Joe splashed in the bedroom and Missie May fanned around in the kitchen. A fresh red and white checked cloth on the table. Big pitcher of buttermilk beaded with pale drops of butter from the churn. Hot fried mullet, crackling bread, ham hock atop a mound of string beans and new potatoes, and perched on the window-sill a pone of spicy potato pudding.

Very little talk during the meal but that little consisted of banter that pretended to deny affection but in reality flaunted it. Like when Missie May reached for a second helping of the tater pone. Joe snatched it out of her reach.

After Missie May had made two or three unsuccessful grabs at the pan, she begged, "Aw, Joe gimme some mo' dat tater pone.''

"Nope, sweetenin' is for us men-folks. Y'all pritty lil frail eels don't need nothin' lak dis. You too sweet already.''

"Please, Joe.''

"Naw, naw. Ah don't want you to git no sweeter than whut you is already. We goin' down de road a lil piece t'night so you go put on yo' Sunday-go-to-meetin' things.''

Missie May looked at her husband to see if he was playing some prank. "Sho nuff, Joe?''

"Yeah. We goin' to de ice cream parlor.''

"Where de ice cream parlor at, Joe?''

"A new man done come heah from Chicago and he done got a place and took and opened it up for a ice cream parlor, and bein' as it's real swell, Ah wants you to be one de first ladies to walk in dere and have some set down.''

"Do Jesus, Ah ain't knowed nothin' 'bout it. Who de man done it?''

"Mister Otis D. Slemmons, of spots and places—Memphis, Chicago, Jacksonville, Philadelphia and so on.''

"Dat heavy-set man wid his mouth full of gold teethes?''

"Yeah. Where did you see 'im at?''

"Ah went down to de sto' tuh git a box of lye and Ah seen 'im standin' on de corner talkin' to some of de mens, and Ah come on back and went to scrubbin' de floor, and he passed and tipped his hat whilst Ah was scourin' de steps. Ah thought Ah never seen *him* befo'."

Joe smiled pleasantly. "Yeah, he's up to date. He got de finest clothes Ah ever seen on a colored man's back."

"Aw, he don't look no better in his clothes than you do in yourn. He got a puzzlegut on 'im and he so chuckle-headed, he got a pone behind his neck."

Joe looked down at his own abdomen and said wistfully, "Wisht Ah had a build on me lak he got. He ain't puzzle-gutted, honey. He jes' got a corperation. Dat make 'm look lak a rich white man. All rich mens is got some belly on 'em."

"Ah seen de pitchers of Henry Ford and he's a spare-built man and Rockefeller look lak he ain't got but one gut. But Ford and Rockefeller and dis Slemmons and all de rest kin be as many-gutted as dey please, Ah'm satisfied wid you jes' lak you is, baby. God took pattern after a pine tree and built you noble. Youse a pritty man, and if Ah knowed any way to make you mo' pritty still Ah'd take and do it."

Joe reached over gently and toyed with Missie May's ear. "You jes' say dat cause you love me, but Ah know Ah can't hold no light to Otis D. Slemmons. Ah ain't never been nowhere and Ah ain't got nothin' but you."

Missie May got on his lap and kissed him and he kissed back in kind. Then he went on. "All de womens is crazy 'bout 'im everywhere he go."

"How you know dat, Joe?"

"He tole us so hisself."

"Dat don't make it so. His mouf is cut cross-ways, ain't it? Well, he kin lie jes' lak anybody else."

"Good Lawd, Missie! You womens sho is hard to sense into things. He's got a five-dollar gold piece for a stick-pin and he got a ten-dollar gold piece on his watch chain and his mouf is jes' crammed full of gold teethes. Sho wisht it wuz mine. And whut make it so cool, he got money 'cumulated. And womens give it all to 'im."

"Ah don't see whut de womens see on 'im. Ah wouldn't give 'im a wink if de sheriff wuz after 'im."

"Well, he tole us how de white womens in Chicago give 'im all dat gold money. So he don't 'low nobody to touch it at all. Not even put dey finger on it. Dey tole 'im not to. You kin make 'miration at it, but don't tetch it."

"Whyn't he stay up dere where dey so crazy 'bout 'im?"

"Ah reckon dey done made 'im vast-rich and he wants to travel some. He say dey wouldn't leave 'im hit a lick of work. He got mo' lady people crazy 'bout him than he kin shake a stick at."

"Joe, Ah hates to see you so dumb. Dat stray nigger jes' tell y'all anything and y'all b'lieve it."

"Go 'head on now, honey and put on yo' clothes. He talkin' 'bout his pritty womens—Ah want 'im to see *mine*."

Missie May went off to dress and Joe spent the time trying to make his stomach punch out like Slemmons' middle. He tried the rolling swagger of the stranger, but found that his tall bone-and-muscle stride fitted ill with it. He just had time to drop back into his seat before Missie May came in dressed to go.

On the way home that night Joe was exultant. "Didn't Ah say ole Otis was swell? Can't he talk Chicago talk? Wuzn't dat funny whut he said when great big fat ole Ida Armstrong come in? He asted me, 'Who is dat broad wid de forte shake?' Dat's a new word. Us always thought forty was a set of figgers but he showed us where it means a whole heap of things. Sometimes he don't say forty, he jes' say thirty-eight and two and dat mean de same thing. Know whut he tole me when Ah wuz payin' for our ice cream? He say, 'Ah have to hand it to you, Joe. Dat wife of yours is jes' thirty-eight and two. Yessuh, she's forte!' Ain't he killin'?"

"He'll do in case of a rush. But he sho is got uh heap uh gold on 'im. Dat's de first time Ah ever seed gold money. It lookted good on him sho nuff, but it'd look a whole heap better on you."

"Who, me? Missie May youse crazy! Where would a po' man lak me git gold money from?"

Missie May was silent for a minute, then she said, "Us might find some goin' long de road some time. Us could."

"Who would be losin' gold money round heah? We ain't even seen none dese white folks wearin' no gold money on dey watch chain. You must be figgerin' Mister Packard or Mister Cadillac goin' pass through heah."

"You don't know whut been lost 'round heah. Maybe somebody way back in memorial times lost they gold money and went on off and it ain't never been found. And then if we wuz to find it, you could wear some 'thout havin' no gang of womens lak dat Slemmons say he got."

Joe laughed and hugged her. "Don't be so wishful 'bout me. Ah'm satisfied de way Ah is. So long as Ah be yo' husband, Ah don't keer 'bout nothin' else. Ah'd ruther all de other womens in de world to be dead than for you to have de toothache. Less we go to bed and git our night rest.''

It was Saturday night once more before Joe could parade his wife in Slemmons' ice cream parlor again. He worked the night shift and Saturday was his only night off. Every other evening around six o'clock he left home, and dying dawn saw him hustling home around the lake where the challenging sun flung a flaming sword from east to west across the trembling water.

That was the best part of life—going home to Missie May. Their whitewashed house, the mock battle on Saturday, the dinner and ice cream parlor afterwards, church on Sunday nights when Missie out-dressed any woman in town—all, everything was right.

One night around eleven the acid ran out at the G. and G. The fore-man knocked off the crew and let the steam die down. As Joe rounded the lake on his way home, a lean moon rode the lake in a silver boat. If anybody had asked Joe about the moon on the lake, he would have said he hadn't paid it any attention. But he saw it with his feelings. It made him yearn painfully for Missie. Creation obsessed him. He thought about children. They had been married for more than a year now. They had money put away. They ought to be making little feet for shoes. A little boy child would be about right.

He saw a dim light in the bedroom and decided to come in through the kitchen door. He could wash the fertilizer dust off himself before presenting himself to Missie May. It would be nice for her not to know that he was there until he slipped into his place in bed and hugged her back. She always liked that.

He eased the kitchen door open slowly and silently, but when he went to set his dinner bucket on the table he bumped it into a pile of dishes, and something crashed to the floor. He heard his wife gasp in fright and hurried to reassure her.

"Iss me, honey. Don't get skeered."

There was a quick, large movement in the bedroom. A rustle, a thud, and a stealthy silence. The light went out.

What? Robbers? Murderers? Some varmint attacking his helpless wife, perhaps. He struck a match, threw himself on guard and stepped over the door-sill into the bedroom.

The great belt on the wheel of Time slipped and eternity stood still.

By the match light he could see the man's legs fighting with his breeches in his frantic desire to get them on. He had both chance and time to kill the intruder in his helpless condition—half in and half out of his pants—but he was too weak to take action. The shapeless enemies of humanity that live in the hours of Time had waylaid Joe. He was assaulted in his weakness. Like Samson awakening after his haircut. So he just opened his mouth and laughed.

The match went out and he struck another and lit the lamp. A howling wind raced across his heart, but underneath its fury he heard his wife sobbing and Slemmons pleading for his life. Offering to buy it with all that he had. "Please, suh, don't kill me. Sixty-two dollars at de sto'. Gold money."

Joe just stood. Slemmons looked at the window, but it was screened. Joe stood out like a rough-backed mountain between him and the door. Barring him from escape, from sunrise, from life.

He considered a surprise attack upon the big clown that stood there laughing like a chessy cat. But before his fist could travel an inch, Joe's own rushed out to crush him like a battering ram. Then Joe stood over him.

"Git into yo' damn rags, Slemmons, and dat quick."

Slemmons scrambled to his feet and into his vest and coat. As he grabbed his hat, Joe's fury overrode his intentions and he grabbed at Slemmons with his left hand and struck at him with his right. The right landed. The left grazed the front of his vest. Slemmons was knocked a somersault into the kitchen and fled through the open door. Joe found himself alone with Missie May, with the golden watch charm clutched in his left fist. A short bit of broken chain dangled between his fingers.

Missie May was sobbing. Wails of weeping without words. Joe stood, and after awhile he found out that he had something in his hand. And then he stood and felt without thinking and without seeing with his natural eyes. Missie May kept on crying and Joe kept on feeling so much and not knowing what to do with all his feelings, he put Slemmons' watch charm in his pants pocket and took a good laugh and went to bed.

"Missie May, whut you cryin' for?"

"Cause Ah love you so hard and Ah know you don't love *me* no mo'."

Joe sank his face into the pillow for a spell then he said huskily, "You don't know de feelings of dat yet, Missie May."

"Oh Joe, honey, he said he wuz gointer give me dat gold money and he jes' kept on after me—"

Joe was very still and silent for a long time. Then he said, "Well, don't cry no mo', Missie May. Ah got yo' gold piece for you."

The hours went past on their rusty ankles. Joe still and quiet on one bed-rail and Missie May wrung dry of sobs on the other. Finally the sun's tide crept upon the shore of night and drowned all its hours. Missie May with her face stiff and streaked towards the window saw the dawn come into her yard. It was day. Nothing more. Joe wouldn't be coming home as usual. No need to fling open the front door and sweep off the porch, making it nice for Joe. Never no more breakfast to cook; no more washing and starching of Joe's jumper-jackets and pants. No more nothing. So why get up?

With this strange man in her bed, she felt embarrassed to get up and dress. She decided to wait till he had dressed and gone. Then she would get up, dress quickly and be gone forever beyond reach of Joe's looks and laughs. But he never moved. Red light turned to yellow, then white.

From beyond the no-man's land between them came a voice. A strange voice that yesterday had been Joe's.

"Missie May, ain't you gonna fix me no breakfus'?"

She sprang out of bed. "Yeah, Joe. Ah didn't reckon you wuz hongry."

No need to die today. Joe needed her for a few more minutes anyhow.

Soon there was a roaring fire in the cook stove. Water bucket full and two chickens killed. Joe loved fried chicken and rice. She didn't deserve a thing and good Joe was letting her cook him some breakfast. She rushed hot biscuits to the table as Joe took his seat.

He ate with his eyes in his plate. No laughter, no banter.

"Missie May, you ain't eatin' yo' breakfus'."

"Ah don't choose none, Ah thank yuh."

His coffee cup was empty. She sprang to refill it. When she turned from the stove and bent to set the cup beside Joe's plate, she saw the yellow coin on the table between them.

She slumped into her seat and wept into her arms.

Presently Joe said calmly, "Missie May, you cry too much. Don't look back lak Lot's wife aud turn to salt."

The sun, the hero of every day, the impersonal old man that beams as brightly on death as on birth, came up every morning and raced across the blue dome and dipped into the sea of fire every evening. Water ran down hill and birds nested.

Missie knew why she didn't leave Joe. She couldn't. She loved him too much, but she could not understand why Joe didn't leave her. He was polite, even kind at times, but aloof.

There were no more Saturday romps. No ringing silver dollars to stack beside her plate. No pockets to rifle. In fact the yellow coin in his trousers was like a monster hiding in the cave of his pockets to destroy her.

She often wondered if he still had it, but nothing could have induced her to ask nor yet to explore his pockets to see for herself. Its shadow was in the house whether or no.

One night Joe came home around midnight and complained of pains in the back. He asked Missie to rub him down with liniment. It had been three months since Missie had touched his body and it all seemed strange. But she rubbed him. Grateful for the chance. Before morning, youth triumphed and Missie exulted. But the next day, as she joyfully made up their bed, beneath her pillow she found the piece of money with the bit of chain attached.

Alone to herself, she looked at the thing with loathing, but look she must. She took it into her hands with trembling and saw first thing that it was no gold piece. It was a gilded half dollar. Then she knew why Slemmons had forbidden anyone to touch his gold. He trusted village eyes at a distance not to recognize his stick-pin as a gilded quarter, and his watch charm as a four-bit piece.

She was glad at first that Joe had left it there. Perhaps he was through with her punishment. They were man and wife again. Then another thought came clawing at her. He had come home to buy from her as if she were any woman in the long house. Fifty cents for her love. As if to say that he could pay as well as Slemmons. She slid the coin into his Sunday pants pocket and dressed herself and left his house.

Halfway between her house and the quarters she met her husband's mother, and after a short talk she turned and went back home. Never would she admit defeat to that woman who prayed for it nightly. If she had not the substance of marriage she had the outside show. Joe must leave *her*. She let him see she didn't want his old gold four-bits too.

She saw no more of the coin for some time though she knew that Joe could not help finding it in his pocket. But his health kept poor, and he came home at least every ten days to be rubbed.

The sun swept around the horizon, trailing its robes of weeks and days. One morning as Joe came in from work, he found Missie May chopping wood. Without a word he took the ax and chopped a huge pile before he stopped.

"You ain't got no business choppin' wood, and you know it."

"How come? Ah been choppin' it for de last longest."

"Ah ain't blind. You makin' feet for shoes."

"Won't you be glad to have a lil baby chile, Joe?"

"You know dat 'thout astin' me."

"Iss gointer be a boy chile and de very spit of you."

"You reckon, Missie May?"

"Who else could it look lak?"

Joe said nothing, but he thrust his hand deep into his pocket and fingered something there.

It was almost six months later Missie May took to bed and Joe went and got his mother to come wait on the house.

Missie May delivered a fine boy. Her travail was over when Joe came in from work one morning. His mother and the old women were drinking great bowls of coffee around the fire in the kitchen.

The minute Joe came into the room his mother called him aside.

"How did Missie May make out?" he asked quickly.

"Who, dat gal? She strong as a ox. She gointer have plenty mo'. We done fixed her wid de sugar and lard to sweeten her for de nex' one."

Joe stood silent awhile.

"You ain't ast 'bout de baby, Joe. You oughter be mighty proud cause he sho is de spittin' image of yuh, son. Dat's yourn all right, if you never git another one, dat un is yourn. And you know Ah'm mighty proud too, son, cause Ah never thought well of you marryin' Missie May cause her ma used tuh fan her foot round right smart and Ah been mighty skeered dat Missie May wuz gointer git misput on her road."

Joe said nothing. He fooled around the house till late in the day then just before he went to work, he went and stood at the foot of the bed and asked his wife how she felt. He did this every day during the week.

On Saturday he went to Orlando to make his market. It had been a long time since he had done that.

Meat and lard, meal and flour, soap and starch. Cans of corn and tomatoes. All the staples. He fooled around town for awhile and bought bananas and apples. Way after while he went around to the candy store.

"Hellow, Joe," the clerk greeted him. "Ain't seen you in a long time."

"Nope, Ah ain't been heah. Been round in spots and places."

"Want some of them molasses kisses you always buy?"

"Yessuh." He threw the gilded half dollar on the counter. "Will dat spend?"

"Whut is it, Joe? Well, I'll be doggone! A gold-plated four-bit piece. Where'd you git it, Joe?"

"Offen a stray nigger dat come through Eatonville. He had it on his watch chain for a charm—goin' round making out iss gold money. Ha ha! He had a quarter on his tie pin and it wuz all golded up too. Tryin' to fool people. Makin' out he so rich and everything. Ha! Ha! Tryin' to tole off folkses wives from home."

"How did you git it, Joe? Did he fool you, too?"

"Who, me? Naw suh! He ain't fooled me none. Know whut Ah done? He come round me wid his smart talk. Ah hauled off and knocked 'im down and took his old four-bits way from 'im. Gointer buy my wife some good ole lasses kisses wid it. Gimme fifty cents worth of dem candy kisses."

"Fifty cents buys a mightly lot of candy kisses, Joe. Why don't you split it up and take some chocolate bars, too. They eat good, too."

"Yessuh, dey do, but Ah wants all dat in kisses. Ah got a lil boy chile home now. Tain't a week old yet, but he kin suck a sugar tit and maybe eat one them kisses hisself."

Joe got his candy and left the store. The clerk turned to the next customer. "Wisht I could be like these darkies. Laughin' all the time. Nothin' worries 'em."

Back in Eatonville, Joe reached his own front door. There was the ring of singing metal on wood. Fifteen times. Missie May couldn't run to the door, but she crept there as quickly as she could.

"Joe Banks, Ah hear you chunkin' money in mah do'way. You wait till Ah got mah strength back and Ah'm gointer fix you for dat."

FROM
Moses, Man of
the Mountain

MOSES WAS AN OLD MAN with a beard. He was the great law-giver. He
had some trouble with Pharaoh about some plagues and led the Children
of Israel out of Egypt and on to the Promised Land. He died on Mount
Nebo and the angels buried him there. That is the common concept of
Moses in the Christian world.

But there are other concepts of Moses abroad in the world. Asia and
all the Near East are sown with legends of this character. They are so
numerous and so varied that some students have come to doubt if the
Moses of the Christian concept is real. Then Africa has her mouth on
Moses. All across the continent there are the legends of the greatness of
Moses, but not because of his beard nor because he brought the laws
down from Sinai. No, he is revered because he had the power to go up
the mountain and to bring them down. Many men could climb mountains. Anyone could bring down laws that had been handed to them. But
who can talk with God face to face? Who has the power to command God
to go to a peak of a mountain and there demand of Him laws with which
to govern a nation? What other man has ever seen with his eyes even the
back part of God's glory? Who else has ever commanded the wind and
the hail? The light and darkness? That calls for power, and that is what
Africa sees in Moses to worship. For he is worshipped as a god.

In Haiti, the highest god in the Haitian pantheon is Damballa
Ouedo Ouedo Tocan Freda Dahomey and he is identified as Moses, the
serpent god. But this deity did not originate in Haiti. His home is in
Dahomey and is worshipped there extensively. Moses had his rod of
power, which was a living serpent. So that in every temple of Damballa
there is a living snake, or the symbol.

And this worship of Moses as the greatest one of magic is not confined to Africa. Wherever the children of Africa have been scattered by slavery, there is the acceptance of Moses as the fountain of mystic powers. This is not confined to Negroes. In America there are countless people of other races depending upon mystic symbols and seals and syllables said to have been used by Moses to work his wonders. There are millions of copies of a certain book, *The Sixth and Seventh Books of Moses,* being read and consulted in secret because the readers believe in Moses. Some even maintain that the stories of the miracles of Jesus are but Mosaic legends told again. Nobody can tell how many tales and legends of Moses are alive in the world nor how far they travelled, so many have collected around his name.

So all across Africa, America, the West Indies, there are tales of the powers of Moses and great worship of him and his powers. But it does not flow from the Ten Commandments. It is his rod of power, the terror he showed before all Israel and to Pharaoh, and THAT MIGHTY HAND.

—The Author.

HAVE MERCY! Lord, have mercy on my poor soul!'' Women gave birth and whispered cries like this in caves and out-of-the-way places that humans didn't usually use for birthplaces. Moses hadn't come yet, and these were the years when Israel first made tears. Pharaoh had entered the bedrooms of Israel. The birthing beds of Hebrews were matters of state. The Hebrew womb had fallen under the heel of Pharaoh. A ruler great in his newness and new in his greatness had arisen in Egypt and he had said, "This is law. Hebrew boys shall not be born. All offenders against this law shall suffer death by drowning."

So women in the pains of labor hid in caves and rocks. They must cry, but they could not cry out loud. They pressed their teeth together. A night might force upon them a thousand years of feeling. Men learned to beat upon their breasts with clenched fists and breathe out their agony without a sound. A great force of suffering accumulated between the basement of heaven and the roof of hell. The shadow of Pharaoh squatted in the dark corners of every birthing place in Goshen. Hebrew women shuddered with terror at the indifference of their wombs to the Egyptian law.

The province of Goshen was living under the New Egypt and the New Egyptian and they were made to know it in many ways. The sign of the new order towered over places of preference. It shadowed over work, and fear was given body and wings.

The Hebrews had already been driven out of their well-built homes and shoved further back in Goshen. Then came more decrees:

1. Israel, you are slaves from now on. Pharaoh assumes no responsibility for the fact that some of you got old before he came to power. Old as well as young must work in his brickyards and road camps.

   a. No sleeping after dawn. Fifty lashes for being late to work.
   b. Fifty lashes for working slow.
   c. One hundred lashes for being absent.
   d. One hundred lashes for sassing the bossman.
   e. Death for hitting a foreman.

2. Babies take notice: Positively no more boy babies allowed among Hebrews. Infants defying this law shall be drowned in the Nile.

Hebrews were disarmed and prevented from becoming citizens of Egypt, they found out that they were aliens, and from one new decree to the next they sank lower and lower. So they had no comfort left but to beat their breasts to crush the agony inside. Israel had learned to weep.

THE SUN WAS SETTING. Under the brilliant, cloudless Egyptian sun thousands of Hebrew workers were struggling with building stones. Some of their backs were bloody from the lash; many of them were stoopy from age and all of them were sweaty and bent and tired from work. The Egyptian foreman gazed at the drooping sun in awe and breathed with reverence: "Ah, Horus, golden god! Lord of both horizons. The weaver of the beginning of things!"

Amram, struggling with the help of another man to move a heavy stone into place in the foundation, heard him and looked up.

"Horus may be all those good things to the Egyptians, brother, but that sun-god is just something to fry our backs."

"I heard him what he said," the other worker whispered back. "If Horus is the weaver of the beginning of things, he's done put some mighty strange threads in his loom."

"And still and all I used to admire him too, before this new government come in, didn't you?"

"Uhuh. I used to admire everything in Egypt. But the palms and the plains ain't scenery to me no more. They just look like suffering to me now."

"They look that way to me too, now," Amram whispered back, "and the worst part about it is, my wife is going to have another baby."

"I heard about it, Amram. What you going to do? Take her off in the wilderness like I did mine?"

"Don't know exactly, Caleb. One man was telling me he hid his wife out in a boat until it was all over. Turned out to be a girl so it was all right."

"How soon you expecting?"

"Of course you can't never be sure exactly, but we figure in two or three days more. I'm planning on hunting up some good cave or some place like that the secret police don't know about yet. Thought I'd take tonight to locate a place. Will you go along with me?"

"Sure I will. You got the midwife engaged?"

"Yes, that's all fixed up. Going to send my boy Aaron and my girl Miriam along to help around generally. They can do little things around and watch out for spies. Old Puah, the midwife, knows her business all right and she's just as loyal as she can be, but she's getting kind of old, you know."

"That's right. It's good you got a sizeable boy and girl to run errands and to stand watch. It's liable to happen while we are at work, you know."

"Oh, yes, and that's how come I want to find a place and get it sort of fixed up with a quilt or two for my wife to rest on and some water and things like that so when the time comes I won't need to worry. It's a sin and a shame our wives can't even have a baby in peace."

"And that's just the reason I want to go with that delegation to see old Pharaoh tonight. You know a bunch of us are going tonight to see him to protest these new decrees, don't you?"

"Sure, but I don't believe it'll do a bit of good. Still and all I want to go just to see what he's going to say this time. But it makes me fighting mad to see him sit up there, him and his so-called advisors, and laugh right in our faces. Reckon we'll get back from our little cave hunt in time to go along with the rest?"

"Hope so. I just don't see how he can keep on putting out all these decrees and making 'em meaner all the time. He's got to give us some kind of a justice sooner or later."

"You think so, Caleb? I don't. I saw his eyes last time. That man loves to see us suffer. He loves to see us hurt and ache. That's how come he lets us come—to be sure he's griping us good. I've about made up my mind that these protests ain't doing us no good at all." ·

"You reckon, Amram?"

"Sure. You all talk like somebody else made these laws and Pharaoh don't know nothing about 'em. He makes 'em his own self and he's glad when we come tell him they hurt. Why, that's a whole lot of pleasure to him, to be making up laws all the time and to have a crowd like us around handy to pass all his mean ones on. Why, he's got a law about everything under the sun! Next thing you know he'll be saying cats can't have kittens. He figures that it makes a big man out of him to be passing and passing laws and rules. He thinks that makes him look more like a king. Long time ago he done passed all the laws that could do anybody good. So now he sits up and studies up laws to do hurt and harm, and we're the only folks in Egypt he got the nerve to put 'em on. He aims to keep us down so he'll always have somebody to wipe his feet on. He brags that him and the Egyptian nation is eating high on the hog now."

"Well, it's his time now, be mine after while, maybe."

"Maybe is right. He's got us in the go-long and I just don't see no way out unless he was to die and a better man come along."

"It certainly is hard, Amram, getting use to being a slave."

"And look what he done done! Passed a law we can't go in the temples no more. He says their gods ain't our gods."

"Like what other gods do we know anything about. It gives you a real empty feeling not to have no gods anymore. If we can't go to the temples in Thebes and Memphis and Luxor, we could build us one in Goshen and sacrifice, Amram. Maybe if we do that they might help us to get our rights back again."

"Caleb, those temples were built by Egyptians and those gods were made by Egyptians. Gods always love the people who make 'em. We can't put no faith in them."

"Don't say that, Amram. That don't leave me no way to turn at all. Makes me feel like my insides been ripped out."

"Well, Caleb, I'm giving it out just like I figured it out. We just ain't got no out that I can see. Anybody depending on somebody else's gods is depending on a fox not to eat chickens. I don't see no way out but death and, Caleb, you are up against a hard game when you got to die to beat it."

The foreman was coming so they quit whispering and speeded up their work for a while. It was about dark and they knew they couldn't work much longer anyway. The foreman glanced at them in passing and went on. They began to whisper again right away, under pretense of adjusting a rope for lifting a stone.

"Caleb?"

"I hear you, Amram."

"Wouldn't it be swell if some of us hid knives in our clothes when we went to see Pharaoh?"

"It sure would. But they always search us, don't they, before they let us in."

"I know, but it is something nice to think about, ain't it?"

"Sure is."

"Right now, everybody's nerve is gone, but someday, maybe not in our time, but, he's bound to meet his match first and last."

"That's a long time to wait, Amram, but I reckon it is the best we can do. I hate myself for not trying it even if they all kill me for it."

"That's what I hate 'em for too, making me scared to die. It's a funny thing, the less people have to live for, the less nerve they have to risk losing—nothing."

"Where'd you get that good word from, Amram? It sure is the truth. I know it by myself."

"Oh, you learn things as you go along. I hope I don't have another boy, Caleb. Even if the soldiers don't find him and kill him, I don't want him feeling like I feel. I want him to be a man."

AMRAM AND CALEB GOT OFF and plodded on home. Amram was full of feelings about his wife's condition and Caleb talked about the protest meeting. He wanted Amram to go if he could.

"I guess you're right about it not doing no good and I reckon we all know it. But I guess the reason we go is it makes us feel like we still got some say-so over our life. In that way we don't feel quite so much like mules."

Amram said, "Eat your supper just as quick as you can if you going with me and let's locate a hiding place for my wife."

They said goodbye at the door of Amram's hut and Caleb went on home. Amram stepped inside to fate. Jochebed's water had broken and she was in labor. Old Puah was in the back room squatting down by the straw pallet of Jochebed whispering to her to "bear down!" in her harsh old voice.

Amram knelt by his wife and kissed her. She lifted her arms about his neck and hung there.

"Amram," she whispered, "you won't have no time to move me at all. But you mustn't let me scream, hear? No matter how hard the pain gets you mustn't let me scream. Pharaoh's secret police don't never stop prowling."

"I know that. Oh, honey, I hate for our child to come like this. I don't feel like no man at all."

"You can't help it, honey. You done the best you could. Just don't let me scream out when I get so bad I don't know what I'm doing. Hold my mouth good, Amram. Don't let me expose our child to murder, in case it's a boy."

"I promise, Jochebed, but this is a mean moment in life."

She hugged him faintly and smiled up. "The pains took me hard once or twice. I was afraid it was going to come before you got here," she said with a sort of happiness in her voice because her husband was there at her time.

In a little while Amram started to eat his supper. But no sooner did he begin than Jochebed uttered a cry. He flew back to her side and lifted her head in his arms and put one hand over her mouth. She tried hard to scream, but Amram was there.

The back of Amram's hard hand filled her mouth. His rough hand clamped down fiercely over her lower face. Jochebed fought for her breath and for the boon of shrieking out her agony and suffering.

"Shhh! The Egyptians will hear you!"

The woman may have heard, but she struggled harder to release the agony of her loins through cries. Her lungs almost exploded with the pent-in air. She clawed at her husband's hands which so relentlessly smothered her gasping cries. She drew up her knees violently and arched her back.

Now old Puah, the midwife, knelt over Jochebed and laid helping hands upon her belly. "Bear down!" the midwife commanded sternly. "Bear down, Jochebed, and have done with this birthing. It is taking much too long. Bear down, I tell you!" The command was stern but whispered. It was muted by a fear like every other sound in the house. Old Puah put her lips to the other's ear and beseeched, "Ah, Jochebed, will you not hurry up with this child before the soldiers pass again?"

"Shut up, woman," Amram began, but had to turn all of his attention and strength to muffling the agony of his wife. She was flinging her
head from side to side to wrench free of the hands that gripped her lower
face like a vice. Finally the pain wave passed and she subsided on the
straw limp and white.

"Ah, it is awful when a woman cannot even cry out in childbirth,"
Puah said. "When will these Egyptians be punished for their crimes?"

"Hush! Mouth almighty!" Amram said. "The very air in Goshen
has ears. Have you got the medicine fixed for her and ready?"

"Certainly, Amram. I didn't start to delivering babies just yesterday.
As soon as I know a woman's time is near, I boil the herbs for her."

"Where is it then?" Amram whispered anxiously.

"In that pot over against the wall. But do you think it is safe to give
it now? It will speed up her labor but—" She looked fearfully over her
shoulder towards the dark door of the outer room.

Jochebed set her teeth and hissed a groan. Instantly her husband's
hands flew to her mouth. From his kneeling position he looked over his
shoulder into the outer room and whispered "Aaron."

A young voice charged with fear whispered back from the dark outer
room. "Yessir, papa."

"Don't stand there yelling back and forth with me! Come and hear
what I have to say."

Aaron the boy entered the back room lit dimly by the crude oil lamp
on the floor and stood timidly back of the squatting Puah. The lamp
shone between the pale face of his mother on the straw pallet and the
tortured features of his father kneeling over her. He didn't feel so much
like a coward as he had out there in the dark front room for he saw the
fear on the faces of the three grown folks in the room.

"Yessir, papa, what you want with me?"

"Where is your sister?"

"Miriam is out there—" indicating the outer room.

"Tell her to come here."

Aaron tiptoed back into the other room without a sound and came
back shoving Miriam before him. They knelt before Amram and
presented their ears.

"Miriam, you go and squat just inside the front door and watch. If
anyone approaches come quickly. Do not call out."

"Yessir, papa."

"Aaron, you go outside."

"Not outside, papa. Please don't make me go outside," Aaron gasped in terror. "The secret police!"

"Yes, outside!" Amram answered sternly. "These Egyptian scoundrel-beasts must be overcome somehow. There ain't but a few of us Hebrews. We ain't got nothing to fight with. Do as I tell you. Go out to the main street and watch. When you see a band of the plug-uglies coming, run back and whisper to Miriam. She will give us the sign."

"But I ain't but twelve years old. All them Egyptian soldiers—"

"Go on! It's done got so that Israelite boys can't wait to get grown to be men. You will have to be a man right now." Amram gestured towards the pallet, the midwife and the room and Aaron stumbled out into the Egyptian darkness to watch. Miriam took her post by the house door and Puah gave Jochebed the drink she called the "friend of women" while Amram knelt in love and fear beside her head. He looked down on the thick red hair of his wife, her white face with the eyes closed in weariness, the hollows in her neck and her breasts. He saw the tracks of time over all and thought, "Of course, Jochebed ain't a girl no more. We got a son twelve years old and a daughter who is nine. Girl-wives must turn into women some time or other."

The oil in the lamp was getting low and Amram moved to replenish it. Old Puah measured and folded swaddling clothes and the night kept its silence outside the house.

Suddenly screams full of terror, sounds of strife and things overthrown came from another quarter of the village. Screams, gagging cries, metal on metal, metal on softer substances.

Amram rushed to the middle door. "Where is that, Miriam?"

"Beyond the house of Hur," the girl sobbed. "Oh, please let me call in Aaron and let's bar the door, papa. The soldiers will kill us!"

A great scream of pain burst from the throat of Jochebed and Amram flew to her bedside and silenced her as before. The struggle was brief and fierce. Then it all ended with a little sigh of relief at the momentary cessation of pain. Amram smoothed back her hair and put his palm soothingly upon his wife's head.

"You, you let me scream," Jochebed accused Amram weakly between subsiding gasps.

Amram thought to quiet her fears with soothing words, but just then Aaron plunged through the front door, stumbling over Miriam's knees and flung his ghastly face into the back room.

"Papa! Mama! Puah! They had a baby at Jacob's house and the soldiers took it and killed it! It was a boy baby, papa, so the Egyptians took it and killed it. Jacob tried to save his baby so they killed him too. I saw it all from the darkness outside.''

"How did they know the child was there?'' Amram asked.

"They have been skulking around the neighborhood since yesterday, someone told me. Maybe they heard it cry. Perhaps somebody told on them.''

Three pairs of eyes sought the midwife at once.

"We know your loyalty, Puah,'' Amram said, "but some of the midwives have been known to go from the confinement to the Egyptians.''

"And, papa,'' Aaron went on, "the soldiers also killed Jacob's wife. Was it because she cried so loud?''

For a space they all swam in the silence in the room. All their bodies leaned forward as if in flight. The midwife, the husband and the woman on the straw, these were crumbling bags of fear. The naked flame of the rush light on the floor even tried to flee before the tiny breeze from the door. Then suddenly Jochebed clenched her fists and groaned like the earth birthing mountains, and the body and feel of the sound threatened them like a sword until the cry of the newborn baby ended it all.

Old Puah was squatted on her haunches to receive the child. The man heard the cry but did not look behind him. He looked at the pain-struck face of his wife and she begged him with her looks. Puah busied herself around behind him for a minute and then she spoke.

"Amram, your wife has borne you a son.''

AMRAM BOWED HIS HEAD for a space, then straightened tensely as if he listened to every sound in Egypt, however distant. As if he gazed and saw every sight and scene in the Kingdom from end to end. As if he felt every throb and tasted every draught.

"A son?'' he gasped at last.

"A son,'' Puah answered him, "and a beautiful child.''

"It must not live to cry again. Give it to me.''

Jochebed roused herself upon her elbows.

"No.''

"Give me the child, Puah,'' Amram said with a fearful calm in his voice. "It is a whole lot better for it to stop breathing in my hands than for those—"

Jochebed had struggled to her knees. "No! My son is going to live. If the Egyptians come to kill it, then they got to kill me before they do him. If Pharaoh done scared all the love out of its papa, then let all Egypt come against me. I can't die but one time nohow, and it might as well be now. Puah, hand me my son!"

Amram turned his stricken face upon his wife. "Jochebed, there are different kinds of courage. Sometimes ordinary love and courage ain't enough for the occasion. But a woman wouldn't recognize a time like that when it come."

"Is my son got a Hebrew for a father or a Pharaoh?"

"But you heard what Aaron said."

"What of it? Pharaoh may be dead tomorrow. Who knows? Let's take a chance."

Amram looked about him wearily. "Well, if we must fool the crocodiles, let us begin and do it right. Aaron, go and watch up and down the road while I dig out a cave under the inside wall of the house. It must be large enough to hold the child."

Aaron arose sullenly. "But, papa, the soldiers may come along and kill me. They'll ask me what I'm doing out there."

"Go on! As soon as I have finished I will come and stand guard myself and you can go to bed. The sound of my battle with the soldiers will warn you all to hide the child."

Jochebed, clutching her new son to her breast, threw her husband a look so full of love and happiness that Amram felt for the moment that the sacrifice of his own body was a little thing.

The police, the secret police. That was what worried the people of Goshen. Just to look around, they were nowhere, but from the effects they were everywhere. Were ears pressed to their walls at night? It seemed so. A casual conversation might bring a public whipping and extra hours of work. How did Pharaoh find out so much? Hebrew began to suspect Hebrew. Men were accused of treason and revolt for saying Pharaoh was not kind. Everything was treason and subject to labor fines and lashings. No one except women were sent to jail. Pharaoh said it was a waste of man power and groceries to fasten up able-bodied Hebrews in jail. Every crime not punishable by death could be worked out in the brickyards, the stone quarries or on buildings. A beautiful new city bore his name and more were being planned. The Hebrews did not know all this about new plans. They talked together and said that when the new city of Rameses was finished, that Pharaoh would be satisfied. Some of them even thought that they might get back their houses and lands.

But Pharaoh took counsel with his servants. Week after week he called them to listen to his newest ideas that he was going to work into plans. The servants told Pharaoh that all of his thoughts had genius and after ten meetings they told him his plans were perfect. So he called the Hebrew elders together to listen. He was going to speak to them in the public place. His messengers went all through Goshen and they went on all the public works telling them to come to the meeting. Pharaoh was going to be good and kind enough to appear before them in person and speak to them of his own free will. Three days after the announcement he was going to speak on the Hebrew future.

The people in Goshen were excited. Hope burst its binding string and gushed over the province.

Jochebed held her baby on her lap and smiled at her husband. "Maybe we won't have to hide our baby no more, Amram. Maybe we can circumcise it and hold a christening."

"Maybe."

"I could make some little honey cakes and have palm wine and beer. That would be just like old times, wouldn't it?"

"Yes, it would. Like when Aaron and Miriam come."

"Only this baby is so much prettier than either one of them ever was, ain't he?"

"I think so. He's awful fine looking. Too bad we can't show him around some. Finest looking baby in Egypt."

"You know, Amram, I just felt all along that Pharaoh couldn't keep up his meanness. It was too awful to last."

"What makes you think he's changed his mind? Him sending for us got everybody to hoping and wishing, but it don't have to be what we hope at all."

"Oh, there you go again! Amram, what makes you always looking for the dark side of everything? I declare to my rest you just like an old sorehead bear. Naturally, Pharaoh is fixing to free us and leave our boy babies alone. He couldn't do nothing else."

"Oh, yes, he could, too. Everybody to their own nature. He don't have to smell through our nose at all, and I don't believe nothing until I see it."

"Aw, Amram, you wrong this time. I done talked to a heap of people and they all think like I do."

"You all ain't thinking, you wishing. Anyhow, keep our baby in the hole just like we been doing for the last three months. Keep him hid till we hear further. 'Tain't no use in taking chances."

"He's getting so strong! Look at him trying to sit alone! Look at him! He's mad now cause he can't quite make it. Listen at the voice he's got on him!"

"That's just the thing I'm scared of. I can't half work for worrying. Some of them secret spies is bound to hear him before long. Then what we going to do, honey? I thought they had us last night."

"Oh, a couple of days more and we won't have to worry."

"I hope you know what you hoping about, but old Pharaoh is mighty hard, honey, mighty hard."

"You just wait till the meeting and you going to see I'm right. God wouldn't let this thing we're under keep on like it's going. It's bound to come a change."

"What god you talking about, Jochebed? These gods was here in Egypt long before we ever thought of coming here. Don't look to them for too much, honey. Then you won't be disappointed."

Jochebed made to lay the child down on the pallet and it burst into lusty crying. Instantly the woman and her husband became hunted beasts. She grabbed the baby up and pressed its face into her soft bosom and glared towards the window and the door like something at bay. Amram crept to the door and looked around outside. When he returned the child had vanished into the dark hole under the wall, and the hole covered with a mat, but its voice could be heard nevertheless.

"See what I told you?" Amram gasped. "First and last we're all going to be butchered without mercy. Oh, Lord! why didn't I die before I cried? Why did I have to live for this?"

Jochebed seized the child again and pacified him quickly.

"Well, we got by again," she sighed with relief.

"But for how long?" Amram demanded. "Tomorrow, maybe, or in the next half an hour."

"You didn't see no spies around outside, did you?"

"Jochebed, you don't have to see spies for them to see you. Maybe the soldiers are on the way already."

Jochebed started to say something, but her husband shut her off with a gesture. His head hung down and for several minutes the thud-thud-

thudding of his fists against his breast were like a funeral march in drum tones; a tearless sorrow throbbing over death; a muted wail without words. Finally he could bear his feelings and he stopped.

"Listen, woman, Pharaoh is a flesh and blood man just like you and me, strange as it may seem. This won't be the first of his hearing how bad off we is here in Goshen. We ain't in the fix we're in by no accident, neither. He knows the feelings of a husband and a father. It is a terrible thing to strip a man of his meaning to his wife and children. Pharaoh knows all that. He means to do all that he is doing and maybe more. He has hunted around in his own heart for something to measure one's feelings by and the things that would hurt us the most. Then when he found them, he has done those things with calculated spite. You're just dumb to the fact. And another thing, he ain't sending for us to better our condition. He hates the very sight of us. The only reason he consents to look at us at all is because he wants to destroy us some more and enjoy seeing it gripe us."

The woman bent like a willow and cried softly over the child like a thin soprano sob song. Amram carried the bass part with his fists against his chest. Finally they crept to bed without eating. But all night the woman soothed herself by thinking "maybe." Amram dreamed dreams of smiting out with a bloody sword. Then it was time for him to get up and go to work again.

Everybody at work was whispering about the meeting with Pharaoh and everybody had made up their minds what would happen there, each one according to his courage. Some rolled over and over in a wallow of hope and scratched their backs with wishes. These men were afraid to think. Some stared in the face of probabilities and braced themselves for the shock.

So the meeting came. The Hebrew Elders went and stood in the public place that was full of soldiers fully armed. Then Pharaoh came in surrounded by his highborn servants and took his place. After his chief scribe got through telling the Hebrews what a blessing it was for Pharaoh to not only let them see his sacred body, he was actually going to let them listen to his voice. He was going to speak to them, using his own sacred voice and lips. They had done nothing to deserve such a great blessing. It just went to show how very kind and gentle and gracious great Pharaoh was. Always considering others before he did himself, and so on and so forth. Then Pharaoh himself rose to speak.

He said that his goodness and mercies were tõo well known to waşte time talking about. The only reason he mentioned it at all was because he could see all over Goshen that it was not appreciated as he had hoped and expected. Here they were, Hebrews, who had come down into Egypt as the allies and aides of those oppressors of the Egyptian people, and as such had trampled on the proud breast of Egyptian liberty for more than three hundred years. But the gods had used the magnificent courage of the real Egyptians to finally conquer and expel those sheep-herding interlopers whom the Hebrews had aided in every way they could to deprive the real Egyptians of their homes and their liberties. And now that they, the Hebrews, were conquered and beaten, he might have killed them all. That would have been right and just, seeing the great injury his beloved country had suffered at their hands. But did he do that? No! He was gentle and he spared them and allowed them to continue to live in the country. All he had required of them was that they work and build him a few cities here and there to pay back in a small way for all the great benefits they had received in their long residence in Egypt and also to give back some of the wealth they had so ruthlessly raped from the helpless body of Egypt when she was in no position to defend herself.

And now, what does he discover? He finds that these same Hebrews, instead of setting to work with glad hearts, happy that they have been given a chance, even in a small way, to make some sort of pay back on their huge debt to Egypt, and to redeem themselves in the eyes of the world, were congregating in Goshen and planning protests against his mild and beneficent decrees! It was hard to believe, but he happened to have the facts. So what did it prove? It was too plain for even the most merciful to ignore that these Hebrews whom he had saved from the fury of his people and against the advice of his wise counsellors, did not want to pay their debt to Egypt and decency. They were doing all they could to evade it. This show of ingratitude and hardness of heart was bound to arouse the mild but courageous Egyptian nation to fury unless something was done to show the loyal nation, who had suffered so much already, that its ruler would not further encourage such iniquities. His piercing eyes and all-hearing ears had discovered a well-organized plot to swindle Egypt out of her just amount of work out of them, by slowing up their work—a most reprehensible and low-down trick worthy only of Hyksos and Hebrews! But he had a remedy for this. The overseers had been instructed to use the lash more freely to speed up work and to rub salt in the welts raised by the whip. But still that did not repay poor suffering Egypt for the work they had lost in the past. So he now decreed that Hebrews must begin work one hour earlier in the morning and work one hour more in the evening.

Just in passing he wanted to acknowledge a petition with many signatures that had reached him. In it the Hebrews had again raised that question of leaving Egypt. He just wanted to say neither in this generation nor yet in the generations of their great grandchildren would they be allowed to escape their just punishments. Did the Egyptians run away when they were being robbed and oppressed by these same malefactors and their friends? No!

Then he went on to say that even greater wickedness had been uncovered. His laws and most royal decrees were being flouted. He, after taking counsel with his wise advisors, had decreed that all boy babies born to the Hebrews must be destroyed. But he found that certain people were plotting together to make his laws come to nothing. And something was going to be done about it. The strong arm of Pharaoh had never failed against his enemies, in spite of his merciful nature.

Pharaoh paused and looked at the faces of the Hebrew Elders grouped below and before him. He saw the uncomfortable stir that moved them almost imperceptibly. The slight shifting of feet; the nervous movements of hands, the gaping, stricken faces of the less wary among them, and he smiled.

"I see that I got you by the short hair when I told you I know what is going on about those boy babies. That is not the worst yet. My police have captured several of those midwives who have been waiting on your womenfolks in secret. They claimed that they wouldn't talk, but when my men got through with them they talked and talked aplenty, from old Puah on down."

Amram started violently and then hated himself for his weakness, but he couldn't help himself. It looked like Pharaoh was looking straight at him. He could see the gleam in Pharaoh's eyes as he went on. "So now I know all about those births behind rocks and in caves and such as that. And I know all about those babies hidden out in the woods and in holes dug under house walls. My soldiers will be around to call on you, and when they come to call, they won't miss nobody. I done told you."

The Elders looked at one another and finally Hur spoke up. "Give us a chance, Great Pharaoh. We proved ourselves builders and generally constructive under the last regime. We love Egypt. It is the only home we know. Trust us and see if we are good citizens or not."

"Why should I trust people without monuments and memories? It looks bad to me—a people who honor nobody. It is a sign that you forget your benefactors as soon as possible after the need is past."

"We don't build monuments, but we do have memories."

"How is anyone to know that? Take for instance your great man Joseph. As long as you have been in Egypt you have not raised one stone to his memory."

"Look at it another way. Perhaps we do not need stones to remind us. It could be that some folks need stones to remind them. It could be that memorial stones are signs of bad memories. We just don't trust our memories to stones."

Pharaoh's face darkened at this. He laughed in a harsh way.

"Well, anyway, you won't need no stones to remind your children and your great-great-grandchildren of the punishment that Rameses put on you. You are going to work and work and work. You are going to weep and you are going to bleed and bleed until you have paid in a measure for your crimes against Egypt. I done told you now. Don't give me no trouble unless you want to make me mad."

The Elders shuffled out of the place somehow and started on home. "No rest, no property, no babies, no gods," Amram gasped. "Why would anybody want to live? Why don't we kill ourselves and be done with the thing?"

"Maybe we hope we'll beat the game somehow without dying. That's human, ain't it?" somebody said and so they dragged themselves on home to tell what was said. They ground their souls between their teeth as they went but there was nothing to spit out. It was just a grinding and an aching.

Jochebed was asleep when Amram got home, so he wouldn't wake her to hear what he had to say. Tomorrow was time enough to start the weeping. So he stepped over the straw bed of his two older children and stretched out beside his wife till daylight. Then he told her.

She didn't say anything and she didn't stand up. She took the sleeping baby in her arms and sat there on the straw pallet staring down in its face. Amram squatted down before her and stared down at the baby too. Its little hands and feet and the helpless soft body was between the man and the woman and they huddled over it in silence for a long time. Then Amram said huskily, "Shall we grant it merciful escape, Jochebed?" and felt in her lap for her hand and pressed it. He could not bear to look at her eyes.

"No, Amram."

"Those brutal soldiers, Jochebed, grin with pleasure when they hunt down one of our children like hounds after rabbits."

"I don't care, honey. If my child is murdered, old Pharaoh has got to do the murdering his own self. I ain't going to allow him to make me do his murdering for him. If the gods want the life of my innocent boy, then they got to make a move and show me. I mean to hold out till they do. Let's hide it on the river like some others I know."

"All right, honey. I sure do want him to live and do well."

Impulsively he caught the child up in his arms.

"To think that we have not had the joy of giving it a name, nor fondling it, nor circumcising it lest it cry out and be found."

"It sure is sad. But you hurry on to work, Amram, before the soldiers come to hunt you up. It sure would hurt me to my heart to have to see 'em lay that salted lash on your back."

"But what will you do about this big, fat son of ours?"

"Go on to work, Amram, and I will find some way. One of the children is always on guard."

Amram hurried off and Jochebed called the children to her. "Go and cut me rushes from the marshes," she told them. "Go and hurry back fast. I got to make a good basket. Get me the best rushes you can."

The basket was scarcely started when Amram reached home after dark. Jochebed had given way to her despair more than once and crumpled on the straw beside her growing child. Twice he had cried so loud that Jochebed knew he could be heard all over the neighborhood and prayed that no prowling Egyptians were near.

So four people forgot hunger that night and sleep was not present in them. Four pairs of ears strained towards the night outside the house and four hearts fainted at every creeping sound as four pairs of fingers toiled over the basket until it was woven strong and tight and daubed and calked with pitch and mud.

"You think, Amram, if I took the baby before Pharaoh and begged him, he might get sorry for me and let me keep my child?"

"Get sorry for you? No. He plans harsher measures for us. The horn that is hooking us gets stiffer day by day. If you could only run away with him or hide him for a while!"

"There ain't no other way then, but the river. All the roads is full of spies. Goshen is ringed with steel. Amram, do you think this basket will be safe?''

"I hope so, Jochebed. It is a real good basket, even if we was in a hurry. I don't believe the water will get in to it. Hand me the baby and let us see how he fits in it.''

Jochebed lined the basket lovingly with one of her garments and then with goose feathers before she laid the child inside. Then she knew the basket was ready, so it was the time for tears. There was nothing any more with which to busy her hands and brace her spirits. She beat her breasts and wept without restraint for several minutes. Amram bowed his head in silence. Aaron and Miriam sat in dumb terror watching their parents and occasionally smiting their breasts to show their sympathy of grief.

"We must put him on the river, Amram,'' Jochebed said at last. "That is why I made the boat—the basket for him.''

"But why upon the river?''

"We ain't never been nowhere, Amram, so we don't know. It could be other people besides those we know live along the Nile. It may even run outside of Egypt. Maybe someone among them may find him and love him. Maybe even in Egypt there might be somebody with a heart.'' She broke down into sobbing again. "Anyway, there ain't nothing left for us to do. One thing I know Pharaoh can't make out of me. He can't take my son away from me and make me a murderer at the same time. That's one thing I don't aim to let him do.''

Amram looked at his wife's face and was fed inwardly by her look. So the night of the morning found them with the basket moving stealthily down to the Nile. At the river, Amram withdrew with Aaron and Miriam to watch. Jochebed fed the child copiously from her breasts and put him back into the basket. Then the thought assailed her that perhaps her basket was not seaworthy after all. She took him out again and held him across her knees as she tried her woven boat upon the water. It floated dry and lightly upon the stream. She drew it back to her and placed her baby in it for the last time and covered it with the lid. The little bark was propelled out from the shore among the tall bulrushes and rested there with the Nile lapping it gently and lulling the child to sleep.

Jochebed squatted there watching until her husband sent Miriam to call her lest she be found there by some Egyptians. She rose stiffly after a while and closed her bosom slowly. She spoke to Miriam and told the girl to station herself beneath the clump of palms not too far away to see what happened to the child. She must go home and sprawl on the earthen floor with her fears. Then she spoke to the morning, and the Nile: "Nile, youse such a great big river and he is such a little bitty thing. Show him some mercy, please."

ALL THE LITTLE STARS CREPT BACK into heaven and the sun rose. Miriam, standing on the watch wall among the palms, calmed herself and sat down. Her eyes wandered from the particular spot among the bulrushes to bulrushes in general. Then she regarded the river and the activities on the river. Far up-stream, several fishing boats were out. A group was drawing water with oxen for the fields. Water birds swooping and diving, and occasionally feeding-fishes, flinging their bodies out of the water in the exultation of the kill. Then Miriam went to sleep.

She woke up with a guilty start and looked for the little ark on the river which contained her baby brother. It was not there. She looked all around her to see if anyone was watching her and feeling sure on that score, she crept down to the spot where the basket had been and parted the bulrushes. The child and his basket were gone, that was all. And she had not the least idea of where he had gone, nor how. What should she tell her parents? She began to cry.

But her tears did not flow long. Down-stream at some distance she saw a glorious sight. A large party of young women dressed in rich clothing was clustered on the bank. The morning sun struck against shining metal ornaments and drew Miriam away from her search for her brother and from her tired and frightened self. She crept downstream, keeping as close to the shrubbery growing along the river as best she could.

Ten young women stood out in the stream holding up a long piece of cloth that shielded another young woman from public view, or almost shielded her. Two others washed and massaged her for several minutes while Miriam watched from her hiding place. It was a marvelous scene to her and she felt uplifted from gazing on it. This could be nobody else but the Princess Royal—only daughter of Pharaoh, newly widowed by the death of the Assyrian crown prince and returned to Egypt. Miriam noted her person, her trappings and her attendants and said to herself: "Royalty is a wonderful thing. It sure is a fine happening. It ought to be so that everybody that wanted to could be a queen. I wish I could get close enough to touch that princess. I wish I was one of those girls waiting on her, even.''

The Princess came up out of the river. The girls holding the screening cloth moved up with her on dry land and kept shielding her until she was rubbed down, oiled and dressed. There was chatting and laughter. The lift of a thin, sweet tone came to where she crouched in the bushes and the child Miriam stood up and craned her neck to see where it came from. And now she saw two black eunuchs squatting on their heels at a distance from the bathing party playing, one on a flute and the other on a stringed instrument. Some of the girls took positions and began to dance. The others went on folding garments, packing caskets with toilet articles and generally preparing to leave the bathing place. The dance ended and then the music. The Princess rose from the stool placed for her and was instantly surrounded by her party. One eunuch carried a sunshade over her head. Two girls waved ornate fans on long handles. Miriam's heart beat fast as she realized that they were coming in her direction. Now she would be able to see them at close range.

But the party did not move off at once. Something in the water had attracted the attention of the Princess. She was directing someone in the party to it. One of the girls removed her sandals and went down into the stream and came out with a dark, oval object. "Aha!" thought Miriam, "they had forgotten the casket in which is kept the things for washing the Princess. They will get a good scolding for that. But I wish they had left it so I could have seen what was in it. That would have been wonderful! I could have run after her and returned it to her and maybe she might have made me one of her ladies in waiting. Oh, a lady in waiting to the Princess! Nothing could be greater than that.''

The party moved off leisurely and came abreast of Miriam. They were not more than thirty feet from where she hid. She was so entranced that she stood up, the better to see, and one of the ladies saw her.

"It is a Hebrew!" she all but screamed. "What is she doing here? Catch her!"

"She is only a child," the Princess said lightly. "She can do nothing harmful.''

"But she might be a spy," one of the ladies pointed out.

"Yes, these Hebrews may be planning to assassinate you."

The eunuchs drew their swords at this and looked threateningly at Miriam.

"Nonsense!" the Princess rejoined. "No one knew we were coming here today and no one—not even I—knows where we go tomorrow.''

"Still she should be questioned. Never can tell what these Hebrews might do to overthrow the government."

"Governments are not overthrown by little girls," the Princess retorted, and the party swept on its way towards the palace of Pharaoh.

Miriam stood blinking for a long time. She was completely beside herself with ecstasy. She had seen the daughter of Pharaoh. The daughter of Pharaoh had spoken to her. Well, anyhow she had spoken of her. All her life she was going to remember the gait of the Princess when she walked. She wondered if that movement was a special gift to royalty or if people like her could copy it. She certainly meant to try it before her play-mates. "This is the way the Princess walks," she would tell them. "I know, because I saw her and she spoke to me." She flew home as fast as her legs could move to tell what she had seen.

She burst into the house and found her mother stretched upon the floor facing the little cave where she had hidden the baby so often, and her mother was holding one of his little garments and weeping bitterly. Then Miriam remembered, not just that she had seen the Princess and heard her speak, but why she had been posted at that lonely place on the bank of the Nile at all. She recoiled from her mother's face in panic.

"What happened to my child, Miriam?"

"Oh—er—" Miriam came back to herself from her dreams of the palace. "I—I don't know, mama."

"You don't know?" Jochebed sprang to her feet in fury. "You don't know when you were left there to find out? You stupid dunce! Why *don't* you know? Didn't you stay where I put you?"

"Yes. Yes, mama, but I—I went to sleep. I was so tired from last night that I couldn't help it. I went to sleep after sun-up."

Seeing her frenzied mother searching for something with which to strike her made Miriam come alive inside more thoroughly than she ever had done before in her life and suddenly an explanation flashed across her brain.

"You see, mama, while I was asleep, the basket with your baby in it floated down-stream and the Princess saw it and took him home to the palace with her."

"The Princess? You mean Pharaoh's daughter?"

"Yes, mama, she's the very one. She was bathing herself in the river down below me and the basket with the baby in it floated down to where she was after she had finished her bath and was perfumed and anointed and dressed with a whole heap of pretty things in her hair. Then when she was ready to go she saw the baby and sent and took it with her. I met the party on the road and tried to ask 'em what they was doing with your child, but they took and drawed a sword on me and made like they was going to kill me.''

Jochebed wept bitterly. She felt her heart crowding her throat. She felt like the whole of Egypt was crowded into her middle and still she felt empty of joy.

''Now I know my poor little baby will be killed,'' she wailed and bowed herself again upon the floor. ''The sea-buzzards will kill it just for fun.''

No, mama, she was real nice. She walked like this and smiled at me. And when some of her servants threatened me she told them to leave me alone. She had music played when she found the child and took it to the palace like she was proud. I love the Princess, mama. I wish she would take me to the palace too.''

''Miriam, I ain't to be fooled with today: is you telling me the truth, or is you trying to dodge a whipping for not minding the baby?''

''But mama, I *did* see her send for the casket and take it home with her. One of her ladies in waiting carried it herself.''

''Oh, I am so sorry that I did not stay myself to watch! Maybe I won't never know what become of my baby. Miriam, are you sure it was the same basket which we made to hold the baby?''

''Yes, ma'am. I could see them get it even from a distance. And the Princess had on red sandals and her toenails was red.''

''And how did she treat the baby?''

She made them play music and they danced for her because she was so glad because she had found the child. I could see everything they did, mama. I wasn't far from the Princess. She told 'em she loved the child a lot already.''

Jochebed stiffened her back and stood up suddenly. ''I ain't a bit surprised to hear the Princess loved him. He is a mighty pretty child, and smart as a whip for his age.'' A glow began to gleam through her seamed face. ''So my child is in the palace! I'll go let the neighbors know.'' She tied her best shawl over her head and got as far as the door and stopped. ''No, I reckon I ought to tell my husband about our son getting to be a Prince of the house of Pharaoh before I tell the others.'' She took off her shawl and turned back. ''Get busy, Miriam, folks will be coming in to see us when they hear. The house must look better than it's looking now for

big doings like this. We is kinfolks to the Pharaohs now.'' She thrust the
broom into Miriam's hands and herself began to make up a batch of
honey cookies.

Jochebed began to mix the dough. She took great care with it and all
the time laboring Miriam for more detail.

"Miriam."

"Yes, mama."

"Come here to me. You didn't tell me whether the baby cried or not
when the Princess opened the basket."

"No, ma'am. I did not hear him cry at all. And, mama, the Princess
had a headdress of blue feathers that fell down over her shoulders in a real
pretty way like this." Miriam grabbed a shawl and draped it over her
head and strutted about.

"What did she *say*, Miriam, when she saw him? Tell me her exact
words."

"She said, 'What a beautiful child!' "

"Did she say that? She must be a real fine Princess sure enough."

"Oh, she is. Maybe if I was to go and ask her, she might take me for
a nurse to the baby."

"Hush up talking foolish! Youse too young. She would need a
woman with breast milk. I will go myself tomorrow to the palace and find
out if they need anybody."

Jochebed kneaded dough vigorously and bustled about.

"Blow up the fire, Miriam. I want a bed of coals to bake these hot
cakes." She patted out the little honey cakes and put them on the fire.
"Think I *will* run over to Rachel's, Hur's wife, and tell her about it. We
have always been the best of friends and she would feel hurt if I kept
anything secret from her like this. I'll tell her it's a secret and she won't
tell a soul. Mind you now, Miriam, don't let them cakes burn."

When Amram entered the door that night, very tired and sore from
work, he greeted his wife with "What is this I hear about the daughter of
Pharaoh adopting our son?"

"Oh, you done heard it already?" Jochebed asked with a pleased air.

"Who in Goshen ain't heard? That is all the folks are talking about.
Well, is it so?"

"Certainly, it is so."

"How do you know? Did the palace say anything to you?"

"Why, no. Reckon they didn't count us enough to tell us, us being

Hebrews. But Miriam saw her bathing party at the river and saw them take the child.''

"Humph! Pharaoh's killing every Hebrew boy child he can get his hands on and his daughter taking one home for a son. Ridiculous!''

"Oh, the Egyptians may not be as cruel as you make them out to be. Come here, Miriam, and tell your pa what you saw and what you heard.''

Miriam told again what she had told her mother and added, "And she wanted me to come to the palace to take care of the child for her.''

"See, Mr. Smarty!'' Jochebed cried triumphantly. "Always hunting for something mean and low. You don't even believe butter is greasy.''

"Oh, I'm willing enough to believe if you give me something to go on. I still want to ask Miriam some questions. For instance, if Miriam was *not* close enough to make out any special marks on the casket, how can she know it was the same one? Millions like that been made in Egypt. If Miriam didn't hear the baby cry how could she tell *what* was in the basket? It might have been the toilet articles of the Princess or a hundred other things. And then again even if she had heard a baby cry unless she was close enough to see the baby, how does she know it was the same one? Couldn't the party have brought a baby with them from the palace?''

Jochebed lost her good nature at that. Possibly he touched upon fears already hidden in her heart so she flew hot and turned upon Amram.

"Oh, you make me sick with your doubts and your suspicions! Always looking for a bug under every chip! Throwing cold water on everything! As if your own daughter couldn't tell the truth! I suppose you would rather believe that a crocodile come along while Miriam closed her eyes for a minute and et up our poor child.''

"It could have happened, you know.''

"Shut up!'' Jochebed screamed. "You ain't human! You ain't got no feelings! First you wanted to kill the child yourself and—''

"No, Jochebed, I didn't want to kill my boy. Pharaoh passed that law, not me. I just wanted to keep the soldiers from having the satisfaction of murdering it, that was all.''

"And when I wouldn't let you, you, its papa, I stopped you from killing it, you want to believe now that the crocodiles et it up or either the soldiers found it after all and drowned it. Amram, youse as hard as a flint inside. I hate you.''

"Jochebed,'' Amram said patiently, "I don't want to rob you out of your hope. I dread to think myself. But don't let us not raise up our hope to the throne of truth. Let us go ask at the palace tomorrow. Anyway, you had no business telling this thing all around until you had talked with me.''

They had to stop quarreling because people began dropping in. Soon the house was full of people gloating inwardly and chuckling out loud. ''Ho, ho! Pharaoh hates Hebrews, does he? He passes a law to destroy all our sons and he gets a Hebrew child for a grandson. Ain't that rich?''

And Amram hated it all. It made him feel flimsy and artificial. He felt worse because he could hear Miriam outside, the center of a large crowd, telling and retelling her story. ''The child was crying and that is how she found him. So Pharaoh's daughter asked me to bring mama to the palace to be a nurse for the child.''

''And why not?'' one elder asked. ''There is plenty of Hebrew blood in that family already. That is why that Pharaoh wants to kill us all off. He is scared somebody will come along and tell who his real folks are. The country can't get along without us. Take Joseph for example now: Did Egypt ever amount to anything until he took hold of things? I ask you, did it now? Tell me! We are going to have another great man in the palace when this boy they just took in grows up. This country can't make out without us.''

''You said something just now, but you didn't know it,'' another added. ''The higher-ups who got Hebrew blood in 'em is always the ones to persecute us. I got it from somebody that ought to know, that the grandmother of Pharaoh was a Hebrew woman.''

Why, they tell me that the new commissioner of finance is an out-and-out Hebrew who renounced his race. He won't even be seen speaking to one of us.''

''That would be just like him to do a trick like that. Afraid of being recognized, that's why.''

''For my part,'' one of the women said, ''I think the Princess is a very fine woman. It is time we quit straining against the new order and took an active part in it.'' There was hearty agreement from many women with this viewpoint.

''Oh, you women!'' Amram snorted. ''You are always ready to go with the conquerer. You recognize nothing but power. If it is a woman, a cow, a ewe, a doe or whatever female it is—let the male fight and die for her, and the moment that he is thoroughly beaten or killed, she gives herself to his conqueror. Talk about men being hard! We are the sentimental fools and you are the realists. Phooey!''

The little cakes were finally all gone and the crowd talked far into the night of the Hebrew victory over Pharaoh and went home. They did not question too closely for proof. They wanted to believe, and they did. It kept them from feeling utterly vanquished by Pharaoh. They had something to cherish and chew on, if they could say they had a Hebrew in the palace.

So the next day, Jochebed washed herself and walked the long and dusty way to the palace gate to offer herself as nurse to the baby, but they would not let her in. There was no new baby to be nursed, they told her. The Princess had been summoned home from Assyria on the death of her husband and had brought her infant son with her several months ago. But what is that to you, Hebrew woman? Anyway, no Hebrew servants were being used in the palace. Begone with you!

Still and all, Goshen never gave up their belief in the Hebrew in the palace. It was something for men to dream about. Jochebed became a figure of importance—the mother of our Prince in the palace. Miriam told her story again and again to more believing ears. It grew with being handled until it was a history of the Hebrew in the palace, no less. Men claimed to have seen signs at the birth of the child, and Miriam came to believe every detail of it as she added them and retold them time and time again. Others conceived and added details at their pleasure and the legends grew like grass.

FROM
Their Eyes Were
Watching God

THERE ARE YEARS that ask questions and years that answer. Janie had had no chance to know things, so she had to ask. Did marriage end the cosmic loneliness of the unmated? Did marriage compel love like the sun the day?

In the few days to live before she went to Logan Killicks and his often-mentioned sixty acres, Janie asked inside of herself and out. She was back and forth to the pear tree continuously wondering and thinking. Finally out of Nanny's talk and her own conjectures she made a sort of comfort for herself. Yes, she would love Logan after they were married. She could see no way for it to come about, but Nanny and the old folks had said it so it must be so. Husbands and wives always loved each other, and that was what marriage meant. It was just so. Janie felt glad of the thought for then it wouldn't seem so destructive and mouldy. She wouldn't be lonely anymore.

Janie and Logan got married in Nanny's parlor of a Saturday evening with three cakes and big platters of fried rabbit and chicken. Everything to eat in abundance. Nanny and Mrs. Washburn had seen to that. But nobody put anything on the seat of Logan's wagon to make it ride glorious on the way to his house. It was a lonesome place like a stump in the middle of the woods where nobody had ever been. The house was absent of flavor, too. But anyhow Janie went on inside to wait for love to begin. The new moon had been up and down three times before she got worried in mind. Then she went to see Nanny in Mrs. Washburn's kitchen on the day for beaten biscuits.

Nanny beamed all out with gladness and made her come up to the bread board so she could kiss her.

"Lawd a'mussy, honey, Ah sho is glad tuh see mah chile! G'wan inside and let Mis' Washburn know youse heah. Umph! Umph! Umph! How is dat husband uh yourn?"

Janie didn't go into where Mrs. Washburn was. She didn't say anything to match up with Nanny's gladness either. She just fell on a chair with her hips and sat there. Between the biscuits and her beaming pride Nanny didn't notice for a minute. But after a while she found the conversation getting lonesome so she looked up at Janie.

"Whut's de matter, sugar? You ain't none too spry dis mornin'."

"Oh, nothin' much, Ah reckon. Ah come to get a lil information from you."

The old woman looked amazed, then gave a big clatter of laughter. "Don't tell me you done got knocked up already, less see—dis Saturday it's two month and two weeks."

"No'm, Ah don't think so anyhow." Janie blushed a little.

"You ain't got nothin' to be shamed of, honey, youse uh married 'oman. You got yo' lawful husband same as Mis' Washburn or anybody else!"

"Ah'm all right day way. Ah *know* 'tain't nothin' dere."

"You and Logan been fussin'? Lawd, Ah know dat grass-gut, liver-lipted nigger ain't done took and beat mah baby already! Ah'll take a stick and salivate 'im!"

"No'm, he ain't even talked 'bout hittin' me. He says he never mean to lay de weight uh his hand on me in malice. He chops all de wood he think Ah wants and den he totes it inside de kitchin for me. Keeps both water buckets full."

"Humph! don't 'spect all dat tuh keep up. He ain't kissin' yo' mouf when he carry on over yuh lak dat. He's kissin' yo' foot and 'taint in uh man tuh kiss foot long. Mouf kissin' is on uh equal and dat's natural but when dey got to bow down tuh love, dey soon straightens up."

"Yes'm."

"Well, if he do all dat whut you come in heah wid uh face long as mah arm for?"

"'Cause you told me Ah mus gointer love him, and, and Ah don't. Maybe if somebody was to tell me how, Ah could do it."

"You come heah wid yo' mouf full uh foolishness on uh busy day. Heah you got uh prop tuh lean on all yo' bawn days, and big protection, and everybody got tuh tip dey hat tuh you and call you Mis' Killicks, and you come worryin' me 'bout love."

"But Nanny, Ah wants to want him sometimes. Ah don't want him to do all de wantin'."

"If you don't want him, you sho oughta. Heah you is wid de onliest organ in town, amongst colored folks, in yo' parlor. Got a house bought and paid for and sixty acres uh land right on de big road and. . . . Lawd have mussy! Dat's de very prong all us black women gits hung on. Dis love! Dat's just whut's got us uh pullin' and uh haulin' and sweatin' and doin' from can't see in de mornin' till can't see at night. Dat's how come de ole folks say dat bein' uh fool don't kill nobody. It jus' makes you sweat. Ah betcha you wants some dressed up dude dat got to look at de sole of his shoe everytime he cross de street tuh see whether he got enough leather dere tuh make it across. You can buy and sell such as dem wid what you got. In fact you can buy 'em and give 'em away.''

"Ah ain't studyin' 'bout none of 'em. At de same time Ah ain't takin' dat ole land tuh heart neither. Ah could throw ten acres of it over de fence every day and never look back to see where it fell. Ah feel de same way 'bout Mr. Killicks too. Some folks never was meant to be loved and he's one of 'em.''

"How come?"

"'Cause Ah hates de way his head is so long one way and so flat on de sides and dat pone uh fat back uh his neck.''

"He never made his own head. You talk so silly.''

"Ah don't keer who made it, Ah don't like de job. His belly is too big too, now, and his toe-nails look lak mule foots. And 'tain't nothin' in de way of him washin' his feet every evenin' before he comes tuh bed. 'Taint nothin' tuh hinder him 'cause Ah places de water for him. Ah'd ruther be shot wid tacks than tuh turn over in de bed and stir up de air whilst he is in dere. He don't even never mention nothin' pretty.''

She began to cry.

"Ah wants things sweet wid mah marriage lak when you sit under a pear tree and think. Ah . . .''

"'Tain't no use in you cryin', Janie. Grandma done been long uh few roads herself. But folks is meant to cry 'bout somethin' or other. Better leave things de way dey is. Youse young yet. No tellin' whut mout happen befo' you die. Wait awhile, baby. Yo' mind will change.''

Nanny sent Janie along with a stern mien, but she dwindled all the rest of the day as she worked. And when she gained the privacy of her own little shack she stayed on her knees so long she forgot she was there herself. There is a basin in the mind where words float around on thought and thought on sound and sight. Then there is a depth of thought untouched by words, and deeper still a gulf of formless feelings untouched by thought. Nanny entered this infinity of conscious pain again on her old knees. Towards morning she muttered, "Lawd, you know mah heart. Ah done de best Ah could do. De rest is left to you.''

She scuffled up from her knees and fell heavily across the bed. A month later she was dead.

So Janie waited a bloom time, and a green time and an orange time. But when the pollen again gilded the sun and sifted down on the world she began to stand around the gate and expect things. What things? She didn't know exactly. Her breath was gusty and short. She knew things that nobody had ever told her. For instance, the words of the trees and the wind. She often spoke to falling seeds and said, "Ah hope you fall on soft ground," because she had heard seeds saying that to each other as they passed. She knew the world was a stallion rolling in the blue pasture of ether. She knew that God tore down the old world every evening and built a new one by sun-up. It was wonderful to see it take form with the sun and emerge from the gray dust of its making. The familiar people and things had failed her so she hung over the gate and looked up the road towards way off. She knew now that marriage did not make love. Janie's first dream was dead, so she became a woman.

LONG BEFORE THE YEAR WAS UP, Janie noticed that her husband had stopped talking in rhymes to her. He had ceased to wonder at her long black hair and finger it. Six months back he had told her, "If Ah kin haul de wood heah and chop it fuh yuh, look lak you oughta be able tuh tote it inside. Mah fust wife never bothered me 'bout choppin' no wood nohow. She'd grab dat ax and sling chips lak uh man. You done been spoilt rotten."

So Janie had told him, "Ah'm just as stiff as you is stout. If you can stand not to chop and tote wood Ah reckon you can stand not to git no dinner. 'Scuse mah freezolity, Mist' Killicks, but Ah don't mean to chop de first chip."

"Aw you know Ah'm gwine chop de wood fuh yuh. Even if you is stingy as you can be wid me. Yo' Grandma and me myself done spoilt yuh now, and Ah reckon Ah have tuh keep on wid it."

One morning soon he called her out of the kitchen to the barn. He had the mule all saddled at the gate.

"Looka heah, LilBit, help me out some. Cut up dese seed taters fuh me. Ah got tuh go step off a piece."

"Where you goin'?"

"Over tuh Lake City tuh see uh man about uh mule."

"Whut you need two mules fuh? Lessen you aims to swap off dis one."

"Naw, Ah needs two mules dis yeah. Taters is goin' tuh be taters in de fall. Bringin' big prices. Ah aims tuh run two plows, and dis man Ah'm talkin' 'bout is got uh mule all gentled up so even uh woman kin handle 'im."

Logan held his wad of tobacco real still in his jaw like a thermometer of his feelings while he studied Janie's face and waited for her to say something.

"So Ah thought Ah mout as well go see." He tagged on and swallowed to kill time but Janie said nothing except, "Ah'll cut de p'taters fuh yuh. When yuh comin' back?"

"Don't know exactly. Round dust dark Ah reckon. It's uh sorta long trip—specially if Ah hafter lead one on de way back."

When Janie had finished indoors she sat down in the barn with the potatoes. But springtime reached her in there so she moved everything to a place in the yard where she could see the road. The noon sun filtered through the leaves of the fine oak tree where she sat and made lacy patterns on the ground. She had been there a long time when she heard whistling coming down the road.

It was a cityfied, stylish dressed man with his hat set at an angle that didn't belong in these parts. His coat was over his arm, but he didn't need it to represent his clothes. The shirt with the silk sleeveholders was dazzling enough for the world. He whistled, mopped his face and walked like he knew where he was going. He was a seal-brown color but he acted like Mr. Washburn or somebody like that to Janie. Where would such a man be coming from and where was he going? He didn't look her way nor no other way except straight ahead, so Janie ran to the pump and jerked the handle hard while she pumped. It made a loud noise and also made her heavy hair fall down. So he stopped and looked hard, and then he asked her for a cool drink of water.

Janie pumped it off until she got a good look at the man. He talked friendly while he drank.

Joe Starks was the name, yeah Joe Starks from in and through Georgy. Been workin' for white folks all his life. Saved up some money—round three hundred dollars, yes, indeed, right here in his pocket. Kept hearin' 'bout them buildin' a new state down heah in Floridy and sort of wanted to come. But he was makin' money where he was. But when he heard about 'em makin' a town all outa colored folks, he knowed dat was de place he wanted to be. He had always wanted to be a big voice, but de white folks had all de sayso where he come from and everywhere else, exceptin' dis place dat colored folks was buildin' their-selves. Dat was right too. De man dat built things oughta boss it. Let colored folks build things too if dey wants to crow over somethin'. He was glad he had his money all saved up. He meant to git dere whilst de town wuz yet a baby. He meant to buy in big. It had always been his wish and desire to be a big voice and he had to live nearly thirty years to find a chance. Where was Janie's papa and mama?

"Dey dead, Ah reckon. Ah wouldn't know 'bout 'em 'cause mah Grandma raised me. She dead too."

"She dead too! Well, who's lookin' after a lil girl-chile lak you?"

"Ah'm married."

"You married? You ain't hardly old enough to be weaned. Ah betcha you still craves sugar-tits, doncher?"

"Yeah, and Ah makes and sucks 'em when de notion strikes me. Drinks sweeten' water too."

"Ah loves dat mahself. Never specks to get too old to enjoy syrup sweeten' water when it's cools and nice."

"Us got plenty syrup in de barn. Ribbon-cane syrup. If you so desires—"

"Where yo' husband at, Mis' er-er."

"Mah name is Janie Mae Killicks since Ah got married. Useter be name Janie Mae Crawford. Mah husband is gone tuh buy a mule fuh me tuh plow. He left me cuttin' up seed p'taters."

"You behind a plow! You ain't got no mo' business wid uh plow than uh hog is got wid uh holiday! You ain't got no business cuttin' up no seed p'taters neither. A pretty doll-baby lak you is made to sit on de front porch and rock and fan yo'self and eat p'taters dat other folks plant just special for you."

Janie laughed and drew two quarts of syrup from the barrel and Joe Starks pumped the water bucket full of cool water. They sat under the tree and talked. He was going on down to the new part of Florida, but no harm to stop and chat. He later decided he needed a rest anyway. It would do him good to rest a week or two.

Every day after that they managed to meet in the scrub oaks across the road and talk about when he would be a big ruler of things with her reaping the benefits. Janie pulled back a long time because he did not represent sun-up and pollen and blooming trees, but he spoke for far horizon. He spoke for change and chance. Still she hung back. The memory of Nanny was still powerful and strong.

"Janie, if you think Ah aims to tole you off and make a dog outa you, youse wrong. Ah wants to make a wife outa you."

"You mean dat, Joe?"

"De day you puts yo' hand in mine, Ah wouldn't let de sun go down on us single. Ah'm uh man wid principles. You ain't never knowed what it was to be treated lak a lady and Ah wants to be de one tuh show yuh. Call me Jody lak you do sometime."

"Jody," she smiled up at him, "but s'posin'—"

"Leave de s'posin' and everything else to me. Ah'll be down dis road uh little after sunup tomorrow mornin' to wait for you. You come go wid me. Den all de rest of yo' natural life you kin live lak you oughta. Kiss me and shake yo' head. When you do dat, yo' plentiful hair breaks lak day."

Janie debated the matter that night in bed.

"Logan you 'sleep?"

"If Ah wuz, you'd be done woke me up callin' me."

"Ah wuz thinkin' real hard about us; about you and me."

"It's about time. Youse powerful independent around here sometime considerin'."

"Considerin' whut for instance?"

"Considerin' youse born in a carriage 'thout no top to it, and yo' mama and you bein' born and raised in de white folks back-yard."

"You didn't say all dat when you wuz begging Nanny for me to marry you."

"Ah thought you would 'preciate good treatment. Thought Ah'd take and make somethin' outa yuh. You think youse white folks by de way you act."

"S'posin' Ah wuz to run off and leave yuh sometime."

There! Janie had put words to his held-in fears. She might run off sure enough. The thought put a terrible ache in Logan's body, but he thought it best to put on scorn.

"Ah'm gettin' sleepy, Janie. Let's don't talk no mo'. 'Tain't too many mens would trust yuh, knowin yo' folks lak dey do."

"Ah might take and find somebody dat did trust me and leave yuh."

"Shucks! 'Tain't no mo' fools lak me. A whole lot of mens will grin in yo' face, but dey ain't gwine tuh work and feed yuh. You won't git far and you won't be long, when dat big gut reach over and grab dat little one, you'll be too glad to come back here.''

"You don't take nothin' to count but sow-belly and corn-bread.''

"Ah'm sleepy. Ah don't aim to worry mah gut into a fiddle-string wid no s'posin'.'' He flopped over resentful in his agony and pretended sleep. He hoped that he had hurt her as she had hurt him.

Janie got up with him the next morning and had the breakfast half-way done when he bellowed from the barn.

"Janie!'' Logan called harshly. "Come help me move dis manure pile befo' de sun gits hot. You don't take a bit of interest in dis place. 'Tain't no use in foolin' round in dat kitchen all day long.''

Janie walked to the door with the pan in her hand still stirring the cornmeal dough and looked towards the barn. The sun from ambush was threatening the world with red daggers, but the shadows were gray and solid-looking around the barn. Logan with his shovel looked like a black bear doing some clumsy dance on his hind legs.

"You don't need mah help out dere, Logan. Youse in yo' place and Ah'm in mine.''

"You ain't got no particular place. It's wherever Ah need yuh. Git uh move on yuh, and dat quick.''

"Mah mama didn't tell me Ah wuz born in no hurry. So whut business Ah got rushin' now? Anyhow dat ain't whut youse mad about. Youse mad 'cause Ah don't fall down and wash-up dese sixty acres uh ground yuh got. You ain't done me no favor by marryin' me. And if dat's what you call yo'self doin', Ah don't thank yuh for it. Youse mad 'cause Ah'm tellin' yuh whut you already knowed.''

Logan dropped his shovel and made two or three clumsy steps towards the house, then stopped abruptly.

"Don't you change too many words wid me dis mawnin', Janie, do Ah'll take and change ends wid yuh! Heah, Ah just as good as take you out de white folks' kitchen and set you down on yo' royal diasticutis and you take and low-rate me! Ah'll take holt uh dat ax and come in dere and kill yuh! You better dry up in dere! Ah'm too honest and hard-workin' for anybody in yo' family, dat's de reason you don't want me!'' The last sentence was half a sob and half a cry. "Ah guess some low-lifed nigger is grinnin' in yo' face and lyin' tuh yuh. God damn yo' hide!''

Janie turned from the door without answering, and stood still in the middle of the floor without knowing it. She turned wrongside out just standing there and feeling. When the throbbing calmed a little she gave Logan's speech a hard thought and placed it beside other things she had seen and heard. When she had finished with that she dumped the dough on the skillet and smoothed it over with her hand. She wasn't even angry. Logan was accusing her of her mama, her grandmama and her feelings, and she couldn't do a thing about any of it. The sow-belly in the pan needed turning. She flipped it over and shoved it back. A little cold water in the coffee pot to settle it. Turned the hoe-cake with a plate and then made a little laugh. What was she losing so much time for? A feeling of sudden newness and change came over her. Janie hurried out of the front gate and turned south. Even if Joe was not there waiting for her, the change was bound to do her good.

The morning road air was like a new dress. That made her feel the apron tied around her waist. She untied it and flung it on a low bush beside the road and walked on, picking flowers and making a bouquet. After that she came to where Joe Starks was waiting for her with a hired rig. He was very solemn and helped her to the seat beside him. With him on it, it sat like some high, ruling chair. From now on until death she was going to have flower dust and springtime sprinkled over everything. A bee for her bloom. Her old thoughts were going to come in handy now, but new words would have to be made and said to fit them.

"Green Cove Springs," he told the driver. So they were married before sundown, just like Joe had said. With new clothes of silk and wool.

They sat on the boarding house porch and saw the sun plunge into the same crack in the earth from which the night emerged.

ON THE TRAIN THE NEXT DAY, Joe didn't make many speeches with rhymes to her, but he bought her the best things the butcher had, like apples and a glass lantern full of candies. Mostly he talked about plans for the town when he got there. They were bound to need somebody like him. Janie took a lot of looks at him and she was proud of what she saw. Kind of portly like rich white folks. Strange trains, and people and places didn't scare him neither. Where they got off the train at Maitland he found a buggy to carry them over to the colored town right away.

It was early in the afternoon when they got there, so Joe said they must walk over the place and look around. They locked arms and strolled from end to end of the town. Joe noted the scant dozen of shame-faced houses scattered in the sand and palmetto roots and said, "God, they call this a town? Why, 'tain't nothing but a raw place in de woods."

"It is a whole heap littler than Ah thought." Janie admitted her disappointment.

"Just like Ah thought," Joe said. "A whole heap uh talk and nobody doin' nothin'. I god, where's de Mayor? He asked somebody. "Ah want tuh speak wid de Mayor."

Two men who were sitting on their shoulder-blades under a huge live oak tree almost sat upright at the tone of his voice. They stared at Joe's face, his clothes and his wife.

"Where y'all come from in sich uh big haste?" Lee Coker asked.

"Middle Georgy," Starks answered briskly. "Joe Starks is mah name, from in and through Georgy."

"You and yo' daughter goin' tuh join wid us in fellowship?" the other reclining figure asked. "Mighty glad tuh have yuh. Hicks is the name, Guv'nor Amos Hicks from Buford, South Carolina. Free, single, disengaged."

"I god, Ah ain't nowhere near old enough to have no grown daughter. This here is mah wife."

Hicks sank back and lost interest at once.

"Where is de Mayor?" Starks persisted. "Ah wants tuh talk wid *him*."

"Youse uh mite too previous for dat," Coker told him. "Us ain't got none yit."

"Ain't got no Mayor! Well, who tells y'all what to do?"

"Nobody. Everybody's grown. And then agin, Ah reckon us just ain't thought about it. Ah knows Ah ain't."

"Ah did think about it one day," Hicks said dreamily, "but then Ah forgot it and ain't thought about it since then."

"No wonder things ain't no better," Joe commented. "Ah'm buyin' in here, and buyin' in big. Soon's we find some place to sleep tonight us menfolks got to call people together and form a committee. Then we can get things movin' round here."

"Ah kin point yuh where yuh kin sleep," Hicks offered. "Man got his house done built and his wife ain't come yet."

Starks and Janie moved on off in the direction indicated with Hicks and Coker boring into their backs with looks.

"Dat man talks like a section foreman," Coker commented. "He's mighty compellment.''

"Shucks!" said Hicks. "Mah britches is just as long as his. But dat wife uh hisn! Ah'm uh son of uh Combunction if Ah don't go tuh Georgy and git me one just like her.''

"Whut wid?''

"Wid mah talk, man.''

"It takes money tuh feed pretty women. Dey gits uh lavish uh talk.''

"Not lak mine. Dey loves to hear me talk because dey can't understand it. Mah co-talkin' is too deep. Too much co to it.''

"Umph!''

"You don't believe me, do yuh? You don't know de women Ah kin git to mah command.''

"Umph!''

"You ain't never seen me when Ah'm out pleasurin' and givin' pleasure.''

"Umph!''

"It's uh good thing he married her befo' she seen me. Ah kin be some trouble when Ah take uh notion.''

"Umph!''

"Ah'm uh bitch's baby round lady people.''

"Ah's much ruther see all dat than to hear 'bout it. Come on less go see whut he gointuh do 'bout dis town.''

They got up and sauntered over to where Starks was living for the present. Already the town had found the strangers. Joe was on the porch talking to a small group of men. Janie could be seen through the bedroom window getting settled. Joe had rented the house for a month. The men were all around him, and he was talking to them by asking questions.

"Whut is de real name of de place?''

"Some say West Maitland and some say Eatonville. Dat's 'cause Cap'n Eaton give us some land along wid Mr. Laurence. But Cap'n Eaton give de first piece.''

"How much did they give?''

"Oh 'bout fifty acres.''

"How much is y'all got now?''

"Oh 'bout de same.''

"Dat ain't near enough. Who owns de land joining on to whut yuh got?''

"Cap'n Eaton.''

"Where *is* dis Cap'n Eaton?"

"Over dere in Maitland, 'ceptin' when he go visitin' or somethin'."

"Lemme speak to mah wife a minute and Ah'm goin' see de man. You cannot have no town without some land to build it on. Y'all ain't got enough here to cuss a cat on without gittin' yo' mouf full of hair."

"He ain't got no mo' land tuh give away. Yuh needs plenty money if yuh wants any mo'."

"Ah specks to pay him."

The idea was funny to them and they wanted to laugh. They tried hard to hold it in, but enough incredulous laughter burst out of their eyes and leaked from the corners of their mouths to inform anyone of their thoughts. So Joe walked off abruptly. Most of them went along to show him the way and to be there when his bluff was called.

Hicks didn't go far. He turned back to the house as soon as he felt he wouldn't be missed from the crowd and mounted the porch.

"Evenin', Miz Starks."

"Good evenin'."

"You reckon you gointuh like round here?"

"Ah reckon so."

"Anything *Ah* kin do tuh help out, why you kin call on me."

"Much obliged."

There was a long dead pause. Janie was not jumping at her chance like she ought to. Look like she didn't hardly know he was there. She needed waking up.

"Folks must be mighty close-mouthed where you come from."

"Dat's right. But it must be different at yo' home."

He was a long time thinking but finally he saw and stumbled down the steps with a surly "Bye."

"Good bye."

That night Coker asked him about it.

"Ah saw yuh when yuh ducked back tuh Starks' house. Well, how didju make out?"

"Who, me? Ah ain't been near de place, man. Ah been down tuh de lake tryin tuh ketch me uh fish."

"Umph!"

"Dat 'oman ain't so awfully pretty nohow when yuh take de second look at her. Ah had to sorta pass by de house on de way back and seen her good. 'Tain't nothin' to her 'ceptin' dat long hair."

"Umph!"

"And anyhow, Ah done took uhlikin' tuh de man. Ah wouldn't harm him at all. She ain't half ez pretty ez uh gal Ah run off and left up in South Cal'lina."

"Hicks, Ah'd git mad and say you wuz lyin' if Ah didn't know yuh so good. You just talkin' to consolate yo'self by word of mouth. You got uh willin' mind, but youse too light behind. A whole heap uh men seen de same thing you seen but they got better sense than you. You oughta know you can't take no 'oman lak dat from no man lak him. A man dat ups and buys two hundred acres uh land at one whack and pays cash for it."

"Naw! He didn't buy it sho nuff?"

"He sho did. Come off wid de papers in his pocket. He done called a meetin' on his porch tomorrow. Ain't never seen no sich uh colored man befo' in all mah bawn days. He's gointuh put up uh store and git uh post office from de Goven'ment."

That irritated Hicks and he didn't know why. He was the average mortal. It troubled him to get used to the world one way and then suddenly have it turn different. He wasn't ready to think of colored people in post offices yet. He laughed boisterously.

"Y'all let dat stray darky tell y'all any ole lie! Uh colored man sittin' up in uh post office!" He made an obscene sound.

"He's liable tuh do it too, Hicks. Ah hope so anyhow. Us colored folks is too envious of one 'nother. Dat's how come us don't git no further than us do. Us talks about de white man keepin' us down! Shucks! He don't have tuh. Us keeps our own selves down."

"Now who said Ah didn't want de man tuh git us uh post office? He kin be de king uh Jerusalem fuh all Ah keer. Still and all, 'tain't no use in telling lies just 'cause uh heap uh folks don't know no better. Yo' common sense oughta tell yuh de white folks ain't goin' tuh 'low him tuh run no post office."

"Dat we don't know, Hicks. He say he kin and Ah b'lieve he know whut he's talkin' 'bout. Ah reckon if colored folks got they own town they kin have post offices and whatsoever they please, regardless. And then agin, Ah don't speck de white folks way off yonder give uh damn. Less us wait and see."

"Oh, Ah'm waitin' all right. Specks tuh keep on waitin' till hell freeze over."

"Aw, git reconciled! Dat woman don't want you. You got tuh learn dat all de women in de world ain't been brought up on no teppentine

still, and no sawmill camp. There's some women dat jus' ain't for you
tuh broach. You can't get *her* wid no fish sandwich.''

They argued a bit more then went on to the house where Joe was and
found him in his shirt-sleeves, standing with his legs wide apart, asking
questions and smoking a cigar.

"Where's de closest saw-mill?'' He was asking Tony Taylor.

" 'Bout seben miles goin' t'wards Apopka,'' Tony told him.
"Thinkin' 'bout buildin' right away?''

"I god, yeah. But not de house Ah specks tuh live in. Dat kin wait
till Ah makes up mah mind where Ah wants it located. Ah figgers we all
needs uh store in uh big hurry.''

"Uh store?'' Tony shouted in surprise.

"Yeah, uh store right heah in town wid everything in it you needs.
'Tain't uh bit uh use in everybody proagin' way over tuh Maitland tuh
buy uh little meal and flour when they could git it right heah.''

"Dat would be kinda nice, Brother Starks, since you mention it.''

"I god, course it would! And then agin uh store is good in other
ways. Ah got tuh have a place tuh be at when folks come tuh buy land.
And furthermo' everything is got tuh have uh center and uh heart tuh it,
and uh town ain't no different from nowhere else. It would be natural
fuh de store tuh be meetin' place fuh de town.''

"Dat sho is de truth, now.''

"Oh, we'll have dis town all fixed up tereckly. Don't miss bein' at
de meetin' tuhmorrow.''

Just about time for the committee meeting called to meet on his
porch next day, the first wagon load of lumber drove up and Jody went to
show them where to put it. Told Janie to hold the committee there until
he got back, he didn't want to miss them, but he meant to count every
foot of that lumber before it touched the ground. He could have saved
his breath and Janie could have kept right on with what she was doing. In
the first place everybody was late in coming; then the next thing as soon
as they heard where Jody was, they kept right on up there where the new
lumber was rattling off the wagon and being piled under the big live oak
tree. So that's where the meeting was held with Tony Taylor acting as
chairman and Jody doing all the talking. A day was named for roads and
they all agreed to bring axes and things like that and chop out two roads
running each way. That applied to everybody except Tony and Coker.
They could carpenter, so Jody hired them to go to work on his store bright
and soon the next morning. Jody himself would be busy driving around

from town to town telling people about Eatonville and drumming up citizens to move there.

Janie was astonished to see the money Jody had spent for the land come back to him so fast. Ten new families bought lots and moved to town in six weeks. It all looked too big and rushing for her to keep track of. Before the store had a complete roof, Jody had canned goods piled on the floor and was selling so much he didn't have time to go off on his talking tours. She had her first taste of presiding over it the day it was complete and finished. Jody told her to dress up and stand in the store all that evening. Everybody was coming sort of fixed up, and he didn't mean for nobody else's wife to rank with her. She must look on herself as the bell-cow, the other women were the gang. So she put on one of her bought dresses and went up the new-cut road all dressed in wine-colored red. Her silken ruffles rustled and muttered about her. The other women had on percale and calico with here and there a head-rag among the older ones.

Nobody was buying anything that night. They didn't come there for that. They had come to make a welcome. So Joe knocked in the head of a barrel of soda crackers and cut some cheese.

"Everybody come right forward and make merry. I god, it's mah treat." Jody gave one of his big heh heh laughs and stood back. Janie dipped up the lemonade like he told her. A big tin cup full for everybody. Tony Taylor felt so good when it was all gone that he felt to make a speech.

"Ladies and gent'men, we'se come tuhgether and gathered heah tuh welcome tuh our midst one who has seen fit tuh cast in his lot amongst us. He didn't just come hisself neither. He have seen fit tuh bring his, er, er, de light uh his home, dat is his wife amongst us also. She couldn't look no mo' better and no nobler if she wuz de queen uh England. It's uh pledger fuh her tuh be heah amongst us. Brother Starks, we welcomes you and all dat you have seen fit tuh bring amongst us—yo' belov-ed wife, yo' store, yo' land—"

A big-mouthed burst of laughter cut him short.

"Dat'll do, Tony," Lige Moss yelled out. "Mist' Starks is uh smart man, we'se all willin' tuh acknowledge tuh dat, but de day he comes waggin' down de road wid two hund'ed acres uf land over his shoulder, Ah wants tuh be dere tuh see it."

Another big blow-out of a laugh. Tony was a little peeved at having the one speech of his lifetime ruined like that.

"All y'all know whut wuz meant. Ah don't see how come—"

" 'Cause you jump up tuh make speeches and don't know how,''
Lige said.

"Ah wuz speakin' jus' all right befo' you stuck yo' bill in."

"Naw, you wuzn't, Tony. Youse way outa jurisdiction. You can't
welcome uh man and his wife 'thout you make comparison about Isaac
and Rebecca at de well, else it don't show de love between 'em if you
don't."

Everybody agreed that that was right. It was sort of pitiful for Tony
not to know he couldn't make a speech without saying that. Some
tittered at his ignorance. So Tony said testily, "If all them dat's gointuh
cut de monkey is done cut it and through wid, we'll thank Brother Starks
fuh a respond."

So Joe Starks and his cigar took the center of the floor.

"Ah thanks you all for yo' kind welcome and for extendin' tuh me
de right hand uh fellowship. Ah kin see dat dis town is full uh union and
love. Ah means tuh put mah hands tuh de plow heah, and strain every
nerve tuh make dis our town de metropolis uh de state. So maybe Ah
better tell yuh in case you don't know dat if we expect tuh move on, us
got tuh incorporate lak every other town. Us got tuh incorporate, and us
got tuh have uh mayor, if things is tuh be done and done right. Ah
welcome you all on behalf uh me and mah wife tuh dis store and tuh de
other things tuh come. Amen."

Tony led the loud hand-clapping and was out in the center of the
floor when it stopped.

"Brothers and sisters, since us can't never expect tuh better our
choice, Ah move dat we make Brother Starks our Mayor until we kin see
further."

"Second dat motion!!!" It was everybody talking at once, so it was
no need of putting it to a vote.

"And now we'll listen tuh uh few words uh encouragement from
Mrs. Mayor Starks."

The burst of applause was cut short by Joe taking the floor himself.

"Thank yuh fuh yo' compliments, but mah wife don't know nothin'
'bout no speech-makin'. Ah never married her for nothin' lak dat. She's
uh woman and her place is in de home."

Janie made her face laugh after a short pause, but it wasn't too easy.

She had never thought of making a speech, and didn't know if she cared to make one at all. It must have been the way Joe spoke out without giving her a chance to say anything one way or another that took the bloom off of things. But anyway, she went down the road behind him that night feeling cold. He strode along invested with his new dignity, thought and planned out loud, unconscious of her thoughts.

"De mayor of uh town lak dis can't lay round home too much. De place needs buildin' up, Janie, Ah'll git hold uh somebody tuh help out in de store and you kin look after things whilst Ah drum up things otherwise."

"Oh Jody, Ah can't do nothin' wid no store lessen youse there. Ah could maybe come in and help you when things git rushed, but—"

"I god, Ah don't see how come yuh can't. 'Tain't nothin' atall tuh hinder yuh if yuh got uh thimble full uh sense. You got tuh. Ah got too much else on mah hands as Mayor. Dis town needs some light right now."

"Unh hunh, it *is* uh little dark right long heah."

" 'Course it is. 'Tain't no use in scufflin' over all dese stumps and roots in de dark. Ah'll call uh meetin' bout de dark and de roots right away. Ah'll sit on dis case first thing."

The very next day with money out of his own pocket he sent off to Sears, Roebuck and Company for the street lamp and told the town to meet the following Thursday night to vote on it. Nobody had ever thought of street lamps and some of them said it was a useless notion. They went so far as to vote against it, but the majority ruled.

But the whole town got vain over it after it came. That was because the Mayor didn't just take it out of the crate and stick it up on a post. He unwrapped it and had it wiped off carefully and put it up on a showcase for a week for everybody to see. Then he set a time for the lighting and sent word all around Orange County for one and all to come to the lamp-lighting. He sent men out to the swamp to cut the finest and the straightest cypress post they could find, and kept on sending them back to hunt another one until they found one that pleased him. He had talked to the people already about the hospitality of the occasion.

"Y'all know we can't invite people to our town just dry long so. I god, naw. We got tuh feed 'em something, and 'taint't nothin' people laks better'n barbecue. Ah'll give one whole hawg mah ownself. Seems lak all de rest uh y'all put tuhgether oughta be able tuh scrape up two mo'. Tell yo' womenfolks tuh do 'round 'bout some pies and cakes and sweet p'tater pone."

That's the way it went, too. The women got together the sweets and the men looked after the meats. The day before the lighting, they dug a big hole in back of the store and filled it full of oak wood and burned it down to a glowing bed of coals. It took them the whole night to barbecue the three hogs. Hambo and Pearson had full charge while the others helped out with turning the meat now and then while Hambo swabbd it all over with the sauce. In between times they told stories, laughed and told more stories and sung songs. They cut all sorts of capers and whiffed the meat as it slowly came to perfection with the seasoning penetrating to the bone. The younger boys had to rig up the saw-horses with boards for the women to use as tables. Then it was after sun-up and everybody not needed went home to rest up for the feast.

By five o'clock the town was full of every kind of a vehicle and swarming with people. They wanted to see that lamp lit at dusk. Near the time, Joe assembled everybody in the street before the store and made a speech.

"Folkses, de sun is goin' down. De Sun-maker brings it up in de mornin', and de Sun-maker sends it tuh bed at night. Us poor weak humans can't do nothin' tuh hurry it up nor to slow it down. All we can do, if we want any light after de settin' or befo' de risin', is tuh make some light ourselves. So dat's how come lamps was made. Dis evenin' we'se all assembled heah tuh light uh lamp. Dis occasion is something for us all tuh remember tuh our dyin' day. De first street lamp in uh colored town. Lift yo' eyes and gaze on it. And when Ah touch de match tuh dat lamp-wick let de light penetrate inside of yuh, and let it shine, let it shine, let it shine. Brother Davis, lead us in a word uh prayer. Ask uh blessin' on dis town in uh most particular manner."

While Davis chanted a traditional prayer-poem with his own variations, Joe mounted the box that had been placed for the purpose and opened the brazen door of the lamp. As the word Amen was said, he touched the lighted match to the wick, and Mrs. Bogle's alto burst out in:

We'll walk in de light, de beautiful light
Come where the dew drops of mercy shine bright
Shine all around us by day and by night
Jesus, the light of the world.

They, all of them, all of the people took it up and sung it over and over until it was wrung dry, and no further innovations of tone and tempo were conceivable. Then they hushed and ate barbecue.

When it was all over that night in bed Jody asked Janie, "Well, honey, how yuh lak bein' Mrs. Mayor?"

"It's all right Ah reckon, but don't yuh think it keeps us in uh kinda strain?"

"Strain? You mean de cookin' and waitin' on folks?"

"Naw, Jody, it jus' looks lak it keeps us in some way we ain't natural wid one 'nother. You'se always off talkin' and fixin' things, and Ah feels lak Ah'm jus' markin' time. Hope it soon gits over."

"Over, Janie? I god, Ah ain't even started good. Ah told you in de very first beginnin' dat Ah aimed tuh be uh big voice. You oughta be glad, 'cause dat makes uh big woman outa you."

A feeling of coldness and fear took hold of her. She felt far away from things and lonely.

JANIE SOON BEGAN TO FEEL the impact of awe and envy against her sensibilities. The wife of the Mayor was not just another woman as she had supposed. She slept with authority and so she was part of it in the town mind. She couldn't get but so close to most of them in spirit. It was especially noticeable after Joe had forced through a town ditch to drain the street in front of the store. They had murmured hotly about slavery being over, but every man filled his assignment.

There was something about Joe Starks that cowed the town. It was not because of physical fear. He was no fist fighter. His bulk was not even imposing as men go. Neither was it because he was more literate than the rest. Something else made men give way before him. He had a bow-down command in his face, and every step he took made the thing more tangible.

Take for instance that new house of his. It had two stories with porches, with bannisters and such things. The rest of the town looked like servant's quarters surrounding the "big house." And different from everybody else in the town he put off moving in until it had been painted, in and out. And look at the way he painted it—a gloaty, sparkly white. The kind of promenading white that the houses of Bishop Whipple, W. B. Jackson and the Vanderpool's wore. It made the village feel funny talking to him—just like he was anybody else. Then there was the matter of the spittoons. No sooner was he all set as the Mayor—post master—landlord—storekeeper, than he bought a desk like Mr. Hill or Mr. Galloway over in Maitland with one of those swing-around chairs to it. What with him biting down on cigars and saving his breath on talk and swinging round in that chair, it weakened people. And then he spit in that gold-looking vase that anybody else would have been glad to put on their front-room table. Said it was a spittoon just like his used-to-be bossman used to have in his bank up there in Atlanta. Didn't have to get up and go to the door every time he had to spit. Didn't spit on his floor neither. Had that golded-up spitting pot right handy. But he went further than that. He bought a little lady-size pot for Janie to spit in. Had it right in the parlor with little sprigs of flowers painted all around the sides. It took people by surprise because most of the women dipped snuff and of course had a spit-cup in the house. But how could they know up-to-date folks was spitting in flowery little things like that? It sort of made the rest of them feel that they had been taken advantage of. Like things had been kept from them. Maybe more things in the world besides spitting pots had been hid from them, when they wasn't told no better than to spit in tomato cans. It was bad enough for white people, but when one of your own color could be so different it put you on a wonder. It was like seeing your sister turn into a 'gator. A familiar strangeness. You keep seeing your sister in the 'gator and the 'gator in your sister, and you'd rather not. There was no doubt that the town respected him and even admired him in a way. But any man who walks in the way of power and property is bound to meet hate. So when speakers stood up when the occasion demanded and said "Our beloved Mayor," it was one of those statements that everybody says but nobody actually believes like "God is everywhere." It was just a handle to wind up the tongue with. As time went on and the benefits he had conferred upon the town receded in time they sat on his store porch while he was busy inside and discussed him. Like one day after he caught Henry Pitts with a wagon load of his ribbon cane and took the cane away from Pitts and made him leave town. Some of them thought Starks ought not to have done that. He had so much cane and everything else. But they didn't say that while Joe Starks was on the porch. When the mail came from Maitland and he went inside to sort it out everybody had their say.

Sim Jones started it off as soon as he was sure that Starks couldn't hear him.

"It's uh sin and uh shame runnin' dat po' man way from here lak dat. Colored folks oughtn't tuh be so hard on one 'nother.''

"Ah don't see it dat way atall," Sam Watson said shortly. "Let colored folks learn to work for what dey git lak everybody else. Nobody ain't stopped Pitts from plantin' de cane he wanted tuh. Starks give him uh jub, what mo' do he want?"

"Ah know dat too," Jones said, "but Sam, Joe Starks is too exact wid folks. All he got he done made it offa de rest of us. He didn't have all dat when he come here."

"Yeah, but none uh all dis you see and you'se settin' on wasn't here neither, when he come. Give de devil his due."

"But now, Sam, you know dat all he do is big-belly round and tell other folks what tuh do. He loves obedience out of everybody under de sound of his voice."

"You kin feel a switch in his hand when he's talkin' to yuh," Oscar Scott complained. "Dat chastisin' feelin' he totes sorter give yuh de protolapsis uh de cutinary linin'."

"He's uh whirlwind among breezes," Jeff Bruce threw in.

"Speakin' of winds, he's de wind and we'se de grass. We bend which ever way he blows," Sam Watson agreed, "but at dat us needs him. De town wouldn't be nothin' if it wasn't for him. He can't help bein' sorta bossy. Some folks needs thrones, and ruling-chairs and crowns tuh make they influence felt. He don't. He's got uh throne in de seat of his pants."

"Whut Ah don't lak 'bout de man is, he talks tuh unlettered folks wid books in his jaws," Hicks complained. "Showin' off his learnin'. To look at me you wouldn't think it, but Ah got uh brother pastorin' up round Ocala dat got good learnin'. If he wuz here, Joe Starks wouldn't make no fool outa him lak he do de rest uh y'all."

"Ah often wonder how dat lil wife uh hisn makes out wid him, 'cause he's uh man dat changes everything, but nothin' don't change him."

"You know many's de time Ah done thought about dat mahself. He gits on her ever now and then when she make little mistakes round de store."

"Whut make her keep her head tied up lak some ole 'oman round de store? Nobody couldn't *git* me tuh tie no rag on mah head if Ah had hair lak dat."

"Maybe he make her do it. Maybe he skeered some de rest of us mens might touch it round dat store. It sho is uh hidden mystery tuh me.''

"She sho don't talk much. De way he rears and pitches in de store sometimes when she make uh mistake is sort of ungodly, but she don't seem to mind at all. Reckon dey understand one 'nother.''

The town had a basketful of feelings good and bad about Joe's positions and possessions, but none had the temerity to challenge him. They bowed down to him rather, because he was all of these things, and then again he was all of these things because the town bowed down.

EVERY MORNING THE WORLD flung itself over and exposed the town to the sun. So Janie had another day. And every day had a store in it, except Sundays. The store itself was a pleasant place if only she didn't have to sell things. When the people sat around on the porch and passed around the pictures of their thoughts for the others to look at and see, it was nice. The fact that the thought pictures were always crayon enlargements of life made it even nicer to listen to.

Take for instance the case of Matt Bonner's yellow mule. They had him up for conversation every day the Lord sent. Most especial if Matt was there himself to listen. Sam and Lige and Walter were the ringleaders of the mule-talkers. The others threw in whatever they could chance upon, but it seemed as if Sam and Lige and Walter could hear and see more about that mule than the whole county put together. All they needed was to see Matt's long spare shape coming down the street and by the time he got to the porch they were ready for him.

"Hello, Matt.''

"Evenin', Sam.''

"Mighty glad you come 'long right now, Matt. Me and some others wuz jus' about tuh come hunt yuh.''

"Whut for, Sam?''

"Mighty serious matter, man. Serious!!''

"Yeah man,'' Lige would cut in, dolefully. "It needs yo' strict attention. You ought not tuh lose no time.''

"Whut is it then? You oughta hurry up and tell me.''

"Reckon we better not tell yuh heah at de store. It's too fur off tuh do any good. We better all walk on down by Lake Sabelia.''

"Whut's wrong, man? Ah ain't after none uh y'alls foolishness now.''

"Dat mule uh yourn, Matt. You better go see 'bout him. He's bad off."

"Where 'bouts? Did he wade in de lake and uh alligator ketch him?"

"Worser'n dat. De womenfolks got yo' mule. When Ah come round de lake 'bout noontime mah wife and some others had 'im flat on de ground usin' his sides fuh uh wash board."

The great clap of laughter that they have been holding in, bursts out. Sam never cracks a smile. "Yeah, Matt, dat mule so skinny till de women is usin' his rib bones fuh uh rub-board, and hangin' things out on his hock-bones tuh dry."

Matt realizes that they have tricked him again and the laughter makes him mad and when he gets mad he stammers.

"You'se uh stinkin' lie, Sam, and yo' feet ain't mates. Y-y-y-you!"

"Aw, man, 'tain't no use in you gittin' mad. Yuh know yuh don't feed de mule. How he gointuh git fat?"

"Ah-ah-ah- d-d-does feed 'im! Ah g-g-gived 'im uh full cup uh cawn every feedin'."

"Lige knows all about dat cup uh cawn. He hid round yo' barn and watched yuh. 'Tain't no feed cup you measures dat cawn outa. It's uh tea cup."

"Ah does feed 'im. He's jus' too mean tuh git fat. He stay poor and rawbony jus' fuh spite. Skeered he'll hafta work some."

"Yeah, you feeds 'im. Feeds 'im offa 'come up' and seasons it wid raw-hide."

"Does feed de ornery varmint! Don't keer whut Ah do Ah can't git long wid 'im. He fights every inch in front uh de plow, and even lay back his ears tuh kick and bite when Ah go in de stall tuh feed 'im."

"Git reconciled, Matt," Lige soothed. "Us all knows he's mean. Ah seen 'im when he took after one uh dem Roberts chillun in de street and woulda caught 'im and maybe trompled 'im tuh death if the wind hadn't of changed all of a sudden. Yuh see de youngun wuz tryin' tuh make it tuh de fence uh Starks' onion patch and de mule wuz dead in behind 'im and gainin' on 'im every jump, when all of a sudden de wind changed and blowed de mule way off his course, him bein' so poor and everything, and before de ornery varmint could tack, de youngun had done got over de fence." The porch laughed and Matt got mad again.

"Maybe de mule takes out after everybody," Sam said, "'cause he thinks everybody he hear comin' is Matt Bonner comin' tuh work 'im on uh empty stomach.''

"Aw, naw, aw, naw. You stop dat right now," Walter objected. "Dat mule don't think Ah look lak no Matt Bonner. He ain't dat dumb. If Ah thought he didn't know no better Ah'd have mah picture took and give it tuh dat mule so's he could learn better. Ah ain't gointuh 'low 'im tuh hold nothin' lak dat against me.''

Matt struggled to say something but his tongue failed him so he jumped down off the porch and walked away as mad as he could be. But that never halted the mule talk. There would be more stories about how poor the brute was; his age; his evil disposition and his latest caper. Everybody indulged in mule talk. He was next to the Mayor in prominence, and made better talking.

Janie loved the conversation and sometimes she thought up good stories on the mule, but Joe had forbidden her to indulge. He didn't want her talking after such trashy people. "You're Mrs. Mayor Starks, Janie. I god, Ah can't see what uh woman uh yo' sability would want tuh be treasurin' all dat gum-grease from folks dat don't even own de house dey sleep in. 'Tain't no earthly use. They's jus' some puny humans playin' round de toes uh Time.''

Janie noted that while he didn't like the mule himself, he sat and laughed at it. Laughed his big heh, heh laugh too. But then when Lige or Sam or Walter or some of the other big picture takers were using a side of the world for a canvas, Joe would hustle her off inside the store to sell something. Look like he took pleasure in doing it. Why couldn't he go himself sometimes? She had come to hate the inside of that store anyway. That Post Office too. People always coming and asking for mail at the wrong time. Just when she was trying to count up something or write in an account book. Get her so hackled she'd make the wrong change for stamps. Then too, she couldn't read everybody's writing. Some folks wrote so funny and spelt things different from what she knew about. As a rule, Joe put up the mail himself, but sometimes when he was off she had to do it herself and it always ended up in a fuss.

The store itself kept her with a sick headache. The labor of getting things down off of a shelf or out of a barrel was nothing. And so long as people wanted only a can of tomatoes or a pound of rice it was all right. But supposing they went on and said a pound and a half of bacon and a half pound of lard? The whole thing changed from a little walking and stretching to a mathematical dilemma. Or maybe cheese was thirty-seven cents a pound and somebody came and asked for a dime's worth. She went through many silent rebellions over things like that. Such a waste of life and time. But Joe kept saying that she could do it if she wanted to and he wanted her to use her privileges. That was the rock she was battered against.

This business of the head-rag irked her endlessly. But Jody was set on it. Her hair was NOT going to show in the store. It didn't seem sensible at all. That was because Joe never told Janie how jealous he was. He never told her how often he had seen the other men figuratively wallowing in it as she went about things in the store. And one night he had caught Walter standing behind Janie and brushing the back of his hand back and forth across the loose end of her braid ever so lightly so as to enjoy the feel of it without Janie knowing what he was doing. Joe was at the back of the store and Walter didn't see him. He felt like rushing forth with the meat knife and chopping off the offending hand. That night he ordered Janie to tie up her hair around the store. That was all. She was there in the store for *him* to look at, not those others. But he never said things like that. It just wasn't in him. Take the matter of the yellow mule, for instance.

Late one afternoon Matt came from the west with a halter in his hand. "Been huntin' fuh mah mule. Anybody seen 'im?" he asked.

"Seen 'im soon dis mornin' over behind de schoolhouse," Lum said. "'Bout ten o'clock or so. He musta been out all night tuh be way over dere dat early."

"He wuz," Matt answered. "Seen 'im last night but Ah couldn't ketch 'im. Ah'm 'bliged tuh git 'im in tuhnight 'cause Ah got some plowin' fuh tohmorrow. Done promised tuh plow Thompson's grove."

"Reckon you'll ever git through de job wid dat mule-frame?" Lige asked.

"Aw dat mule is plenty strong. Jus' evil and don't want tuh be led."

"Dat's right. Dey tell me he brought you heah tuh dis town. Say you started tuh Miccanopy but de mule had better sense and brung yuh on heah."

"It's uh l-l-lie! Ah set out fuh dis town when Ah left West Floridy."

"You mean tuh tell me you rode dat mule all de way from West Floridy down heah?"

"Sho he did, Lige. But he didn't mean tuh. He wuz satisfied up dere, but de mule wuzn't. So one mornin' he got straddle uh de mule and he took and brought 'im on off. Mule had sense. Folks up dat way don't eat biscuit bread but once uh week.''

There was always a little seriousness behind the teasing of Matt, so when he got huffed and walked on off nobody minded. He was known to buy side-meat by the slice. Carried home little bags of meal and flour in his hand. He didn't seem to mind too much so long as it didn't cost him anything.

About half an hour after he left they heard the braying of the mule at the edge of the woods. He was coming past the store very soon.

"Less ketch Matt's mule fuh 'im and have some fun."

"Now, Lum, you know dat mule ain't aimin' tuh let hisself be caught. Less watch *you* do it.''

When the mule was in front of the store, Lum went out and tackled him. The brute jerked up his head, laid back his ears and rushed to the attack. Lum had to run for safety. Five or six more men left the porch and surrounded the fractious beast, goosing him in the sides and making him show his temper. But he had more spirit left than body. He was soon panting and heaving from the effort of spinning his old carcass about. Everybody was having fun at the mule-baiting. All but Janie.

She snatched her head away from the spectacle and began muttering to herself. "They oughta be shamed uh theyselves! Teasin' dat poor brute beast lak they is! Done been worked tuh death; done had his disposition ruint wid mistreatment, and now they got tuh finish devilin' 'im tuh death. Wisht Ah had mah way wid 'em all.''

She walked away from the porch and found something to busy herself with in the back of the store so she did not hear Jody when he stopped laughing. She didn't know that he had heard her, but she did hear him yell out, "Lum, I god, dat's enough! Y'all done had yo' fun now. Stop yo' foolishness and go tell Matt Bonner Ah wants to have uh talk wid him right away.''

Janie came back out front and sat down. She didn't say anything and neither did Joe. But after a while he looked down at his feet and said, "Janie, Ah reckon you better go fetch me dem old black gaiters. Dese tan shoes sets mah feet on fire. Plenty room in 'em, but they hurts regardless.''

She got up without a word and went off for the shoes. A little war of defense for helpless things was going on inside her. People ought to have some regard for helpless things. She wanted to fight about it. "But Ah hates disagreement and confusion, so Ah better not talk. It makes it hard tuh git along." She didn't hurry back. She fumbled around long enough to get her face straight. When she got back, Joe was talking with Matt.

"Fifteen dollars? I god you'se as crazy as uh betsy bug! Five dollars."

"L-l-less we strack uh compermise, Brother Mayor. Less m-make it ten."

"Five dollars." Joe rolled his cigar in his mouth and rolled his eyes away indifferently.

"If dat mule is wuth somethin' tuh *you*, Brother Mayor, he's wuth mo' tuh me. More special when Ah got uh job uh work tuhmorrow."

"Five dollars."

"All right, Brother Mayor. If you wants tuh rob uh poor man lak me uh everything he got tuh make uh livin' wid, Ah'll take de five dollars. Dat mule been wid me twenty-three years. It's mighty hard."

Mayor Starks deliberately changed his shoes before he reached into his pocket for the money. By that time Matt was wringing and twisting like a hen on a hot brick. But as soon as his hand closed on the money his face broke into a grin.

"Beatyuh tradin' dat time, Starks! Dat mule is liable tuh be dead befo' de week is out. You won't git no work outa him."

"Didn't buy 'im fuh no work. I god, Ah bought dat varmint tuh let 'im rest. You didn't have gumption enough tuh do it."

A respectful silence fell on the place. Sam looked at Joe and said, "Dat's uh new idea 'bout varmints, Mayor Starks. But Ah laks it mah ownself. It's uh noble thing you done." Everybody agreed with that.

Janie stood still while they all made comments. When it was all done she stood in front of Joe and said, "Jody, dat wuz uh mighty fine thing fuh you tuh do. 'Tain't everybody would have thought of it, 'cause it ain't no everyday thought. Freein' dat mule makes uh mighty big man outa you. Something like George Washington and Lincoln. Abraham Lincoln, he had de whole United States tuh rule so he freed de Negroes. You got uh town so you freed uh mule. You have tuh have power tuh free things and dat makes you lak uh king uh something."

Hambo said, "Yo' wife is uh born orator, Starks. Us never knowed dat befo'. She put jus' de right words tuh our thoughts."

Joe bit down hard on his cigar and beamed all around, but he never said a word. The town talked about it for three days and said that's just what they would have done if they had been rich men like Joe Starks. Anyhow a free mule in town was something new to talk about. Starks piled fodder under the big tree near the porch and the mule was usually around the store like the other citizens. Nearly everybody took the habit of fetching along a handful of fodder to throw on the pile. He almost got fat and they took a great pride in him. New lies sprung up about his free-mule doings. How he pushed open Lindsay's kitchen door and slept in the place one night and fought until they made coffee for his breakfast; how he stuck his head in the Pearsons' window while the family was at the table and Mrs. Pearson mistook him for Rev. Pearson and handed him a plate; he ran Mrs. Tully off of the croquet ground for having such an ugly shape; he ran and caught up with Becky Anderson on the way to Maitland so as to keep his head out of the sun under her umbrella; he got tired of listening to Redmond's long-winded prayer, and went inside the Baptist church and broke up the meeting. He did everything but let himself be bridled and visit Matt Bonner.

But way after awhile he died. Lum found him under the big tree on his rawbony back with all four feet up in the air. That wasn't natural and it didn't look right, but Sam said it would have been more unnatural for him to have laid down on his side and died like any other beast. He had seen Death coming and had stood his ground and fought it like a natural man. He had fought it to the last breath. Naturally he didn't have time to straighten himself out. Death had to take him like it found him.

When the news got around, it was like the end of a war or something like that. Everybody that could knocked off from work to stand around and talk. But finally there was nothing to do but drag him out like all other dead brutes. Drag him out to the edge of the hammock which was far enough off to satisfy sanitary conditions in the town. The rest was up to the buzzards. Everybody was going to the dragging-out. The news had got Mayor Starks out of bed before time. His pair of gray horses was out under the tree and the men were fooling with the gear when Janie arrived at the store with Joe's breakfast.

"I god, Lum, you fasten up dis store good befo' you leave, you hear me?" He was eating fast and talking with one eye out of the door on the operations.

"Whut you tellin' 'im tuh fasten up for, Jody?" Janie asked surprised.

"'Cause it won't be nobody heah tuh look after de store. Ah'm goin' tuh de draggin'-out mahself.''

"'Tain't nothin' so important Ah got tuh do tuhday, Jody. How come Ah can't go long wid you tuh de draggin'-out?''

Joe was struck speechless for a minute. "Why, Janie! You wouldn't be seen at uh draggin'-out, wouldja? Wid any and everybody in uh passle pushin' and shovin' wid they no-manners selves? Naw, naw!''

"You would be dere wid me, wouldn't yuh?''

"Dat's right, but Ah'm uh man even if Ah is de Mayor. But de mayor's wife is somethin' different again. Anyhow they's liable tuh need me tuh say uh few words over de carcass, dis bein' uh special case. But *you* ain't goin' off in all dat mess uh commonness. Ah'm surprised at yuh fuh askin'.''

He wiped his lips of ham gravy and put on his hat. "Shet de door behind yuh, Janie. Lum is too busy wid de hawses.''

After more shouting of advice and orders and useless comments, the town escorted the carcass off. No, the carcass moved off with the town, and left Janie standing in the doorway.

Out in the swamp they made great ceremony over the mule. They mocked everything human in death. Starks led off with a great eulogy on our departed citizen, our most distinguished citizen and the grief he left behind him, and the people loved the speech. It made him more solid than building the schoolhouse had done. He stood on the distended belly of the mule for a platform and made gestures. When he stepped down, they hoisted Sam up and he talked about the mule as a school teacher first. Then he set his hat like John Pearson and imitated his preaching. He spoke of the joys of mule-heaven to which the dear brother had departed this valley of sorrow; the mule-angels flying around; the miles of green corn and cool water, a pasture of pure bran with a river of molasses running through it; and most glorious of all, *No* Matt Bonner with plow lines and halters to come in and corrupt. Up there, mule-angels would have people to ride on and from his place beside the glittering throne, the dear departed brother would look down into hell and see the devil plowing Matt Bonner all day long in a hell-hot sun and laying the raw-hide to his back.

With that the sisters got mock-happy and shouted and had to be held up by the menfolks. Everybody enjoyed themselves to the highest and then finally the mule was left to the already impatient buzzards. They were holding a great flying-meet way up over the heads of the mourners and some of the nearby trees were already peopled with the stoop-shouldered forms.

As soon as the crowd was out of sight they closed in in circles. The near ones got nearer and the far ones got near. A circle, a swoop and a hop with spread-out wings. Close in; close in till some of the more hungry or daring perched on the carcass. They wanted to begin, but the Parson wasn't there, so a messenger was sent to the ruler in a tree where he sat.

The flock had to wait the white-headed leader, but it was hard. They jostled each other and pecked at heads in hungry irritation. Some walked up and down the beast from head to tail, tail to head. The Parson sat motionless in a dead pine tree about two miles off. He had scented the matter as quickly as any of the rest, but decorum demanded that he sit oblivious until he was notified. Then he took off with ponderous flight and circled and lowered, circled and lowered until the others danced in joy and hunger at his approach.

He finally lit on the ground and walked around the body to see if it were really dead. Peered into its nose and mouth. Examined it well from end to end and leaped upon it and bowed, and the others danced a response. That being over, he balanced and asked:

"What killed this man?"
The chorus answered, "Bare, bare fat."
"What killed this man?"
"Bare, bare fat."
"What killed this man?"
"Bare, bare fat."
"Who'll stand his funeral?"
"We!!!!!"
"Well, all right now."

So he picked out the eyes in the ceremonial way and the feast went on. The yaller mule was gone from the town except for the porch talk, and for the children visiting his bleaching bones now and then in the spirit of adventure.

Joe returned to the store full of pleasure and good humor but he didn't want Janie to notice it because he saw that she was sullen and he resented that. She had no right to be, the way he thought things out. She wasn't even appreciative of his efforts and she had plenty cause to be. Here he was just pouring honor all over her; building a high chair for her to sit in and overlook the world and she here pouting over it! Not that he wanted anybody else, but just too many women would be glad to be in her place. He ought to box her jaws! But he didn't feel like fighting today, so he made an attack upon her position backhand.

"Ah had tuh laugh at de people out dere in de woods dis mornin', Janie. You can't help but laugh at de capers they cuts. But all the same, Ah wish mah people would git mo' business in 'em and not spend so much time on foolishness."

"Everybody can't be lak you, Jody. Somebody is bound tuh want tuh laugh and play."

"Who don't love tuh laugh and play?"

"You make out like you don't, anyhow."

"I god, Ah don't make out no such uh lie! But it's uh time fuh all things. But it's awful tuh see so many people don't want nothin' but uh full belly and uh place tuh lay down and sleep afterwards. It makes me sad sometimes and then agin it makes me mad. They say things sometimes that tickles me nearly tuh death, but Ah won't laugh jus' tuh disincourage 'em." Janie took the easy way from a fuss. She didn't change her mind but she agreed with her mouth. Her heart said, "Even so, but you don't have to cry about it."

But sometimes Sam Watson and Lige Moss forced a belly laugh out of Joe himself with their eternal arguments. It never ended because there was no end to reach. It was a contest in hyperbole and carried on for no other reason.

Maybe Sam would be sitting on the porch when Lige walked up. If nobody was there to speak of, nothing happened. But if the town was there like on Saturday night, Lige would come up with a very grave air. Couldn't even pass the time of day, for being so busy thinking. Then when he was asked what was the matter in order to start him off, he'd say, "Dis question done 'bout drove me crazy. And Sam, he know so much into things, Ah wants some information on de subject."

Walter Thomas was due to speak up and egg the matter on "Yeah, Sam always got more information than he know what to do wid. He's bound to tell yuh whatever it is you wants tuh know."

Sam begins an elaborate show of avoiding the struggle. That draws everybody on the porch into it.

"How come you want me *tuh* tell yuh? You always claim God done met you round de cornder and talked His inside business wid yuh. 'Tain't no use in you askin' *me* nothin'. Ah'm questionizin' *you*."

"How you gointuh do dat, Sam, when Ah arrived dis conversation mahself? Ah'm askin' *you*."

"Askin' me what? You ain't told me de subjick yit."

"Don't aim tuh tell yuh! Ah aims tuh keep yuh in de dark all de time. If you'se smart lak you let on you is, you kin find out."

"Yuh skeered to lemme know whut it is, 'cause yuh know Ah'll tear it tuh pieces. You got to have a subjick tuh talk from, do yuh can't talk. If uh man ain't got no bounds, he ain't got no place tuh stop."

By this time, they are the center of the world.

"Well all right then. Since you own up you ain't smart enough tuh find out whut Ah'm talkin' 'bout, Ah'll tell you. Whut is it dat keeps uh man from gettin' burnt on uh red-hot stove—caution or nature?"

"Shucks! Ah thought you had somethin' hard tuh ast me. Walter kin tell yuh dat."

"If de conversation is too deep for yuh, how come yuh don't tell me so, and hush up? Walter can't tell me nothin' uh de kind. Ah'm uh educated man, Ah keeps mah arrangements in mah hands, and if it kept me up all night long studyin' 'bout it, Walter ain't liable tuh be no help to me. Ah needs uh man lak you."

"And then agin, Lige, Ah'm gointuh tell yuh. Ah'm gointuh run dis conversation from uh gnat heel to uh lice. It's nature dat keeps uh man off of uh red-hot stove."

"Uuh huuh! Ah knowed you would going tuh crawl up in dat holler! But Ah aims tuh smoke yuh right out. 'Tain't no nature at all, it's caution, Sam."

"'Tain't no sich uh thing! Nature tells yuh not tuh fool wid no red-hot stove, and you don't do it neither."

"Listen, Sam, if it was nature, nobody wouldn't have tuh look out for babies touchin' stoves, would they? 'Cause dey just naturally wouldn't touch it. But dey sho will. So it's caution."

"Naw it ain't, it's nature, cause nature makes caution. It's de strongest thing dat God ever made, now. Fact is it's de onliest thing God ever made. He made nature and nature made everything else."

"Naw nature didn't neither. A whole heap of things ain't even been made yit."

"Tell me somethin' you know of dat nature ain't made."

"She ain't made it so you kin ride uh butt-headed cow and hold on tuh de horns."

"Yeah, but dat ain't yo' point."

"Yeah it is too."

"Naw it ain't neither."

"Well what *is* mah point?"

"You ain't got none, so far."

"Yeah he is too," Walter cut in, "de red-hot stove is his point."

"He know mighty much, but he ain't proved it yit."

"Sam, Ah say it's caution, not nature dat keeps folks off uh red-hot stove."

"How is de son gointuh be before his paw? Nature is de first of everything. Ever since self was self, nature been keepin' folks off of red-hot stoves. Dat caution you talkin' 'bout ain't nothin' but uh humbug. He's uh inseck dat nothin' he got belongs to him. He got eyes, lak somethin' else; wings lak somethin' else—everything! Even his hum is de sound of somebody else."

"Man, whut you talkin' 'bout? Caution is de greatest thing in de world. If it wasn't for caution—"

"Show me somethin' dat caution ever made! Look whut nature took and done. Nature got so high in uh black hen she got tuh lay uh white egg. Now you tell me, how come, whut got intuh man dat he got tuh have hair round his mouth? Nature!"

"Dat ain't—"

The porch was boiling now. Starks left the store to Hezekiah Potts, the delivery boy, and come took a seat in his high chair.

"Look at dat great big ole scoundrel-beast up dere at Hall's fillin' station—uh great big old scoundrel. He eats up all de folks outa de house and den eat de house."

"Aw 'tain't no sicha varmint nowhere dat kin eat no house! Dat's uh lie. Ah wuz dere yiste'ddy and Ah ain't seen nothin' lak dat. Where is he?"

"Ah didn't see him but Ah reckon he is in de back-yard some place. But dey got his picture out front dere. They was nailin' it up when Ah come pass dere dis evenin'."

"Well all right now, if he eats up houses how come he don't eat up de fillin' station?"

"Dat's 'cause dey got him tied up so he can't. Dey got uh great big picture tellin' how many gallons of dat Sinclair high-compression gas he drink at one time and how he's more'n uh million years old.''

"'Tain't *nothin'* no million years old!''

"De picture is right up dere where anybody kin see it. Dey can't make de picture till dey see de thing, kin dey?''

"How dey goin' to tell he's uh million years old? Nobody wasn't born dat fur back.''

"By de rings on his tail Ah reckon. Man, dese white folks got ways for tellin' anything dey wants tuh know.''

"Well, where he been at all dis time, then?''

"Dey caught him over dere in Egypt. Seem lak he used tuh hang round dere and eat up dem Pharaohs' tombstones. Dey got de picture of him doin' it. Nature is high in uh varmint lak dat. Nature and salt. Dat's whut makes up strong man lak Big John de Conquer. He was uh man wid salt in him. He could give uh flavor to *anything*.''

"Yeah, but he was uh man dat wuz more'n man. 'Tain't no mo' lak him. He wouldn't dig potatoes, and he wouldn't rake hay: He wouldn't take a whipping, and he wouldn't run away.''

"Oh yeah, somebody else could if dey tried hard enough. Me mahself, Ah got salt in *me*. If Ah like man flesh, Ah could eat some man every day, some of 'em is so trashy they'd let me eat 'em.''

"Lawd, Ah loves to talk about Big John. Less we tell lies on Ole John.''

But here come Bootsie, and Teadi and Big 'oman down the street making out they are pretty by the way they walk. They have got that fresh, new taste about them like young mustard greens in the spring, and the young men on the porch are just bound to tell them about it and buy them some treats.

"Heah come mah order right now,'' Charlie Jones announces and scrambles off the porch to meet them. But he has plenty of competition. A pushing, shoving show of gallantry. They all beg the girls to just buy anything they can think of. Please let them pay for it. Joe is begged to wrap up all the candy in the store and order more. All the peanuts and soda water—everything!

"Gal, Ah'm crazy 'bout you,'' Charlie goes on to the entertainment of everybody. "Ah'll do anything in the world except work for you and give you mah money.''

The girls and everybody else help laugh. They know it's not courtship. It's acting-out courtship and everybody is in the play. The three girls hold the center of the stage till Daisy Blunt comes walking down the street in the moonlight.

Daisy is walking a drum tune. You can almost hear it by looking at the way she walks. She is black and she knows that white clothes look good on her, so she wears them for dress up. She's got those big black eyes with plenty shiny white in them and makes them shine like brand new money and she knows what God gave women eyelashes for, too. Her hair is not what you might call straight. It's Negro hair, but it's got a kind of white flavor. Like the piece of string out of a ham. It's not a ham at all, but it's been around ham and got the flavor. It was spread down thick and heavy over her shoulders and looked just right under a big white hat.

"Lawd, Lawd, Lawd," that same Charlie Jones exclaims rushing over to Daisy. "It must be uh recess in heben if St. Peter is lettin' his angels out lak dis. You got three men already layin' at de point uh death 'bout yuh, and heah's uhnother fool dat's willin' tuh make time on yo' gang."

All the rest of the single men have crowded around Daisy by this time. She is parading and blushing at the same time.

"If you know anybody dat's 'bout tuh die 'bout me, yuh know more'n Ah do," Daisy bridled. "Wisht Ah knowed who it is."

"Now, Daisy, *you* know Jim, and Dave and Lum is 'bout tuh kill one 'nother 'bout you. Don't stand up here and tell dat big ole got-dat-wrong."

"Dey a mighty hush-mouf about it if dey is. Dey ain't never told me nothin'."

"Unhunh, you talked too fast. Heah, Jim and Dave is right upon de porch and Lum is inside de store."

A big burst of laughter at Daisy's discomfiture. The boys had to act out their rivalry too. Only this time, everybody knew they meant some of it. But all the same the porch enjoyed the play and helped out whenever extras were needed.

David said, "Jim don't love Daisy. He don't love yuh lak Ah do."

Jim bellowed indignantly, "Who don't love Daisy? Ah know you ain't talkin' 'bout me."

Dave: "Well all right, less prove dis thing right now. We'll prove right now who love dis gal de best. How much time is you willin' tuh make fuh Daisy?"

Jim: "Twenty yeahs!"

Dave: "See? Ah told yuh dat nigger didn't love yuh. Me, Ah'll beg de Judge tuh hang me, and wouldn't take nothin' less than life."

There was a big long laugh from the porch. Then Jim had to demand a test.

"Dave, how much would you be willin' tuh do for Daisy if she was to turn fool enough tuh marry yuh."

"Me and Daisy done talked dat over, but if you just got tuh know, Ah'd buy Daisy uh passenger train and give it tuh her."

"Humph! Is dat all? Ah'd buy her uh steamship and then Ah'd hire some mens tuh run it fur her."

"Daisy, don't let Jim fool you wid his talk. He don't aim tuh do nothin' fuh yuh. Uh lil ole steamship! Daisy, Ah'll take uh job cleanin' out de Atlantic Ocean fuh you any time you say you so desire." There was a great laugh and then they hushed to listen.

"Daisy," Jim began, "you know mah heart and all de ranges uh mah mind. And you know if Ah wuz ridin' up in uh earoplane way up in de sky and Ah looked down and seen you walkin' and knowed you'd have tuh walk ten miles tuh git home, Ah'd step backward offa dat earoplane just to walk home wid you."

There was one of those big blow-out laughs and Janie was wallowing in it. Then Jody ruined it all for her.

Mrs. Bogle came walking down the street towards the porch. Mrs. Bogle who was many times a grandmother, but had a blushing air of coquetry about her that cloaked her sunken cheeks. You saw a fluttering fan before her face and magnolia blooms and sleepy lakes under the moonlight when she walked. There was no obvious reason for it, it was just so. Her first husband had been a coachman but "studied jury" to win her. He had finally become a preacher to hold her till his death. Her second husband worked in Fohnes orange grove—but tried to preach when he caught her eye. He never got any further than a class leader, but that was something to offer her. It proved his love and pride. She was a wind on the ocean. She moved men, but the helm determined the port. Now, this night she mounted the steps and the men noticed her until she passed inside the door.

"I god, Janie," Starks said impatiently, "why don't you go on and see whut Mrs. Bogle want? Whut you waitin' on?"

Janie wanted to hear the rest of the play-acting and how it ended, but she got up sullenly and went inside. She came back to the porch with her bristles sticking out all over her and with dissatisfaction written all over her face. Joe saw it and lifted his own hackles a bit.

Jim Weston had secretly borrowed a dime and soon he was loudly beseeching Daisy to have a treat on him. Finally she consented to take a pickled pig foot on him. Janie was getting up a large order when they came in, so Lum waited on them. That is, he went back to the keg but came back without the pig foot.

"Mist' Starks, de pig feets is all gone!" he called out.

"Aw naw dey ain't, Lum. Ah bought uh whole new kag of 'em wid dat last order from Jacksonville. It come in yistiddy."

Joe came and helped Lum look but he couldn't find the new keg either, so he went to the nail over his desk that he used for a file to search for the order.

"Janie, where's dat last bill uh ladin'?"

"It's right dere on de nail, ain't it?"

"Naw it ain't neither. You ain't put it where Ah told yuh tuh. If you'd git yo' mind out de streets and keep it on yo' business maybe you could git somethin' straight sometimes."

"Aw, look around dere, Jody. Dat bill ain't apt tuh be gone off nowheres. If it ain't hangin' on de nail, it's on yo' desk. You bound tuh find it if you look."

"Wid you heah, Ah oughtn't tuh hafta do all dat lookin' and searchin'. Ah done told you time and time agin tuh stick all dem papers on dat nail! All you got tuh do is mind me. How come you can't do lak Ah tell yuh?"

"You sho loves to tell me whut to do, but Ah can't tell you nothin' Ah see!"

"Dat's 'cause you need tellin'," he rejoined hotly. "It would be pitiful if Ah didn't. Somebody got to think for women and chillun and chickens and cows. I god, they sho don't think none theirselves."

"Ah knows uh few things, and womenfolks thinks sometimes too!"

"Aw naw they don't. They just think they's thinkin'. When Ah see one thing Ah understands ten. You see ten things and don't understand one."

Times and scenes like that put Janie to thinking about the inside state of her marriage. Time came when she fought back with her tongue as best she could, but it didn't do her any good. It just made Joe do more. He wanted her submission and he'd keep on fighting until he felt he had it.

So gradually, she pressed her teeth together and learned how to hush. The spirit of the marriage left the bedroom and took to living in the parlor. It was there to shake hands whenever company came to visit, but it never went back inside the bedroom again. So she put something in there to represent the spirit like a Virgin Mary image in a church. The bed was no longer a daisy-field for her and Joe to play in. It was a place where she went and laid down when she was sleepy and tired.

She wasn't petal-open anymore with him. She was twenty-four and seven years married when she knew. She found that out one day when he slapped her face in the kitchen. It happened over one of those dinners that chasten all women sometimes. They plan and they fix and they do, and then some kitchen-dwelling fiend slips a scrochy, soggy, tasteless mess into their pots and pans. Janie was a good cook, and Joe had looked forward to his dinner as a refuge from other things. So when the bread didn't rise and the fish wasn't quite done at the bone, and the rice was scorched, he slapped Janie until she had a ringing sound in her ears and told her about her brains before he stalked on back to the store.

Janie stood where he left her for unmeasured time and thought. She stood there until something fell off the shelf inside her. Then she went inside there to see what it was. It was her image of Jody tumbled down and shattered. But looking at it she saw that it never was the flesh and blood figure of her dreams. Just something she had grabbed up to drape her dreams over. In a way she turned her back upon the image where it lay and looked further. She had no more blossomy openings dusting pollen over her man, neither any glistening young fruit where the petals used to be. She found that she had a host of thoughts she had never expressed to him, and numerous emotions she had never let Jody know about. Things packed up and put away in parts of her heart where he could never find them. She was saving up feelings for some man she had never seen. She had an inside and an outside now and suddenly she knew how not to mix them.

She bathed and put on a fresh dress and head kerchief and went on to the store before Jody had time to send for her. That was a bow to the outside of things.

Jody was on the porch and the porch was full of Eatonville as usual at this time of the day. He was baiting Mrs. Tony Robbins as he always did when she came to the store. Janie could see Jody watching her out of the corner of his eye while he joked roughly with Mrs. Robbins. He wanted to be friendly with her again. His big, big laugh was as much for her as for the baiting. He was longing for peace but on his own terms.

"I god, Mrs. Robbins, whut make you come heah and worry me when you see Ah'm readin' mah newspaper?" Mayor Starks lowered the paper in pretended annoyance.

Mrs. Robbins struck her pity-pose and assumed the voice.

"'Cause Ah'm hongry, Mist' Starks. 'Deed Ah is. Me and mah chillun is hongry. Tony don't fee-eed me!"

This was what the porch was waiting for. They burst into a laugh.

"Mrs. Robbins, how can you make out you'se hongry when Tony comes in here every Satitday and buys groceries lak a man? Three weeks' shame on yuh!"

"If he buy all dat you talkin' 'bout, Mist' Starks, God knows whut he do wid it. He sho don't bring it home, and me and mah po' chillun is *so* hongry! Mist' Starks, please gimme uh lil piece uh meat fur me and mah chillun."

"Ah know you don't need it, but come on inside. You ain't goin' tuh lemme read till Ah give it to yuh."

Mrs. Tony's ecstasy was divine. "Thank you, Mist' Starks. You're noble! You'se du most gentlemanfied man Ah ever did see. You'se uh king!"

The salt pork box was in the back of the store and during the walk Mrs. Tony was so eager she sometimes stepped on Joe's heels, sometimes she was a little before him. Something like a hungry cat when somebody approaches her pan with meat. Running a little, caressing a little and all the time making little urging-on cries.

"Yes, indeedy, Mist' Starks, you'se noble. You got sympathy for me and mah po' chillun. Tony don't give us nothin' tuh eat and we'se *so* hongry. Tony don't fee-eed me!"

This brought them to the meat box. Joe took up the big meat knife and selected a piece of side meat to cut. Mrs. Tony was all but dancing around him.

"Dat's right, Mist' Starks! Gimme uh lil piece 'bout dis wide." She indicated as wide as her wrist and hand. "Me and mah chillun is *so* hongry!"

Starks hardly looked at her measurements. He had seen them too often. He marked off a piece much smaller and sunk the blade in. Mrs. Tony all but fell to the floor in her agony.

"Lawd a'mussy! Mist' Starks, you ain't gointuh gimme dat lil teeninchy piece fuh me and all mah chillun, is yuh? Lawd, we'se *so* hongry!''

Starks cut right on and reached for a piece of wrapping paper. Mrs. Tony leaped away from the proffered cut of meat as if it were a rattlesnake.

"Ah wouldn't tetch it! Dat lil eyeful uh bacon for me and all mah chillun! Lawd, some folks is got everything and they's so gripin' and so mean!''

Starks made as if to throw the meat back in the box and close it. Mrs. Tony swooped like lightning and seized it, and started towards the door.

"Some folks ain't go no heart in dey bosom. They's willin' tuh see uh po' woman and her helpless chillun starve tuh death. God's gointuh put 'em under arrest, some uh dese days, wid dey stingy gripin' ways."

She stepped from the store porch and marched off in high dudgeon! Some laughed and some got mad.

"If dat wuz *mah* wife," said Walter Thomas, "Ah'd kill her cemetery dead.''

"More special after Ah done bought her everything mah wages kin stand, lak Tony do," Coker said. "In de fust place Ah never would spend on *no* woman whut Tony spend on *her*.''

Starks came back and took his seat. He had to stop and add the meat to Tony's account.

"Well, Tony tells me tuh humor her along. He moved here from up de State hopin' tuh change her, but it ain't. He say he can't bear tuh leave her and he hate to kill her, so 'tain't nothin' tuh do but put up wid her.''

"Dat's 'cause Tony love her too good," said Coker. "Ah could break her if she wuz mine. Ah'd break her or kill her. Makin' uh fool outa me in front of everybody.''

"Tony won't never hit her. He says beatin' women is just like steppin' on baby chickens. He claims 'tain't no place on uh woman tuh hit," Joe Lindsay said with scornful disapproval, "but Ah'd kill uh baby just born dis mawnin' fuh uh thing lak dat. 'Tain't nothin' but low-down spitefulness 'ginst her husband make her do it.''

"Dat's de God's truth," Jim Stone agreed. "Dat's de very reason.''

Janie did what she had never done before, that is, thrust herself into the conversation.

"Sometimes God gits familiar wid us womenfolks too and talks His

inside business. He told me how surprised He was 'bout y'all turning out
so smart after Him makin' yuh different; and how surprised y'all is goin'
tuh be if you ever find out you don't know half as much 'bout us as you
think you do. It's so easy to make yo'self out God Almighty when you
ain't got nothin' tuh strain against but women and chickens.''

"You gettin' too moufy, Janie," Starks told her. "Go fetch me de
checker-board *and* de checkers. Sam Watson, you'se mah fish.''

THE YEARS TOOK ALL THE FIGHT out of Janie's face. For a while she
thought it was gone from her soul. No matter what Jody did, she said
nothing. She had learned how to talk some and leave some. She was a rut
in the road. Plenty of life beneath the surface but it was kept beaten
down by the wheels. Sometimes she stuck out into the future, imagining
her life different from what it was. But mostly she lived between her hat
and her heels, with her emotional disturbances like shade patterns in the
woods—come and gone with the sun. She got nothing from Jody except
what money could buy, and she was giving away what she didn't value.

Now and again she thought of a country road at sun-up and
considered flight. To where? To what? Then too she considered thirty-
five is twice seventeen and nothing was the same at all.

"Maybe he ain't nothin'," she cautioned herself, "but he is
something in my mouth. He's got tuh be else Ah ain't got nothin' tuh
live for. Ah'll lie and say he is. If Ah don't, life won't be nothin' but uh
store and uh house."

She didn't read books so she didn't know that she was the world and
the heavens boiled down to a drop. Man attempting to climb to painless
heights from his dung hill.

Then one day she sat and watched the shadow of herself going about
tending store and prostrating itself before Jody, while all the time she
herself sat under a shady tree with the wind blowing through her hair and
her clothes. Somebody near about making summertime out of lonesome-
ness.

This was the first time it happened, but after a while it got so
common she ceased to be surprised. It was like a drug. In a way it was
good because it reconciled her to things. She got so she received all things
with the stolidness of the earth which soaks up urine and perfume with
the same indifference.

One day she noticed that Joe didn't sit down. He just stood in front of a chair and fell in it. That made her look at him all over. Joe wasn't so young as he used to be. There was already something dead about him. He didn't rear back in his knees any longer. He squatted over his ankles when he walked. That stillness at the back of his neck. His prosperous-looking belly that used to thrust out so pugnaciously and intimidate folks, sagged like a load suspended from his loins. It didn't seem to be a part of him anymore. Eyes a little asbsent too.

Jody must have noticed it too. Maybe, he had seen it long before Janie did, and had been fearing for her to see. Because he began to talk about her age all the time, as if he didn't want her to stay young while he grew old. It was always, "You oughta throw somethin' over yo' shoulders befo' you go outside. You ain't no young pullet no mo'. You'se uh ole hen now." One day he called her off the croquet grounds. "Dat's somethin' for de young folks, Janie, you out dere jumpin' round and won't be able tuh git out de bed tuhmorrer." If he thought to deceive her, he was wrong. For the first time she could see a man's head naked of its skull. Saw the cunning thoughts race in and out through the caves and promontories of his mind long before they darted out of the tunnel of his mouth. She saw he was hurting inside so she let it pass without talking. She just measured out a little time for him and set it aside to wait.

It got to be terrible in the store. The more his back ached and his muscle dissolved into fat and the fat melted off his bones, the more fractious he became with Janie. Especially in the store. The more people in there the more ridicule he poured over her body to point attention away from his own. So one day Steve Mixon wanted some chewing tobacco and Janie cut it wrong. She hated that tobacco knife anyway. It worked very stiff. She fumbled with the thing and cut way away from the mark. Mixon didn't mind. He held it up for a joke to tease Janie a little.

"Looka heah, Brother Mayor, whut yo' wife done took and done." It was cut comical, so everybody laughed at it. "Uh woman and uh knife—no kind if uh knife, don't b'long tuhgether." There was some more good-natured laughter at the expense of women.

Jody didn't laugh. He hurried across from the post office side and took the plug of tobacco away from Mixon and cut it again. Cut it exactly on the mark and glared at Janie.

"I god amighty! A woman stay round uh store till she get old as Methusalem and still can't cut a little thing like a plug of tobacco! Don't stand dere rollin' yo' pop eyes at me wid yo' rump hangin' nearly to yo' knees!''

A big laugh started off in the store but people got to thinking and stopped. It was funny if you looked at it right quick, but it got pitiful if you thought about it awhile. It was like somebody snatched off part of a woman's clothes while she wasn't looking and the streets were crowded. Then too, Janie took the middle of the floor to talk right into Jody's face, and that was something that hadn't been done before.

"Stop mixin' up mah doings wid mah looks, Jody. When you git through tellin' me how tuh cut uh plug uh tobacco, then you kin tell me whether mah behind is on straight or not.''

"Wha—whut's dat you say, Janie? You must be out yo' head.''

"Naw, Ah ain't outa mah head neither.''

"You must be. Talkin' any such language as dat.''

"You de one started talkin' under people's clothes. Not me.,'

"Whut's de matter wid you, nohow? You ain't no young girl to be gettin' all insulted 'bout yo' looks. You ain't no young courtin' gal. You'se uh ole woman, nearly forty.''

"Yeah, Ah'm nearly forty and you'se already fifty. How come you can't talk about dat sometimes instead of always pointin' at me?''

"T'ain't no use in gettin' all mad, Janie, 'cause Ah mention you ain't no young gal no mo'. Nobody in heah ain't lookin' for no wife outa yuh. Old as you is.''

"Naw, Ah ain't no young gal no mo' but den Ah ain't no old woman neither. Ah reckon Ah looks mah age too. But Ah'm uh woman every inch of me, and Ah know it. Dat's uh whole lot more'n *you* kin say. You big-bellies round here and put out a lot of brag, but 'tain't nothin' to it but yo' big voice. Humph! Talkin' 'bout *me* lookin' old! When you pull down yo' britches, you look lak de change uh life.''

"Great God from Zion!'' Sam Watson gasped. "Y'all really playin' de dozens tuhnight.''

"Wha—whut's dat you said?'' Joe challenged, hoping his ears had fooled him.

"You heard her, you ain't blind,'' Walter taunted.

"Ah ruther be shot with tacks than tuh hear dat 'bout mahself,'' Lige Moss commiserated.

Then Joe Starks realized all the meanings and his vanity bled like a flood. Janie had robbed him of his illusion of irresistible maleness that all men cherish, which was terrible. The thing that Saul's daughter had done to David. But Janie had done worse, she had cast down his empty armor before men and they had laughed, would keep on laughing. When he paraded his possessions hereafter, they would not consider the two together. They'd look with envy at the things and pity the man that owned them. When he sat in judgment it would be the same. Good-for-nothing's like Dave and Lum and Jim wouldn't change place with him. For what can excuse a man in the eyes of other men for lack of strength? Raggedy-behind squirts of sixteen and seventeen would be giving him their merciless pity out of their eyes while their mouths said something humble. There was nothing to do in life anymore. Ambition was useless. And the cruel deceit of Janie! Making all that show of humbleness and scorning him all the time! Laughing at him, and now putting the town up to do the same. Joe Starks didn't know the words for all this, but he knew the feeling. So he struck Janie with all his might and drove her from the store.

AFTER THAT NIGHT Jody moved his things and slept in a room downstairs. He didn't really hate Janie, but he wanted her to think so. He had crawled off to lick his wounds. They didn't talk too much around the store either. Anybody that didn't know would have thought that things had blown over, it looked so quiet and peaceful around. But the stillness was the sleep of swords. So new thoughts had to be thought and new words said. She didn't want to live like that. Why must Joe be so mad with her for making him look small when he did it to her all the time? Had been doing it for years. Well, if she must eat out of a long-handled spoon, she must. Jody might get over his mad spell any time at all and begin to act like somebody towards her.

Then too she noticed how baggy Joe was getting all over. Like bags hanging from an ironing board. A little sack hung from the corners of his eyes and rested on his cheek-bones; a loose-filled bag of feathers hung from his ears and rested on his neck beneath his chin. A sack of flabby something hung from his loins and rested on his thighs when he sat down. But even these things were running down like candle grease as time moved on.

He made new alliances too. People he never bothered with one way or another now seemed to have his ear. He had always been scornful of root-doctors and all their kind, but now she saw a faker from over around Altamonte Springs, hanging around the place almost daily. Always talking in low tones when she came near, or hushed altogether. She didn't know that he was driven by a desperate hope to appear the old-time body in her sight. She was sorry about the root-doctor because she feared that Joe was depending on the scoundrel to make him well when what he needed was a doctor, and a good one. She was worried about his not eating his meals, till she found out he was having old lady Davis to cook for him. She knew that she was a much better cook than the old woman, and cleaner about the kitchen. So she bought a beef-bone and made him some soup.

"Naw," thank you," he told her shortly. "Ah'm havin' uh hard enough time tuh try and git well as it is."

She was stunned at first and hurt afterwards. So she went straight to her bosom friend, Pheoby Watson, and told her about it.

"Ah'd ruther be dead than for Jody tuh think Ah'd hurt him," she sobbed to Pheoby. "It ain't always been too pleasant, 'cause you know how Joe worships de works of his own hands, but God in heben knows Ah wouldn't do one thing tuh hurt nobody. It's too underhand and mean."

"Janie, Ah thought maybe de thing would die down and you never would know nothin' 'bout it, but it's been singin' round here ever since de big fuss in de store dat Joe was 'fixed' and you wuz the one dat did it."

"Pheoby, for de longest time, Ah been feelin' dat somethin' set for still-bait, but dis is—is—oh Pheoby! What *kin* I do?"

"You can't do nothin' but make out you don't know it. It's too late fuh y'all tuh be splittin' up and gittin' divorce. Just g'wan back home and set down on yo' royal diasticutis and say nothin'. Nobody don't b'lieve it nohow."

"Tuh think Ah been wid Jody twenty yeahs and Ah just now got tuh bear de name uh poisonin' him! It's 'bout to kill me, Pheoby. Sorrow dogged by sorrow is in mah heart."

"Dat's lie dat trashy nigger dat calls hisself uh two-headed doctor brought tuh 'im in order tuh git in wid Jody. He seen he wuz sick— everybody been knowin' dat for de last longest, and den Ah reckon he hear y'all wuz kind of at variance, so dat wuz his chance. Last summer dat multiplied cock-roach wuz round heah tryin' tuh sell gophers!"

"Phoeby, Ah don't even b'lieve Jody b'lieve dat lie. He ain't never took no stock in de mess. He just make out he b'lieve it tuh hurt me. Ah'm stone dead from standin' still and tryin' tuh smile."

She cried often in the weeks that followed. Joe got too weak to look after things and took to his bed. But he relentlessly refused to admit her to his sickroom. People came and went in the house. This one and that one came into her house with covered plates of broth and other sick-room dishes without taking the least notice of her as Joe's wife. People who had never known what it was to enter the gate of the Mayor's yard unless it were to do some menial job now paraded in and out as his confidants. They came to the store and ostentatiously looked over whatever she was doing and went back to report to him at the house. Said things like "Mr. Starks need *somebody* tuh sorta look out for 'im till he kin git on his feet again and look for hisself."

But Jody was never to get on his feet again. Janie had Sam Watson to bring her the news from the sick room, and when he told her how things were, she had him bring a doctor from Orlando without giving Joe a chance to refuse, and without saying she sent for him.

"Just a matter of time," the doctor told her. "When a man's kidneys stop working altogether, there is no way for him to live. He needed medical attention two years ago. Too late now."

So Janie began to think of Death. Death, that strange being with the huge square toes who lived way in the West. The great one who lived in the straight house like a platform without sides to it, and without a roof. What need has Death for a cover, and what winds can blow against him? He stands in his high house that overlooks the world. Stands watchful and motionless all day with his sword drawn back, waiting for the messenger to bid him come. Been standing there before there was a where or a when or a then. She was liable to find a feather from his wings lying in her yard any day now. She was sad and afraid too. Poor Jody! He ought not to have to wrassle in there by himself. She sent Sam in to suggest a visit, but Jody said No. These medical doctors wuz all right with the Godly sick, but they didn't know a thing about a case like his. He'd be all right just as soon as the two-headed man found what had been buried against him. He wasn't going to die at all. That was what he thought. But Sam told her different, so she knew. And then if he hadn't, the next morning she was bound to know, for people began to gather in the big yard under the palm and chinaberry trees. People who would not have dared to foot the place before crept in and did not come to the house. Just squatted under the trees and waited. Rumor, that wingless bird, had shadowed over the town.

She got up that morning with the firm determination to go in there and have a good talk with Jody. But she sat a long time with the walls creeping in on her. Four walls squeezing her breath out. Fear lest he depart while she sat trembling upstairs nerved her and she was inside the room before she caught her breath. She didn't make the cheerful, casual start that she had thought out. Something stood like an oxen's foot on her tongue, and then too, Jody, no Joe, gave her a ferocious look. A look with all the unthinkable coldness of outer space. She must talk to a man who was ten immensities away.

He was lying on his side facing the door like he was expecting somebody or something. A sort of changing look on his face. Weak-looking but sharp-pointed about the eyes. Through the thin counterpane she could see what was left of his belly huddled before him on the bed like some helpless thing seeking shelter.

The half-washed bedclothes hurt her pride for Jody. He had always been so clean.

"Whut you doin' in heah, Janie?"

"Come tuh see 'bout you and how you wuz makin' out."

He gave a deep-growling sound like a hog dying down in the swamp and trying to drive off disturbance. "Ah come in heah tuh git shet uh you but look lak 'tain't doin' me no good. G'wan out. Ah needs tuh rest."

"Naw, Jody, Ah come in heah tuh talk widja and Ah'm gointuh do it too. It's for both of our sakes Ah'm talkin'."

He gave another ground grumble and eased over on his back.

"Jody, maybe Ah ain't been sich uh good wife tuh you, but Jody—"

"Dat's 'cause you ain't got de right feelin' for nobody. You oughter have some sympathy 'bout yo'self. You ain't no hog."

"But, Jody, Ah meant tuh be awful nice."

"Much as Ah done fuh yuh. Holdin' me up tuh scorn. No sympathy!"

"Naw, Jody, it wasn't because Ah didn't have no sympathy. Ah had uh lavish uh dat. Ah just didn't never git no chance tuh use none of it. You wouldn't let me."

"Dat's right, blame everything on me. Ah wouldn't let you show no feelin'! When, Janie, dat's all Ah ever wanted or desired. Now you come blamin' me!"

" 'Tain't dat, Jody. Ah ain't here tuh blame nobody. Ah'm just tryin' tuh make you know what kind a person Ah is befo' it's too late."

"Too late?" he whispered.

His eyes buckled in a vacant-mouthed terror and she saw the awful surprise in his face and answered it.

"Yeah, Jody, don't keer whut dat multiplied cock-roach told yuh tuh git yo' money, you got tuh die, and yuh can't live."

A deep sob came out of Jody's weak frame. It was like beating a bass drum in a hen-house. Then it rose high like pulling in a trombone.

"Janie! Janie! don't tell me Ah got tuh die, and Ah ain't used tuh thinkin' 'bout it."

" 'Tain't really no need of you dying, Jody, if you had of—de doctor—but it don't do no good bringin' dat up now. Dat's just whut Ah wants tuh say, Jody. You wouldn't listen. You done lived wid me for twenty years and you don't half know me atall. And you could have but you was so busy worshippin' de works of yo' own hands, and cuffin' folks around in their minds till you didn't see uh whole heap uh things yuh could have."

"Leave heah, Janie. Don't come heah—"

"Ah knowed you wasn't gointuh lissen tuh me. You changes everything but nothin' don't change you—not even death. But Ah ain't goin' outa here and Ah ain't gointuh hush. Naw, you gointuh listen tuh me one time befo' you die. Have yo' way all yo' life, trample and mash down and then die ruther than tuh let yo'self heah 'bout it. Listen, Jody, you ain't de Jody Ah run off down the road wid. You'se whut's left after he died. Ah run off tuh keep house wid you in uh wonderful way. But you wasn't satisfied wid me de way Ah was. Naw! Mah own mind had tuh be squeezed and crowded out tuh make room for yours in me."

"Shut up! Ah wish thunder and lightnin' would kill yuh!"

"Ah know it. And now you got tuh die tuh find out dat you got tuh pacify somebody besides yo'self if you wants any love and any sympathy in dis world. You ain't tried tuh pacify *nobody* but yo'self. Too busy listening tuh yo' own big voice."

"All dis tearin' down talk!" Jody wishpered with sweat globules forming all over his face and arms. "Git outa heah!"

"All dis bowin' down, all dis obedience under yo' voice—dat ain't whut Ah rushed off down de road tuh find out about you."

A sound of strife in Jody's throat, but his eyes stared unwillingly into a corner of the room so Janie knew the futile fight was not with her. The icy sword of the square-toed one had cut off his breath and left his hands in a pose of agonizing protest. Janie gave them peace on his breast, then she studied his dead face for a long time.

"Dis sittin' in de rulin' chair is been hard on Jody," she muttered out loud. She was full of pity for the first time in years. Jody had been hard on her and others but life had mishandled him too. Poor Joe! Maybe if she had known some other way to try, she might have made his face different. But what the other way could be, she had no idea. She thought back and forth about what had happened in the making of a voice out of a man. Then thought about herself. Years ago, she had told her girl self to wait for her in the looking glass. It had been a long time since she had remembered. Perhaps she'd better look. She went over to the dresser and looked hard at her skin and features. The young girl was gone, but a handsome woman had taken her place. She tore off the kerchief from her head and let down her plentiful hair. The weight, the length, the glory was there. She took careful stock of herself, then combed her hair and tied it back up again. Then she starched and ironed her face, forming it into just what people wanted to see, and opened up the window and cried, "Come heah people! Jody is dead. Mah husband is gone from me."

JOE'S FUNERAL WAS THE FINEST THING Orange County had ever seen with Negro eyes. The motor hearse, the Cadillac and Buick carriages; Dr. Henderson there in his Lincoln; the hosts from far and wide. Then again the gold and red and purple, the gloat and glamor of the secret orders, each with its insinuations of power and glory undreamed of by the uninitiated. People on farm horses and mules; babies riding astride of brothers' and sisters' backs. The Elks band ranked at the church door and playing "Safe in the Arms of Jesus" with such a dominant drum rhythm that it could be stepped off smartly by the long line as it filed inside. The Little Emperor of the cross-roads was leaving Orange County as he had come—with the out-stretched hand of power.

Janie starched and ironed her face and came set in the funeral behind her veil. It was like a wall of stone and steel. The funeral was going on outside. All things concerning death and burial were said and done. Finish. End. Nevermore. Darkness. Deep hole. Dissolution. Eternity. Weeping and wailing outside. Inside the expensive black folds were resurrection and life. She did not reach outside for anything, nor did the things of death reach inside to disturb her calm. She sent her face to Joe's funeral, and herself went rollicking with the springtime across the world. After a while the people finished their celebration and Janie went on home.

Before she slept that night she burnt up every one of her head rags and went about the house the next morning wth her hair in one thick braid swinging well before her waist. That was the only change people saw in her. She kept the store in the same way except of evenings she sat on the porch and listened and sent Hezekiah in to wait on late custom. She saw no reason to rush at changing things around. She would have the rest of her life to do as she pleased.

AFTERWORD
By Alice Walker

Looking for Zora

"On January 16, 1959, Zora Neale Hurston, suffering from the effects of a stroke and writing painfully in longhand, composed a letter to the 'editorial department' of Harper & Brothers inquiring if they would be interested in seeing 'the book I am laboring upon at present—a life of Herod the Great.' One year and twelve days later, Zora Neale Hurston died without funds to provide for her burial, a resident of the St. Lucie County, Florida, Welfare Home. She lies today in an unmarked grave in a segregated cemetery in Fort Pierce, Florida, a resting place generally symbolic of the black writer's fate in America.

"Zora Neale Hurston is one of the most significant unread authors in America, the author of two minor classics and four other major books."
—Robert Hemenway; "Zora Hurston and the Eatonville Anthropology," from *The Harlem Renaissance Remembered*, edited by Arna Bontemps (Dodd, 1972)

ON AUGUST 15, 1973, I wake up just as the plane is lowering over Sanford, Florida, which means I am also looking down on Eatonville, Zora Neale Hurston's birthplace. I recognize it from Zora's description in *Mules and Men*: "the city of five lakes, three croquet courts, three hundred brown skins, three hundred good swimmers, plenty guavas, two schools, and no jailhouse." Of course I cannot see the guavas, but the five lakes are still there, and it is the lakes I count as the plane prepares to land in Orlando.

From the air, Florida looks completely flat, and as we near the ground this impression does not change. This is the first time I have seen the interior of the state, which Zora wrote about so well, but there are the acres of orange groves, the sand, mangrove trees, and scrub pine that I know from her books. Getting off the plane I walk through the hot moist air of midday into the tacky but air-conditioned airport. I search for Charlotte Hunt, my companion on the Zora Hurston expedition. She lives in Winter Park, Florida, very near Eatonville, and is writing her graduate dissertation on Zora. I see her waving—a large pleasant-faced white woman in dark glasses. We have written to each other for several weeks, swapping our latest finds (mostly hers) on Zora, and trying to make sense out of the mass of information obtained (often erroneous or simply confusing) from Zora herself—through her stories and autobiography— and from people who wrote about her.

Eatonville has lived for such a long time in my imagination that I can hardly believe it will be found existing in its own right. But after 20 minutes on the expressway, Charlotte turns off and I see a small settlement of houses and stores set with no particular pattern in the sandy soil off the road. We stop in front of a neat gray building that has two fascinating signs: EATONVILLE POST OFFICE and EATONVILLE CITY HALL.

Inside the Eatonville City Hall half of the building, a slender, dark brown-skin woman sits looking through letters on a desk. When she hears we are searching for anyone who might have known Zora Neale Hurston, she leans back in thought. Because I don't wish to inspire foot-dragging in people who might know something about Zora they're not sure they should tell, I have decided on a simple, but I feel profoundly *useful*, lie.

"I am Miss Hurston's niece," I prompt the young woman, who brings her head down with a smile.

"I think Mrs. Moseley is about the only one still living who might remember her," she says.

"Do you mean *Mathilda* Moseley, the woman who tells those 'woman-is-smarter-than-man' lies in Zora's book?"

"Yes," says the young woman. "Mrs. Moseley is real old now, of course. But this time of day, she should be at home."

I stand at the counter looking down on her, the first Eatonville resident I have spoken to. Because of Zora's books, I feel I know something about her; at least I know what the town she grew up in was like years before she was born.

"Tell me something," I say, "do the schools teach Zora's books here?"

"No," she says, "they don't. I don't think most people know anything about Zora Neale Hurston, or know about any of the great things she did. She was a fine lady. I've read all of her books myself, but I don't think many other folks in Eatonville have."

"Many of the church people around here, as I understand it," says Charlotte in a murmured aside, "thought Zora was pretty loose. I don't think they appreciated her writing about them."

"Well," I say to the young woman, "thank you for your help." She clarifies her directions to Mrs. Moseley's house and smiles as Charlotte and I turn to go.

"The letter to Harper's does not expose a publisher's rejection of an unknown masterpiece, but it does reveal how the bright promise of the Harlem Renaissance deteriorated for many of the writers who shared in its exuberance. It also indicates the personal tragedy of Zora Neale Hurston: Barnard graduate, author of four novels, two books of folklore, one volume of autobiography, the most important collector of Afro-American folklore in America, reduced by poverty and circumstance to seek a publisher by unsolicited mail."—Robert Hemenway

"Zora Hurston was born in 1901, 1902, or 1903—depending on how old she felt herself to be at the time someone asked."—Librarian, Beinecke Library, Yale University

THE MOSELEY HOUSE IS SMALL AND WHITE and snug, its tiny yard nearly swallowed up by oleanders and hibiscus bushes. Charlotte and I knock on the door. I call out. But there is no answer. This strikes us as peculiar. We have had time to figure out an age for Mrs. Moseley—not dates or a number, just old. I am thinking of a quivery, bedridden invalid when we hear the car. We look behind us to see an old black-and-white Buick—paint peeling and grillwork rusty—pulling into the drive. A neat old lady in a purple dress and white hair is straining at the wheel. She is frowning because Charlotte's car is in the way.

Mrs. Moseley looks at us suspiciously. "Yes, I knew Zora Neale," she says, unsmilingly and with a rather cold stare at Charlotte (who I imagine feels very *white* at that moment), "but that was a long time ago, and I don't want to talk about it."

"Yes ma'am," I murmur, bringing all my sympathy to bear on the situation.

"Not only that," Mrs. Moseley continues, "I've been sick. Been in the hospital for an operation. Ruptured artery. The doctors didn't believe I was going to live, but you see me alive, don't you?"

"Looking well, too," I comment.

Mrs. Moseley is out of her car. A thin, sprightly woman with nice gold-studded false teeth, uppers and lowers. I like her because she stands *straight* beside her car, with a hand on her hip and her straw pocketbook on her arm. She wears white T-strap shoes with heels that show off her well-shaped legs.

"I'm eighty-two years old, you know," she says. "And I just can't remember things the way I used to. Anyhow, Zora Neale left here to go to school and she never really came back to live. She'd come here for material for her books, but that was all. She spent most of her time down in South Florida."

"You know, Mrs. Moseley, I saw your name in one of Zora's books."

"You did?" she looks at me with only slightly more interest. "I read some of her books a long time ago, but then people got to borrowing and borrowing and they borrowed them all away."

"I could send you a copy of everything that's been reprinted," I offer. "Would you like me to do that?"

"No," says Mrs. Moseley promptly. "I don't read much any more. Besides, all of that was *so* long ago. . . ."

Charlotte and I settle back against the car in the sun. Mrs. Moseley tells us at length and with exact recall every step in her recent operation, ending with: "What those doctors didn't know—when they were expecting me to die (and they didn't even think I'd live long enough for them to have to take out my stitches!)—is that Jesus is the best doctor, and if *He* says for you to get well, that's all that counts."

With this philosophy, Charlotte and I murmur quick assent: being Southerners and church bred, we have heard that belief before. But what we learn from Mrs. Moseley is that she does not remember much beyond the year 1938. She shows us a picture of her father and mother and says that her father was Joe Clarke's brother. Joe Clarke, as every Zora Hurston reader knows, was the first mayor of Eatonville; his fictional counterpart is Jody Starks of *Their Eyes Were Watching God.* We also get directions to where Joe Clarke's store *was*—where Club Eaton is now. Club Eaton, a long orange-beige nightspot we had seen on the main road, is apparently famous for the good times in it regularly had by all. It is, perhaps, the modern equivalent of the store porch, where all the men of Zora's childhood came to tell "lies," that is, black folktales, that were "made and used on the spot," to take a line from Zora. As for Zora's exact birthplace, Mrs. Moseley has no idea.

After I have commented on the healthy growth of her hibiscus bushes, she becomes more talkative. She mentions how much she *loved* to dance, when she was a young woman, and talks about how good her husband was. When he was alive, she says, she was completely happy because he allowed her to be completely free. "I was so free I had to pinch myself sometimes to tell if I was a married woman."

Relaxed now, she tells us about going to school with Zora. "Zora and I went to the same school. It's called Hungerford High now. It *was* only to the eighth grade. But our teachers were so good that by the time you left you knew college subjects. When I went to Morris Brown in Atlanta, the teachers there were just teaching me the same things I had already learned right in Eatonville. I wrote Mama and told her I was going to come home and help her with her babies. I wasn't learning anything new."

"Tell me something, Mrs. Moseley," I ask, "why do you suppose Zora was against integration? I read somewhere that she was against school desegregation because she felt it was an insult to black teachers."

"Oh, one of them [white people] came around asking me about integration. One day I was doing my shopping. I heard 'em over there talking about it in the store, about the schools. And I got on out of the way because I knew if they asked me, they wouldn't like what I was going to tell 'em. But they came up and asked me anyhow. 'What do you think about this integration?' one of them said. I acted like I thought I had heard wrong. 'You're asking *me* what *I* think about integration?' I said. 'Well, as you can see I'm just an old colored woman'—I was seventy-five or seventy-six then—'and this is the first time anybody ever asked me about integration. And nobody asked my grandmother what she thought, either, but her daddy was one of you all.' " Mrs. Moseley seems satisfied with this memory of her rejoinder. She looks at Charlotte. "I have the blood of three races in my veins," she says belligerently, "white, black, and Indian, and nobody asked me *anything* before."

"Do you think living in Eatonville made integration less appealing to you?"

"Well, I can tell you this: I have lived in Eatonville all my life, and I've been in the governing of this town. I've been everything but Mayor and I've been *assistant* Mayor. Eatonville was and is an all-black town. We have our own police department, post office, and town hall. Our own school and good teachers. Do I need integration?

"They took over Goldsboro, because the black people who lived there never incorporated, like we did. And now I don't even know if any black folks live there. They built big houses up there around the lakes. But we didn't let that happen in Eatonville, and we don't sell land to just anybody. And you see, we're still here.''

When we leave, Mrs. Moseley is standing by her car, waving. I think of the letter Roy Wilkins wrote to a black newspaper blasting Zora Neale for her lack of enthusiasm about the integration of schools. I wonder if he knew the experience of Eatonville she was coming from. Not many black people in America have come from a self-contained, all-black community where loyalty and unity are taken for granted. A place where black pride is nothing new.

There is, however, one thing Mrs. Moseley said that bothered me.

"Tell me, Mrs. Moseley," I had asked, "why is it that thirteen years after Zora's death, no marker has been put on her grave?"

And Mrs. Moseley answered: "The reason she doesn't have a stone is because she wasn't buried here. She was buried down in South Florida somewhere. I don't think anybody really knew where she was."

"Only to reach a wider audience, need she ever write books—because she is a perfect book of entertainment in herself. In her youth she was always getting scholarships and things from wealthy white people, some of whom simply paid her just to sit around and represent the Negro race for them, she did it in such a racy fashion. She was full of sidesplitting anecdotes, humorous tales, and tragicomic stories, remembered out of her life in the South as a daughter of a traveling minister of God. She could make you laugh one minute and cry the next. To many of her white friends, no doubt, she was a perfect 'darkie,' in the nice meaning they give the term—that is, a naïve, childlike, sweet, humorous, and highly colored Negro.

"But Miss Hurston was clever, too—a student who didn't let college give her a broad 'a' and who had great scorn for all pretensions, academic or otherwise. That is why she was such a fine folklore collector, able to go among the people and never act as if she had been to school at all. Almost nobody else could stop the average Harlemite on Lenox Avenue and measure his head with a strange-looking, anthropological device and not get bawled out for the attempt, except Zora, who used to stop anyone whose head looked interesting, and measure it."—Langston Hughes, *The Big Sea* (Knopf)

"What does it matter what white folks must have thought about her?"—Student, "Black Women Writers" class, Wellesley College

MRS. SARAH PEEK PATTERSON is a handsome, red-haired woman in her late forties, wearing orange slacks and gold earrings. She is the director of Lee-Peek Mortuary in Fort Pierce, the establishment that handled Zora's burial. Unlike most black funeral homes in Southern towns that sit like palaces among the general poverty, Lee-Peek has a run-down, *small* look. Perhaps this is because it is painted purple and white, as are its Cadillac chariots. These colors do not age well. The rooms are cluttered and grimy, and the bathroom is a tiny, stale-smelling prison, with a bottle of black hair dye (apparently used to touch up the hair of the corpses) dripping into the face bowl. Two pine burial boxes are resting in the bathtub.

Mrs. Patterson herself is pleasant and helpful.

"As I told you over the phone, Mrs. Patterson," I begin, shaking her hand and looking into her penny-brown eyes, "I am Zora Neale Hurston's niece, and I would like to have a marker put on her grave. You said, when I called you last week, that you could tell me where the grave is."

By this time I am, of course, completely into being Zora's niece, and the lie comes with perfect naturalness to my lips. Besides, as far as I'm concerned, she *is* my aunt—and that of all black people as well.

"She was buried in 1960," exclaims Mrs. Patterson. "That was when my father was running this funeral home. He's sick now or I'd let you talk to him. But I know where she's buried. She's in the old cemetery, the Garden of the Heavenly Rest, on Seventeenth Street. Just when you go in the gate there's a circle and she's buried right in the middle of it. Hers is the only grave in that circle—because people don't bury in that cemetery any more."

She turns to a stocky, black-skinned woman in her thirties, wearing a green polo shirt and white jeans cut off at the knee. "This lady will show you where it is," she says.

"I can't tell you how much I appreciate this," I say to Mrs. Patterson, as I rise to go. "And could you tell me something else? You see, I never met my aunt. When she died, I was still a junior in high school. But could you tell me what she died of, and what kind of funeral she had?"

"I don't know exactly what she died of," Mrs. Patterson says. "I know she didn't have any money. Folks took up a collection to bury her. . . . I believe she died of malnutrition."

"Malnutrition?"

Outside, in the blistering sun, I lean my head against Charlotte's even more blistering cartop. The sting of the hot metal only intensifies my anger.

"*Malnutrition,*" I manage to mutter. "Hell, our condition hasn't changed *any* since Phillis Wheatley's time. *She* died of malnutrition!"

"Really?" says Charlotte, "I didn't know that."

"One cannot overemphasize the extent of her commitment. It was so great that her marriage in the spring of 1927 to Herbert Sheen was short-lived. Although divorce did not come officially until 1931, the two separated amicably after only a few months, Hurston to continue her collecting, Sheen to attend Medical School."—Robert Hemenway

"WHAT IS YOUR NAME?" I ask the woman who has climbed into the back seat.

"Rosalee," she says. She has a rough, pleasant voice, as if she is a singer who also smokes a lot. She is homely, and has an air of ready indifference.

"Another woman came by here wanting to see the grave," she says, lighting up a cigarette. "She was a little short, dumpty white lady from one of these Florida schools. Orlando or Daytona. But let me tell you something before we gets started. All I know is where the cemetery is. I don't know one thing about that grave. You better go back in and ask her to draw you a map."

A few moments later, with Mrs. Patterson's diagram of where the grave is, we head for the cemetery.

We drive past blocks of small, pastel-colored houses and turn right onto 17th Street. At the very end, we reach a tall curving gate, with the words "Garden of the Heavenly Rest" fading into the stone. I expected, from Mrs. Patterson's small drawing, to find a small circle—which would have placed Zora's grave five or ten paces from the road. But the "circle" is over an acre large and looks more like an abandoned field. Tall weeds choke the dirt road and scrape against the sides of the car. It doesn't help either that I step out into an active anthill.

"I don't know about y'all," I say, "but I don't even believe this." I am used to the haphazard cemetery-keeping that is traditional in most Southern black communities, but this neglect is staggering. As

far as I can see there is nothing but bushes and weeds, some as tall as
my waist. One grave is near the road, and Charlotte elects to
investigate it. It is fairly clean, and belongs to someone who died in
1963.

Rosalee and I plunge into the weeds; I pull my long dress up to
my hips. The weeds scratch my knees, and the insects have a feast.
Looking back, I see Charlotte standing resolutely near the road.

"Aren't you coming?" I call.

"No," she calls back. "I'm from these parts and I know what's
out there." She means snakes.

"Shit," I say, my whole life and the people I love flashing
melodramatically before my eyes. Rosalee is a few yards to my right.

"How're you going to find anything out here?" she asks. And I
stand still a few seconds, looking at the weeds. Some of them are
quite pretty, with tiny yellow flowers. They are thick and healthy, but
dead weeds under them have formed a thick gray carpet on the
ground. A snake could be lying six inches from my big toe and I
wouldn't see it. We move slowly, very slowly, our eyes alert, our legs
trembly. It is hard to tell where the center of the circle is since the
circle is not really round, but more like half of something round.
There are things crackling and hissing in the grass. Sandspurs are
sticking to the inside of my skirt. Sand and ants cover my feet. I look
toward the road and notice that there are, indeed, *two* large curving
stones, making an entrance and exit to the cemetery. I take my
bearings from them and try to navigate to exact center. But the center
of anything can be very large, and a grave is not a pinpoint. Finding
the grave seems positively hopeless. There is only one thing to do:

"Zora!" I yell, as loud as I can (causing Rosalee to jump), "are
you out here?"

"If she is, I sho hope she don't answer you. If she do, I'm gone."

"Zora!" I call again. "I'm here. Are you?"

"If she is," grumbles Rosalee, "I hope she'll keep it to herself."

"Zora!" Then I start fussing with her. "I hope you don't think
I'm going to stand out here all day, with these snakes watching me
and these ants having a field day. In fact, I'm going to call you just
one or two more times." On a clump of dried grass, near a small
bushy tree, my eye falls on one of the largest bugs I have ever seen. It
is on its back, and is as large as three of my fingers. I walk toward it,
and yell "Zo-ra!" and my foot sinks into a hole. I look down. I am

standing in a sunken rectangle that is about six feet long and about three or four feet wide. I look up to see where the two gates are.

"Well," I say, "this is the center, or approximately anyhow. It's also the only sunken spot we've found. Doesn't this look like a grave to you?"

"For the sake of not going no farther through these bushes," Rosalee growls, "yes, it do."

"Wait a minute," I say, "I have to look around some more to be sure this is the only spot that resembles a grave. But you don't have to come."

Rosalee smiles—a grin, really—beautiful and tough.

"Naw," she says, "I feels sorry for you. If one of these snakes got ahold of you out here by yourself I'd feel *real* bad." She laughs. "I done come this far, I'll go on with you."

"Thank you, Rosalee," I say. "Zora thanks you too."

"Just as long as she don't try to tell me in person," she says, and together we walk down the field.

"The gusto and flavor of Zora Neal[e] Hurston's storytelling, for example, long before the yarns were published in 'Mules and Men' and other books, became a local legend which might . . . have spread further under different conditions. A tiny shift in the center of gravity could have made them best-sellers."—Arna Bontemps, *Personals* (Paul Bremen, Ltd., London; 1963)

"Bitter over the rejection of her folklore's value, especially in the black community, frustrated by what she felt was her failure to convert the Afro-American world view into forms of prose fiction, Hurston finally gave up."—Robert Hemenway

WHEN CHARLOTTE AND I DRIVE UP to the Merritt Monument Company, I immediately see the headstone I want.

"How much is this one?" I ask the young woman in charge, pointing to a tall black stone. It looks as majestic as Zora herself must have been when she was learning voodoo from those root doctors down in New Orleans.

"Oh, *that* one," she says, "that's our finest. That's Ebony Mist."

"Well, how much is it?"

"I don't know. But wait," she says, looking around in relief, "here comes somebody who'll know."

A small, sunburned man with squinty green eyes comes up. He must be the engraver, I think, because his eyes are contracted into slits, as if he has been keeping stone dust out of them for years.

"That's Ebony Mist," he says. "That's our best."

"How much is it?" I ask, beginning to realize I probably *can't* afford it.

He gives me a price that would feed a dozen Sahelian drought victims for three years. I realize I must honor the dead, but between the dead great and the living starving, there is no choice.

"I have a lot of letters to be engraved," I say, standing by the plain gray marker I have chosen. It is pale and ordinary, not at all like Zora, and makes me momentarily angry that I am not rich.

We go into his office and I hand him a sheet of paper that has:

ZORA NEALE HURSTON
"A GENIUS OF THE SOUTH"
NOVELIST   FOLKLORIST
ANTHROPOLOGIST
1901   1960

"A genius of the South" is from one of Jean Toomer's poems.

"Where is this grave?" the monument man asks. "If it's in a new cemetery, the stone has to be flat."

"Well, it's not a new cemetery and Zora—my aunt—doesn't need anything flat because with the weeds out there, you'd never be able to see it. You'll have to go out there with me."

He grunts.

"And take a long pole and 'sound' the spot," I add. "Because there's no way of telling it's a grave, except that it's sunken."

"Well," he says, after taking my money and writing up a receipt, in the full awareness that he's the only monument dealer for miles, "you take this flag" (he hands me a four-foot-long pole with a red-metal marker on top) "and take it out to the cemetery and put it where you think the grave is. It'll take us about three weeks to get the stone out there."

I wonder if he knows he is sending me to another confrontation with the snakes. He probably does. Charlotte has told me she will cut my leg and suck out the blood, if I am bit.

"At least send me a photograph when it's done, won't you?"

He says he will.

"Hurston's return to her folklore-collecting in December of 1927 was made possible by Mrs. R. Osgood Mason, an elderly white patron of the arts, who at various times also helped Langston Hughes, Alain Locke, Richmond Barthe, and Miguel Covarrubias. Hurston apparently came to her attention through the intercession of Locke, who frequently served as a kind of liaison between the young black talent and Mrs. Mason. The entire relationship between this woman and the Harlem Renaissance deserves extended study, for it represents much of the ambiguity involved in white patronage of black artists. All her artists were instructed to call her 'Godmother'; there was a decided emphasis on the 'primitive' aspects of black culture, apparently a holdover from Mrs. Mason's interest in the Plains Indians. In Hurston's case there were special restrictions imposed by her patron: although she was to be paid a handsome salary for her folklore collecting, she was to limit her correspondence and publish nothing of her research without prior approval."—Robert Hemenway

"You have to read the chapters Zora left out of her autobiography."—Student, Special Collections Room, Beinecke Library, Yale University

DR. BENTON, a friend of Zora's and a practicing M.D. in Fort Pierce, is one of those old, good-looking men whom I always have trouble not liking. (It no longer bothers me that I may be constantly searching for father figures; by this time I have found several and dearly enjoyed knowing them all.) He is shrewd, with steady brown eyes under hair that is almost white. He is probably in his seventies, but doesn't look it. He carries himself with dignity, and has cause to be proud of the new clinic where he now practices medicine. His nurse looks at us with suspicion, but Dr. Benton's eyes have the penetration of a scalpel cutting through skin. I guess right away that if he knows anything at all about Zora Hurston, he will not believe I am her niece.
"Eatonville?" Dr. Benton says, leaning forward in his chair, looking first at me, then at Charlotte. "Yes, I know Eatonville, I grew up not far from there. I knew the whole bunch of Zora's family." (He looks at the shape of my cheekbones, the size of my eyes, and the nappiness of my hair.) "I knew her daddy. The old man. He was a hardworking, Christian man. Did the best he could for his family. He was the mayor of Eatonville for a while, you know.
"My father was the mayor of Goldsboro. You probably never

heard of it. It never incorporated like Eatonville did, and has just about disappeared. But Eatonville is still all-black.''

He pauses and looks at me. ''And you're Zora's niece,'' he says wonderingly.

''Well,'' I say with shy dignity, yet with some tinge, I hope, of a 19th-century blush, ''I'm illegitimate. That's why I never knew Aunt Zora.''

I love him for the way he comes to my rescue. ''You're *not* illegitimate!'' he cries, his eyes resting on me fondly. ''All of us are God's children! Don't you even *think* such a thing!''

And I hate myself for lying to him. Still, I ask myself, would I have gotten this far toward getting the headstone and finding out about Zora Hurston's last days without telling my lie? Actually, I probably would have. But I don't like taking chances that could get me stranded in Central Florida.

''Zora didn't get along with her family. I don't know why. Did you read her autobiography, *Dust Tracks on a Road*?''

''Yes, I did,'' I say. ''It pained me to see Zora pretending to be naive and grateful about the old white 'Godmother' who helped finance her research, but I loved the part where she ran off from home after falling out with her brother's wife.''

Dr. Benton nodded. ''When she got sick, I tried to get her to go back to her family, but she refused. There wasn't any real hatred; they just never had gotten along and Zora wouldn't go to them. She didn't want to go to the county home, either, but she had to, because she couldn't do a thing for herself.''

''I was surprised to learn she died of malnutrition.''

Dr. Benton seems startled. ''Zora *didn't* die of malnutrition,'' he says indignantly. ''Where did you get that story from? She had a stroke and she died in the welfare home.'' He seems peculiarly upset, distressed, but sits back reflectively in his chair: ''She was an incredible woman,'' he muses. ''Sometimes when I closed my office, I'd go by her house and just talk to her for an hour or two. She was a well-read, well-traveled woman and always had her own ideas about what was going on . . . ''

''I never knew her, you know. Only some of Carl Van Vechten's photographs and some newspaper photographs. . . . What did she look like?''

''When I knew her, in the fifties, she was a big woman, *erect*.

Not quite as light as I am [Dr. Benton is dark beige], and about five foot, seven inches, and she weighed about two hundred pounds. Probably more. She . . . ''

"What! Zora was *fat*! She wasn't, in Van Vechten's pictures!"

"Zora loved to eat," Dr. Benton says complacently. "She could sit down with a mound of ice cream and just eat and talk till it was all gone."

While Dr. Benton is talking, I recall that the Van Vechten pictures were taken when Zora was still a young woman. In them she appears tall, tan, and healthy. In later newspaper photographs—when she was in her forties—I remembered that she seemed heavier and several shades lighter. I reasoned that the earlier photographs were taken while she was busy collecting folklore materials in the hot Florida sun.

"She had high blood pressure. Her health wasn't good . . . . She used to live in one of my houses—on School Court Street. It's a block house . . . I don't recall the number. But my wife and I used to invite her over to the house for dinner. *She always ate well*," he says emphatically.

"That's comforting to know," I say, wondering where Zora ate when she wasn't with the Bentons.

"Sometimes she would run out of groceries—after she got sick—and she'd call me. 'Come over here and see 'bout me,' she'd say. And I'd take her shopping and buy her groceries.

"She was always studying. Her mind—before the stroke—just worked all the time. She was always going somewhere, too. She once went to Honduras to study something. And when she died, she was working on that book about Herod the Great. She was so intelligent! And really had perfect expressions. Her English was beautiful." (I suspect this is a clever way to let me know Zora herself didn't speak in the "black English" her characters used.)

"I used to read all of her books," Dr. Benton continues, "but it was a long time ago. I remember one about . . . it was called, I think, 'The Children of God' [*Their Eyes Were Watching God*], and I remember Janie and Teapot [Teacake] and the mad dog riding on the cow in that hurricane and bit old Teapot on the cheek . . . ''

I am delighted that he remembers even this much of the story, even if the names are wrong, but seeing his affection for Zora I feel I must ask him about her burial. "Did she *really* have a pauper's funeral?"

"She *didn't* have a pauper's funeral!" he says with great heat. "Everybody around here *loved* Zora."

"We just came back from ordering a headstone," I say quietly, because he *is* an old man and the color is coming and going on his face, "but to tell the truth, I can't be positive what I found is the grave. All I know is the spot I found was the only grave-size hole in the area."

"I remember it wasn't near the road," says Dr. Benton, more calmly. "Some other lady came by here and we went out looking for the grave and I took a long iron stick and poked all over that part of the cemetery but we didn't find anything. She took some pictures of the general area. Do the weeds still come up to your knees?"

"And beyond," I murmur. This time there isn't any doubt. Dr. Benton feels ashamed.

As he walks us to our car, he continues to talk about Zora. "She couldn't really write much near the end. She had the stroke and it left her weak; her mind was affected. She couldn't think about anything for long.

"She came here from Daytona, I think, She owned a houseboat over there. When she came here, she sold it. She lived on that money, then she worked as a maid—for an article on maids she was writing—and she worked for the *Chronicle* writing the horoscope column.

"I think black people here in Florida got mad at her because she was for some politician they were against. She said this politician *built* schools for blacks while the one they wanted just talked about it. And although Zora wasn't egotistical, what she thought, she thought; and generally what she thought, she said."

When we leave Dr. Benton's office, I realize I have missed my plane back home to Jackson, Mississippi. That being so, Charlotte and I decide to find the house Zora lived in before she was taken to the county welfare home to die. From among her many notes, Charlotte locates a letter of Zora's she has copied that carries the address: 1734 School Court Street. We ask several people for directions. Finally, two old gentlemen in a dusty gray Plymouth offer to lead us there. School Court Street is not paved, and the road is full of mud puddles. It is dismal and squalid, redeemed only by the brightness of the late afternoon sun. Now I can understand what a "block" house is. It is a house shaped like a block, for one thing, surrounded by others just like it. Some houses are blue and some are green or yellow. Zora's is light green. They are tiny—about 50 by 50 feet, squatty with flat roofs. The house Zora lived in looks worse than the others, but that is its only distinction. It also has three ragged and dirty children sitting on the steps.

"Is this where y'all live?" I ask, aiming my camera.

"No, ma'am," they say in unison, looking at me earnestly. "We live over yonder. This Miss So-and-So's house; but she in the horspital."

We chatter inconsequentially while I take more pictures. A car drives up with a young black couple in it. They scowl fiercely at Charlotte and don't look at me with friendliness, either. They get out and stand in their doorway across the street. I go up to them to explain. "Did you know Zora Hurston used to live right across from you?" I ask.

"Who?" They stare at me blankly, then become curiously attentive, as if they think I made the name up. They are both Afro-ed and he is somberly dashiki-ed.

I suddenly feel frail and exhausted. "It's too long a story," I say, "but tell me something, is there anybody on this street who's lived here for more than thirteen years?"

"That old man down there," the young man says, pointing. Sure enough, there is a man sitting on his steps three houses down. He has graying hair and is very neat, but there is a weakness about him. He reminds me of Mrs. Turner's husband in *Their Eyes Were Watching God.* He's rather "vanishing"-looking, as if his features have been sanded down. In the old days, before black was beautiful, he was probably considered attractive, because he has wavy hair and light-brown skin; but now, well, light skin has ceased to be its own reward.

After the preliminaries, there is only one thing I want to know: "Tell me something," I begin, looking down at Zora's house, "did Zora like flowers?"

He looks at me queerly. "As a matter of fact," he says, looking regretfully at the bare, rough yard that surrounds her former house, "she was crazy about them. And she was a great gardener. She loved azaleas, and that running and blooming vine [morning glories], and she really loved that night-smelling flower [gardenia]. She kept a vegetable garden year-round, too. She raised collards and tomatoes and things like that.

"Everyone in this community thought well of Miss Hurston.

When she died, people all up and down this street took up a collection for her burial. We put her away nice."

"Why didn't somebody put up a headstone?"

"Well, you know, one was never requested. Her and her family didn't get along. They didn't even come to the funeral."

"And did she live down there by herself?"

"Yes, until they took her away. She lived with—just her and her companion, Sport."

My ears perk up. "Who?"

"Sport, you know, her dog. He was her only companion. He was a big brown-and-white dog."

When I walk back to the car, Charlotte is talking to the young couple on their porch. They are relaxed and smiling.

"I told them about the famous lady who used to live across the street from them," says Charlotte as we drive off. "Of course they had no idea Zora ever lived, let alone that she lived across the street. I think I'll send some of her books to them."

"That's real kind of you," I say.

"I am not tragically colored. There is no great sorrow damned up in my soul, nor lurking behind my eyes. I do not mind at all. I do not belong to the sobbing school of Negrohood who hold that nature somehow has given them a lowdown dirty deal and whose feelings are all hurt about it. . . . No, I do not weep at the world—I am too busy sharpening my oyster knife."—Zora Neale Hurston, "How It Feels to Be Colored Me," *World Tomorrow*, 1928

THERE ARE TIMES—and finding Zora Hurston's grave was one of them—when normal responses of grief, horror, and so on, do not make sense because they bear no real relation to the depth of the emotion one feels. It was impossible for me to cry when I saw the field full of weeds where Zora is. Partly this is because I have come to know Zora through her books and she was not a teary sort of person herself; but partly, too, it is because there is a point at which even grief feels absurd. And at this point, laughter gushes up to retrieve sanity.

It is only later, when the pain is not so direct a threat to one's own existence that what was learned in that moment of comical lunacy is understood. Such moments rob us of both youth and vanity. But perhaps they are also times when greater disciplines are born.

ALICE WALKER is the author of many highly acclaimed books of poetry and prose, including *In Love and Trouble, Revolutionary Petunias, Meridian,* and *Good Night Willie Lee, I'll See You in the Morning.* She is a contributing and consulting editor to *Ms.* magazine and to *Freedomways,* and has taught literature and writing at Jackson State, Tougaloo, Wellesley, University of Massachusetts, and Yale.

MARY HELEN WASHINGTON is the Director of the Center for Black Studies at the University of Detroit. She has edited two collections of stories by black women, *Black-Eyed Susans* and *Midnight Birds.* In 1979, Washington received a fellowship from the Bunting Institute at Radcliffe to work on an historical anthology of black women writers.

THE REPRINTS ADVISORY BOARD of The Feminist Press is a group of feminist historians and literary scholars who work with the Press to bring the work of lost or neglected writers to a wide audience: Mari Jo Buhle, American Civilization, Brown University; Ellen Cantarow, writer, Cambridge, Massachusetts; Ellen DuBois, American Studies / History, SUNY / Buffalo; Moira Ferguson, English / Women's Studies, University of Nebraska; Elaine R. Hedges, English / Women's Studies, Towson State University; Florence Howe, American Studies, SUNY / Old Westbury; Gloria Hull, English, University of Delaware; Louis Kampf, Literature, Massachusetts Institute of Technology; Joan Kelly, History / Women's Studies, City College / CUNY; Alice Kessler-Harris, Labor Studies / History, Hofstra University; Paul Lauter, American Studies, SUNY / Old Westbury; Ellen Rosen, Sociology, Vassar College; Catharine Stimpson, English, Barnard College; Amy Swerdlow, History, Rutgers University.

THE FEMINIST PRESS offers alternatives in education and in literature. Founded in 1970, this nonprofit, tax-exempt educational and publishing organization works to eliminate sexual stereotypes in books and schools, providing instead a new or neglected literature with a broader vision of human potential. The publishing program includes reprints of important works by women, feminist biographies of women, and nonsexist children's books. Curricular materials, bibliographies, directories, and a newsletter provide information and support for women's studies at every educational level. Inservice projects help teachers develop new methods to encourage students to become their best and freest selves. Through publications and projects, The Feminist Press is beginning to recreate the forgotten history of women and attempting to create a more humane and equitable society for the future.